You and the Law in New Jersey

W9-BND-951

YOU AND THE LAW IN NEW JERSEY

A RESOURCE GUIDE

Second Edition

**Melville D. Miller, Jr., and Leighton A. Holness
and the Staff of Legal Services of New Jersey**

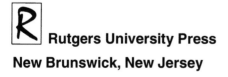 Rutgers University Press

New Brunswick, New Jersey

Library of Congress Cataloging-in-Publication Data

Miller, Melville D.
    You and the law in New Jersey : a resource guide / Melville D.
Miller, Jr., Leighton A. Holness, and the staff of Legal Services of
New Jersey. — 2nd ed.
        p.   cm.
    Includes bibliographical references and index.
    ISBN 0-8135-2531-4 (cloth : alk. paper). — ISBN 0-8135-2532-2
(pbk. : alk. paper)
    1. Law—New Jersey—Popular works.   I. Holness, Leighton A.
II. Legal Services of New Jersey.   III. Title.
KFN1881.M55 1998
349.749—dc21   97-43070
                                                                    CIP

British Cataloging-in-Publication data for this book is available from
the British Library

Copyright © 1998 by Rutgers, The State University
All rights reserved
No part of this book may be reproduced or utilized in any form or by
any means, electronic or mechanical, or by any information storage
and retrieval system, without written permission from the publisher.
Please contact Rutgers University Press, 100 Joyce Kilmer Avenue,
Piscataway, New Jersey 08854. The only exception to this prohibition
is "fair use" as defined by U.S. copyright law.

Manufactured in the United States of America

Contents

CONTENTS

Preface

For more than thirty years, Legal Services programs in New Jersey have, in civil matters, provided lawyers without charge to people who could not afford them. Funded primarily by the federal and state governments, the programs have only enough resources to provide legal representation to one-fifth of those people who need it. For many years Legal Services of New Jersey (LSNJ), which coordinates New Jersey's Legal Services network, has struggled to find ways to close this gap between available resources and actual need. One of the ways in which we have tried to help the remaining four-fifths is by offering at least some basic information about various areas of the law so that people could be in a better position to help themselves. We have published a series of booklets on housing, consumer, and education law; domestic violence; lead paint poisoning; entitlement programs; and expungement of arrest records. Since 1981 we have also published a monthly legal informational newsletter, *Looking Out for Your Legal Rights,* which focuses on a host of legal issues in some depth.

In 1987, we knitted much of this material together to publish the first edition of this book, a resource without precedent in New Jersey. Nancy Goldhill, then and now a senior attorney at LSNJ, had the primary responsibility for pulling together that first edition, writing major portions and serving as principal editor for the rest. This second edition, while fully updated and very substantially revised, depends enormously on Nancy's pioneering and extraordinary efforts.

As with the prior publication, the evolution of this book was made possible by a broad collaborative effort among people on the staff of LSNJ, in other Legal Services programs in the state, in private and public interest legal practice, and in the larger New Jersey legal community.

Civil law evolves significantly over time, ever more rapidly. In the eleven years since the first edition, whole new areas of legal focus and specialization have emerged. For several years, Leighton Holness, another senior attorney at LSNJ, has coordinated the research and writing necessary to convey the current state of the law in this second edition. In addition to doing much of the writing, with great patience and skill he guided the teams of contributors, listed below, in each legal subject area. As with Nancy's contribution to the 1987 edition, there would be no second edition without him.

Other current and former LSNJ attorneys made key contributions: Nancy Goldhill and Beatrix Shear on the family law chapter; Francisco Marinas and former staffer Dawn Miller on the chapters concerning consumer law, credit, and utilities; Harris David, Connie Pascale, and former staffer David Sciarra on housing; and former staffer Peggy Stevenson on lead poisoning. Donna Hildreth, senior advocate, contributed to the family law chapter. Sue Perger, who for a miraculous two decades has been responsible for all of LSNJ's publications, oversaw the precursors of many of these chapters in LSNJ's manuals and the *Looking Out* newsletter. Charlotte Adams, Angie Williams, Louisa West, and Adona Oglivie carried the critical tasks of editing and production.

Other key contributors from the New Jersey legal community and elsewhere, as writers, reviewers, or commenters, included the following:

Citizen: Kathleen Holness, economist at AT&T.

Consumer: Gail Chester, Middlesex County Legal Services; Neil Forgarty, Hudson County Legal Services.

Criminal Justice: Joanna Boretti, private practitioner; Harold Creacy, Union County Legal Services; Abel Garcia, Stockton State College.

Disabled: Richard J. Bennett, Middlesex County Legal Services; Bonnie Karg, Passaic County Legal Aid Society; Linda Headley and Pat Reilly, formerly of the public advocate's office.

Education: Elizabeth Athos, formerly of Hudson County Legal Services; Kit Ellenbogen, formerly of the Education Law Center.

Employment: Denzil Dunkley, Balk, Mandel & Oxfeld (workers' compensation); Joseph Fine (unions); Neil Mullen (employment discrimination); Jesse H. Strauss (state and federal employees); Keith Talbot, Camden Regional Legal Services (rights of agricultural workers). Bennett D. Zurofsky made a major contribution to the research and initial drafting of the sections on job safety and whistle-blower protection. Fine, Strauss, and Zurofsky were all of the firm of Reitman, Parsonnet & Duggan.

Family: Adena Adler, Legal Aid Society of Mercer County; Diana Bodeen, Passaic County Legal Aid Society; Joyce Helfman, Middlesex County Legal Services; Ann Kloeckner, formerly of Union County Legal Services; Judith McKay, formerly of Middlesex County Legal Services.

Health: Russell Gale, Middlesex County Legal Services; Pat Reilly; Jacqueline Stevens, Legal Aid Society of Morris County; Michelle Munsat. The section on charity care is an adaptation of the LSNJ pamphlet on charity care written by Gail Chester, Middlesex County Legal Services.

Public Benefits: Donna Arons, formerly of Legal Aid Society of Mercer County; Ted Gardner, Hudson County Legal Services.

Seniors: Marilyn Askin and Mark Levin, private practitioners (wills and estates); Janice Chapin, Union County Legal Services; Richard J. Bennett, Middlesex County Legal Services (Social Security and SSI); Paula Palewicz, actuary at AT&T (pensions and other retirement benefits); Cecelia Urban.

Veterans: Lisa Day, Community Legal Services; Guy A. Weiner, state of New Jersey.

We are deeply grateful for their assistance. We stress that LSNJ itself remains responsible for the final product; our contributors should get full credit for the strengths of these chapters but merit no share of the blame for the weaknesses and failings.

We hope this volume will be a service to the people of New Jersey and that it will promote greater justice.

Edison, New Jersey

Melville D. Miller, Jr.
President, Legal Services of New Jersey

You and the Law in New Jersey

How to Use This Book

This book is intended to help you better understand the laws that affect you as a New Jersey resident. Most of us will face dozens of situations in our lives when we need to understand our rights or obligations under the law. By referring to this book, you should be better able to

- Approach legal situations and problems on your own, perhaps resolving them and avoiding more complex difficulties.
- Understand the legal system.
- Know when and how to get a lawyer.
- Effectively use a lawyer you have hired.
- Be confident when you are confronted by lawsuits, opposing lawyers, judges, sheriffs, police, and others involved with the law.

This book is designed for use in two ways. Most important, it is a reference source, which you can consult when you find yourself confronted by a legal situation. The chapter titles, organization, headings, and index should make it easy for you to find what you need.

This book can also provide you with an overview of the legal system in New Jersey, quite apart from any specific problem. This comprehensive perspective will be of interest to general readers and would serve well as a companion text for practical law segments of high school or college courses.

This book is *not* designed to replace lawyers or make them unnecessary. For many legal problems, you will still need the help of an attorney. Reading the book will, however, make you better able to judge when an attorney should be consulted and how the attorney should be used.

Do not try to rely solely on what you read here in dealing with a legal problem, for several reasons:

- Laws change every day and it is very possible that something you read about in this book may have changed dramatically since it was written. This book reflects the state of the law as of May 1997. It is essential for you to check the most current law, by using the tools in Chapter 1 or seeing a lawyer, before you proceed.
- This book provides basic information about the law, but very often the facts of a particular situation have a major effect on how a law is applied. Special facts can even lead a court to change a previous interpretation of the law. Lawyers can help advise you about how specific laws may be applied to your own particular facts.
- This book is intended not as a step-by-step guide for following a particular legal procedure, but rather as a source of basic information. Consequent-

ly, if you want to pursue a legal case on your own, you will still need to consult the courts and court clerks described later in this book to get the necessary forms and instructions.

As explained more fully in the first chapter, this book contains information about New Jersey state law as well as federal law, which affects you as a resident of the United States.

Many people find the legal system complex and even threatening. From the black robes of judges to the difficult wording of legal forms, much about this system tends to scare or confuse those who are not lawyers. There is no real need for this mystery and intimidation. We are convinced that if people are armed with greater knowledge about the law, they will be better able to participate in our society, which aspires to the unquestionably noble goal of equal justice under the law.

1. You and the Law

This chapter will advise you how to find the law, do legal research, find lawyers and use them more effectively, start and respond to lawsuits, and follow the proceedings of a court case. It includes tables that describe the federal and state courts in New Jersey.

SOURCES OF THE LAW

The word *law* includes more than just statutes of the U.S. Congress and state legislatures. Federal and state courts, administrative agencies, and cities and towns also make law. This section will explain some of the sources of the law.

CONSTITUTIONS. A *constitution* sets up the power and duties of a government and guarantees rights to the citizens who are living under that government. The U.S. Constitution, which went into effect in 1789, defined the structure of the federal government, dividing it into three branches: the executive branch (the president), the legislative branch (Congress), and the judicial branch (the federal court system). It also divided the power to govern the United States between the federal government and the states. Each state is empowered to control all areas not specifically given to the federal government by the Constitution.

The first ten amendments to the U.S. Constitution, known as the Bill of Rights, grant basic guaranties to the people including freedom of speech, religion, and press; the right to trial by jury in criminal cases; and the right to be treated fairly under the law. These rights are protected from interference both by the federal government and, under the Fourteenth Amendment, by the individual states.

States also have constitutions. The current version of the New Jersey Constitution was adopted in 1947. The state constitution also sets up a three-part system of government and guarantees New Jersey citizens certain basic rights similar to those granted by the U.S. Constitution. Typical of most state constitutions, it also contains many special provisions which are not in the U.S. Constitution. For example, all New Jersey residents are given the right to join labor unions and the right to a "thorough and efficient" public education.

STATUTES. The U.S. Congress and the New Jersey legislature make laws by passing *statutes*. Congress has the power to enact federal laws on subjects delineated in the U.S. Constitution as matters of national attention. For example, the federal government controls job safety, minimum wages, and

3

pension funds. State laws, on the other hand, generally govern local matters such as landlord-tenant rights and family relationships. For many matters, such as protection of consumers and the environment, there are both federal and state laws that apply. If the federal government has properly passed a law on a particular subject, that federal mandate usually will take precedence over (*preempt*) conflicting state provisions.

REGULATIONS. Congress and state legislatures create administrative agencies to administer the laws they pass. These administrative agencies, part of the executive branch of government, make law by passing *regulations* that help them to enforce the statutes they are responsible for administering. Before a federal agency passes a regulation, it is required to publish the regulation in a daily publication called the *Federal Register,* available in many libraries and from the Government Printing Office. New Jersey agencies must publish their proposed rules in the bimonthly *New Jersey Register,* also available in many libraries and through the U.S. Department of State. Members of the public have a short period of time—thirty days in New Jersey—in which to comment on these proposed regulations before they are finally adopted. Once an agency properly adopts a regulation, it has the weight of law.

ORDINANCES. Cities and towns can make their own laws on certain subjects by passing *ordinances.* Zoning regulations, building codes, and rent control laws are examples of local ordinances. Proposed ordinances must be published in the legal section of a local newspaper prior to final adoption.

CASE LAW. Courts and administrative agencies also create law by deciding disputes between parties. Court decisions are sometimes called the *common law.* When these decisions are published, they can be used as *precedent* by courts and agencies to decide future cases. Decisions frequently interpret statutes, regulations, or case precedent. The decisions of higher appellate courts are binding on lower trial courts in the same court system. (See the charts of the federal and state court systems in tables 1.1 and 1.2.)

Generally, the federal courts decide cases that involve federal statutes or the U.S. Constitution and the state courts decide cases relating to state statutes or the state constitution. Federal and state agencies typically have the power to decide cases that arise under the regulations they administer.

In addition to deciding cases, courts and administrative agencies make procedural rules that control how they will handle cases. The rules of the New Jersey courts are set forth in the *New Jersey Court Rules,* which is published every year. The rules of the federal courts are contained in a separate book. In addition, the U.S. District Court for New Jersey has some of its own local rules, which appear in the *New Jersey Court Rules* book mentioned above.

4

TABLE 1.1. The Federal Court System

UNITED STATES SUPREME COURT

Hears the most important appeals from highest state courts and federal appellate courts.

Composed of nine justices appointed by the president.

Located in Washington, D.C.

UNITED STATES COURT OF APPEALS

Hears appeals from federal district court cases and many agency decisions.

Panels of three judges hear most cases.

Divided into circuits by geographical area. New Jersey, along with Pennsylvania and Delaware, is in the third circuit. The court is located in Philadelphia.

UNITED STATES DISTRICT COURT

Hears cases in which the

Issue involves federal law or the federal Constitution.

United States is suing or being sued.

Person suing and person being sued are from different states and the amount being sued for is more than $75,000.

The New Jersey district courts are located in Newark, Trenton, and Camden.

NOTE: There are also courts that hear special kinds of cases, for example, a bankruptcy court.

CRIMINAL LAW AND CIVIL LAW. Both federal and state laws can be divided into criminal and civil categories. Criminal laws define crimes and punishment for acts that hurt other people, property, or the interests of the community as a whole.

The majority of laws are civil, not criminal, and govern conduct such as commercial dealings, landlord-tenant disputes, divorces, liability for auto accidents, and many other problems.

DOING LEGAL RESEARCH

To learn more about a legal area or a problem you are having, you may want to do some legal research on your own. The following suggestions should help you get started. We stress, however, that many problems require the help of a lawyer. This information on basic legal research is in no way a suggestion that you try to solve all legal problems by yourself.

WHERE TO FIND THE LAWS. Although there is now a great deal of legal information to be found on the Internet, perhaps the best places to go are the libraries of the two public law schools in New Jersey: Rutgers Law School, in Newark and in Camden. In addition, Seton Hall University has a private law school in Newark. The Rutgers libraries are open to the public and have the books and people who can help you find the laws or cases you need.

TABLE 1.2. The New Jersey State Court System

SUPREME COURT
(located in Trenton)

Hears important cases and appeals in which there is a dissent in the Appellate Division

SUPERIOR COURT, APPELLATE DIVISION

Hears appeals from Law and Chancery Division cases, administrative agencies, and tax court

Law Division[a]		Chancery Division[a]	
Civil Division[a]	Criminal Division[a]	General Equity[a]	Family Part[a]
Hears cases in which a person is suing for more than $10,000	Hears cases in which a person is accused of a serious crime	Hears cases in which the person suing is not seeking money	Hears divorces, child custody cases, adoptions, and juvenile matters
Special Civil Part	Hears appeals from municipal court		
Hears cases in which a person is suing for less than $10,000			
Landlord-tenant cases			
Small-claims cases, in which a person is suing for less than $2,000			

Probate Part[a]

Hears matters involving estates and challenges to wills

MUNICIPAL COURT

Hears cases involving minor crimes, traffic tickets, and ordinance violations

NOTE: There is also a tax court, which hears cases involving tax issues and rebates.

You can also read law books in some public libraries, many college libraries, and law libraries located in county courthouses. Check your local public library first; you may find everything you need right there. You can also go to the State Law Library in Trenton.

DECIDING WHICH LAW APPLIES. Each state has its own legislature, its own courts, and its own distinct set of laws. The law of each state applies to the people living within that state or to events that take place or have an effect there. When you are researching a question about something that occurred in New Jersey, you should start with New Jersey law. You need to check, however, whether the issue you are researching is in one of the areas governed by federal law.

The statutes made in Trenton by the New Jersey legislature are kept in a set of green books called *New Jersey Statutes Annotated (N.J.S.A.)*. These books are numbered by titles, chapters, and sections. A *citation* (or *cite*)— which tells you what book to look in—to a New Jersey statute would look like this: *N.J.S.A.* 2A:18-53 (*N.J.S.A.* Title 2A, chapter 18, section 53). To find out which *N.J.S.A.* book contains the law you want to study, you should first look for your topic in the *N.J.S.A.* index.

Statutes passed by the U.S. Congress are published in a set of books called the *U.S. Code Annotated (U.S.C.A.)*. Like the New Jersey statutes, these books have many titles, chapters, and sections, which can be located by using the *U.S.C.A.* index.

Because some of the *U.S.C.A.* and *N.J.S.A.* books were printed many years ago, updates with new or recent laws are published each year. The updates, called *pocket parts,* are found at the end of each *U.S.C.A.* and *N.J.S.A.* book. Even if the law you want is in the main text of the book, you should always check the pocket parts to see if any changes to the law have been made.

Records of opinions in court cases are kept in books called *reporters.* Opinions of the New Jersey Supreme Court, the highest state court, are kept in a set of books called *New Jersey Reports*. A cite to a case opinion starts with the name of the people or organizations that were in court against each other. After the names, the number of the book where you can find the court opinion is listed. So, *Marini v. Ireland,* 56 *N.J.* 130 (1970), means that the court opinion in a case in which a person named Marini sued a person named Ireland is found in the fifty-sixth volume of *New Jersey Reports*, starting at page 130. The year the case was decided is 1970.

Opinions of the superior court, including the Appellate Division and the Law and Chancery divisions, are kept in a set of green books called *New Jersey Superior Court Reports (N.J. Super.)*. Opinions of other states' courts are kept in a system of books called *regional reporters,* issued by West Publishing Company. The regional reporters, organized by regional groups of states, are

Atlantic (A.), Northeastern (N.E.), Northwestern (N.W.), Southern (So.), Southeastern (S.E.), Southwestern (S.W.), and *Pacific (P.).*

Opinions of the U.S. Supreme Court can be found in three sets of books: *United States Reports (U.S.), Supreme Court Reporter (S. Ct.),* and *Lawyers Edition (L.E.* and *L.E. 2d).* These are published by three different companies; each is a complete set of U.S. Supreme Court decisions. Opinions of federal appellate courts are contained in a set of books called the *Federal Reporter (F.* and *F. 2d).* Opinions of federal district courts (the lowest federal courts) are contained in a set of books called the *Federal Supplement (F. Supp.).*

Federal administrative agency decisions are usually not found in published books but are retained by the agencies themselves. New Jersey state administrative decisions are kept in *New Jersey Administrative Reports (N.J.A.R.).*

Federal agency regulations are contained in the *Code of Federal Regulations (C.F.R.).* New Jersey state agency regulations are found in the *New Jersey Administrative Code (N.J.A.C.).* Both have an index to help you find the right volume.

LEGAL FORMS. If you need to find a legal form, such as for a lease or a business contract, a number of books have legal forms. These include

- The *Appendix of the New Jersey Court Rules.*
- *New Jersey Forms—Legal and Business* (a set of green books published by the Lawyers Co-operative Publishing Company).
- *New Jersey Practice* (a set of red books published by West Publishing Company).
- Books on different subjects published by the Institute of Continuing Legal Education (ICLE), located at The Law Center, 1 Constitution Square, New Brunswick, New Jersey 08901-1500.

Most of the form books have indexes that will help you find the form you want. Sometimes the form will have blanks for you to fill in. Other times the form will have sample information and you will have to draw up your own document, substituting the information that applies to your situation. You can either photocopy the form or check your local stationery store to see if you can buy the form.

GENERAL SOURCES. It is easiest to do research if you have one or more specific questions to answer. Sometimes, however, you will need to understand an area of law better before you can narrow down your questions. In this case, you should begin by looking at a general book covering the particular area that concerns you to get an idea about the basic principles in a particular area of law, and begin to form specific questions.

General sources include

- Legal encyclopedias such as *American Jurisprudence* and *Corpus Juris Secundum.*
- Treatises written by experts in the field.
- A series of books called *Nutshells*, published by West Publishing Company.

If your question involves a federal or state statute, you should begin researching with the index to the *United States Code Annotated* (for federal law) or the index to the *New Jersey Statutes Annotated* (for state law). Remember to check the pocket parts for the most recent cites. The annotations to the statute will refer you to relevant cases that rely on the statute.

If you cannot find a case by looking in the statute books, you can look in a set of books called a *digest.* Each reporter system has a digest. New Jersey's is called *West's New Jersey Digest 2d.*

A digest divides the law into different topics. The topics are listed alphabetically and divided into subtopics. If you can find even one case that is relevant, it will probably enable you to find other similar cases. You can also find additional cases by using a book called *Shepard's Citations.* There is a set of *Shepard's Citations* for each reporter system. If you look up your case in the right *Shepard's*, it will refer you to all other cases which mention your case. It will also tell you if courts still follow your case. Ask the librarian how to use it.

When you read a case, try to identify the question the court was answering. Compare your question with that question. The closer your question is to that question, the more useful the case will be. Also, try to find out what facts the court relied on and found important.

GETTING LEGAL HELP

Every person has the right to represent himself or herself in court. This is called appearing *pro se* or *pro per.* Although you are never required to have a lawyer in court, most of the time it is a good idea to have one. Only one New Jersey court, the Small-Claims Section of the Special Civil Part, is designed for pro se appearances. Representing yourself is not easy. Figuring out what the law is and how to follow the court rules properly can be difficult. You cannot count on the judge to explain what you do not know or to assume the role of your lawyer.

Whether or not to hire a lawyer is a decision you must make based on your finances and what you stand to lose. You should almost definitely see a lawyer if you have been seriously injured, if you are accused of a crime, if you are sued for a large amount of money, or if you are sued and the other side is represented by a lawyer. You should also strongly consider seeing a lawyer if you want to make a will, buy a house, get divorced, or start a business.

CHOOSING A LAWYER. Unfortunately, there are no consumer guides listing the best lawyers. The best way to choose a lawyer is to ask your friends to recommend a lawyer they have used and liked. Remember that many lawyers specialize in one particular area. For example, there are lawyers who know a lot about divorce law but very little about labor law. The lawyer who may have been helpful with your friend's divorce may not be helpful in your workers' compensation case.

Most county bar associations have a *lawyer referral service,* which is listed in your local telephone directory or Yellow Pages. You can also call the New Jersey State Bar Association for the local referral service number. The referral service will give you the name and telephone number of an attorney in your area who specializes in the particular area of law related to your problem. Lawyers who register with lawyer referral services usually agree to hold an initial consultation at a low price.

Lawyers can and do advertise on radio, on television, and in local newspapers. Sometimes lawyers will offer a fixed rate for certain services. But be careful. A lawyer's advertisement, like any other advertisement, is only that lawyer's opinion of himself or herself. It may not be an accurate representation of his or her services.

WORKING WITH A LAWYER. At your first meeting or consultation with a lawyer, you will explain your problem. You should bring copies of all important documents with you. Do not be afraid to ask the lawyer if he or she has handled your type of case before or to ask about the lawyer's fee. If the lawyer has not represented you before, he or she must give you a written explanation of how your bill will be calculated, either before or shortly after he or she begins to represent you. Usually this will be spelled out in a document called a *retainer agreement,* which is a contract for the lawyer's services. It is always a good idea to have a written retainer agreement. Make sure you understand everything in it before you sign.

The lawyer you choose should keep you informed about the progress of your case and should follow your wishes in all important decisions. At the same time, a lawyer should be able to expect that you will be cooperative. Provide all information the lawyer requests. Show up on time for all appointments, hearings, or court appearances. Finally, tell your lawyer all of the facts. Do not leave out information because it is embarrassing or because you think it will hurt you. Without all of the facts, a lawyer cannot make a good decision about how to proceed. Remember that there is an attorney-client privilege, which requires your lawyer to keep what you say to him or her confidential, unless you let him or her know that you are going to commit a crime or a fraud.

THE ATTORNEY-CLIENT PRIVILEGE. Communications between a lawyer and client are *confidential* and *privileged.* The client has the right to refuse to disclose any such communication and to prevent the lawyer and anyone working for the lawyer from disclosing any such communication. Confidentiality means that the information cannot be disclosed to any person at any time; privilege means that the lawyer cannot be forced to disclose the information in court.

The lawyer must keep these client confidences. The privilege must be *claimed* by the lawyer, unless the client instructs the lawyer not to claim the privilege. The privilege, of course, can be claimed by the client or, if the client is incompetent or has died, by his or her guardian or personal representative. This duty of silence does not, however, extend to a communication made between a lawyer and a client during which the client sought or used legal representation to help the client in committing a crime or a fraud. It does not apply if the subject of the communication is a serious crime or fraud that the client is about to commit. It also does not cover communications made between a client and lawyer when (1) the client is suing the lawyer because the lawyer did not do what the lawyer promised to do, *or* (2) the lawyer is suing the client because the client did not pay him or her for the legal work done.

The purpose of the confidence and privilege rule is to encourage clients to make full disclosure to their lawyers. In order for a lawyer to prepare a case properly, there must be full and free discussion between the client and the lawyer.

PROBLEMS WITH YOUR LAWYER. If you think that your lawyer is not doing a good job, you should let him or her know. If a conversation with the lawyer is not enough to solve the problem, you should write a letter to the lawyer explaining how you feel.

If you are still unhappy, you can fire your lawyer, with or without a reason. If you have given the lawyer a *retainer* (money in advance), the lawyer must return to you any part of it which he or she has not earned. If you still owe the lawyer money, your lawyer has the right to be paid for the value of the work that has been done on your behalf. If you do not pay, your lawyer can sue you or get a *lien* (an interest) on any money you may recover later.

Ethics Complaints. Lawyers must follow the Rules of Professional Conduct, which are published in the *New Jersey Court Rules.* These rules set out what lawyers can and cannot do. If you think your lawyer has broken these rules or behaved unethically, you can file a *grievance* against the lawyer. The grievance must be in writing and must be filed with the *district ethics committee* nearest to the lawyer's office. To find the nearest district ethics committee, you can call the Office of Attorney Ethics in Trenton. The district committee will review all grievances. If the committee believes that the lawyer has behaved unethically, it will file a complaint and hold a hearing. If the hearing panel finds that a reprimand is not sufficient discipline, the matter

11

will be referred to the Disciplinary Review Board. That board can recommend sanctions, such as suspension or disbarment. Recommendations as to attorney discipline are then reviewed by the New Jersey Supreme Court. All ethics complaints and their outcomes are now public information.

Fee Arbitration. If you think that you were overcharged by a lawyer, you can ask for *fee arbitration*. A fee arbitration will be conducted by a hearing panel, which will then decide whether the fee is reasonable and, if not, set a reasonable fee. You must request fee arbitration at the district fee arbitration committee nearest to the lawyer's office. Before a lawyer sues you for a fee, he or she must tell you about fee arbitration. The Office of Attorney Ethics can provide you with more information about fee arbitration.

Lawyers Fund for Client Protection. If your lawyer took money that belonged to you, you may be able to get this amount back from the Lawyers Fund for Client Protection. All lawyers in the state are required to pay money into this fund to provide protection to clients who lose money as a result of a lawyer's dishonest conduct.

Before you file a claim, you must let the local county prosecutor and the district ethics committee know about your loss. Then you must get a claim form and file it with the Lawyers Fund for Client Protection in Trenton.

Usually, you have one year to make the claim from the time the attorney was suspended, disbarred, or convicted. There is a limit on how much the fund will pay for all of the claims against any one attorney.

WHAT TO DO IF YOU CANNOT AFFORD A LAWYER. You still may be able to pay for a lawyer on your own, even if you have little or no money. Some lawyers will agree to charge only a small, fixed fee, depending on the type of case. Some lawyers will arrange for you to pay in installments or will accept payments through a credit card.

In certain types of cases, particularly cases in which you are suing because of personal injury, you will be able to work out a *contingent fee* agreement. This is a contract in which the lawyer agrees to represent you without charge unless and until you recover money damages. If you do recover damages, the lawyer gets a certain percentage of the award; the maximum amounts are set by court rule. If you do not recover money, you do not have to pay a fee for the lawyer's time. However, you probably will have to pay the lawyer for any expenses, such as court filing fees, costs of discovery, and other payments made by the lawyer. Contingent fee agreements must be in writing. A lawyer cannot agree to a contingent fee in a matrimonial case or a criminal case.

Legal Services. If you have very little or no money, you may qualify for free legal assistance from the Legal Services program in your county. Legal Services is a publicly and privately funded nonprofit agency that represents and advises low-income people in civil cases. To find the telephone number of the office in your county, look in the white pages or Yellow Pages of your phone book, or contact Legal Services of New Jersey (LSNJ) in Edison, New Jersey, (732) 572-9100.

American Civil Liberties Union. You also may want to seek help from other agencies. The American Civil Liberties Union (ACLU), based in Newark, generally represents people who have cases involving serious violations of constitutional or civil rights. These cases are usually test cases in which new and important issues are raised.

Law School Clinics. The three New Jersey law schools have clinics where third-year law students, under the supervision of attorneys, can represent clients who have low incomes or who have problems in special areas such as women's rights, constitutional law, prison issues, or environmental matters.

Public Defender. The New Jersey Public Defender, a state agency that is part of the Department of State, provides legal representation to low-income people charged with major crimes. The program has offices in each of New Jersey's twenty-one counties. To get the telephone number or address of the office of the public defender in your county, look in your telephone directory or call the main office of the public defender in Trenton.

Other Government Agencies. Some government agencies will investigate complaints for you. They may be able to settle your complaint or file suit on your behalf. Agencies that may help are mentioned in later chapters, in connection with particular legal problems.

WHEN YOU WANT TO SUE IN STATE COURT

The legal process has certain basic stages and procedures. Some of the most fundamental information is offered in the following pages. More detail about specific legal areas is given in later chapters.

THE COMPLAINT. A *complaint* is a legal document in which the person bringing the lawsuit (the *plaintiff*) explains why he or she is suing the other party (the *defendant*). The complaint should include

- A *caption* (who you are, who the defendant is, which court you are suing in, and what county the court is in),
- The facts (what happened and when),
- The reason you are suing (what legal wrong has been done to you), *and*
- What you want the court to do.

When you file suit in superior court, Chancery or Law Division, you will first send an original and a copy of your complaint with a check for the required *filing fee* to the superior court. If you cannot afford to pay the filing fee, you can file an *in forma pauperis* motion seeking permission to file without paying a fee. You will have to submit an *affidavit* setting forth your financial situation

---

DECIDING IN WHICH COUNTY TO SUE

The following rules apply when you are trying to figure out in which county your suit belongs:

✔ In cases involving real estate, your case belongs in the county where the property is located.
✔ In cases against government, public agencies, or officials, your case belongs in the county where the claim arose.
✔ In all other actions (except receivership, attachments, family, and probate actions, which have their own rules), you can sue in the county where the claim arose, where any party lives at the time the suit is filed, or where a nonresident defendant was served with the summons.

---

and inability to pay. Check with the clerk of the county in which you file for the exact filing procedure. The clerk will file your complaint and will send you a copy with a *docket number* on it. You will use this docket number on all future court papers.

A separate document called a *summons* must then be prepared, with the name and address of the defendant and certain other information, such as how long the defendant has to file an answer to the complaint. You must send a copy of the summons and complaint, with an additional copy for each defendant, to the sheriff of the county where each defendant lives. The sheriff will then serve that defendant with the summons and complaint. You must tell the sheriff the defendant's address and pay a fee for service, plus an additional amount for the sheriff's mileage. The sheriff will let you know the total after the defendant has been served.

When you file suit in the Special Civil Part, you send a summons and complaint—with an additional copy for each defendant—to the county clerk of the Special Civil Part. You should include an extra copy and an envelope and ask the clerk to return a copy to you. You will have to pay a filing fee. The amount of the fee depends on whether you have a small-claims case, a landlord-tenant case, or otherwise. You will also have to pay a fee to have the summons and complaint served. This fee will vary from county to county. Some counties have established a service-by-mail program; the initial service is by mail in those counties and whenever the summons must be served in a county other than the one in which you filed your complaint. You should, therefore, call the clerk of the county in which you are suing and ask what you should do.

STATUTES OF LIMITATIONS. You cannot wait forever to file a lawsuit. To protect defendants from being put at a disadvantage because witnesses and evidence have disappeared by the time suit is filed, the law limits the time to file suit. These time limits are enacted by legislative bodies and are called *statutes of limitations.*

Statutes of limitations generally start to run as soon as the events that created the right to sue someone have taken place. Two examples of such statutes are a limit of two years for personal injury cases and a limit of six years for cases involving contracts and injury to property. Other time limits apply to other types of cases. If a defendant shows that you have waited too long to sue and that the statute of limitations has run, your case will be dismissed.

There are some instances in which the statute of limitations will not apply. One exception is a situation in which the defendant fooled the plaintiff into waiting until the statute had run. Another exception is a situation in which the plaintiff was not aware within the statutory period that he or she had suffered an injury that would create a right to sue. In such a case, the statute starts to run when the plaintiff does become aware of the injury.

SUING THE GOVERNMENT OR A GOVERNMENT AGENCY. Your right to sue federal, state, or local governments and their agencies may be limited by the doctrine of *sovereign immunity.* Both the federal and state legislatures have passed laws which permit suits to be filed against public entities only under certain circumstances. Most notably, the New Jersey Tort Claims Act[1] allows people to sue the state and any subdivisions or other public agencies for their acts of *negligence* (improper conduct that causes harm to other persons or property). However, before you can sue the state or any other entity under this law, you must comply with certain procedural requirements.

Before you sue, you must file a *tort claim notice* with the state, county, town, or agency within ninety days of the events that gave rise to your claim. This will give them notice of the facts underlying your claim. Your claim should state

- Your name and address.
- What happened.
- What your loss was.
- Who caused your loss.
- How much money you want.

You must present the claim to the government or agency you are suing, either in person or by certified mail. After the state, county, or town gets your claim notice, you must wait six months to file a lawsuit.

If you miss the ninety-day time limit, you can file suit only if you get a court's permission to file a late claim. To do this, you will have to file a motion with a superior court judge explaining why you did not file on time.

15

WHEN YOU ARE SUED

If you are sued, the mail carrier or a sheriff will bring you a summons and complaint. The summons is often delivered by certified mail, and you must sign for it. Under certain circumstances you can be served by regular mail.

Generally, you have only twenty days to respond to a complaint. You should see a lawyer right away. The following information will give you a general idea of court procedure.

You should file a written response, called an *answer*, to the complaint, or judgment can be entered against you. If you choose to represent yourself, at a minimum you should write a letter to the court. The letter should

- State that you received a summons and complaint,
- Briefly outline any respects in which the complaint is untrue, *and*
- State that you want to appear in court to defend yourself.

If possible, when you outline why the complaint is untrue, you should go through each statement made in the complaint and briefly state your side of the story. Make sure that when you write this response you are accurate.

When you have finished writing your answer, you must send two copies to the clerk of the court with a self-addressed, stamped envelope. Ask the court clerk to send you back a filed copy. You must also send a copy of this same answer to the attorney for the plaintiff. (The attorney's address is in the top left-hand corner of the papers.)

If you do not file an answer within the time limit, the court clerk may enter *default* against you. A final *judgment of default* may later be entered. This means you will automatically lose the lawsuit, whether you are right or wrong.

STAGES OF A COURT CASE

After a complaint is filed and answered, the case moves to a stage called *discovery*. This is a time when each party can get information from all other parties, before the case goes to trial. You can ask specific questions about what the other party thinks the facts of the case are, what evidence he or she plans to use in court, and any other item that may help your case. The questions can be written out and sent to the other party, in which case they are called *interrogatories*. If a party fails to respond to interrogatories, the court can decide the case against that party. You must tell the truth when you answer interrogatories.

One party can also force another to answer questions in person, under oath, before a shorthand reporter who records the questions and answers. These accounts are called *depositions*. In special circumstances, depositions may be videotaped.

THE COURT HEARING. If an answer has been filed, the court will schedule a hearing date. The court clerk will notify you of the date and time; you must appear in court on time.

At the hearing, the plaintiff has the *burden of proof.* This means that it is up to the plaintiff to prove his or her claims first. Bring all of your papers, receipts, and other documents to court to back up your claims. You should also bring any witnesses who can testify about the facts of the case.

The plaintiff begins the suit in a civil trial. Before any witnesses are called, the lawyers for each side may make *opening statements* to the judge or to the jury, if there is one. These statements are to inform the judge and jurors of the nature of the case and the evidence that will be offered at trial. Such opening statements are not evidence.

After the opening statements, the plaintiff calls witnesses and conducts the *direct examination* to prove his or her case. After each witness completes his or her direct testimony, the defendant's attorney may *cross-examine* him or her. Should he or she wish to do so, the plaintiff's attorney may then *reexamine* the witness. When the plaintiff has completed presenting his or her entire side of the case, the defendant may call witnesses to establish his or her contentions and to disprove the plaintiff's case. The plaintiff may cross-examine the defendant's witnesses. The defendant has the opportunity to reexamine those witnesses who have been cross-examined. The plaintiff may then call other witnesses to rebut new matter advanced by the defendant's witnesses.

After all the evidence has been presented by both sides, each of the attorneys has the right to sum up, analyze the proof, and present arguments in favor of his or her client. The attorney for the defendant sums up first. Statements made in *summations* are not evidence.

If it is a jury trial, the judge then instructs the jurors about their duties and responsibilities and about the law that they must apply to the evidence in the case. This is known as the *charge* to the jury. The case is then turned over to the jury for its *deliberation.* A jury in a civil trial consists of six members, unless for good reason the court allows a twelve-person jury. Agreement by five of the six jurors is required for a *verdict.* In order for the jury to decide in favor of the plaintiff, the jury must conclude that, on balance, the evidence supported the plaintiff's case more than the defendent's case. In coming to this conclusion, the jury may consider only that evidence defined as believable by the judge.

After the trial, the judge will enter a *judgment* deciding the case, or, if there is a jury, the jury will return a verdict, which will then be incorporated into the judgment. If you win the case, the judgment will be for you. If you lose the case, the judgment will be against you. If the case involves money, the judgment will allow the winning party to collect money from the other side. A money judgment can be enforced by a *wage execution (garnishment)* or a *property execution.*

GOING TO SMALL-CLAIMS COURT

The Small-Claims Division of the Special Civil Part of superior court is a fast, inexpensive way of suing someone for small amounts of money. These amounts change from time to time, but generally are in the low thousands of dollars.

You do not need a lawyer in small-claims court. The rules in small-claims court are less complicated than in other New Jersey courts. Many of the people who use small-claims court are not represented by a lawyer. But if your case is very complicated, it might be a good idea to have a lawyer.

You will have to use the small-claims court in the county in which the person you are suing lives, or in the county where the business you are suing is located. Go to the county courthouse building and look for the clerk's office of the Special Civil Part. Tell the clerk you want to start a small-claims suit.

You must obbtain a complaint form from the court clerk and fill it out. When you fill out the complaint form, you should give

- A short, clear statement that explains the facts of your case and why you are suing (this can be as short as one or two sentences),
- The amount of money for which you are suing,
- Your name and address (you are the *plaintiff*), *and*
- The name and address of the person you are suing (the *defendant*).

If you are suing on a contract, you may want to attach a photocopy of the contract to the court papers.

You also have to fill out a summons. This notifies the person you are suing to show up in court. Ask the court clerk for help if you have questions about filling in the complaint or summons. You should also ask the court clerk to check that your papers are filled out properly. You must pay a filing fee. When you complete the complaint, make sure you give the clerk the correct amount.

Next, find out the date and time your case will be heard. Also, find out the *docket number* (case number). Before the court date, gather all the information you need to present your case and to prove your side of the story, such as the contract, canceled checks, and receipts. If you are suing about a small item such as a radio, plan on bringing that to court. If it is something too large to bring to court, like a car or a sofa, take pictures to help the judge understand the problem. You might also want to get a witness, such as a car mechanic if your suit involves a car, to come to court with you to explain the problem and the cost of repair.

OUT-OF-COURT SETTLEMENTS. Before the court date, to save both sides the hassle of going to court, the person you are suing may make you an offer to

18

settle out of court. He or she will probably offer you less than the amount you are asking for. You can accept a *settlement* if you decide to do so. But you should know that you cannot sue the same person again for the same problem to get back the rest of the money.

If you decide to settle, write to the court clerk before the court date, or call if you do not have enough time, and explain that the case has been settled and that you want to drop your lawsuit. Make sure you receive the settlement money before you cancel the court date.

AT THE HEARING. On the court date, bring all the evidence you have that you feel will help prove your case. This includes the contract, canceled checks, photos, receipts, and witnesses. If you are going to ask a witness to testify on your behalf, spend a few minutes before you go to court reviewing what he or she is going to say.

At the hearing, both you and the person you are suing will get a chance to tell your sides of the story. The judge will listen to the facts and decide who is right.

If the defendant does not show up for the court date, you will be required to sign an affidavit stating that your complaint was true and that the defendant does owe you the money for which you are suing.

THE JUDGMENT. If the judge decides in your favor, he or she will enter a *judgment* for you, telling you the amount you have won. However, the judge does not order the defendant to pay you. Fortunately, some people pay voluntarily after a judge gives a decision.

Do not sign anything releasing the defendant from liability unless you are paid with cash, a certified check, or a money order. If the defendant was not in court, contact that person and let him or her know that the judge decided in your favor. Ask the defendant to pay you the amount of money the judge ordered.

COLLECTING THE AMOUNT WON. If the defendant refuses to pay a judgment, go to the clerk at small-claims court and explain the situation. The court clerk will tell you how to collect the money owed to you. It might be necessary for the constable of the Special Civil Part to collect the money for you. You will have to pay a small fee plus the constable's mileage costs for this service. But you have to help the constable by finding out where the defendant's money is. One easy way is to locate the defendant's bank. If you originally paid the defendant by check, the name of the defendant's bank will be stamped on the back of the check when it is returned to you. Also, if you find out where the defendant works, his or her salary can be *garnished*. If the defendant owns a house, there is a procedure for placing a lien on the house.

Collecting a small-claims court judgment from a reluctant defendant can be a complicated process. Depending on the amount of money the judge has awarded you, you may want to hire an attorney to collect your judgment.

THE RIGHT TO AN INTERPRETER

It is difficult to understand court or agency proceedings when you are not a lawyer. It is impossible if you are deaf or do not understand English. In most court and agency proceedings, a deaf person has the right to a sign language interpreter if he or she is a party or a witness. The interpreter must be certified and the court or agency must pay for the interpreter. If a deaf person is arrested, an interpreter must give him or her *Miranda warnings* (an explanation of legal rights). A sign language interpreter can be obtained by calling the Division of the Deaf.

A non-English-speaking person has the right to an interpreter during a criminal trial. Each county must provide interpreting services necessary for civil cases in the Law Division and the Family Part of the Chancery Division. There are standards, which are being used but have not yet been officially adopted, covering who can act as an interpreter in cases involving non-English-speaking persons.

APPEALS

If you lose a case in the Law or Chancery Division of superior court, you may *appeal* to the Appellate Division. You may also appeal to the Appellate Division of superior court if you lose a case before an administrative agency. However, it is very difficult to appeal without a lawyer. The deadline for appealing is forty-five days after the judgment is entered or after the final decision of an administrative agency is issued.

An appeal is not a second trial or hearing. Appellate judges do not listen to testimony or review documents. Instead, they review the written record of a trial or other proceeding and decide if there was something legally wrong with the decision so that it should be reversed. You can sometimes appeal from the Appellate Division to the New Jersey Supreme Court.

During the appeal process, if you cannot pay for a lawyer and are not eligible for Legal Services, there are two places you can get help. First, you can go to a law library and ask if they have the *New Jersey Appellate Practice Handbook*. Second, you can call the Appellate Division at (609) 292-4822. The Appellate Division will send you a package with all the papers you need for filing an appeal. The Appellate Division also has a lawyer who helps non-lawyers file appeals.

To start an appeal, you must first file a *notice of appeal* with the appeals court and you must serve a *request for transcript* on the court reporter or person in charge of the tape recording. You must include with the request for transcript a deposit for each day of trial or hearing. Copies of the notice of appeal must be sent to all parties to the case and to the trial court. You must also fill in a *case information statement* with some basic information about the case. You must send a filing fee with these papers. Within thirty days of filing the appeal, you must send the court a deposit to cover the costs of the appeal. If you cannot afford to pay the filing fee or deposit, you may be excused from the requirement by filing a motion, as in trial court. If you were declared to be an *indigent* in the trial court, simply send the Appellate Division the order and show that you are still indigent. You can also file a new motion to be declared an indigent. But even if you do not have to pay the filing fee or deposit, you may still have to pay for the transcripts. The transcript fee is waived only in very limited circumstances.

Once the trial transcript or other statement of the proceedings in the trial court or agency has been received, you have forty-five days to file a *brief*. A brief sets out the facts of the case and your legal arguments. You will need to get legal assistance to file a proper legal brief. Also, within seven days of receiving the transcript, you must send to all other parties a copy of the *transcript delivery certification* that comes with the transcript. The opposing party will have thirty days from the date of receiving your brief to file an answering brief.

Once the Appellate Division has all the papers, it will decide your appeal. If you lose in the Appellate Division, the New Jersey Supreme Court (the highest state court) *may* hear your appeal. You have the automatic right to appeal to the supreme court if your case involves an important question under either the U.S. Constitution or the state constitution, if one of the panel of three Appellate Division judges filed a *dissenting opinion* (an opinion disagreeing with the other judges), or in a case in which the death penalty was imposed. In all other cases, you can appeal to the supreme court only if the court agrees to hear the case. In such cases, you must file a *petition for certification* to get the court's permission to appeal. Certification will generally be granted only if the appeal presents a question of general public importance that should be resolved by the state's highest court, or if the decision is in conflict with other Appellate Division decisions. If you have a case that might be appealed to the New Jersey Supreme Court, you will need legal assistance.

2. Your Rights as a Tenant

This chapter discusses your rights as a tenant, from using rental referral agencies to find a place to live, to your rights under the eviction process. In addition, the chapter discusses issues concerning security deposits, lease terms and regulations, housing discrimination, how to have repairs done by the landlord, and what to do if you have received notice of your apartment's conversion to a condominium.

FINDING A PLACE TO RENT

Tenants often seek help in searching for an apartment or house to rent and sometimes go to rental referral agencies, also called apartment locators or apartment finders. There have been many complaints about some of these agencies, which charge $100 or more just for a list of apartments for rent. These lists are often copied out of the local newspapers. Often, people are referred to apartments that are already rented or to apartments that don't even exist.

There are regulations that rental referral agencies must follow:

- The agency must provide you with a written contract stating the services to be provided and the fee to be charged, as well as the length of the contract, the actions you must take to use the service, and the policy for refunds.
- The agency is prohibited from advertising or referring you to nonexisting addresses or properties that the agency has not checked for availability.
- The agency cannot refer you to a rental property unless it has the permission of the landlord or the landlord's agent to refer prospective tenants.
- The agency must check regularly with the landlord to see if the apartment remains available by confirming the availability of all units advertised in a newspaper each day the ad appears, *and* by confirming all units to which tenants are referred every three working days.
- The agency must tell you when it last checked the unit for availability. Agencies may not refer you to any apartment not checked within the previous seven calendar days. The regulations require agencies to have enough telephone lines and workers to receive and answer phone calls from their clients.
- The agency cannot charge you a fee over $25 before you obtain housing, unless the fee is deposited promptly in the agency's escrow account and held until the agency performs all of the services required by your

contract, or the agency posts a cash security in an amount approved by the New Jersey Real Estate Commission.

- An agency must keep copies of all contracts between consumers and the agency for one year. It must also keep copies of written statements showing that landlords gave the agency permission to refer tenants and that the agency checked that rental units were available before referring tenants.
- An agency must post the regulations in its offices and give consumers a copy on request.

Ask questions about the referral service before you use an agency. Ask to examine their contract and look through their agreements with landlords. Make sure the agency lists available apartments and does not simply copy ads from newspapers. To make a complaint about a referral agency, contact the New Jersey Real Estate Commission in Trenton.

You can also get help finding an apartment from real estate agencies. These agencies will not ask you for money unless they are going to take you to see a specific apartment. Agencies that actually rent and sell homes and apartments can be a big help in finding a place to live.

CONDITION OF THE APARTMENT

Moving in marks the real beginning of your relationship with your landlord. This is the moment at which you first occupy your rental unit. This is a good time to make sure the apartment or house is safe and in good condition and, if it is not, to make an agreement with the landlord to make any necessary repairs.

Documenting the condition of the apartment when you move in is also important when you move out. Some landlords try to blame tenants for damages that were there when the tenant moved in as a way to keep all or part of the security deposit. To avoid this, follow the steps outlined in the box on the next page.

After you have checked each of these items, make a list of what is broken or in poor condition. Ask the landlord or superintendent to sign the list. If he or she refuses, get one of your friends or neighbors to sign and date it. It is a very good idea to take pictures. You can also talk to other tenants who already live there. For example, if you are renting in the summer the other tenants can tell you whether there is enough heat in the winter.

Ask the landlord to make all necessary repairs immediately. Get this agreement in writing with the date and the landlord's signature. Any promises to repair which are not in writing will be difficult to enforce.

If you cannot get the landlord to sign a written agreement or statement, then you should send your list of defective conditions in a letter to the landlord.

CHECKING THE CONDITION OF AN APARTMENT

Before you move in, make sure that the apartment has been issued with a Certificate of Occupancy (CO). Also, do the following:

- ✔ *Bathroom*—Check the water pressure and hot water and look for leaks. Make sure that the toilet works. Check for loose tiles on the walls and floor and look for bugs or signs of bugs.
- ✔ *Kitchen*—Check the water pressure, leaks, hot and cold water, stove, and refrigerator, if any; look for bugs.
- ✔ *Ceiling and walls*—Check for water-leak stains, dampness, loose plaster, holes, or cracks.
- ✔ *Windows*—Check the locks, screens, glass, and frames.
- ✔ *Floors*—Look for rotten wood, loose tiles, splinters, water stains, and cigarette burns.
- ✔ *Electricity*—Make sure that the light switches and fixtures work. Take a lamp and try all of the outlets and look for hanging or open wires. It is sometimes not possible to check the working condition of electrical switches and outlets since the power may have been shut off in the apartment.
- ✔ *Heat*—Turn on the heating system and make sure that it works properly, even if you rent in the summer.
- ✔ *Basement*—Look for rat holes, dirt, trash, leaks, loose wires, broken windows, crumbling walls, sewage, and termites.
- ✔ *Smoke detectors*—Check for installation and make sure that they work properly.
- ✔ *Doors*—Check for dead-bolt locks and peepholes on the entrance door.
- ✔ *Paint*—Look in all rooms to make sure the paint is fresh; check for peeling, flaking, or chipped paint.

Explain in the letter that you expect that the landlord will make the repairs. Send the letter by certified mail, return receipt requested. Keep a copy of the letter and the return receipt. You will need these documents should the landlord seek to wrongfully evict you or keep your security deposit.

SECURITY DEPOSITS

Most agreements to rent housing or leases require you to pay the first month's rent before you move in. Most leases also require you to pay a *security deposit*. The Rent Security Deposit Act (*N.J.S.A.* 46:8-19) specifies how a landlord must collect, maintain, and return a security deposit. Under this law, a security deposit is money that belongs to the tenant but is held by the landlord in trust. A security deposit is made to protect the landlord against the tenant's failure to follow his or her responsibilities as stated in the lease. These can include failure to pay the rent or damages by the tenant to the apartment other than ordinary wear and tear. Read your lease carefully before you sign it. The lease should state clearly where the landlord will hold your security deposit and under what conditions it will be returned to you when you move out.

The Rent Security Deposit Act applies to all rental units, including tenant-occupied, single-family homes. The only exception is for rental units in owner-occupied buildings that have no more than two units other than the owner-landlord's unit. The law applies even to tenants in these small, owner-occupied buildings if the tenant sends a thirty-day written notice to the landlord stating that he or she will apply the law if the landlord does not comply with the law's provisions.

The most a landlord can collect as a security deposit is one and one-half times the monthly rent. There are no exceptions to this limit.

Ask for a receipt when you pay the security deposit. The receipt should include the date, the landlord's signature, and the amount of the security deposit paid. The receipt should show that this money is for a security deposit. Also, make sure that your written lease states the amount of the security deposit you have paid.

NOTICE OF DEPOSIT. The Rent Security Deposit Act requires the landlord to put your security deposit in a separate bank account that pays interest. The landlord must tell you *in writing* the name and address of the bank where the deposit is being kept and the amount of the deposit. The law also states that if the landlord does not give you this written notice within thirty days after you pay the security deposit, the landlord loses the right to hold the security deposit. If you do not receive this written notice, the law gives you the right to give the landlord a written notice that you will use the security deposit to pay your rent. This notice should be sent to the landlord by certified mail, return receipt requested, and you should keep a copy. If you follow this procedure, the landlord *must* apply your security deposit toward your rent and cannot ask you for another security deposit for as long as you live in the apartment.

Even if the landlord sends you the notice within thirty days, the notice still violates the law if it is not accurate. If you receive the notice, call the bank and find out if the money has been deposited. If the money was *not* deposited, you can tell the landlord in writing to use the security deposit to pay your rent just as if the landlord had not sent you a notice at all.

INTEREST ON YOUR DEPOSIT. The Rent Security Deposit Law requires landlords who rent ten or more apartments to place tenants' security deposits in either an insured money market fund *or* a federally insured bank account. The account must pay a rate of interest set at least quarterly and equal to the average rate of interest paid by the bank on money market accounts. These higher-interest accounts must be in New Jersey–based institutions.

The law requires landlords who rent fewer than ten apartments to place security deposits in bank accounts that pay at least the regular rate of interest.

The interest earned on your security deposit is yours; the law allows the landlord to keep only a small amount to cover his or her administrative expenses. This amount is equal to 1 percent of the security deposit per year, or 12.5 percent of the total interest earned on the security deposit, whichever is greater, less the amount of any service fee charged by the investment company or bank involved.

The law also requires that your share of the interest earned on the deposit be (1) allowed to remain in the account and add up to your benefit, (2) paid in cash to you, *or* (3) subtracted from the amount of rent you owe. This must be done either when your lease is to be renewed or at least once every twelve months.

GETTING YOUR DEPOSIT BACK. Even if you move out before your lease has expired, within thirty days after you move out the landlord must return your security deposit and interest, less any charges for repairing damage to the property or rent you owe. If the landlord deducts any amounts for damages or rent, he or she must give you a complete list of the damages he or she claims you did to the property and the cost of repairs. The list of damages must be sent by the landlord by registered or certified mail, and the landlord must return to you any money left over from your security deposit.

The landlord can only charge you for property damage that is more than ordinary wear and tear. "Ordinary wear and tear" means damage that takes place from the normal, careful use of the property. Examples of normal wear and tear are faded paint on the walls, loose tile in the bathroom, window cracks caused by winter weather, or leaky faucets or radiators. Examples of damages that might not be ordinary wear and tear are large holes in the walls caused by nailing up decorations, cigarette burns on floors, or a broken mirror on the bathroom cabinet.

Landlords cannot charge cleaning fees to tenants who leave their apartments "broom clean." Landlords often try to deduct such fees, as well as fees for painting. There are steps you can take to prevent a landlord from charging you for ordinary wear and tear, cleaning, or painting. Before you move out, ask the landlord or superintendent to inspect the apartment personally. Then ask that person to sign a note stating that you left the apartment clean and undamaged. If you cannot get the landlord or superintendent to inspect the unit, have a friend do so. Ask your friend to take photographs and sign and date them. If you have a friend do this, make sure the friend can go to court with you if necessary. If you end up in court, the judge will not accept a letter from your friend as evidence.

You can file a complaint against the landlord in small-claims court if the landlord has not returned your security deposit after thirty days. The landlord must pay you double the amount of the entire security deposit if no amount was returned, or double any amount that was wrongfully deducted from your deposit. When you file your small-claims court complaint, make sure you ask for double the amount of the deposit or double the amount that you feel the landlord should not have deducted from your deposit. You should also ask for interest and costs of the suit. The court may also award you reasonable attorney's fees if you hired a lawyer.

SECURITY DEPOSITS AFTER THE SALE OF A BUILDING. If your former landlord sells the building without returning your security deposit or without turning it over to your new landlord, you are protected under the Rent Security Deposit Act. The law makes the new owner automatically responsible for returning a tenant's security deposit, even if the new owner never received the deposit from the seller. This recognizes that most tenants can't track down a former landlord and that it is easier for the new owner to find out whether any money is due to tenants. Buyers of rental property have the responsibility to make sure that the seller doesn't walk away with the tenants' security deposits.

RETURN OF SECURITY DEPOSITS AFTER DISPLACEMENT. If you are forced to move because of fire, flood, condemnation, or evacuation, the landlord must return your security deposit plus your portion of the interest earned on it within five days. Before returning your money, the landlord may deduct any charges you owe under the lease agreement. This includes any rent you owed when you were displaced. The security deposit must be made available to you during normal business hours for thirty days in the city in which the property is located. The landlord must also give you a detailed statement of interest earned by the deposit and a list of any deductions. If the city clerk agrees, the landlord can turn your money over to the clerk. The city clerk must then make it available to you.

Within three business days after the owner is notified of the displacement, the owner must give you written notice by personal delivery or by mail to your last known address stating where and when your security deposit will be available. The owner must send a duplicate notice to the relocation officer, if the city has one, or to the city clerk. When your last known address is that from which you were displaced and the mailbox at that address is no longer useable, the owner must also post such notice at each outside entrance of that property. If you do not ask for the money within thirty days, the owner must redeposit it in an interest-bearing account in the same bank from which it was withdrawn.

If you move back into the same property later, you must immediately return to the landlord one-third of the security deposit. You must return another third within thirty days and the last third within sixty days from the date you moved back in. If you do not repay the security deposit, the landlord may bring an eviction action against you for nonpayment of rent.

LEASES

A *lease* is a contract between a landlord and a tenant for the rental of an apartment or house. A lease can be in written or oral form.

Sometimes, landlords will try to include *unreasonable* or unfair terms in the lease. For example, a lease may require a tenant to get the landlord's permission to have overnight guests or visitors. This rule is unreasonable. A tenant has the right to have friends or relatives visit for a few days without getting permission from the landlord.

Before signing a written lease, read it carefully. Do not sign a lease with blank spaces. Make sure that the terms in the lease are the same as those to which you and the landlord agreed when you discussed renting the unit. If you do not understand any part of the lease, don't sign it. Tell the landlord you first want to take it to a friend or lawyer who will help you to understand it. If you do sign a lease, be sure you are given a copy. This will prevent the landlord from making changes afterward.

If your lease is oral, make sure you discuss with your landlord all of the responsibilities you have and all of the responsibilities the landlord has. It is important that you understand what you must do before you make a final agreement with the landlord.

COMMON LEASE REQUIREMENTS. Most leases, whether written or oral, have several requirements or terms in common. In addition, the law requires certain conduct by landlords and tenants under any lease. This section reviews some of the more common lease requirements and discusses how the law treats them.

Term of the Lease. A lease will define its *term,* the length of time that you agree to rent the property—usually one month, six months, or a year. If your lease has no set length of time, the term is automatically one month if the rent is paid on a monthly basis. This means that your agreement runs from month to month.

The lease will state the amount of rent that you agree to pay for the apartment or house. If you sign a one-year lease for $500 a month, you are entering into a contract to pay $500 for twelve months, or $6,000.

Receipts. You should always pay your rent by personal check or money order. This way you have a receipt for each payment. You should not pay rent with cash unless you get a signed receipt! Be careful if you use money orders.

Sometimes a landlord will claim that he or she did not receive your money order. You will then have to ask the bank to find out what happened to it. If the landlord tries to evict you for nonpayment of rent, you will need proof to show the judge that you did pay the rent. Therefore, always get a signed receipt from your landlord when you pay by money order. Always keep copies of all of your rent receipts.

Security Deposit. The lease may require a security deposit. If a security deposit is required, the written lease should state that it was received and indicate the amount.

Late Charge. Many leases require a late charge if the rent is not paid by a certain date. This charge is supposed to cover the money lost by the landlord as a result of the late payment. Courts will enforce late charges if reasonable and spelled out in writing in the lease. Late charges are not allowed unless there is an agreement stating that late charges are to be considered part of the rent. Late charges are also not allowed if the tenant's failure to pay the rent on time was due to the landlord's failure to make needed repairs. Under the Anti-Eviction Act, a tenant who repeatedly pays rent after its due date can be sued for eviction. A landlord must wait at least five days before adding a late charge if the tenant receives Social Security retirement benefits or certain government pensions.

Attorneys' Fees. Some leases require a tenant to pay the landlord's attorney's fee if the landlord uses a lawyer to take the tenant to court. If your lease has such a term and the landlord takes you to court for eviction and wins the case, you *will* be responsible for paying a "reasonable" fee for the landlord's attorney.

If the judge finds that you are responsible for paying a reasonable fee for the landlord's attorney, you can be evicted if you do not pay that amount on the day of the hearing. Some judges will even grant an eviction in cases in which the tenant paid the rent owed before the court date but failed to include with the rent payment the fee the attorney asked for in the complaint.

LEASE RULES. A lease will often include rules that the landlord wants the tenant to follow. Lease rules require you to conduct yourself in a certain way or not to do certain things in your apartment or in the common areas of your building or complex. For example, your lease may contain rules about using a washing machine in your apartment; about your responsibility to pay for electric, gas, heat, or other utilities if not included in the rent; about how you are to dispose of trash; and about how you must use common facilities, such as laundries or playgrounds.

Before entering into a lease, you should make sure that you are willing to follow the rules and regulations. If you do not follow the requirements, you can be evicted under the Anti-Eviction Act for breaking a rule, as long as the rule is reasonable.

Damages. A lease will usually state that you are responsible for any damage done to the property by your children, guests, or pets if it is more than normal wear and tear. The law requires tenants to be responsible for the proper care of the landlord's property, even if your written lease contains nothing about this or if you have an oral lease. Under the Anti-Eviction Act, you can be evicted for destroying the landlord's property.

Repairs. Tenants have a legal responsibility to notify the landlord of needed repairs even if there is no written lease. Most leases state that the tenant is responsible for giving the landlord prompt notice of any repairs that are needed. There are several reasons why you should promptly report any defect, particularly such problems as water leaks. These problems can cause additional damage if they are not corrected right away. By giving notice of such problems, you can also avoid any attempt by the landlord to claim that you must pay for the additional damage. You can also avoid giving the landlord a claim against all or part of your security deposit. You should make sure that, when possible, you give notice in writing, keeping a copy for your records.

Other Tenants' Rights. A lease requires the landlord to make sure that each tenant respects the rights of other tenants. If one tenant is disturbing the other tenants by playing loud music at night or destroying the property, it is the landlord's responsibility to make that tenant stop. But in order for the landlord to be held responsible for any damages suffered by the tenants, one of the tenants must tell the landlord about the situation.

Under any lease, whether written or oral, you cannot interfere with the rights of other tenants. This means that you and your family members, guests, and pets cannot act in ways that disturb the peace and quiet of other tenants and neighbors. Under the Anti-Eviction Act, you can be evicted for being disorderly, making too much noise, or disturbing other tenants.

Pets. A written lease usually will state whether the tenant is allowed to have a pet. If your landlord says that it's okay to have a pet, make sure that you get his or her permission in writing. Many landlords do not permit pets and the lease will have a "no-pets" clause in it.

If a tenant has a pet but the property is sold to a new owner-landlord who wants to prohibit pets, the new landlord might try to offer the tenant a new lease with a no-pets clause. The law now prohibits a new owner-landlord from forcing tenants to give up pets they were allowed to have by the previous owner. However, the new landlord can still prohibit *new* tenants from having pets and can try to force an existing tenant to get rid of any pet that is causing problems for other tenants.

There are special rules regarding pets for senior citizens who live in rental housing for the elderly. Federal law allows the elderly and disabled to own and keep common household pets in federally assisted elderly rental housing. New Jersey law also gives residents of *all* senior citizen projects the right to have pets. This law applies to buildings containing three apartments or more, condominium projects, and cooperative buildings, as long as all of the apartments are for senior citizens. Senior citizens are defined as people sixty-two years of age or older and include the surviving spouse of a senior as long as he or she is at least fifty-five years old.

Under the law, the landlord cannot refuse to renew a tenant's lease because the tenant owns a pet. The landlord can make reasonable rules concerning the care and control of pets by tenants and can require a tenant to give away any offspring from the tenant's pet within eight weeks of birth. The landlord can't require that the pet be spayed or neutered. The law also allows a landlord to demand that a tenant get rid of a pet if

- The tenant does not follow the reasonable rules adopted by the landlord and this causes a violation of any health or building code.
- The tenant does not take good care of the pet.
- The tenant does not control the pet, such as keeping a dog on a leash when taking it out for a walk.
- The tenant does not clean up the pet's waste when asked to do so by the landlord.
- The tenant does not keep his or her pet from making waste on the sidewalks, doorways, hallways, or other common areas in and around the complex.

LANDLORD INSPECTION. All leases, whether written or oral, give the tenant *exclusive possession* of the dwelling unit. This means that only the tenant, or members of the tenant's household, or people the tenant allows in the house or apartment, have the right to be there. *The landlord does not have the right to come into the house or apartment any time that he or she wants.* In a written lease, the landlord's duty not to enter the tenant's house or apartment is called the *covenant of quiet enjoyment.* This covenant or promise means that the *tenant* has control over who can or can't come into the apartment or house.

There are a few exceptions to this covenant:

- If the tenant invites or asks the landlord or one of the landlord's workers to come in.
- If the landlord needs to inspect the apartment, but only at *reasonable frequencies* (every day is probably not reasonable; every month or two may be all right); at a *reasonable* time of day (4 A.M. is unreasonable; 4 P.M. might be okay, depending on whether the tenant will be home at that time); *and* only after giving the tenant *reasonable notice* that he or she is coming to inspect. Reasonable notice usually means a written notice given *at least one day* before the landlord wants to come in. There is a regulation, for buildings containing three apartments or more, requiring one day's notice before a landlord can come into an apartment to make an inspection or do repairs.

- If the landlord or one of the landlord's workers needs to come into the apartment to do maintenance or make repairs. If the repairs are not an emergency, workers can come into the house or apartment only at a reasonable time and only after giving reasonable notice as mentioned above.
- If the landlord or the landlord's workers need to come into the house or apartment to do *emergency* repairs. Under this circumstance, the landlord may not have to give one day's notice—or any notice—if the emergency is very serious or a dangerous condition exists.

If the landlord or one of the landlord's workers comes into your house or apartment and does not have your permission or does not have one of the other reasons discussed above, he or she is breaking the law. You should send a letter by certified mail to the landlord complaining about what happened and keep a copy for your records. You can also call the police or go to the police station or local court and file a complaint against the person who came in for *trespass* or *harassment*.

RENEWAL OR TERMINATION OF THE LEASE. A yearly lease that is not automatically renewed becomes a month-to-month lease when the lease year ends.

A *month-to-month* lease will renew itself automatically for another month unless the tenant or the landlord acts to end the lease. This rule applies even if the lease agreement is oral and not in writing.

Changing Lease Terms upon Renewal. When your lease ends, the landlord can offer you a new lease with changes in the terms and conditions of the lease. To do this, the landlord must give you a written notice ending your existing lease and offering to enter into a new lease with you if you accept the changes. The landlord's notice must clearly spell out the changes.

A tenant's refusal at the end of a lease to accept reasonable changes in the terms and conditions of the lease can result in eviction under the Anti-Eviction Act. To be "reasonable," the changes must take into account the circumstances and interests of *both* the landlord *and the tenant.* This means that your landlord cannot make lease changes *that he or she knows will cause you unnecessary hardship,* unless he or she has very strong reasons for doing so. If your landlord sends you a written notice containing lease changes you think are unreasonable, send a letter to the landlord describing what you consider to be the unreasonable changes. Your letter should also state that you will not accept the new lease unless the landlord offers to make changes that are reasonable.

For example, assume that at the end of your lease your landlord wants to change the lease by putting in late charges if your rent is paid after the fifth day of the month. The landlord knows that you do not get paid or receive your assistance check until the third or fourth day of the month and that it will be very hard for you to pay the rent money by the fifth. You refuse to sign the new lease and the landlord takes you to court to try to evict you. In court, the judge should decide that the lease change is not reasonable because the landlord knows that you could not pay the rent by the fifth and should have picked a date later in the month.

Terminating a Lease. Before you end or break a lease, you must understand a basic rule about landlord-tenant law in New Jersey. Because of the Anti-Eviction Act, you cannot be evicted simply because your lease ends. A tenant can be evicted only if the landlord can prove one of the good causes for eviction under the law (see the section in this chapter entitled "Evictions"). The ending or expiration of a lease is not a good cause for eviction. However long your lease, you do not have to move just because your lease has ended. Unless you (or the landlord) end your lease, all yearly leases and month-to-month leases automatically renew themselves. The only exception to this rule is if you live in a building with no more than three apartments and the landlord lives in one of the apartments.

To end a lease, either the tenant or the landlord must give the other a written notice before the end of the lease stating that the lease will not be renewed. If this written notice is not given or is not given in the required time, then the lease will renew itself automatically at least on a month-to-month basis, generally with the same terms and conditions.

Unless the lease says otherwise, to end a yearly lease you must give the landlord a written notice at least one full month before the end of the lease. The notice must tell the landlord that you are moving out when the lease ends. Likewise, unless the lease says otherwise, the landlord must give you at least one full month's notice before the end of the lease to terminate a yearly lease. The landlord must first terminate the old lease before he or she can raise the rent or change other lease terms. Remember that you cannot be evicted just because the landlord ends your lease.

If your current lease—or a notice from your landlord—says that you must either sign a new lease by a certain date or else move out by the date your present lease expires, your failure to renew your lease will put the landlord on notice that you intend to move out at the end of the lease period. If you object to the changes in the lease, let the landlord know. (Lease changes must be reasonable.) If you then choose not to move out, you will become a month-to-month tenant. You will, however, be subject to eviction for refusing to sign a new lease.

To end a month-to-month lease or any rental agreement that does not have a specific lease term, you must give a written one-month notice before the month starts. You can then move out at the end of the month.

Moving Out before the Lease Ends. If you move out before the end of the lease, the landlord can hold you responsible for the rent that becomes due until the apartment or house is rented again, or until the lease ends. However, the landlord must try to rent the apartment.

33

For example, if you move out during July and your lease ends on October 31, you could be held responsible for the rents of August, September, and October. But if another tenant moves in on September 1, then the landlord may sue you only for August's rent. This does not apply if the landlord agrees in writing to let you move before the lease ends.

If you have to move before the end of the lease term, notify your landlord in writing as soon as possible. Try to get your landlord's written permission to break the lease. If your landlord refuses to give you permission and you know of people who are interested in your apartment, send their names in a letter to your landlord.

You do not have to leave a forwarding address when you move. But if you want your security deposit back, you may have to give your former landlord your new address.

Tenants sometimes notify the landlord that they are moving because they have found another apartment that is more affordable or in better condition. What can you do if the new apartment becomes unavailable or some other problem comes up that makes the move impossible? If this happens, you do not have to move out just because you gave notice. There may be other financial consequences, however. In these situations, you should seek help from an attorney, Legal Services, or a state or local tenants' association. Your landlord can't evict you simply because you did not leave when you said you would.

CONSTRUCTIVE EVICTIONS. If your landlord refuses to make needed repairs to your apartment, you can move out before the lease ends and still not be held responsible for rent for the time left on the lease. It is important to have proof of these bad conditions. You can get this proof by having a building inspection done and taking pictures before you move out. The law in this situation holds the landlord responsible for breaking the lease by failing to fulfill his or her duty to provide you with safe and decent housing. This is called *constructive eviction.*

Certain rules apply to constructive evictions:

- You can break your lease under this rule only if your rental unit is in such bad condition that your and your family's health and safety are at risk and your landlord does not make repairs after receiving notice from you in writing.
- It is important that you give the landlord notice of the defective conditions and a reasonable amount of time to make repairs before moving out and claiming constructive eviction. Your notice should be in writing and by certified mail, return receipt requested.
- If serious conditions in your apartment force you to move before the end of your lease, you are still entitled to have your security deposit returned to you.

34

- If you move because of bad conditions before your lease ends, your landlord may try to sue you for rent for the time left on the lease. The landlord will almost certainly refuse to return your security deposit. You may find yourself in court either because the landlord has sued you for back rent or because you are suing the landlord for the return of your security deposit. Whether you win or lose in court will depend on how serious the judge believes the conditions were that you claim forced you to move.

TENANT DEATH OR ILLNESS. The law recognizes that death or serious illness often requires households to search for less expensive housing, including moving in with other family members. The law provides that any lease for one year or more may be ended before it expires if the tenant or the tenant's spouse dies. The tenant, the tenant's executor or administrator, or the surviving spouse must give the landlord written notice of the lease termination if the names of both spouses are on the lease. The lease termination becomes valid forty days after the landlord receives written notice if (1) the rent owed up to that point has been paid, (2) the property is vacated at least five working days before the fortieth day, *and* (3) the tenant's lease does not prohibit early termination upon the tenant's death.

When a lease is terminated because of the tenant's death, any property tax rebate or credit due and owing to the tenant before the lease termination must be paid to the executor or administrator of the tenant's estate or to the tenant's surviving spouse. Any landlord who fails to do this becomes liable to the tenant's estate or surviving spouse for twice the amount of the property tax rebate to which the tenant was entitled, or $100, whichever is greater.

The law also allows the lease to survive the death of the tenant. The Anti-Eviction Act requires the landlord to show good cause to evict before the court can evict the tenant's family, sub-tenants, or legal representatives. This means that after the main tenant dies, a landlord must prove that he or she is entitled under the Anti-Eviction Act to evict that tenant's remaining family members or legal representatives. The landlord cannot bring trespass charges in municipal court against such persons.

You must be careful if the landlord tries to include a section in your lease that requires family members to leave the apartment immediately or shortly after the death of the tenant named in the lease. The courts have held that the tenant may have to accept the lease with this section for the present, but have refused to decide whether family members remaining after a named tenant's death would be protected by the Anti-Eviction Act. The courts left this question to be decided when the issue arises, after the named tenant's death. If the landlord asks you to sign a lease with this type of section in it, write on the lease that you are signing "under protest."

Any lease for at least one year may be ended before it expires if the tenant or the tenant's spouse becomes disabled due to an illness or accident. In such a case, the tenant or spouse must notify the landlord on a form available from the New Jersey Department of Community Affairs (DCA). The form requires (1) certification of a treating doctor that the tenant or spouse is unable to continue to work; (2) proof of loss of income; *and* (3) proof that any pension, insurance, or other assistance to which the tenant or spouse is entitled is not enough to pay the rent, even when added with other income. The lease termination becomes effective forty days after the landlord receives the written notice. The property must also be vacated and possession returned to the landlord at least five days before the fortieth day.

HOUSING ACCESSIBLE TO PEOPLE WITH DISABILITIES. The law permits tenants who are disabled to break their lease if the landlord, after notice, has failed to make the dwelling unit accessible to the disabled tenant or a disabled member of the household. To break your lease under these circumstances, you must notify the landlord in advance and the notice must contain (1) a statement from your physician that you are permanently disabled, *and* (2) a statement that you asked the landlord to make the house or apartment accessible at the landlord's expense and that the landlord was unable or unwilling to do so.

LANDLORD REGISTRATION

The law requires landlords who rent houses, apartments, or buildings to register certain information with the clerk of the city or town where the building is located. If your building contains three or more apartments, the landlord must also register with the New Jersey DCA in Trenton. The law requires that the landlord list his or her name and address and the telephone number of someone—such as the superintendent or janitor—who can be reached at any time and is responsible for ordering emergency repairs and receiving complaints from tenants. The landlord must display this information at the property itself in a place where tenants can see it and the landlord must give this information in writing to each tenant.

The registration law prevents a landlord from evicting you if the building is not properly registered. If your landlord has not registered the property or has not given you a copy of the registration, the court cannot enter a judgment to evict you. In most eviction cases in which a landlord has not registered, the judge will postpone hearing the case to give the landlord time to register. Once the landlord registers, the court can then hear the case and enter a judgment for eviction. The postponement can give you extra time to move or to pay rent you may owe.

If your landlord is not registered, you can file a complaint in superior or municipal court. A landlord can be fined up to $500 for failing to register.

YOUR RIGHT TO SAFE AND DECENT HOUSING

Tenants frequently complain that their landlord will not repair such things as windows, locks, toilets, faucets, and heating systems when these break from normal wear and tear. Tenants also complain that their landlord does not do routine maintenance, such as pest extermination. You have a right as a tenant to live in housing that is safe, clean, and decent.

WARRANTY OF HABITABILITY. Landlords have a duty under New Jersey landlord-tenant law to maintain their rental property in a safe and decent condition. This duty applies to all leases, whether written or oral. The duty to keep rental units safe and decent is called the *warranty of habitability*. The warranty of habitability is based upon common sense: In return for receiving rent from the tenant, the landlord must make sure that the housing is fit to be occupied by the tenant.

The warranty of habitability has been held to include keeping the basic elements of your housing unit in good condition. This includes taking care of the physical structure, such as the roof, windows, and walls; the systems which supply you heat, hot and cold water, and electricity and gas; and appliances, such as the stove, refrigerator, and dishwasher. It also includes keeping apartments pest free and common areas clean, and providing security against crime, such as locks on doors and windows to deter break-ins.

MULTIPLE-DWELLING CODE. In addition, there are several codes adopted by the state or local governments that establish standards for maintaining rental property. There are trained personnel who inspect rental properties to enforce the code and who are available to take complaints about violations of the code from individual tenants.

Landlords of buildings with three or more units must meet the standards in the New Jersey housing- or property-maintenance *multiple dwelling* code. This code is contained in regulations issued by the New Jersey DCA.

This code has detailed and specific rules that cover a wide range of issues: locks, window screens, ventilation, pests, plumbing, painting, garbage, living space, and more. You can find these regulations in your public or courthouse library, or you can call the DCA, Bureau of Housing Inspection, in Trenton for more information.

OTHER CODES. Most towns and cities also have their own housing or property maintenance codes. These codes usually apply to *all* buildings or apartments, not just multiple dwellings. Single-family and two-family houses are covered by these codes. Call your city hall or municipal building department and ask for the building inspector or housing inspector if you have any questions or problems or would just like to see a copy of the local housing code.

HEATING REQUIREMENTS. If your lease requires the landlord to provide heat, the landlord must give you the amount of heat required by either the state code or the local town or city ordinance. Under the state health code, from October 1 to May 1, whenever the outside temperature falls below fifty-five degrees, the landlord must provide enough heat so that the temperature in the apartment stays at least sixty-eight degrees from 6 A.M. to 11 P.M. Between the hours of 11 P.M. and 6 A.M., the temperature in the apartment must be at least sixty-five degrees.

Many local boards of health have the power to make repairs to heating systems so that you can receive heat. There must be an ordinance adopted by your local government that gives the board of health the power to make repairs to heating systems. Even with an ordinance, the board of health can act only if the temperature outdoors is below fifty-five degrees. To get action, you must call the board of health and say that you tried to get the landlord to fix the heat. The board will then wait twenty-four hours before having someone make the repairs.

Some New Jersey cities have programs to provide an emergency delivery of oil, at government expense, when tenants have no heat because the landlord did not buy oil. The city then collects the money directly from the landlord. Check with your local government to find out about such programs.

The housing inspector or board of health in your town enforces the heat requirements in the state health code. Larger cities often have special no-heat hot lines which are set up especially to handle complaints. The inspector can file a complaint in court on your behalf, or you can file your own complaint. The landlord must then appear in court and explain why he or she is not providing heat. The court can impose stiff penalties, including fines or jail sentences.

LEAD PAINT AND LEAD POISONING. Lead poisoning is a dangerous health problem for many tenants, especially children. Lead poisoning is the presence of too much lead in the body. Children and unborn fetuses are particularly at risk of harm from lead poisoning since their bodies and nervous systems are still developing. Lead poisoning can cause serious physical and mental harm to adults and children. Don't wait to do something about it if you think you or your children may be exposed to lead in your apartment or home.

A person can be poisoned by eating lead or breathing lead dust. Tenants—especially children under age six—are frequently poisoned by the paint in their apartment or house. Until 1977, lead could be used in house paints. There is usually a lot of lead paint in older buildings. Peeling or cracking paint in older houses and apartments can be dangerous. Exterior paint can also have lead in it. Peeling paint on the outside of houses or porches can fall on the ground.

Children like the taste of paint chips and may chew on window sills and paint chips that fall on the floor. Babies, toddlers, and preschool-age children like to put things into their mouths. In houses with peeling or cracking lead paint, lead dust can get on children's hands, pacifiers, and toys. When children then put these items into their mouths, they can swallow lead dust and poison themselves.

Lead can enter your body or your children's bodies by breathing air with lead dust in it. Scraping paint off walls or vacuuming up paint chips from floors can spread lead dust around the house. Lead can poison an unborn child if the mother breathes lead dust.

There is a blood test that shows if you or your children have been poisoned by lead. The law requires every doctor, registered nurse, or health care facility to perform lead screening on every child under age six to whom they have provided health services. Whenever the screening shows an elevated blood level (currently fifteen micrograms per deciliter or above), the doctor, nurse, or health care facility must make reasonable efforts to obtain a confirmatory blood test. Children participating in the Medicaid program must be tested for lead poisoning for free. For information on testing, call your local health department.

Lead poisoning is a serious health hazard. If you or your children test high for levels of lead in your blood there may be lead paint in your apartment or home. You should immediately get advice and help from Legal Services on how to have your landlord remove the lead paint as quickly as possible.

Because lead poisoning is so harmful, laws help protect exposed tenants. The law prohibits using lead paint on many surfaces, including the inside or outside of apartments or houses. For lead paint that is already there, the law says that such paint is a *public nuisance* that must be removed by the landlord.

The local health department must investigate violations of lead paint laws and force the landlord to remove lead paint. If anyone in your family is tested and has a high level of lead in their blood, call the health department and ask them to inspect your home immediately.

If the health department finds a child under six years old with a high blood-lead level, then the health department must order the owner of the building to remove the lead. To correct the problem, the owner can cover the surface with hard material such as siding or wallpaper or remove the lead paint and repaint with nonlead paint.

The health department will give tenants or occupants a copy of its notice to the owner so that they know what the health department has ordered the owner to do.

CRIME INSURANCE. If you live in an apartment building of ten or more units, your landlord must tell you about the availability of federal crime insurance within thirty days after you move in. The law requires the landlord to tell you where you can apply for crime insurance. Even more important, the law requires landlords to make whatever improvements are necessary to make tenants insurable, including improving defective window and door locks.

If the landlord does not tell you about crime insurance and where you can get it, you can file a complaint in superior court. The court may fine the landlord up to $200 for each violation.

WINDOW GUARDS. Landlords of multiple-dwelling units are required, at the tenant's request, to install and maintain window guards in the public halls and in the apartment of any tenant who has a child ten years old or younger living in the apartment. The law requires landlords to give tenants an annual notice which tells tenants that they can make a written request to have window guards installed. This notice should also be contained in the lease. The cost of installing window guards may be passed on to the tenants. Note that window guards are *not* required on any first-floor windows or on any windows that give access to a fire escape. Owner-occupied buildings and some other buildings are also exempt from this requirement. If you have small children and have not been notified about window guards, you may want to talk to a lawyer to find out if this law covers you.

HOW TO GET YOUR LANDLORD TO MAKE REPAIRS

The law gives you several ways to assert your right as a tenant to safe and decent housing and to make your landlord repair defective conditions in your rental unit. You have the legal right to

- Call in the building or health inspector.
- Use your rent to make repairs.
- Withhold your rent.
- Take legal action.

USING THE HOUSING AND HEALTH CODES. As discussed earlier, rental units must meet city and state housing and health codes. The codes list the requirements that the landlord's property must meet so that it can be approved as a safe or *standard* building. The codes deal with heat, plumbing, roofing, pests, and other serious defects like weak walls.

If you feel that the conditions in your apartment or house are defective, unliveable, or dangerous, tell your landlord. If your landlord fails to make the repairs in a reasonable period of time, call the local building inspector and ask him or her to inspect the property as soon as possible. If you can, be present when the inspection is done so that you can point out all of the problems. Ask the inspector's name and ask him or her to send you a copy of the report.

If the needed repairs present a sanitation problem, such as a sewage leak, call the city or county board of health. Ask for an inspector to check the condition. When the inspector comes, get his or her name.

If the inspector finds violations of the code, he or she will send a letter to the landlord listing the code violations. This letter will advise the landlord that a reinspection will take place on a certain date to check whether the repairs have been made.

Some housing and health code inspectors do not send the tenant a copy of the inspection reports or inform the tenant of the results of the inspection. As a tenant in the property, you have a right to receive a copy of these reports and you should make sure to ask that copies of all reports be sent to you.

Reinspecting a Housing Unit. If your housing unit fails the inspection, the housing or health code inspector must reinspect it. You might find that the landlord has not made the necessary repairs. If this happens, you should call the inspector and inform him or her that the landlord has not made the required repairs.

If, on reinspection, the inspector finds that the landlord has not made the repairs, another inspection will be scheduled. If violations are still not corrected, the building inspector should then give a summons to the landlord to appear in municipal court. If found guilty, the landlord can be fined.

Condemning or Closing a Building. The housing- and property-maintenance codes allow inspectors to declare a house or apartment building *unfit for human habitation* if there are serious defects in the rental unit or building. These defects must pose a threat to the health and safety of the tenants. A collapse in the structure of a building or absence of heat or hot water are the types of situations that may warrant declaring a building unfit. By declaring the building unfit, the inspector can order you to leave your rental unit and close the building.

There have been cases in which an inspector condemned a building even though the defective conditions were not serious enough to force tenants to leave. For example, a landlord seeking to convert a building into condominiums could get the tenants out of the building with the inspector's help, thereby avoiding the requirements of the condominium-conversion laws. If you suspect that the actions of the housing inspector or your landlord in trying to force you out are wrong, get advice from a lawyer.

If the building inspector tells you in writing to move because the building has been declared unfit, you might be entitled to relocation assistance from the local government. Relocation assistance includes help in finding a new place to live, moving expenses, and up to $4,000 in assistance toward buying or renting a house or apartment.

USING THE RENT TO MAKE REPAIRS: REPAIR AND DEDUCT. Another way tenants can get repairs made is by using rent money to make the repairs. After making

---

RULES FOR REPAIR AND DEDUCT

✔ The conditions that are in need of repair must be serious enough to affect the tenant's health or well-being.

✔ The tenant must first give the landlord proper notice stating that repairs are needed and also give the landlord a reasonable amount of time to make the repairs. The notice should be in writing and sent by certified mail, return receipt requested.

✔ After waiting a reasonable amount of time, the tenant should have the repair done and pay for it with all or part of the rent money.

✔ The cost of the repair must be reasonable.

✔ The tenant then deducts the amount from the next rent payment and gives the landlord a copy of the receipt for the repair.

---

the repairs, the tenant subtracts the cost of the repairs from the rent instead of paying it to the landlord as rent. This is called *repair and deduct.* There are certain rules for repair and deduct that you must follow (see the box above).

In an emergency situation, if you can't reach the landlord in person or by telephone, you can have the repairs made and then tell the landlord.

The use of repair and deduct sometimes leads to disputes between the landlord and tenant. A landlord may try to hold the tenant responsible for the full rent even the tenant used the rent money to repair a serious defect. In this situation, the landlord may try to evict you in court for nonpayment of rent. If you show the judge a copy of the letter you sent telling the landlord to make the repair and a copy of the repair receipt, the judge should not hold you responsible for the full rent.

WITHHOLDING RENT. When a landlord simply refuses to make needed repairs, tenants often have little choice but to withhold rent. There are two steps you must take if you decide to withhold rent to force the landlord to make repairs:

1. You must send a letter to the landlord explaining what conditions must be corrected. The letter should explain that you will stop paying rent until all of the repairs are completed. You should also explain that, once the repairs are completed, you will pay a reduced rent from the time the repairs were needed until the time the repairs are completed. The letter should be sent by certified mail, return receipt requested, and you should keep a copy of the letter since you may need it later in court.

2. You must save the rent you withhold each month and put it in a safe place. A bank account is a good place to deposit the rent each month because you will earn interest on the money. Saving the rent is the most important thing you can do.

Landlords need the rent money to pay bills and make a profit. Rent withholding denies the landlord this money each month. Some landlords will decide to make all of the repairs or make an agreement with you to make repairs in return for your paying the withheld back rent and starting to pay your rent again. Make sure that any agreement is in writing.

RENT ABATEMENT HEARING. A landlord may take you to court for not paying rent. This is where saving the rent you withheld becomes very important. You cannot be evicted for nonpayment of rent if you have saved all of the rent and you appear in court with the money on the day you are summoned. You should tell the judge that you withheld your rent because of the bad conditions. The judge will require you to deposit the withheld rent with the court clerk. If you don't have the money that day, you can be evicted. If you deposit the money, the judge will then schedule a second hearing, called a *rent abatement hearing*, to accept evidence about the conditions in your apartment.

The rent abatement hearing gives you the chance to show the judge just how bad the conditions are in your apartment and in the common areas of the building. Make a list and bring it with you to court when you testify. You also should bring the copy of the letter that you sent notifying the landlord of your decision to withhold rent and of the defective conditions in the apartment or house. Also, bring any reports by housing or health code inspectors about the conditions. If you can, take pictures of holes, stains, and other problems and show them to the judge.

The judge hearing your case has the power to lower the rent for the months in which you withheld your rent. The judge can then allow you to keep the difference between your regular rent and the lower rent for the months you withheld rent. The judge can also allow you to pay the lower rent in the future until the landlord makes all of the repairs. The judge will list each repair that must be made before the rent can be returned to its regular amount. This is called a *rent abatement order.*

It is important that you use rent withholding only if the problems in your house or apartment are serious and only after you have given the landlord notice. At a rent abatement hearing, the judge could also decide that the conditions are not bad enough and require that you pay all of the withheld rent. If this happens, you may be responsible for paying court costs, late charges, and the cost of the landlord's attorney's fee.

COURT ORDER TO REPAIR. Instead of rent withholding, tenants can now go directly to court and ask the judge to order the landlord to make repairs. This type of lawsuit is filed in small-claims court and can include a request that the judge order the landlord to pay money back for repairs made by the tenants.

Tenants should talk with their local Legal Services office, tenants' organization, or a private lawyer if they want to know more about using small-claims court or if they are not sure about how they should fill out the papers required to file a small-claims complaint.

RENT RECEIVERSHIP. The law also allows tenants to file a petition with the court to appoint a *receiver* to run the building or complex. The petition, which must be filed in superior court, asks the judge to name someone to collect all the rents and to use the money to make repairs to the building. The person who is named by the court to collect rents and order repairs is a *rent receiver.*

A judge will usually consider granting the petition when the landlord has a history of refusing to correct conditions that deprive the tenants of heat, water, electricity, or other essential services. The judge usually appoints a rent receiver only when repair and deduct, rent withholding, and other attempts to have repairs made have failed.

Petitioning for a rent receiver is a complex legal procedure that requires the help of an attorney. You should keep in mind that if the landlord is trying to evict you because you withheld rent due to very bad conditions in your building, the judge *on his or her own* can begin the process of having a receiver appointed. You may want to ask the judge about this during a rent abatement hearing if your landlord is completely uncooperative and the conditions in your building are serious.

GOING TO THE LANDLORD'S INSURANCE COMPANY. Another way to put pressure on the landlord to make repairs is to complain to the landlord's property insurance company about conditions that are a safety hazard. In towns with rent control, the name of the insurance company will appear in bills the landlord submits in connection with a *hardship increase application.* In other places, it may be more difficult to learn the name of the landlord's insurance company.

For example, a broken stairway could cause a tenant to fall and get hurt. The insurance company would then have to pay if the tenant sued the landlord and won. But if the tenant complains to the insurance company about the broken stairway, the company might force the landlord to repair the stairway by threatening to cancel the policy.

RENT INCREASES

Tenants often ask if they have any rights when the landlord asks for a rent increase, especially if their landlord has raised the rent in the past and the tenant is at the point where he or she can no longer afford to pay any more.

The answer to this question is yes. Landlords can increase the rent only if they follow the correct procedure by ending the lease at the old rent and creating a new lease at the increased rent. A landlord also cannot ask for a rent increase that is unconscionable, and, if the tenant lives in a community with rent control, the rent increase cannot exceed the amount allowed under the rent control ordinance. Your landlord cannot increase the rent during the term of your lease.

NOTICE OF INCREASE. For a landlord to raise your rent, you must be given proper written notice informing you that the present written or oral lease is being ended and you can stay in the rental unit by signing a new lease at the higher rent. If you decide to sign the lease and stay on as a tenant, you must pay the rent increase.

If your lease is monthly, a proper notice must explain that your present lease will be terminated in one full calendar month. You must receive this notice at least one month before your lease ends. The notice period may be greater, depending on what your current lease says.

Any notice of a rent increase that is not in writing and is not divided into two parts—ending the old lease and beginning a new lease at a higher rent—is not legal, and you do not have to pay the increase.

CONTESTING OR EVALUATING THE INCREASE. If the landlord asks for a rent increase and you decide to stay but not pay the increase, you are not agreeing to the increase. You should be aware that if you do this, the landlord can try to evict you in court under the Anti-Eviction Act. The law allows landlords to evict tenants for nonpayment of a rent increase.

Under the Anti-Eviction Act, a landlord cannot make you pay an increase in rent that is so large that it is *unconscionable.* This means extremely harsh or so unreasonable as to be shocking. Whether an increase is unconscionable depends on the facts of each case. For example, an increase of over 20 percent, if made by the landlord without a very good reason, could be unconscionable. Even a 5 percent increase could be unconscionable if the conditions in the building are very bad and the landlord has failed to make needed repairs.

Unconscionability does not apply if your apartment, house, or mobile home is covered by a rent control ordinance adopted by your city or township. In all places where there is no rent control, an unconscionable increase is the only limitation on your landlord's right to increase the rent. If you believe that your landlord is asking for an unconscionable rent increase, you can refuse to pay the increase. Your landlord can then take you to court to try to evict you for nonpayment of the rent increase. If the notice ending your lease and increasing your rent is proper, you can defend against the increase in court by arguing that the increase is unconscionable.

45

The judge should require the landlord to show that the large increase sought is justified because the expenses are more than the rental income, or that there is an insufficient profit.

In addition, the landlord should be required to show that improvements were made to the rental units or the building and that these improvements mean better living conditions for tenants. A landlord should not be given credit for improvements needed to bring the building into compliance with housing and health codes. Tenants have a right to safe and decent housing and should not be penalized simply because a present or former landlord did not make repairs to the building. Some judges do not, however, take these factors into account when ruling on whether a rent increase is unconscionable. Instead, there are judges who believe that landlords can double or triple the rent simply by showing that other apartments in the area are renting for a similar amount.

INCREASES UNDER RENT CONTROL ORDINANCES.   Rent increases are also limited to the amounts allowed under a local rent control ordinance, if the community has adopted rent control and the rental unit is covered by rent control. More than 100 cities and townships in New Jersey have passed rent control ordinances. To learn if your city or township has rent control and if it covers your unit, you should call your city or town hall. The ordinance will state how much and how often your rent can be raised.

There are two types of rent increases allowed by most rent control ordinances. First, the ordinances allow landlords to automatically increase the rent by a certain percentage each year. This is called a *fair-return* increase. Second, the ordinances allow landlords to apply to the rent control board for an increase above the fair-return amount. This is called a *hardship* increase.

Fair-Return Increases. Under the law, rent control must allow landlords a fair rate of return. This is commonly referred to as a *cost-of-living* increase. As a general rule, a fair return is equal to the return on an investment in other businesses having similar risks. A fair return should not be so high as to allow landlords to charge tenants more than the fair value of the property and services which are provided. Most rent control ordinances use a formula to determine fair return and the amount of the automatic yearly increase a landlord can obtain.

Hardship Increases. Rent control ordinances also allow landlords the chance to apply to the rent control board for a hardship increase. Tenants must be notified if the landlord applies for a hardship increase. The rent control board will then hold a public hearing on the landlord's request and, after the hearing, make a decision on the request. The rent control hearing gives tenants a chance to contest the rent increase sought in the application.

If you receive notice that your landlord is applying for a hardship increase, there are several steps you can take. You should immediately contact your rent control board and ask them for (1) a copy of the ordinance, (2) a copy of the landlord's application for a hardship increase, *and* (3) information when the hearing on the hardship increase will be held by the rent control board. You may also want to seek the advice of an attorney and get any help you can from the tenants' organization in your building, complex, or community.

At the hearing on a request for a hardship increase, the landlord will try to show why he or she should get the increase. To defeat the hardship application, you must show that the landlord should not recover unfair or unreasonable costs being claimed. This means that you must carefully go through the hardship application and examine each item to make sure it is fair and reasonable. You should also make sure that the landlord is properly reporting all income. For example, you should challenge any cost the landlord is not entitled to recover under the ordinance, any cost that appears inflated or false, or any cost that is unreasonable or too high, such as financing.

If you find out that your rent is higher than the legal rent set by the rent control ordinance, you should contact your rent control board. You can file a complaint with the board to get the rent lowered to the correct amount and to recover the amount of illegal rent you paid. Your local Legal Services program, a private attorney, or your local tenants' organization can also help.

Landlords may not be allowed to include in a hardship increase any costs that result from a planned conversion of the building to a condominium or cooperative. For example, a court has held that where a building had its property taxes doubled when it was converted into a cooperative, the rent control board was justified in not allowing the increase. The court also ruled that the Anti-Eviction Act requires that tenants who choose not to buy ownership in a condominium or cooperative be protected against conversion-related rent increases.

The law does not allow your landlord to increase your rent in order to "get even" with you because you are using your legal rights as a tenant, because you have reported housing and health code violations to official inspectors, or because you belong to a tenants' organization.

EVICTIONS

In New Jersey, the only way a tenant can be evicted or removed from his or her rental unit is if a superior court judge orders the eviction. An order for eviction can come only after the landlord has sued the tenant for eviction in superior court and won. There is no other way that you can be legally evicted from your home or apartment. You do not have to move out simply because the landlord tells you to or threatens to evict you if you don't leave.

SELF-HELP EVICTIONS. It is illegal for a landlord or anyone else to force you to move out without going through the legal eviction process. This kind of self-help eviction is called a *forcible entry and detainer* or a *lockout.* A lockout occurs when the landlord padlocks your door or changes your locks while you are gone and then won't allow you back into the apartment or house. A lockout can also happen when the landlord shuts off the water, electricity, or gas to try to force you to move out.

It is also against the law for a landlord to hold or take your clothing or furniture to force you to pay rent. This is called a *distraint* and is illegal, even if you owe rent to the landlord.

If you are locked out, you should immediately call the police. You should then see an attorney or contact your Legal Services program for help. A landlord who locks you out of your apartment or house or holds your personal belongings for rent is breaking the law. You can file a complaint in the Special Civil Part of the superior court. The judge has the power to (1) order the landlord to let you back in your rental unit and return your personal belongings, (2) award you money damages for the loss of your housing or property, *and* (3) award you attorneys' fees.

ROOMING AND BOARDINGHOUSE EVICTIONS. Residents of licensed rooming and boardinghouses are protected from self-help evictions. Owners must evict residents through the same court process as any other tenant. Some hotels and motels are really rooming or boardinghouses because people live there as their only residence for extended periods of time. The law considers a hotel or motel a rooming or boardinghouse if at least 15 percent of the rooms are occupied by people who have lived there for more than ninety days. This means that *all of the residents* (but *not* the guests) at the hotel or motel have the same rights as rooming and boardinghouse residents, including the right to be evicted only through the court process. You may need an attorney or help from Legal Services to figure out if this law applies to you.

NOTICES REQUIRED BEFORE AN EVICTION SUIT. As mentioned above, the only person who can legally evict you is a judge. The judge can order your eviction only after a court hearing at which the landlord has proven one or more of the *causes* for eviction under the Anti-Eviction Act, *N.J.S.A.* 2A:18-61.1 et seq. In addition, the law requires that the landlord give the tenant certain notices before going to court, except for nonpayment of rent. These notices must describe in detail the cause for eviction and must be given within certain time periods.

The Anti-Eviction Act requires that for every cause for eviction except nonpayment of rent, the landlord must serve you with a notice to *quit,* and, in some cases, a notice to *cease.*

The most common cause for eviction is nonpayment of rent. For this cause, and only for this cause, the landlord does not have to send you any advance notice before filing a complaint for eviction in court. This means that if you fail to pay rent, the landlord can go directly to court and you may not get any warning from the landlord before receiving the court summons and complaint. You *do* have to receive advance notice before the landlord can take you to court for not paying an increase in rent.

If you don't owe rent but the landlord is trying to evict you for one of the other causes under the Anti-Eviction Act, the landlord must give you certain written notices before taking you to court. For some causes, you must be given a notice to cease first, then a notice to quit. For other causes, you must be given only a notice to quit.

Notice to Cease. A notice to cease is a notice or letter telling you to stop certain conduct that is not allowed under your lease or under the Anti-Eviction Act. The notice must tell you exactly what conduct the landlord is complaining about. The notice must also tell you that if you stop the wrong conduct, you won't be evicted. If you stop the conduct that is described in the notice, the landlord cannot evict you.

A notice to cease is not required for every cause for eviction. A notice to cease is necessary only if you are charged with being disorderly, breaking rules and regulations, breaking an agreement in the lease, or paying rent late.

Notice to Quit. A notice to quit is a notice or letter from the landlord that tells you to move out by a certain date because you have engaged in certain conduct that is not allowed under your lease or under the Anti-Eviction Act. For those eviction causes that also require a notice to cease, the notice to quit will also tell you that since you have ignored the notice to cease, you must move out by a certain date. The notice to quit must tell you specifically what you have done wrong. For causes that do not require the landlord to give you a notice to cease, this is the first and only notice you will get before the landlord can file an eviction suit.

A notice to quit must be given to you directly; left at your house, apartment, or mobile home with someone who is at least fourteen years old; or sent by certified mail. The notice can be sent by regular and certified mail at the same time. If the certified mail is not claimed and the regular mail is not returned, the court will presume that you have been served.

The Anti-Eviction Act requires the landlord to give you a certain period of time before filing a suit in court for your eviction. This time period must be described in the notice to quit. The time periods vary depending on the cause for eviction in the Anti-Eviction Act. Some examples are given below:

- Only three days' notice is required if the landlord wants to evict you for being disorderly or destroying property.
- A one-month notice is required if the landlord wants to evict you for breaking lease rules or for refusing to accept a change in the lease.
- Two months' notice is required if the landlord wants to move into your house or apartment.
- Three months' notice is required if the landlord is trying to board up or demolish the building because of code violations.

49

- Eighteen months' notice is required if the landlord wants to permanently retire your apartment building from residential use.

If you are still in your apartment or house after the time in the notice to quit has run out, the landlord can prepare a *complaint* for your eviction. The complaint will state that the landlord wants you out of the rental unit and must describe the specific causes for the eviction under the Anti-Eviction Act. The complaint is filed in superior court, Special Civil Part, the court that hears landlord-tenant cases.

COURT HEARING. A *summons*, a notice from the court that tells you when and where the court will hear your case, will be attached to the complaint when you receive it. The summons and complaint can be either mailed to you by the court, delivered to you by an officer of the court, or left at your home.

The summons and complaint will tell you when to appear in court. The court rules require that there be at least ten days between the day you receive the summons and the day you must appear in court.

If the hearing is scheduled for a date that is less than ten days from the date on which you received the summons and complaint, tell the judge when you appear in court and ask him or her to postpone the hearing.

You must appear in court on the right date and time if you want to defend against the eviction or try to get more time to pay rent or move out. The first thing that will happen in court is that the judge will *call the list,* announcing the names of the landlord and tenant in each case. It is important that you be present to answer when the judge calls your name and case. If you do not answer, the judge will enter a *default judgment* against you. This means that the landlord has the right to evict you just because you failed to appear.

Postponements. You should call the clerk of the superior court, Special Civil Part, or the judge's office if for some reason you can't make it to court on the day of your case. You should explain why you need a new court date and ask for a postponement. You should also call the landlord or the landlord's attorney and ask the landlord to agree to postpone the case. A request for a postponement should be made several days before the day of your case. Last-minute requests for postponements are usually not allowed.

In some counties, postponements are rarely given. In those counties, the landlord has to agree and there has to be a very good reason to get your case postponed.

Settling before the Hearing. You can settle your case with your land-lord—even after you have received a summons and complaint—until the judge actually begins a hearing in your case. If you reach an agreement to settle your case, get the agreement in writing and be sure that you and your landlord fully understand the terms of the agreement. You should make an agreement with your landlord only if it is both fair and realistic. An agreement that you cannot keep will only lead to your eviction at a later time.

Be careful if you settle your case before the court hearing. If you reach an agreement before the court date, be sure that the landlord agrees to dismiss the complaint to officially end the case against you. This requires the landlord to notify the court clerk. You should also check with the court clerk yourself to make sure that the complaint has been dismissed.

If you reach an agreement with the landlord on the day of court to dismiss the complaint, the landlord has to tell the judge directly. You should remain in court until the landlord tells the judge that the case has been settled.

Mediation. In most courts, *mediation* is required in eviction cases. This means that before a judge will hear an eviction case, you and your landlord must first meet with a law clerk or other court worker to see if the case can be settled. The law clerk or court worker is called a *mediator.* In some counties, including Essex and Passaic, the mediator is an employee of the county welfare agency. A mediator is not supposed to take sides. The mediator's job is to help you and your landlord find a way to reach an agreement without having to go to trial.

In mediation, for example, if you don't have all the rent you owe, you may be able to get your landlord to agree to allow you to pay part of the back rent each month until the whole amount is paid. If the landlord agrees to this, the mediator will usually write down the agreement and give each of you a copy. As long as you keep your part of the agreement, the landlord can't evict you without first starting a new case and proving to the court that he or she has the right to evict you. If you don't live up to your agreement, your landlord can evict you right away.

You are not required to reach an agreement in mediation. You do not have to accept the mediator's suggestions. You always have the right to go before the judge and have the judge decide your case.

A mediator should not offer you any legal advice that could be confusing, especially if you don't have a lawyer or if you are not sure of your legal rights. A mediator is not a judge. If a mediator pressures you, ask to end the mediation.

DEFENDING YOUR CASE IN COURT. The judge will hold hearings in individual cases after he or she calls the list of all the cases. You must be ready to defend yourself against the cause or causes for eviction that are listed by your landlord in the complaint.

There are some common defenses to eviction used by tenants. These defenses could include, for example, showing that the landlord has not sent you the proper notice to cease or notice to quit, or showing that the conduct about which the landlord is complaining did not happen.

Evidence. You must be prepared to present proof to back up your defense. This evidence can include written documents, photographs, and the testimony of witnesses. You must bring with you to court any and all evidence you think you need for your defense. Documents may include receipts for rent or repairs, canceled checks, inspection reports (the court may require the inspector to come to court and may not consider reports without the inspector being there), a copy of your lease, and letters to the landlord. Any witnesses whom you call to testify on your behalf must be present in court on the day of the hearing. The court will not accept a letter from your witness. You will also testify on your own behalf.

The judge will hear from the landlord and the landlord's witnesses first. At this point, the landlord may introduce or give the judge written letters or documents. You have the right to examine the documents to make sure the documents are what the landlord says they are. After the landlord and his witnesses have testified before the judge, you can ask them questions about what they have said. You should not be afraid to ask any questions you have. You do not tell your side of the story at this time.

The judge will hear from you and your witnesses next. You will explain why the landlord should not be able to evict you. It is also your time to give the judge any letters or other documentation and to show the judge any pictures you have of the conditions in your apartment. You may be questioned by the landlord or his or her lawyer. You may then present any evidence or other witnesses you think are important to your defense.

The Judge's Decision. The judge makes a decision after hearing all of the evidence. The judge usually announces his or her decision immediately after hearing the evidence. If you win, the judge will *dismiss* or throw out the landlord's case. This means that you are not evicted and you may remain in your rental unit.

If you lose, the judge enters a *judgment for possession* in favor of the landlord. A judgment for possession is an order for your eviction. It gives the landlord the legal right to have you removed from your apartment or house.

The next step in the eviction process is the act of removing you from your rental unit. This does not happen right away and takes some time to complete. You also have some rights even after the judge gives the eviction order.

CLAIMS FOR RENT. An important rule of New Jersey landlord-tenant law is that a landlord cannot collect rent or any money from you in a lawsuit to evict you under the Anti-Eviction Act. A successful suit for eviction can only give the landlord possession of the rental property. It cannot be combined with a claim for money. In order to sue you for rent or other charges, the landlord must file a separate complaint for money damages, usually in small-claims court.

TENANTS IN A FORECLOSED PROPERTY. Your rights under eviction for cause continue even when a bank or mortgage lender files an action to foreclose on your rental property because your landlord has not paid the mortgage. This means that the foreclosing bank or mortgage lender must follow the law and can only evict you for one of the causes under the law.

SUMMARY OF COMMON DEFENSES TO EVICTION. The next sections discuss some common defenses a tenant may use against an eviction proceeding.

Unauthorized Practice of Law. The judge cannot hear an eviction case if your landlord is a corporation, unless the corporation is represented in court by a lawyer. The letters "Inc." after the landlord's name mean that it is a corporation. Unless the corporation is represented in court by a lawyer, the case must be dismissed, even if the corporation's complaint and summons were prepared by someone who is not a lawyer. Unfortunately, some courts may bend the court rules and allow property managers, stockholders, and others who are not lawyers to act for the corporate landlord. This is improper under New Jersey law.

Failure of Landlord to Register. You cannot be evicted if the landlord has not filed a landlord registration statement with the municipal clerk or New Jersey DCA, or if he or she has not given you written notice of the registration.

Improper Notice or No Notice. You can get an eviction complaint dismissed if the landlord did not give you a proper notice to cease and/or a proper notice to quit before taking you to court.

Improper Eviction Complaint. An eviction suit can be dismissed by the judge if the eviction complaint was not prepared in the right way. This often happens and you should read the complaint you receive to make sure it is correct. Some reasons why an eviction complaint may be improper are as follows:

- The complaint does not say why the landlord wants you out or does not describe the cause for eviction under the Anti-Eviction Act. Remember that the amount of rent the landlord claims you owe must be stated in an eviction complaint for nonpayment of rent.
- The reason stated in the complaint for your eviction is not one of the sixteen causes for eviction specified in the Anti-Eviction Act (see table 2.1).
- The reason stated in the complaint is not the same as the one in the landlord's notice to cease and/or repeated in the notice to quit. The cause for eviction in the complaint must match the cause given in the notice to cease and/or notice to quit.

The judge should dismiss an improper eviction complaint because eviction cases are set up to be quick and the landlord can always start the eviction process over again. Some judges will incorrectly allow a landlord to amend or change the complaint in court so that the complaint is proper and the case can proceed to hearing. You should object if the judge allows an on-the-spot change to the complaint. If the judge allows the amendment anyway, ask to postpone the hearing so that you have time to prepare a defense to the amended or changed complaint.

TABLE 2.1. Summary of Reasons for Eviction for Cause under the Anti-Eviction Act (N.J.S.A. 2A:18-61.1)

Reason	Notice(s) Required before Filing Eviction Suit	Comments
Not paying rent	None required	Homelessness Prevention Program and Emergency Assistance may help with back rent.
Disorderly conduct	Notice to cease	Must describe disorderly conduct and demand cessation or face eviction. Must also state that cessation of conduct will result in not being evicted. If conduct continues after notice is given, tenant may be evicted.
	Notice to quit	Must be served at least three days before filing eviction suit.
Damage or destruction of landlord's property	Notice to quit	Must be served at least three days before filing eviction suit. Damage must have been intentionally caused (you cannot be evicted because of damage accidentally caused).
Violation of landlord's rules or regulations (must be in writing or part of lease and accepted by tenant at beginning of lease term)	Notice to cease	Must describe violation of rules and demand cessation of violation or face eviction.
	Notice to quit	Must be served at least one calendar month before filing eviction suit. Rules and regulations must be "reasonable" and violation must be "substantial."
Violation of lease agreement	Notice to cease	Must describe lease violation and demand cessation or face eviction.
	Notice to quit	Must be served at least one month before filing eviction suit. Lease agreement must be "reasonable" and violation must be "substantial." Landlord must reserve *right of reentry* in lease.
Not paying a rent increase	One-month notice ending tenancy and notice of rent increase	Increase must not be "unconscionable" or must comply with local rent control laws.

Reason	Notice	Requirements
Housing or health code violations when a. Landlord is ordered to board up or tear down building after government housing inspection. b. Landlord cannot correct violations without removing tenant. c. Landlord must end overcrowding or an illegal occupancy. d. Government agency wants to close building as part of a redevelopment project.	Notice to quit	Must be served at least three months before filing eviction suit. Violations must be "substantial"; landlord must be financially unable to make repairs. Tenant cannot be evicted until relocation assistance is provided. For reason b, state must report to the court whether repairs can be made with tenant present.
Landlord wants to permanently retire building from residential use	Notice to quit	Must be served at least eighteen months before filing eviction suit. Must say in detail what the landlord plans to do with the building. Notice is defective (and eviction cannot occur) if future use of property is not clearly stated. Notice must be sent to Department of Community Affairs and rent control office. Conversion of building to nonresidential use must be approved prior to eviction. Cannot use this ground for eviction to avoid relocation assistance available for housing and health code violations. Landlord must pay damages if rerenting to another tenant.
Not accepting changes in the lease	Notice to quit	Must be served at least one month before filing eviction suit. Changes in lease must be "reasonable" as determined by court. Tenant can avoid eviction by agreeing to changes (if reasonable) and paying any overdue rent.
Paying rent habitually late	Notice to cease	Must demand that tenant cease paying rent late. To be evicted, tenant must continue to pay rent late at least *two* times *after* receiving notice to cease.
	Notice to quit	Must be served at least one month before filing eviction suit.

(continued)

TABLE 2.1. (continued)

Reason	Notice(s) Required before Filing Eviction Suit	Comments
Conversion to condominium or cooperative	Notice to quit	Must be served at least three years before filing eviction suit. Tenant cannot be evicted if a senior citizen tenant or disabled tenant has "protected tenancy status."
Conversion to condominium or cooperative (continued)	Notice of intent to convert	Must also include plan for conversion and notice of right to rent comparable housing.
Owner wants to live in apartment or house; only applies when a. Landlord is converting apartment into a condominium and is selling to a buyer who will move in. b. Landlord owns condominium and wants to move in. c. Owner of building with three or fewer units wants to move in or is selling to a buyer who will move in.	Notice to quit	Must be served at least two months before filing eviction suit. Contract for sale between owner and buyer who will be moving in must state that the building will be vacant at time of closing. Buyer must intend to live in building and not convert it to commercial use.
Tenant loses a job that includes rental unit when tenant a. Works for landlord as janitor, as superintendent, or in some other capacity. b. Gets to live in the unit as part of the job. c. Is dismissed by the landlord.	Notice to quit	Must be served at least three days before filing eviction suit.

Conviction of a drug offense or of a theft offense; applies when a. Drug offense has taken place anywhere in the building. b. Tenant is convicted of the drug offense. c. Tenant lets someone who has been convicted of a drug offense in the building live in the tenant's rental unit, or has in the past allowed that person to live in the unit within two years after the person was convicted or released from jail. d. When the theft is of the landlord's property, or is theft from the leased premises, or is theft from other tenant(s) in the same building or complex.	Notice to quit	Must be served at least three days before filing eviction suit.
Assaulting, attacking, or threatening the landlord; applies when a. Tenant is convicted of assaulting or threatening harm to landlord or landlord's employees. b. Tenant lets someone who has been convicted of assault or threats to live in tenant's rental unit, or has in the past allowed that person to live in the unit within two years after the person was convicted or released from jail.	Notice to quit	Must be served at least three days before filing eviction suit.
Engaging or being involved in drug activity; applies when a. Tenant engages in drug activity anywhere in the building. b. Tenant lets someone who has engaged in drug activity in the building to live in tenant's rental unit, or in the past has allowed that person to live in the unit.	Notice to quit	Must be served at least three days before filing eviction suit. Landlord may show conviction for drug offense, or an arrest for a drug offense, or that the activity would violate criminal drug law.

Paying the Rent. A common defense to an eviction for nonpayment of rent is to show that the rent has already been paid. You can do this by bringing receipts to court to show the judge. If you agree that you owe the rent or you have a hearing and the judge finds you owe rent, you can still have the eviction dismissed by paying the rent and court costs owed to the court before the court closes on the day of the hearing.

The rent money and court costs are paid to the clerk of the Special Civil Part of the superior court. The court clerk will give you a receipt and send the money to your landlord. The court clerk also will dismiss the eviction complaint against you. If you pay all the rent to the court clerk before the hearing on your complaint, you should go to the hearing anyway to make sure the judge knows you have paid the rent and dismisses the complaint.

Failure to Provide Safe and Decent Housing. Review the earlier sections explaining repair and deduct, withholding rent, and rent abatement. It is important to remember that if you use repair and deduct and rent withholding as a defense to nonpayment of rent, you will have to show the court how serious the problems are in your apartment. For rent withholding, you will also be required to deposit with the court the full amount of rent you have withheld before you can get a hearing on your defense that your housing is unsafe and in need of repair. This means that when you come to court, you must bring with you the full amount of rent you have withheld in cash, a certified check, or a money order. The court will not accept personal checks.

The Landlord Is Wrong or Is Lying. If what the landlord says in the complaint is not true, you have the right to deny it. The landlord then must prove that what he or she says is true. The law requires the landlord to prove that the complaint is based on facts. But be careful; sometimes a judge will believe the landlord over a tenant, so you should be ready to prove that you are right and the landlord is wrong. You can do this by bringing with you witnesses, photos, letters to or from the landlord, receipts, and anything else which might help prove your case.

Landlord Waiver of Right to Evict. The landlord can waive or give up his or her right to evict you if he or she knows that you have been breaking the lease or any rules of the tenancy but still accepts rent during this period.

Some examples of a waiver are as follows:

- The landlord sends you a notice to cease playing loud music and then sends you a notice to quit by March 31. If the landlord accepts April's rent, the landlord has waived the notice to quit. Although the acceptance of rent is a very important factor in determining whether the landlord has waived the right to evict, it may not be sufficient, depending upon the facts of a particular case.

- Your lease says that no pets are allowed, but the landlord has allowed you to have a pet since you moved in and other tenants have also been allowed to have pets.
- The landlord sends a notice to cease but then later sends you other notices that contradict the notice to cease or that do not threaten the tenant with eviction.

The Landlord Wants to Retaliate. The law does not allow a landlord to evict you to get even for asserting your rights under the law or for enforcing your rights under the lease. The landlord also cannot evict you to get even for your complaining about conditions in your house or apartment to the board of health, building inspector, housing authority, or any other government agency. Finally, the landlord cannot evict you to get even for your involvement with a tenants' association or any other lawful organization. Each of these types of getting even—or retaliation—are defenses to the eviction action. If you can prove that your landlord is trying to evict you in retaliation, the case will be dismissed.

WHEN COURT IS OVER: REMOVALS, STAYS, AND VACATING JUDGMENTS. If the judge decides in favor of the landlord and enters an order or judgment evicting the tenant, the landlord must still follow certain steps to actually have the tenant removed from the apartment or house. During this time, there are opportunities for the tenant to avoid eviction altogether or to get more time to move out.

Warrant for Removal. The *warrant for removal* is an order from the judge telling the constable to evict you. The constable is an officer of the court. An *affidavit of proof* is sent to the court clerk by the landlord, and the court clerk, in turn, issues a warrant for removal to the constable. The law does not allow the warrant for removal to be issued by the court clerk until at least three days after the judge enters a judgment for possession or order of eviction in court. The three-day period is the legal amount of time a landlord must wait to start the process of removing you after the judge orders an eviction.

When the constable gets the warrant for removal from the court clerk, the constable then serves a copy of the warrant on the tenant. The warrant states that the tenant has three choices:

1. Move out within three days to avoid being evicted by the constable. The three days *do not* include weekends or legal holidays.
2. Contest the warrant. This means asking for a new court date so that you can show why you should not be evicted and the warrant should be stopped. You must be up to date in your rent to do this.
3. Be evicted by the constable. This means that the constable will come to your apartment or house and remove you from the premises.

If you do not voluntarily leave the apartment or you do not contest the warrant, the constable will come to your apartment or house and evict you. If you are home at the time, the constable will put you out and padlock the door. The warrant gives the constable power to use force or arrest if you try to stop the eviction. This act is legal in New Jersey. It is important that you leave the premises peaceably. By all means, do not argue or fight with the constable.

How to Contest the Warrant and Hardship Stays. If you need more than three days to move out, you can contest the warrant for removal when you receive it. To do this, you must go to the court clerk's office. Bring with you your copy of the warrant and ask the clerk for a new court date. You can get a new court date to contest the warrant if

- You did not get the summons and complaint, and the warrant for removal is the first court paper telling you of any legal action against you,
- You have new proof showing that you should have won the case,
or
- You need more time to move out and you have reasons for which the court should give you more time to move. Getting more time to move is called getting a *stay* of the warrant for removal.

In some counties, such as Essex, the courts require tenants to prepare a formal *order to show cause* when requesting more time to move out. This practice requires the tenant to get legal help in order to appear before the court. Almost always, if you owe rent, the court will not stop the lockout while you are waiting for your court date.

The judge is allowed under the law to give you a stay of eviction for up to six months, if certain conditions are met. This stay of removal is called a *hardship stay* of eviction. To get a hardship stay, you must show that you have not been able to find any other place to live. You must also show that all rent has been paid and you must agree to pay the rent during the stay period. This means that you cannot get a hardship stay if you are evicted for nonpayment of rent, unless you can pay all of the rent owed and future rent by the time you appear in court to contest the warrant for removal. If, however, you are evicted and your rent is current, a hardship stay can give you up to six more months to find another place to live.

The law allows a judge to grant one-year stays of eviction if the tenant is terminally ill. To be eligible for this type of stay, the tenant must meet all of the following conditions:

- Owe no back rent.
- Be terminally ill and so certified by a doctor.
- Have been a tenant of the landlord for at least two years before the granting of the stay.

- Show that there is a strong chance that the tenant would not be able to find and move to another place without suffering medical harm.

This law applies to all buildings, including owner-occupied buildings.

Vacating the Judgment to Prevent Homelessness. In certain cases, you may be able to avoid being evicted *even after* the judge has ordered your eviction and the warrant for removal has been served on you by the constable. You may also be able to get back into your apartment after the lockout. Under court rules, to prevent an injustice, a judge has the power to set aside a court decision or *vacate a judgment* or order. The New Jersey Supreme Court has ruled that judges can use this court rule to set aside judgments for eviction because of nonpayment of rent whenever tenants are able to pay all the rent due, any attorney's fee, and court costs and such action is necessary in order to prevent tenants from becoming homeless.

An order to show cause or motion must be filed with the court in order to ask the judge in your case to set aside an eviction judgment. To set aside a judgment under this procedure, you must have all of the rent that is due, plus any of the landlord's court costs or attorneys' fees. You should ask the court clerk to help you file the order to show cause or motion if you can't get a lawyer to help you. The judge will conduct a hearing on your motion after it is filed with the court.

There are many programs—such as Emergency Assistance (EA) and the Homelessness Prevention Program (HPP)—that provide funds to certain low-income tenants to pay back rent in order to prevent eviction. Often, by the time a tenant learns of these programs, applies for help, and is granted assistance with back rent, the judgment for eviction is already entered by the court and the warrant for removal may have been issued and served on the tenant. If, at this point, you offer to pay all of the rent but the landlord insists on evicting you, you can then file a motion asking the court to vacate the judgment against you. You can even file for relief after you are locked out.

RELOCATION ASSISTANCE FOR DISPLACED TENANTS

Tenants are often forced to move from their homes because of action taken by a government agency. This is called *displacement*. The reasons an agency could order a tenant to move include the following:

- The building is to be boarded up or torn down with government approval.
- The landlord is ordered by the housing or building inspector to make repairs that cannot be made unless the tenants move.
- The landlord has allowed more people to live in a unit than is allowed by law or the landlord has rented apartments that do not meet government housing and safety laws.

- The building is being taken over by a government agency to be used to build a school playground, a highway, a police station, a neighborhood renewal project, or some other public project.

The law stipulates that tenants forced to move for any of the above reasons are eligible for relocation assistance.

Relocation assistance is money and other assistance to help displaced tenants find a new place to live. Eligible tenants may be able to receive the following payments:

- Money for temporary housing until the tenant finds a permanent home if the government agency forces the tenant to move out immediately because of an emergency. This is limited to $500.
- A payment to cover the tenant's actual moving costs, or a dislocation allowance of $200 and a fixed moving payment of up to $300 based on the number of rooms occupied.
- Up to $4,000 payable over three years to meet rental expenses, or up to $4,000 to help with the required down payment expenses in the purchase of a house.
- Help to locate a new place to live that the tenant can afford.

The law makes the government agency that orders you to move responsible for relocation payments, including money payments. The government agency will usually be a city, town, or other agency that is involved in any of the actions described above, such as the housing inspection office, health department, or fire department. Many cities have a relocation officer who must make sure relocation assistance is available whenever any city agency causes displacement. The operation of local relocation assistance programs is monitored by the New Jersey DCA in Trenton.

CAUTIONS. Cities and towns do not like to pay relocation assistance benefits even to people who are eligible for them. Displaced tenants are often told that they are not eligible for these benefits when they clearly should receive them. Sometimes tenants are told that towns don't give relocation assistance. If you think you are eligible for relocation assistance and are not satisfied with the response of your local agency, contact a lawyer or your county Legal Services office for further advice.

To protect your right to receive relocation assistance:

- Do not move from your apartment or home until you get a notice from the relocation office telling you that you are eligible for relocation assistance and that you must move.
- If you find housing on your own, ask the relocation officer to inspect the housing before you move to make sure the housing is safe and decent.

- If the relocation officer finds housing for you to move into, make sure the housing is decent, safe, and sanitary; near your work, transportation, and public facilities; affordable; and large enough for you and your family.
- File an application for relocation assistance benefits as soon as possible, but no later than twelve months after your moving date.

DISPLACEMENT BY FIRE

Tenants who have lost their housing because of fire do not have an absolute right to receive relocation assistance benefits. Under New Jersey law, cities may, if they wish, provide fire victims with limited benefits. You must check with your local housing or fire inspector to see if your city or town provides relocation assistance to fire victims. Another law allows tenants to sue to force their landlord to repair their fire-damaged apartments. This law states that if a tenant's apartment or rented house is damaged by fire and the fire is not the tenant's fault, the landlord must repair the fire damage as quickly as possible. The law also excuses a tenant from paying rent until the repairs are made. However, this law may not help you if your lease contains provisions different from those in the law.

PROPERTY TAX REBATES FOR TENANTS

There are two kinds of tax rebates for tenants in New Jersey. One is the Tenants' Property Tax Rebate; the other is the Homestead Rebate.

Both programs provide tenants with a return or rebate on property taxes paid to the state by the landlord. The laws allow tenants to receive these rebates because the rent paid by tenants is used by landlords to pay property taxes. State law provides that, if property taxes are going to be lowered or given back by the state, the money should be passed on to tenants since tenants paid these taxes in the first place in their monthly rent. See Chapter 11, "The Rights and Obligations of Citizenship."

CONDOMINIUM AND COOPERATIVE CONVERSIONS

If a building or apartment is being converted into a condominium or cooperative, the Anti-Eviction Act protects all tenants from eviction due to condominium conversion for at least three years, and possibly for several more. The law also protects senior citizens and their spouses, handicapped tenants and their families, and lower-income residents of Hudson County against conversion-related eviction.

The legal process to convert a rental building to a condominium or a cooperative is complicated, as are the laws protecting tenants. If you learn that your building is undergoing conversion or will be converted in the future, it is important that you seek legal advice from a lawyer who knows about these laws.

BASIC STEPS IN CONVERSION. Landlords must follow certain steps to convert rental housing to condominiums or cooperatives. Landlords must follow four different laws: (1) the Planned Real Estate Development Full Disclosure Act, *N.J.S.A.* 45:22A-21; (2) the Senior Citizen and Disabled Protected Tenancy Act, *N.J.S.A.* 2A:18-61.22; (3) the Anti-Eviction Act, *N.J.S.A.* 2A:18-61.1(k) and 2A:18-61.8; *and* (4) the Tenant Protection Act of 1992, *N.J.S.A.* 2A:18-61.40.

    Notice Requirements. An owner who plans to convert a building or a mobile home park must first give each tenant two separate documents: (1) a notice of intent to convert *and* (2) a full plan of conversion. Both the notice of intent to convert and the conversion plan must be sent by certified mail. In addition, the owner must give tenants a three-year notice to quit to vacate the rental unit because of the conversion. The notice of intent to convert and the conversion plan documents must be given to all affected tenants at least sixty days before giving the tenants the three-year notice to quit.

    The laws concerning conversion must be strictly followed by the owner. If the owner does not provide all of the information required in the proper form and in the proper way, the owner may not be able to evict the tenants at the end of the three-year notice period.

    The notice of intent to convert must contain three separate items:

1. A notice to the tenants of their right to buy ownership in the property at a set price.
2. A notice that each tenant has an exclusive right to buy his or her apartment for the first ninety days after receiving the notice of intent to convert. The notice must also state that during the ninety days, the apartment cannot be shown to anyone else unless the tenant has given up his or her right to buy in writing.
3. A copy of the *regulations* on conversions approved by the New Jersey DCA. These regulations explain the tenants' rights under the Anti-EvictionAct.

The full plan of conversion must contain very specific information. For example, the plan must contain a legal description of the property, the price of the apartment, the terms of sale, and a copy of the deed to the apartment, if purchased. The plan is *defective* if it does not contain all of the required information. The requirements for a conversion plan are very complicated, and you should have a skilled attorney review them for you.

    After giving tenants the notice of intent to convert and the plan for conversion, the owner must give tenants who choose not to buy ownership in a condominium or cooperative a three-year notice to vacate or quit the rental unit. This means that tenants have a minimum of three years before their landlord can take them to court to ask that they be evicted because of the conversion. In addition, any time left on a written lease must also expire before an eviction case can be started, even after the end of the three-year notice period.

Comparable Housing. Tenants who have received the notice to quit can ask the landlord in writing for a reasonable opportunity to look at and rent *comparable housing.* This right to ask for comparable housing extends for eighteen months after receipt of the notice to quit. Comparable housing means housing that meets all local and state housing codes and is equivalent to the apartment in which the tenant then lives in size, number of rooms, major facilities, rent, and other ways. The requirements on the owner to offer reasonable opportunities for comparable housing are detailed, and tenants should consult with a knowledgeable attorney for further advice.

Rent Protection. Tenants are given some protection against unfair rent increases during the three-year notice period and for the entire time they remain in the apartment, including during any hardship stays of eviction (postponements). Tenants continue to be covered by rent control if it applies to the building. Also, an owner who asks the rent control board for a hardship increase cannot use any increases in costs resulting from the conversion to justify his or her claim of hardship.

Tenants in towns without rent control can receive only reasonable rent increases. The owner cannot use any increases in costs resulting from the conversion to justify a rent increase.

Tenants should also seek legal advice when faced with a court action for eviction after the three-year notice period. There are complicated rules on the circumstances under which the judge can grant further stays or postponements of eviction.

SPECIAL PROTECTIONS FOR SENIOR CITIZENS AND THE DISABLED. For qualified senior citizens and the disabled who live in buildings being converted to condominiums or cooperatives, the law protects from eviction for up to 40 years. During this protected period these tenants must continue to pay rent and follow reasonable rules and regulations or they can be evicted for some other reason, such as nonpayment of rent.

Senior citizens qualify for protection from eviction if they (1) have an income not higher than three times the *per capita* (average) income in the county in which they live or $50,000, whichever is greater; (2) have lived in the building for one year or have a lease with longer than a one-year term; (3) are over sixty-two years old; *and* (4) live in a building containing at least five rental apartments. Disabled persons qualify if they are unable to work because of a physical or mental impairment or blindness or if they are veterans who have a service-connected disability of 60 percent or more. Disabled persons must also meet the income standards and have lived in a building with at least five rental units for one year, or have a lease with longer than a one-year term.

Before a landlord converts a building, the city or town will send an application form for protected tenancy to every tenant in it. Seniors or disabled tenants who wish to apply must fill out the form and return it to the town within sixty days of receipt. The tenant must also sign a written statement sworn before a notary public giving his or her income and stating that he or she either has lived in the apartment for one year or has a long-term lease.

The city must decide in writing if the tenant qualifies for protection within thirty days after the application is filed. A tenant who qualifies is eligible for protection if the landlord goes ahead with the conversion.

The application form should be sent to the city *within sixty days* of receiving it. Tenants can still apply for protection *even weeks or months later,* as long as the application is made before a court actually enters a judgment for eviction or before the apartment is sold to a person who intends to live in it. Tenants who applied for and were not given protection because they did not qualify (because their income exceeded the limit or for other reasons) can *apply again.* This can be done even a year or more later, as long as they do so before a court judgment or before the apartment is sold.

SPECIAL HUDSON COUNTY PROTECTIONS. The law provides additional protections for certain tenants living in Hudson County (*N.J.S.A.* 2A:18-61.40). Qualified Hudson County tenants are permanently protected from eviction due to the conversion of their building. Qualified tenants must continue to pay rent and follow reasonable lease rules. They can still be evicted if their landlord can prove in court one of the other legal reasons for eviction.

ROOMING AND BOARDINGHOUSES AND MOBILE HOME PARKS

An estimated 40,000 people, most of them poor and elderly, live in New Jersey's 3,500 rooming and boardinghouses. Some of these buildings are old and greatly in need of repair. Some have narrow hallways with poor lighting and don't have proper electrical and heating systems. This makes them fire hazards and hard to escape from when a fire occurs. The poor and elderly who live in these homes are often victimized by landlords who take advantage of the residents' fear of eviction by demanding high rents for poor living conditions.

Thousands of other families reside in mobile home parks throughout New Jersey. Mobile home residents are in an unusual situation: They usually own their mobile home but have to lease the lot on which the home sits from a mobile-home-park owner. The number of licensed and approved mobile home parks is limited. Almost none of these parks accepts homes moved from another park. For this reason, mobile home residents have little room to bargain if they have a dispute with a park owner.

Special laws have been passed to protect residents of rooming and boardinghouses and mobile homes.

ROOMING AND BOARDINGHOUSE ACT. The Rooming and Boardinghouse Act is designed to protect residents living in rooming and boardinghouses. Under the law, DCA is responsible for licensing and inspecting every rooming and boardinghouse. DCA must make sure that each home is safe and decent. DCA must also make sure that the owner or manager of the house respects the rights of residents. For example, DCA must make sure that the building is fire safe, has no serious plumbing or electrical problems, has enough light and air, is clean, and is secure. DCA must also make sure that the house is well run. They must also make sure that there are no violations of the residents' legal rights, such as the right to have visits from family, friends, and social workers.

The law says that every resident of a boardinghouse has the following rights:

- To manage his or her own financial affairs.
- To wear his or her clothing in the style he or she prefers.
- To style his or her hair according to his or her preference.
- To keep and use personal property in his or her room, except where the boardinghouse can show that this would be unsafe or impractical or that it would interfere with the rights of others.
- To receive and send unopened mail.
- To unaccompanied use of a telephone at a reasonable hour and to a private phone at the resident's expense.
- To privacy.
- To hire his or her personal doctor at his or her own expense or under a health care plan.
- To privacy concerning his or her medical condition and treatment.
- To unrestricted personal visits with any person of his or her choice, at any reasonable hour.
- To be active in the community.
- To present complaints for his or her own self or others to government agencies or other persons without threat of reprisal in any form or manner.
- To a safe and decent living environment and care that recognizes the dignity and individuality of the resident.
- To refuse to work for the boarding facility, except as contracted for by the resident and the operator.
- To practice his or her religion.
- To not be deprived of any legal right solely because he or she lives in a boardinghouse.
- To be free from retaliation by the owner if the resident tries to stand up for or enforce his or her rights.

Required Notices of Rights. The owner must give each resident written notice of these rights and the notice must be posted in the home. The notice must include the name, address, and telephone number of social services agencies, including the Office of the Ombudsman for the Institutionalized Elderly, the county welfare agency, and the county Office on Aging.

Any resident whose rights are violated can sue the offender. The resident can ask for actual and punitive damages, reasonable attorneys' fees, and costs of the action.

Same Rights as Other Tenants. The protections in the Anti-Eviction Act apply to rooming and boardinghouse residents. This means that these residents are entitled to the same protections as all other tenants. In addition, if a resident is displaced from a rooming or boardinghouse due to code enforcement, the resident is eligible for relocation assistance.

Mobile home owners are also tenants because they rent space in mobile home parks. For this reason, mobile home owners are protected from eviction under the Anti-Eviction Act. They are also covered by the Tenants' Property Tax Rebate program. Court decision has also established that other landlord-tenant laws covering security deposits, receivership, truth in lending, landlord identity, discrimination against children, self-help eviction, distraint, and reprisal also apply to mobile home owners, even though mobile homes are not specifically mentioned in these laws. In addition, mobile home tenants have special protections under the Mobile Home Act. These protections are explained in the sections that follow.

MOBILE HOME ACT. The Mobile Home Act requires park owners to give at least a one-year written lease to all renters of space within one month of moving in. This is the only form of residential tenancy in New Jersey in which a written lease for a particular period of time is required.

However, the park owner may have a written rule about the style or quality of the type of equipment to be used by the homeowner. A mobile home owner cannot be forced to buy equipment from a park owner or a particular outlet. The mobile home owner may sue the park owner in civil court if this happens.

A mobile-home-park owner cannot require a resident to buy either a mobile home or necessary equipment from a particular seller.

A mobile-home-park owner cannot ask a tenant to move his or her mobile home within the park unless the move is reasonably necessary. The owner must also serve the tenant with a thirty-day notice. In an emergency, the operator may move the mobile home but is responsible for all costs for any damages to the mobile home resulting from the move.

Selling a Mobile Home. A mobile home owner who plans to sell his or her home must give written notice to the park owner. Sales that are attempted without the park owner's consent or knowledge are unlawful. Before selling a mobile home, the seller must give the buyer an *application for park tenancy.* The buyer must then return the application in person to the park owner or operator. A park owner has the right to approve who buys a mobile home in the park but cannot deny anyone without reason. A valid reason for refusal would be an unsatisfactory credit report on the prospective buyer. If the park owner unreasonably refuses to approve the buyer, the home owner or the intended buyer can sue in superior court. The court can award damages, costs of the lawsuit, and attorneys' fees. The court may also require the park owner to rent to the prospective buyer.

A park owner can refuse to approve an interested buyer if the park is designated for senior citizens and the tenant is below the minimum age requirement. However, in a park that is not reserved for seniors, discrimination against buyers with children may be against state and federal law. Seek legal advice if you think you are experiencing this type of discrimination.

Disclosures. A mobile-home-park owner must make known to the tenants and the public all fees, charges, assessments, and rules. These disclosures must be in writing and must be given to tenants before they move in. Any additional fees, charges, assessments, rules, or changes must also be in writing and given to mobile home tenants at least thirty days before the effective date. If the written notice is not given, the park owner cannot use a mobile home owner's failure to comply as a cause for eviction.

Unlawful Payments. It is unlawful for a mobile-home-park owner to ask for or receive a donation or gift directly or indirectly from someone who wants to rent a space in the park. This is a *disorderly persons offense* and the owner can be prosecuted in municipal court. If such a payment is made, the home owner can sue to recover the amount paid. The judge can award double the amount of the unlawful payment, court costs, and attorneys' fees.

Rent Increases. Rent increases for mobile home owners are subject to the same notice requirements and other limits—including rent control if applicable—as those for all other tenants. The mobile-home-park owner is responsible for the general upkeep of the park. This includes the maintenance of all services agreed to in the lease. If the park owner does not maintain the area or services properly, this constitutes a breach of the warranty of habitability and the tenant may seek justice in the same ways any other tenant would.

HOUSING DISCRIMINATION

Federal and New Jersey laws prohibit discrimination in the rental of housing. These laws are called *fair-housing laws.*

Under federal and state laws, it is illegal for a landlord or real estate agency to refuse to rent to you because of race, religion, color, national origin, ancestry, marital status, sex, or physical or mental disabilities. These laws also make it illegal for a landlord or real estate agency to refuse to rent to you because you are pregnant or if your family includes children under fourteen years of age.

New Jersey law makes it illegal to refuse to rent housing to someone who is homosexual. New Jersey law also makes it illegal to refuse to rent to anyone solely because they will pay their rent with rental assistance or welfare.

Federal and state laws make it illegal for a landlord or real estate agency to refuse to rent to families with children. There are, however, some exceptions. A landlord can refuse to rent to families with children if the building was built only for senior citizens, but every apartment in such a building must be occupied by people over the age of sixty-two. Retirement communities for people over fifty-five can refuse to rent to families with children, but only if they provide special services and equipment designed for senior citizens.

Under New Jersey law, it is illegal for a landlord to refuse to rent to a couple because they are not married. Additionally, a court has ruled that it is illegal for a landlord to refuse to rent to homosexuals because of the landlord's fear that they may have or get AIDS.

If you are disabled, federal and state laws provide additional protections against discrimination. It is illegal for a landlord to refuse to rent to you just because of your disability. The landlord also cannot refuse to make reasonable changes to your apartment in order to make it easier for you to live there. This means that the landlord must provide handrails, ramps, or any other special equipment you need. For the landlord to make these improvements, you must pay the reasonable cost of removing the ramps or handrails or other changes after you move out of the apartment. The law also says that the landlord must change the rules and regulations to make it possible for you to live in and enjoy an apartment, as long as the changes you are asking for are legal.

The landlord may be able to require that you deposit money into a special bank account each month to cover the cost of removing the ramps and other equipment when you move out. The landlord can make you deposit this money only if he or she can prove that the changes you need will be very expensive. However, the payments must be low enough that you can afford them and must stop after the amount needed to make the changes has been deposited. The landlord must give you the interest earned on this special account.

State law also permits a tenant with a disability to terminate a lease because the apartment or home is not *handicapped accessible*. You can break your lease only if you ask your landlord to make the unit accessible and the landlord is unwilling or unable to do so.

HOW TO FILE A DISCRIMINATION COMPLAINT. There are government agencies set up to investigate complaints of housing discrimination.

If you feel that a landlord will not rent you an apartment because of your race, religion, color, national origin, ancestry, marital status, sex, handicap, sexual preference, or because you have children, you can do several things.

You can file a discrimination complaint directly with one of three government agencies: (1) the U.S. Department of Housing and Urban Development (HUD), (2) the New Jersey Division on Civil Rights, *and* (3) the New Jersey Real Estate Commission. These agencies are required to investigate your complaint and take action to help you if they find discrimination. They can make landlords who discriminate against you pay money damages and can even get you into the apartment you wanted but were denied.

It is important to call or write to these agencies *immediately* if you believe you are the victim of housing discrimination. You will want these agencies to investigate your complaint right away.

Two main agencies—one federal and one state—handle housing discrimination complaints: the HUD Office of Fair Housing and Equal Opportunity in New York City, and the New Jersey Division on Civil Rights in Trenton. Both agencies handle complaints about the various forms of illegal discrimination described above. Only the state agency, the Division on Civil Rights, handles complaints about discrimination based on sexual orientation.

If you have a complaint against a *real estate broker or agent,* the New Jersey Real Estate Commission in Trenton can investigate and punish any broker or agent whom they find to have discriminated against you. The commission cannot award money damages or force the broker to rent to you.

You can also go directly to court and sue the landlord and/or broker who you believe has discriminated against you without using these agencies. This means, however, that you may need your own lawyer and have to do your own investigation. If you succeed in court, you may be able to get money damages, the apartment that was wrongfully denied you, and attorneys' fees.

Some counties have fair-housing organizations that can help you with your discrimination complaint. They can investigate your complaint for free and help you get the housing you want. They can also help you bring charges against the landlord and/or real estate broker, find you an attorney, or help you file a complaint with HUD or the Division on Civil Rights.

LEGAL REASONS FOR REFUSAL TO RENT. There are certain reasons a landlord may refuse to rent to you that are not illegal discrimination. A landlord doesn't have to rent to you if your income is not high enough to afford the rent or if your family is too large for the size of the apartment. For example, landlord can refuse to rent a one-bedroom apartment to a couple with two children. Also, a landlord can refuse to rent to you if a check of your financial background shows that you have failed to pay rent for apartments in the past or have been unable to pay other debts. It is important that you ask the landlord to be specific about why he or she is refusing to rent to you. If you suspect *illegal* discrimination, get help from a fair-housing group, Legal Services, or a private attorney.

3. About Your Home

This chapter discusses the laws protecting you as a homeowner when buying a house and financing and refinancing your home, and what your rights are under foreclosure. The chapter also discusses home repairs and improvements and the Truth-in-Lending Act (TILA) (*N.J.S.A.* 17:3B-1 *et seq.*).

BUYING A HOME

Buying a home may be the largest investment you ever make. Therefore, it is important to consider your alternatives and know your rights before you agree to purchase. This chapter reviews some of the important laws you should know about before you buy your home.

REAL ESTATE CONTRACTS. Whenever you are buying or selling real estate, it is best to consult with an attorney *before* you sign any agreements. The law requires all real estate contracts to be in writing. An oral agreement to buy or sell real estate has no effect. When you sign a real estate contract prepared by a licensed real estate broker for the purchase of a home in New Jersey, you have three business days to have the contract reviewed by an attorney. This period is called the *attorney review period.* During this period, your attorney can review the contract, make changes, or even cancel the contract. For this reason, it is very important that you get a lawyer to review your real estate contract *immediately.* If you change your mind for any reason, your attorney can cancel the contract for you within the three-day period. After that, the contract is legally binding.

The three-day review period applies to those contracts for purchase of real estate that are prepared by a licensed real estate broker. However, you can (and should) put an attorney review period clause in any real estate contract. Although this also allows the other side to back out, if you change your mind within the three days *you are protected.* In order to put an attorney review period clause into a contract, the seller and buyer must both agree to it and it must be put in writing on the contract. All parties must sign and date the contract. Proper wording of the attorney review period clause should specify that the contract is not binding on either party until three business days *after* the date of the signing, excluding Saturdays, Sundays, and legal holidays.

To protect you as buyer, the real estate contract should deal with a host of issues. You need to discuss each of these issues with your attorney. Among other topics, you should make the contract *conditional* on (subject to)

- Passing structural inspection by an engineer (for all inspections this contract should say who will pay for the inspection).

- Passing a radon inspection.
- Passing a water quality inspection.
- Passing a test of the septic system if the house is not hooked up to a city sewer system.
- Passing a termite inspection.
- The owner having marketable title (no liens or other encumbrances on the house or against the seller, and the seller has full power to convey title with no restrictions).

The contract should also include a firm date for the closing. It should be made subject to your ability to get acceptable financing for a specific amount and interest rate. It should provide for apportionment of real estate taxes paid (depending on the date of sale) and, if the land is five acres or more, it should state who is responsible for any possible rollback taxes from loss of a farmland assessment. The contract should apportion all utility charges, based upon the date of closing. If sewers have recently been installed or are planned, there may be special, very high sewer assessments, and the parties should be clear as to how these costs will be allocated.

HOME WARRANTIES

New Homes. Most new homes purchased in New Jersey are covered by an owner's warranty contract. This is usually a contract between the builder and warranty company, and as the purchaser, you become the *beneficiary.* This means that you will receive the benefit of the warranty. The warranty generally covers structural defects for up to ten years and gives a full warranty for the first year you live in your new home. This is why it is very important to notify the manufacturer and the contractor immediately when you notice any problem, even if you are not sure whether or not you are covered.

Mobile Homes. Mobile homes are covered under the National Mobile Home Construction and Safety Standards Act of 1974 (42 *U.S.C.* Section 5401). This federal law covers mobile homes built after June 14, 1976 and requires a minimal level of construction and safety standards. Furthermore, when a mobile home is bought with certain Department of Housing and Urban Development (HUD)–insured loans, you get a one-year mobile home warranty from the manufacturer (24 *C.F.R.* Section 201.520). The warranty says that the mobile home must conform to all HUD safety and construction standards and ensures that the home is free of defects in materials and workmanship. If defects are found, you can sue the manufacturer for breach of warranty.

FINANCING. When you take out a loan to purchase a home, the lender will require that you give them a *mortgage* on your home. When you give a lender

73

a mortgage on your home, you are giving the lender a *lien,* or *security interest.* This means that if you fail to pay the loan back, the lender will sell your home. This is called a *foreclosure.* The mortgage that you give to the lender when you purchase a home is called a *first mortgage* or *purchase-money mortgage.* Because you are the party giving the mortgage, you are called the *mortgagor;* the lender is called the *mortgagee.*

Loans for first mortgages are covered by a federal law called the Truth-in-Lending Act. TILA requires that the lender provide you with certain disclosures (discussed later in this chapter). The purpose of the disclosures is to make sure you know what you are getting into and that you can afford the payments. Note, however, that the *right of rescission* does not apply to first mortgages which are used to buy or build a house. (See the section in this chapter entitled "Your Rights under the Truth-in-Lending Act.")

When you buy a house and take out a loan, you are conducting three transactions. First, the seller will transfer title to the real estate to you. You will sign a *deed,* which must be recorded in the county clerk's office where the real estate is located. The deed will say that you are the legal owner of the property. Second, you are taking a loan from the lender. You will have to sign a *promissory note,* agreeing to pay the lender back. Finally, you are giving the lender a mortgage on your property. You will have to sign a security instrument, the mortgage, which will be recorded with the county clerk's office. It will act as a lien against your property. Usually, your attorney will represent you at the closing on your house. He or she will prepare all of the legal documents discussed above and should be available to answer all of your questions.

BORROWING AGAINST THE HOME YOU OWN

Now let's say that you already own your home and are thinking of taking out a loan and borrowing against it. When you put your house up as collateral for a loan, you are taking a very serious step because now another person has the right to sell your home if you miss a payment. Never do it without a very good reason. Because it is such a serious step, there are some important laws you should know.

TYPES OF LOANS

Refinancing Loans. These are mortgage loans you take out when you want to pay off your existing mortgage or mortgages in full (for example, you may already have two mortgages on your home so you take out a new loan that pays off both mortgages), or borrow against the equity in your home. You can refinance a loan to get a better interest rate and lower your monthly payments.

Note: If you refinance the equity that you have in your home in order to pay bills, such as credit cards, be careful. This is not always a good idea because you are subjecting your home to foreclosure in order to pay off those bills.

74

Revolving Home Equity Loans. Revolving home equity loans (sometimes called *open-end credit*) permit you to take out credit from time to time up to a certain amount, secured by your house. The lender sets the maximum amount of credit (the credit line) available to you. The amount you actually borrow is up to you. A revolving home equity loan is like a charge account with a mortgage attached. Each time you borrow money on such an account, you increase the mortgage on your house.

If you borrow money against your house with someone else (such as a spouse or relative who lives with you), that person may be able to borrow more money and mortgage your home without seeking any extra permission from you. A revolving home equity loan can be a first mortgage, or you can already have a mortgage on your home and have a revolving home equity loan as a second or third mortgage. The important thing to remember is that you will be able to borrow only a percentage of what equity you have in your home.

Second Mortgages. These are mortgage loans you get when you already have a mortgage on your house. Second mortgages can be *open-* or *closed-end credit*. With closed-end credit, borrowers receive a certain sum of money with a set payback schedule. Unlike the revolving home equity loan, you cannot get any additional credit over what you initially received when you took out the loan. Most second mortgages are closed-end mortgages.

Both revolving home equity loans and second mortgages have similar effects on the borrower: (1) they lower the amount of equity (cash value) the homeowner has in the house, i.e., they lower the amount of money the house is worth to the owner; *and* (2) if the borrower *defaults* (does not make payments) on the loan, the creditor may foreclose on the house.

YOUR RIGHTS UNDER THE TRUTH-IN-LENDING ACT

Most loans that result in a mortgage on your home are also covered by TILA. TILA gives consumers some very important rights. First, it requires lenders to give certain facts to you in advance of taking out your loan. These disclosures are designed to make sure you understand what you are getting yourself into. The exact type of disclosure will vary depending on the type of loan that you have. Details about the disclosures are discussed in Chapter 7, "Credit, Debt, and Banking." Second, for *some* mortgage loans, TILA also gives you the right to change your mind and cancel the contract within three business days (or, in certain cases, within three years). This is called your *right of rescission*. This means that you have extra time to think about the loan agreement and reconsider whether you want to put your house up as collateral to pay back the loan. When you rescind, you are canceling the deal. Generally, you have three business days from the date you sign the mortgage loan to cancel. You may cancel for *any reason* within the three-day period. However, in certain circumstances you do not have this right (see below). The right applies as long as the home is your principal residence; it could be a townhouse, a condominium, or a mobile home.

RIGHT OF RESCISSION. Generally, if a loan or credit contract gives a creditor a *security interest* in your home (other than a first mortgage you use to buy or build the house), you have the right to rescind. This is often called a "cooling-off" period because it gives you a chance to think about the serious step you have taken, away from the pressure of a sales situation. However, the right to cancel under TILA does *not* apply to all transactions that result in a security interest on your home. For example, your right to cancel *does not* apply to the following transactions:

- The initial-purchase mortgage on a home (but it *does* apply to most refinancing loans and most second mortgages).
- Any loan under which the creditor does not take a security interest in your home.
- A refinancing loan with the same creditor that already has your home as a security interest and you do not borrow any more money.
- A loan from a state agency.

Note: Although you do not have a right to cancel the above loans under TILA, you may have a cooling-off period for some of these loans under New Jersey state law. For example, if your loan is covered by the Door-to-Door Sales Act or the Home Repair Financing Act, you will have a three-day right to cancel under state law.

If applicable, this three-day period gives you the unconditional right to cancel for any reason *until midnight of the third business day after* the latest of the following events:

- The date of consummation of the transaction (the date you sign a contract or open an account).
- The date you receive the truth-in-lending disclosure statement from the creditor (up to three years).
- The date you receive a proper notice of your right to cancel from the creditor (up to three years).

Under TILA, a business day means Monday through Saturday but does not include legal holidays. For example, if all of the above events take place a Friday, you have until midnight the following Tuesday to cancel.

If the creditor does not give you a notice of your right to *rescind* (cancel) and an accurate truth-in-lending disclosure statement, you have up to *three years* from the date you signed the contract to cancel.

Creditor's Requirements. When you sign your loan, the creditor must give to *each owner* one copy of a truth-in-lending disclosure statement and two copies of a written notice of the right to cancel. The TILA disclosure statement must provide accurate information about the credit terms of the transaction, including the annual percentage rate and the finance charge. Other required disclosures will vary depending on whether you have a closed-end transaction or an open-end transaction.

The two copies of the notice of the right to rescind must

- State that the creditor has taken a security interest in your home,
- Inform you of your right to cancel (rescind),
- Explain how to cancel (including a form for that purpose, with the creditor's business address on it),
- Explain what happens when you cancel, *and*
- State the last day you may cancel.

Borrower's Requirements. If you decide to cancel your contract within the three-day period, you must sign the notice that the creditor gave you and mail the notice to the creditor by certified mail, return receipt requested. Be sure to keep a copy of the notice and the green receipt card proving the mail was received when it is mailed back to you. To be effective, you must mail the notice to the creditor before midnight of the third business day after you signed the contract.

Before the three-day cooling-off period is up, the creditor is not supposed to take any action on your loan. This means that you should not receive any money, mortgages should not be paid off, and home repairs should not begin. Within twenty days after receiving your notice to cancel, the creditor must return any money you paid, such as a deposit or down payment. You do not have to pay any charges, and the creditor's security interest in your home ends when you cancel your contract.

If you cancel, you can keep any money or property that the creditor gave you until you get your money back. Then you must offer to return the creditor's money or property. If the creditor does not take back its money or property within twenty days of your offer, you can keep it without obligation.

WAIVER OF THE RIGHT TO RESCIND. If you have an immediate need for the money and cannot afford to wait the three days, you can give up your right to wait. This is called a *waiver of right to rescind or cancel.* To waive your right to cancel, you must give the creditor a written statement describing the emergency. The statement must be dated, signed by you, and state that you waive your right to cancel. The creditor should give you notice of your right to cancel before you sign the waiver. The right to cancel and change your mind about a contract that you have signed is in the law for your protection. *Do not give up this very important right unless there is a true emergency.*

SECONDARY MORTGAGE LOAN ACT. Both home equity loans and second mortgage loans are covered by the New Jersey Secondary Mortgage Loan Act (*N.J.S.A.* 17:11A-1) if the property is located in New Jersey, or if the loan was advertised in New Jersey no matter where the lender is located. However, loans made by federal and state savings and loan associations or national and state banks are *not* covered by the act. When making a home equity loan or a second mortgage, the Secondary Mortgage Loan Act requires a lender to

- Give you a copy of every paper you sign.
- Give you a receipt every time you make a cash payment.
- Give you a free statement of your mortgage account at your written request, as often as twice a year.
- Put the words "Secondary Mortgage Loan" in large print on the note you sign.
- Warn you to read the note before you sign and not to sign if there are any blank spaces.
- Notify you if you are turned down for a loan.
- Return all the papers you gave the lender if you are turned down or if you decide not to take the loan.

The act forbids a lender to

- Make any false or misleading statements, including advertisements, in order to attract business.
- Charge more than three percentage points (a point is 1 percent of the loan amount).
- Charge an application fee before the secondary mortgage is closed.
- Charge you brokers' or finders' fees, commissions, premiums, or any other charges for the loan, except interest.
- Charge a penalty if you pay the loan off early.
- Take anything else but real estate as *collateral.*
- Charge you attorneys' fees, except for closing on the loan. (The lender can also charge attorneys' fees if it actually sues you after you have defaulted on the loan and this arrangement is specified in your agreement. The lender can then charge no more than 15 percent of the first $500 you owe, 10 percent of the next $500, and 5 percent of any amount over $1,000 in attorneys' fees.)
- Make or offer to make an unwise second mortgage or home equity loan.

A lender *may* require you to have property insurance. However, you *cannot* be made to purchase credit life or accident and health insurance for a second mortgage or home equity loan.

SPECIAL RULES FOR HOME EQUITY LOANS

Home Ownership and Equity Protection Act. Effective October 5, 1995, Congress passed a law called the Home Ownership and Equity Protec-

DISCLOSURE REQUIREMENTS FOR FIXED-RATE LOANS

Creditors must

- ✔ Tell you the annual percentage rate (APR) and give you a statement saying that costs other than interest are not included in the APR.
- ✔ Give you a list of any fees charged to open the account, use the account, or maintain the account.
- ✔ Tell you that a default can result in the loss of your home.
- ✔ Tell you the dangers of *negative amortization* (your mortgage debt growing larger with time instead of smaller—meaning that your homeowner's equity shrinks).
- ✔ Tell you of the need to consult a tax advisor about the tax deductibility of any interest payment.
- ✔ Tell you that you may get back any fees you paid the lender if the terms of the loan (other than a variable interest rate) change after you apply for the loan and as a result you decide not to take the loan before the loan is closed.
- ✔ Tell you how long it would take to pay off $10,000 if only the minimum payments were made and, if applicable, the fact that making only the minimum payments will result in a large, final *balloon payment.*

tion Act of 1994 (15 *U.S.C.* Section 1639). This law provides added protections and disclosures for consumers who enter into high-interest-rate home equity mortgages. For covered loans, HOEP prohibits balloon payment, negative amortization, and increases of interest rates in the event of default. If you think you are covered by HOEP and have questions or are having problems, see a lawyer to protect your rights. This law is new and can be complicated.

Home Equity Loan Consumer Protection Act. The federal Home Equity Loan Consumer Protection Act of 1988 (15 *U.S.C.* Section 1601 *et seq.*) requires that consumers receive certain information that is easy to understand whenever they receive an application for home equity lines of credit. Unlike the New Jersey Secondary Mortgage Loan Act, which does not cover loans from loan associations or banks, the federal law applies to loans from *all* creditors. The federal law provides consumers with protections when entering into a home equity loan. For example, the law says that a lender can *accelerate* the loan and declare you in default for only three reasons: (1) you fail to pay, (2) you fail to maintain insurance or you otherwise act irresponsibly

79

**DISCLOSURE REQUIREMENTS FOR
VARIABLE-RATE LOANS**

Creditors must

- ✔ Tell you how and when rate changes are made.
- ✔ Tell you the highest interest rate that can be charged over the lifetime of the loan.
- ✔ Tell you the smallest payment you must make if the highest interest rate is charged.
- ✔ Tell you the maximum increases in the interest rate allowed within one year.
- ✔ Give you an example showing what the APR and the minimum payments would have been for the past 15 years.
- ✔ Give you a pamphlet explaining how home equity loans work, discussing their advantages and disadvantages.

---

with regard to the property, *or* (3) you committed fraud when you obtained the loan.

When creditors give you an application for home equity lines of credit, they must disclose certain information to you (see the boxes above and on the preceding page).

New Jersey has no legal limits on the interest rates for mortgages except that provided by the Criminal Usury Law, 30 percent. This means that it's up to you to shop around and compare rates.

FORECLOSURE

If you fail to make payments on your loan, the lender can collect the debt by filing a lawsuit against you to obtain possession and ownership of your home. This is called a *foreclosure*. If the foreclosure lawsuit results in a final judgment against you, it may result in a sale of your home, called a *foreclosure sale*. Foreclosure sales usually bring less money than the property is actually worth.

FAIR FORECLOSURE ACT. A New Jersey law called the Fair Foreclosure Act (FFA) (*N.J.S.A.* 2A:50-58) took effect on December 4, 1995. It applies to all residential mortgage foreclosure lawsuits filed on or after December 5, 1995, and to residential mortgages and residential mortgage debtors. This law applies to you if you own a one-, two-, three-, or four-family dwelling in New Jersey and either you or a member of your immediate family lives in the house. (It could also apply if neither you nor an immediate family member presently lives in the house, as long as you intended to live in the house or intended that an immediate family member live in the house when you signed the loan and mortgage.)

Homeowner Rights. If it applies to you, the FFA gives you some very important rights. First, you have the right to be given a notice that the lender intends to file a lawsuit for foreclosure against you before the complaint is actually filed. You also have the right to *cure* the loan (make payments). If you cure the loan before the bank files its complaint, you will not have to pay court costs or other fees.

In addition to other rights you may have, the FFA says you *must* be advised in the notice that you have the following eleven rights. You have the right

1. To be advised of the particular mortgage or real estate security interest.
2. To be told the nature of the default (for example, to be informed that you are late with your monthly mortgage payment).
3. To be advised that you have the right to cure the default before the lender may file foreclosure proceedings.
4. To be informed of what you must do in order to cure the default before the complaint for foreclosure is filed.
5. To be told the date by which you must cure in order to avoid foreclosure proceedings and to be told the name, address, and phone number of a person to whom the payment or *tender* shall be made. *The lender must give you thirty days to do this.*
6. To be informed about what will happen if you do not cure the default. That is, that the lender may take steps to terminate your ownership of the property by filing a foreclosure suit against you.
7. To be advised that you have the right to cure even if the lender files a foreclosure complaint, but that you will be responsible for the lender's court costs and attorneys' fees.
8. To be advised of the right to transfer the real estate to another person if the mortgage documents allow you to do so. The person to whom you transfer the property will also have the right to cure the default.
9. To be advised to seek counsel from an attorney of your own choosing or from a lawyer referral service; if you are unable to afford an attorney you may communicate with a local Legal Services program.
10. To be given information about the possible availability of financial assistance for curing the default. You may be given a list of agencies identified by the Commissioner of Banking.
11. To be given the name and address of the lender and the telephone number of a representative whom you should call if you disagree with the amount of money the lender says you owe, or if you think you are not in default.

Note: You should not wait until you receive a notice of intention to foreclose (see below) before seeking the advice of a lawyer or credit counseling service. You should seek help at the very first sign of trouble.

In the case of an uncontested foreclosure suit, you have the right to be informed before a final judgment is entered against you. You also have the right to ask the sheriff to delay the foreclosure sale, which the sheriff is allowed to do only twice, for fourteen days each time. A court could also order further delays if there is a good reason to do so.

Lender Rights. Under the new law, lenders have been given some rights, too. In some cases, a lender is permitted to choose an alternate procedure to foreclose. Where this applies, it means that the lender will be allowed to foreclose on your property and gain possession and title without going through a sheriff's sale. This is called the *optional foreclosure procedure without sale.* It is available to lenders in only three instances: (1) if you voluntarily surrender the property and sign over a deed to the lender, (2) if you abandon the property, *or* (3) if there is no equity in your home. These three instances are discussed below.

A lender usually must declare that you are in *default* on your mortgage before it files for foreclosure. In order to determine if you are in default, the lender will have to look at the terms of the agreement into which you entered. Most often, a default will result because you failed to pay the amount due on the monthly principal and interest as required by the agreement, but it could be because of other things. Most mortgage agreements will also declare you in default for failing to pay real estate taxes on time or for not keeping the property adequately insured.

NOTICE OF INTENTION TO FORECLOSE. If you are late with a mortgage payment, the lender must send you a *notice of intention to foreclose* before it is allowed to *accelerate your mortgage* or file a foreclosure complaint against you. Accelerating your mortgage means that the lender will say that you now owe the total amount left due on the loan.

The lender is required to send you the notice of intention to foreclose by certified mail, return receipt requested, or by registered mail. This notice is required in all cases in which the lender decides that it wants to file foreclosure proceedings against a residential mortgage debtor. The only time a lender is not required to send this notice is if you *voluntarily surrender* the property to the lender. Voluntarily surrender means that you sign over a deed to the lender. You should *never* do this without first receiving legal advice or at least credit counseling from a reputable nonprofit organization.

The notice of intention to foreclose will tell you that you have thirty days to make the required payment on the mortgage (curing the default). If you do not make the payment within thirty days, the lender can then accelerate the loan and file a lawsuit against you to foreclose the mortgage. The law says that the notice of intention to foreclose must inform you that you have certain rights. Each right must be provided clearly and conspicuously in the notice. The notice should contain language that is clear, direct, and not misleading.

YOUR RIGHT TO CURE (MAKE YOUR LOAN CURRENT). The right to cure a default on your mortgage loan is important. Prior to the FFA, a lender could arbitrarily decide whether or not it wanted to accept late mortgage payments. If it didn't, there wasn't much a debtor could do to prevent foreclosure except pay the entire amount owed on the mortgage loan. The new law no longer permits lenders to have this discretion. Now, a lender must accept your late payment to cure the mortgage default. But there are conditions on your right to cure.

There are two distinct time periods for a debtor to cure. The *thirty-day right to cure* lasts until the date given you on the notice of intention to foreclose. This date will be approximately thirty days from the date the notice is mailed but could be longer. The notice must tell you the exact date by which you may use this unlimited right to cure the default. If you cure by this date by paying the monthly amounts which are due plus late fees, you will stop the foreclosure process. The lender may not charge you any penalties for using your right to cure. You can use this right an unlimited number of times. However, if you do not cure by using the thirty-day right to cure, the lender may file a foreclosure complaint against you. Even if it does, you can still prevent foreclosure by using what is called the *eighteen-month limited right to cure*.

Unlike the thirty-day right to cure, which can be used repeatedly for the life of the mortgage, the eighteen-month right to cure is limited to use once every eighteen months from the date you cure and the lender reinstates your loan. If you cure the default at this stage, it is likely that a foreclosure action has been filed against you. You may be responsible for attorneys' fees and court costs. However, attorneys' fees and costs are limited to those provided by court rule. Your right to cure under this law ends on the date the court enters a final judgment against you.

Neither the thirty-day nor the eighteen-month right to cure applies if you voluntarily surrender your property. This means that if you sign over a deed to the lender, you have no right to cure unless there is some other defect in the procedure.

If you exercise one of your rights to cure under the new law, you are required to pay what you owe in cash or with a certified or cashier's check. In addition to the amount of the mortgage payments that you owe, you may have to pay late charges if your mortgage agreement requires you to do so. However, the new law specifically forbids the lender from charging you any fee or penalty just for exercising your right to cure. Once you have paid the amount you owe, the lender must reinstate your loan and put you back in the same position you would have been in if you had never been late with your mortgage payments.

NOTICE BEFORE ENTRY OF FINAL JUDGMENT. If you have failed to cure the default and a foreclosure complaint has been filed, the FFA states you have the right, in some cases, to be informed that the lender will be asking the court for a final judgment of foreclosure against you. This is called the *notice before entry of final judgment.* This notice is required to be given to you if a complaint for foreclosure has been filed and served on you and you fail to answer the complaint, or you do file an answer but the court says your answer is *uncontested.*

This notice must state that the lender will apply for the entry of final judgment at least fourteen days prior to doing so.

The notice must tell you that if you fail to respond to the notice, the lender will do what is necessary to enter judgment. Once the lender is able to get a final judgment, you will lose your right to cure the default. However, under certain circumstances, you may still take some steps to delay the judgment and protect your home from foreclosure. (You may also be able to save your home from foreclosure by filing for bankruptcy. See a lawyer concerning this option.)

You have the right to ask the lender to delay entering the final judgment if you have a reasonable likelihood that you will be able to get the money to cure the default within forty-five days. To delay the final judgment, you must do the following:

- Within ten days after receiving the notice before entry of final judgment, you must send the lender a statement.
- The statement must be sent by certified mail, return receipt requested.
- The statement must be made in good faith and certify as true that there is a reasonable likelihood that you will be able to provide payment necessary to cure the default. You should be aware, however, that you will not have an unlimited—or even long—period of time to cure the default. The amount of time that you will have may vary according to when the notice you receive becomes effective, but it will likely be around forty-five days.

Once the lender receives such a statement, it may not obtain a judgment against you until the time you have to cure expires (around forty-five days) and you have still not made the required payment.

OPTIONAL FORECLOSURE PROCEDURE WITHOUT SALE. In some cases, a lender is allowed to foreclose on your property without going through a sheriff's sale. This is called the *optional foreclosure procedure without sale.* A lender's use of this procedure is very limited. It is allowed to be used only under limited circumstances, and a debtor or other interested defendant is allowed to opt out of this alternative procedure for any reason.

The FFA says that a lender can use this procedure only in the following three circumstances:

1. If you abandon the property and the lender submits proof from someone who has such personal knowledge.
2. If you voluntarily surrender the property, which means that you signed over a deed in lieu of foreclosure to the lender (which you should never do unless you have talked to a lawyer first). (In order to voluntarily surrender, you must first be given a notice of intention to foreclose, described above. Also, the deed must clearly say that you have the right to rescind the deed in seven days without penalty, excluding Saturdays, Sundays, and legal holidays and that your rescission is effective upon delivery of a written notice to the lender.)
3. If you have only a small amount of equity in the property. This is determined by knowing the fair market value of your home (i.e., what you could get for it if you sold it) and subtracting any mortgages, liens, or judgments against your property. If the amount that you get after subtracting your liens is 92 percent or more of the fair market value, then the law states that you have no equity. The lender can then use the optional foreclosure procedure to take possession of your home.

Once you have received the *notice of entry of order for redemption* and you do not cure the default or ask for an additional forty-five days, the lender may initiate the optional procedure. It does this by filing an affidavit or *certification* with the court (a request for the court's permission to use the optional foreclosure procedure) that tells the court why the lender believes it is entitled to use the optional foreclosure procedure. This statement must be supported by some other documents or proofs (i.e., the lender must submit proof either of abandonment, of no equity, or that you voluntarily signed a deed in lieu of foreclosure).

The lender must wait at least fourteen days after mailing you the notice of entry of order for redemption, or if you sent the lender a statement requesting more time, it must wait at least forty-five days before it can send these documents to the court.

ORDER FOR REDEMPTION. The next thing you will receive is an *order for redemption,* signed by a judge, and a notice of the order. Once the order is entered, you no longer have the right to cure under the FFA. However, you still may have the right to cure under bankruptcy law (see Chapter 7).

The order for redemption will tell you the time, amount, and place for redemption, which should be not less than forty-five days or more than sixty days after the date the order is entered. The amount for redemption will include the amount that is left on your mortgage plus the lender's costs, including interest and attorneys' fees.

In order to *redeem,* that is, get back your property and save it from foreclosure, you will have to pay the entire amount set forth in the order for redemption by cash, certified check, or cashier's check. You must bring the amount to the attorney's office or other designated place, between 9 A.M. and 4 P.M. on or before the date on the order.

The order and notice are to be mailed to you and each defendant and, if different, to the address of the property being foreclosed. They must be sent by ordinary mail *and* certified mail, return receipt requested, within twenty days after the date of the entry of the order.

The notice must state three things:

1. That the lender is proceeding under the optional foreclosure procedure.
2. That you or any of the other defendants named in the foreclosure complaint (there are usually many) may request a public sale of the mortgaged premises and the method for doing so (i.e., that you, or any of the defendants can opt out of the optional foreclosure procedure).
3. That you or any of the defendants must opt out within thirty days of the date of service of the notice, except if you have a very good reason for being late.

Under the FFA, any defendant can opt out and get a public sale by simply mailing to the Office of Foreclosure or the court a written request for a public sale within thirty days of the date the order or notice is served. The court is then required to enter a judgment of foreclosure, which provides for a public sale.

PUBLIC SALE. If you are the owner of the property and you request a public sale there is no further requirement—you simply get a public sale of the premises, held by a county sheriff.

If the person requesting a public sale is any other person or entity, a 10 percent cash deposit or bond is required to be made prior to the date fixed for redemption. The deposit is to secure the plaintiff-lender against any additional interest and costs as well as any deficiency which may result from the public sale. Also, such a person will be responsible for all expenses and costs associated with the public sale, including sheriffs' fees and commissions.

There are some benefits to requesting a public sale. First, you will probably get a little more time to stay in the home because the sheriff will have to schedule a sale and you have the right to request two adjournments. Also, you may be able to get someone you know to attend the public sale and bid on the property. The property is sold to the highest bidder, which is usually the lender. But, if someone else bids on the property and the amount is more than what the lender is entitled to, there may be a surplus. Finally, you may be able to get someone to buy the property privately or through a real estate agent before the public sale takes place. This usually results in more money, and there may be some left over for you.

Once a judgment of foreclosure is entered, the lender issues a *writ of execution* to the county sheriff who will set a date for a foreclosure sale by auction. The sheriff is required to publish the date of the auction sale and has discretion to adjourn the sale twice, for a period of fourteen days each time. If you do not pay off what is owed in full plus any costs added by the lender and you do not file for bankruptcy protection, the sheriff will hold a public sale by auction of the premises. Usually only the foreclosing lender appears at the public sale to bid, although any member of the public is able to attend. Frequently, the lender buys the property for a nominal amount.

After the public sale, you are given ten additional days to redeem the property. After the ten days have expired, a deed is issued and you are forever foreclosed from any rights, equitable or otherwise, to the property. The lender can then require that you leave the premises. The lender then usually sells the property and attempts to get, at a minimum, the amount of the outstanding mortgage amount, plus costs.

Sheriffs are required to schedule foreclosure sales within 120 days of receipt of a writ of execution. If a sheriff cannot schedule the foreclosure sale within 120 days, a lender can ask the court to appoint a *special master* to hold the foreclosure sale.

Sheriffs are now required to obtain a 20 percent cash deposit from any successful bidder. If the successful bidder does not have the deposit, new bidding is to take place immediately without any further notification or publication. The defaulting bidder suffers penalties and is liable for additional costs, including any difference between the defaulting bidder's highest bid and the highest bid during subsequent bidding.

The FFA states that sheriffs or special masters may make only two adjournments, not exceeding fourteen days each. However, the new law also allows a court to order further adjournments for good reason, although the law does not say what a good reason is. If you think you have a good reason to delay a sheriff sale beyond this twenty-eight-day period, you should see a lawyer.

The lender cannot force you to give up any of your rights, but the law gives you the option to *waive,* or give up, your rights in certain circumstances. In order for a waiver of your rights under the FFA to be effective, you must first be in default and must have received notice of your rights through the notice of intention to foreclose. Then, if a lender works out an agreement with you that you sign, you may waive your rights. But, the waiver must be on a separate piece of paper from the agreement and must also be signed by you.

Note: The FFA was enacted to protect homeowners. *Do not give up any of these important rights* unless you have a very good reason. Also, you should contact a lawyer *before* doing so.

HOME REPAIRS AND IMPROVEMENTS

Home renovations and repairs are essential in order to maintain the value of your home. However, according to the New Jersey Division of Consumer Affairs, problems related to home improvement transactions are a major category of the complaints it receives each year. The complaints from homeowners range from work not performed, missed deadlines, and poor-quality workmanship, to cost overruns, inflated prices, and financing problems.

CONSUMER FRAUD ACT. Regulations under the New Jersey Consumer Fraud Act (*N.J.S.A.* 56:8-19) protect your rights when you hire a contractor to make improvements or repairs to your home. Home repairs and improvements include modernizing, remodeling, altering, painting, and other repairs. Homeowners as well as tenants who buy such services are protected.

Home Repair Cons. Under the regulations, home repair and improvement contractors are not supposed to mislead you to get you to sign a contract. The following typical tricks used by some home repair contractors are specifically forbidden:

- Tricking you into believing you will get a reduced price by using your house as a model or to advertise their work.
- Lying about the quality of the materials they will use.
- Using a bait and switch trick, such as advertising that a supposedly inferior product is on sale, with the intent of enticing you into buying a higher-priced product. (A home repair contractor cannot advertise a bargain price and switch to a more expensive product, claiming that the cheaper product is not as good or is no longer available.)
- Substituting other products for those specified in the contract.
- Offering you a gift to get you to sign a contract unless they tell you all the conditions of the offer, such as how long it lasts and when they will give you the gift.
- Lying about the costs to do the job and what is or is not included, such as delivery or installation.
- Starting work to force you to sign a contract.
- Falsely telling you that your home is dangerous and needs repair.
- Falsely stating that the contractor works for a government agency or for a government energy program.

PRECAUTIONS AND CONTRACTS. Before you sign a contract for any work to be done on your home you should take the steps outlined in the box on the facing page.

All home improvement contracts for more than $100 must be in writing; all changes and conditions thereafter must also be in writing and must be signed by all parties. The contract must be legible and in simple language.

STEPS TO TAKE BEFORE SIGNING A
HOME IMPROVEMENT CONTRACT

✔ Get estimates from more than one contractor. Get at least two, preferably three, written estimates. This may be difficult and time consuming but if it avoids shoddy work, the time and effort are well spent. For some items, such as storm windows, the factory which sells the product may install it. You may not need to get your own contractor in this instance.

✔ Get the names of some of the contractor's past customers. Talk with them to see if they are happy with the contractor's work.

✔ Check with the municipal or county Division of Consumer Affairs where the business is located, the state Office of Consumer Protection's Action Line, and the Better Business Bureau in your area to find out if any complaints have been filed against the contractor.

✔ Get all of the contractor's promises in writing.

✔ Make sure you can find the contractor if there is a problem later. Get the name and address of the owner of the business and the business name and address. Also get the names and addresses of any salespersons, if different from those of the home repair company. Write down the license plate numbers of their cars and trucks. This information may become necessary if the contractor leaves town and you need to contact him or her. (New Jersey does not license or keep track of people who do home improvements for cash. It only licenses those who sell home repairs on credit.)

✔ Read the contract carefully *before* you sign it. If anything is missing, write it in and have the contractor initial it.

✔ Find out if the contractor has insurance, such as workers' compensation. You should make sure that the insurance coverage includes the contractor, workers, and visitors to your home.

✔ Beware of your contractor "arranging" financing for you. Often you get a bad deal. It is best to get your own loan.

✔ Pay by check. If you need to find a contractor who leaves town, his or her checking account number and bank should appear on the back of the returned check.

DISCLOSURE REQUIREMENTS FOR HOME IMPROVEMENT CONTRACTS

The contract must include

- ✔ The names and addresses of everyone involved in the work, including salespeople and contractors.
- ✔ A description of the work to be done and the goods and services that you are buying.
- ✔ The total price that you must pay, including any finance charge. The hourly labor rate and any other conditions affecting the price must be clearly specified if the contract is for time and labor.
- ✔ The disclosure statement about the credit charges, required by TILA, if you pay in installments.
- ✔ The date or time period within which the contractor will start and finish the job.
- ✔ A statement of any guarantee or warranty the contractor makes on products, materials, labor, or services.
- ✔ A description of any mortgage or security interest the contractor takes in your home.

Contracts for home improvements are also required to include all of the information listed in the box above.

CONTRACTOR SECURITY INTERESTS AND LIENS. Remember that a security interest in your home means that the contractor has a mortgage on your property and may be able to foreclose on your house. Sometimes contractors will want to place a lien on your home to cover the cost of repairs.

If the contractor takes a *security interest* (mortgage) in your home, TILA gives you at least three business days after you sign to change your mind and cancel the contract. You should see a lawyer in such a case since you risk losing your home.

If you signed a contract with a door-to-door home repair salesperson you also have up to three business days after you sign the contract to change your mind for any reason and cancel it. Such a contract is treated as a *door-to-door sale*.

A contractor or subcontractor who performs work on your home—or a supplier of materials—may be entitled to a *construction lien* on your property. This type of lien is created by New Jersey law and can have significant consequences. Under the law, before a construction lien can be filed against your home, the contractor or supplier must file a *notice of unpaid balance and right to file a lien.* This triggers *arbitration,* at which time it will be determined whether or not a lien should be placed on your home, and if so, for how much.

If a lien is placed on your home, it can be very troublesome. If you want to sell or refinance your home and there is a lien against it, you will first have to clear the title by getting the lien *discharged,* i.e., paying the total lien amount in full. However, if you have paid the contractor in full but he or she has failed to pay a supplier, the law does not allow the supplier to have a lien against your home.

FINANCING HOME IMPROVEMENTS. You can finance the work by paying the contractor in installments or by getting a loan through a *home financing agency.* Sometimes the contractor will arrange for the contract to be financed by a home financing agency or other lender. If you sign a home repair contract and agree to pay for the goods and services in installments over a period of time greater than ninety days, you are protected by the New Jersey Home Repair Financing Act. Contractors, salespeople, and home financing agencies who offer contracts with these terms must be licensed by the New Jersey Department of Banking.

Home repair contracts *must* contain the following information:

- A statement that notifies you *not* to sign a blank contract and that you are entitled to a copy of the contract at the time you sign it.
- A statement as to whether the contractor carries workers' compensation and public liability insurance. If the contractor is *not* covered by workers' compensation, *you* are responsible for any accidents during the repair.
- The payment schedule, which should list equal payments separated by equal periods of time.
- The disclosure statement about the cost of credit as required by TILA.

The contract may *not* include

- An agreement to pay anything other than the price of the goods and services furnished under the contract.
- A *power of attorney to confess to judgment.* This means that you agree in advance to allow another party to enter a judgment against you.
- A statement that says you cannot sue the holder of your loan if you have a claim against the contractor under the contract.

To file a complaint about a financed home repair contract, contact the New Jersey Department of Banking in Trenton. You can also contact the state Office of Consumer Protection.

You should also see a lawyer. The Consumer Fraud Act also allows you to sue anyone who violates this law, and the fraudulent contractor can be forced to pay for your attorney. There may also be violations of TILA disclosure requirements. Very often you will have a right to cancel the home repair mortgage under TILA.

4. Utilities

This chapter discusses consumer rights to utility services and consumer protections against utility companies, including protections in billing disputes or when shutoffs are threatened for late payment.

In New Jersey, as almost everywhere else, people do not have a choice as to where they buy their utilities. There is usually only one company from which people can buy electricity, gas, telephone, water, or sewer services. For this reason New Jersey has set up some legal rights for utility consumers.

The New Jersey agency in charge of seeing that the electric, gas, telephone, water, and sewer utility companies follow the laws that protect consumers is the New Jersey Board of Public Utilities (BPU). This board is appointed by the governor and has its offices at 2 Gateway Center, Newark, New Jersey 07102.

In order to help consumers know and understand their rights, the BPU developed the Utility Customer's Bill of Rights, a list of fourteen rights that every utility customer has (see the box on the facing page).

DEPOSITS

When you first ask the utility company to turn on the gas or electricity, they might ask you for a deposit if

- At your previous residence you did not have an account with them (for example, your landlord paid for utilities or you lived in an area served by another utility company),

  or
- You have a bad payment record—you paid your bills late or owe money.

The utility company cannot ask that a deposit be more than what the utility company estimates your average monthly bill will be for two months. When you pay your deposit, the utility company must give you a receipt. If you have made a deposit and do not pay your bill, the utility company may use the deposit to pay the bill. The utility company may then require you to make a new deposit.

Once the utility company has your deposit for three months, it must pay you interest on the deposit. The utility company will review your account one year after you close your account and pay your final bill. The utility must then refund the deposit and pay you interest earned on the deposit.

THE UTILITY CUSTOMER'S BILL OF RIGHTS

1. You have the right to utility service if you are a qualified applicant.
2. You shall not be asked to pay unreasonably high deposits as a condition of service nor to make unreasonable payments on past-due bills.
3. You have the right to budget billing or payment plans if you are an electric or gas customer.
4. You are entitled to at least one deferred-payment plan in a year.
5. You have the right to have any complaint against your utility handled promptly by that utility.
6. You have the right to call the New Jersey BPU to investigate your utility complaints and inquiries. Your service may not be terminated for nonpayment of disputed charges during a BPU investigation.
7. You have the right to have your meter tested, free of charge, once a year by your utility if you suspect it is not working properly. For a $5 fee, the meter test will be conducted under the supervision of the staff of the BPU.
8. You have the right to receive a written notice of termination seven days prior to discontinuance of service.
9. Residential service may be shut off, after proper notice, Monday through Thursday, 8:00 A.M. to 4:00 P.M. A utility may not shut off residential service on Friday, Saturday, Sunday, a holiday, or the day before a holiday, or if a valid medical emergency exists in your household.
10. If you are elderly or a low-income customer having financial problems paying your bill, you have the right, under the Winter Termination Program, to request that the company enroll you in a budget plan in accordance with your ability to pay. You are required to make good-faith payments of all reasonable bills for service and, in return, are assured of the right to have gas and electric service from November 15 to March 15 without fear of termination of such service.
11. If you live in a multifamily dwelling, you have the right to posted notice, in common areas, of any discontinuance of service. Individual notice is required to occupants of single- and two-family dwellings.
12. You have the right to have a *diversion of service* investigation if you suspect that the level of consumption reflected in your utility bill is inexplicably high.
13. Service shall not be shut off for nonpayment of repair charges, merchandise charges, or yellow page charges, nor shall notice threatening such discontinuance be given.
14. You have the option of having a deposit refund applied to your account as a credit or of having the deposit refunded by separate check.

The law also requires utility companies to review your account at least once a year. If you have been paying your bills on time, they must then refund your deposit and pay you interest on the deposit.

LATE PAYMENTS AND SHUTOFFS

When you receive your bill, the utility company must give you at least ten days to pay it. If, at the end of the ten days you still have not paid your bill, the utility company may send you a *notice of discontinuance.* This notice will tell you that unless you pay your bill immediately, your services will be cut off in seven days.

The utility company may not cut off services to residential customers for nonpayment

- On Saturdays or Sundays
- On holidays on which the company's payment offices are closed
- After 1 P.M. of its last business day before a weekend or holiday

In addition, the utility cannot turn off services when there is a legitimate bill dispute, a medical emergency, a deferred payment agreement, or when you are covered by the ban on winter shutoffs.

DISPUTING THE BILL. If you have not paid your bill because you disagree with the amount, the utility company cannot cut off your service if (1) you have paid the amount that you think you owe *and* (2) you have asked the BPU for an investigation of the disputed bill.

As long as your complaint is before the BPU and as long as you pay the amount of the bills you do *not* dispute, the utility company is not allowed to turn off your services.

MEDICAL EMERGENCIES. The utility company also may not turn off your service for nonpayment if (1) you have a medical emergency that would worsen if your service was turned off *and* (2) you give proof that you are not able to pay.

To prove to the utility company that you have a medical emergency, you must provide it with a letter from your doctor stating that (1) you have a medical emergency (you must explain what it is and how long it might last) *and* (2) turning off your service would make the emergency worse.

The doctor's letter will stop the utility company from turning off service, but only for thirty days. After that, you can give the utility company another letter from your doctor. This will get you another thirty days of service. If you still have a medical emergency after the sixty days, then you should write or call the BPU. Do not wait until they have cut off your service.

DEFERRED PAYMENT AGREEMENT. If you have not paid your bill and neither of the two preceding situations applies, the utility company may send you a *notice of discontinuance.* If this happens, you have a right to ask for a *deferred payment agreement.* This means requesting the utility company to give you more time to pay the bill. To get such an agreement, call the collection department at the utility company. Give them your account number and explain that you cannot pay the whole bill at once. Tell them how much you can pay and when you can pay the rest. The most the utility company can require as a down payment is 25 percent of the unpaid bill.

If you ask for a deferred payment agreement, the utility company must try to reach an agreement with you. They will ask you to pay future bills on time. They will also ask you to pay part of the unpaid bill each month until it is all paid.

You have a right to *one* deferred payment agreement each year. If you make an agreement and do not keep it, the utility company may send you a notice of discontinuance and turn off your service. If the company refuses to give you a deferred payment agreement, complain immediately to the BPU. Do not wait until your service has been cut off.

Note: A current BPU ruling allows PSE&G to shut off power from the street under certain conditions, even if you have paid your bill. If you live in a multifamily dwelling of four or more units and all but one or two tenants have paid utility bills, your power can be cut off if the utility asks you to let them in to shut off your neighbor's service and you either refuse or are unable to do so. If you are threatened with this type of utility shutoff you should complain to the BPU and contact your local Legal Services office immediately.

If you make a complaint in writing, keep a copy of your letter to prove that you wrote it. Also, keep notes on your conversations with the utility and the BPU.

BAN ON WINTER SHUTOFFS. The ban on winter shutoffs (also called the Winter Termination Program) protects customers from being without heat or hot water during the winter months. The law says that your utility company cannot shut off your gas or electricity from November 15 to March 15 if you receive any of the following:

- Lifeline Credit Program benefits.
- Home Energy Assistance Program (HEAP) benefits (or if you are eligible to receive HEAP benefits).
- Welfare (now called Work First New Jersey).
- Supplemental Security Income (SSI).
- Pharmaceutical Assistance for the Aged and Disabled (PAAD).

The utility company may still send you a notice that they will shut off your service if you do not pay. But if you receive any of the above benefits or can't pay due to circumstances beyond your control and can prove it to the utility company, your service cannot be shut off. If the utility company does, or wants to, shut off your service, you can appeal to the BPU. If the BPU finds that the utility company is wrong and agrees that you are unable to pay, your service will be kept on or turned back on.

Even if you are not in one of these programs, the utility may not shut off your service during the winter if you can't pay your bills because of circumstances beyond your control, such as unemployment, illness, recent death of a spouse, etc.

If your utility service is already shut off, you can get it turned back on during the winter. But you will have to make a down payment (which can't be more than 25 percent of the outstanding bill) and agree to make installment payments each month.

If your income is low, you may qualify for HEAP payments. Call your county welfare board for details.

PARTIAL SERVICE. If you cannot afford both gas and electricity, you can have the company turn off one service. For example, if you owe $200 for electricity and $1,000 for gas, you can ask the company to turn off your gas. You could then make an agreement to pay off the $200 electric bill and keep the electric service.

ESTIMATED BILLS

The utility company must send you bills on a regular basis. They must also try to read your meter regularly. Sometimes the company will send you bills without having looked at your meter. This is called an *estimated bill*. Usually, the amount of the estimated bill is about the same as what your bill would be if the meter had been read.

Sometimes the estimated bill may be much higher than what you usually pay. If this happens, call the utility company and ask them to read your meter. If they say they cannot send someone right away, you may ask the company for a special postcard telling you how to read your meter. Contact the meter-reading department at your utility company for a card. They must give you a card if you ask for one. You may then either telephone the company and tell them what your meter reading is, or you may mail them the postcard with your meter reading on it. The card is postage paid. If you do this right away, they cannot require you to pay the estimated bill but must bill you for the amount you mailed in on the postcard.

Sometimes, after sending estimated bills for several months, the utility company may find out that the estimated bills were too low. If they then send you a bill that is more than 25 percent over your last bill, you can ask for more time to pay the extra amount. They must let you pay back the extra amount over a period of time equal to the period of time they sent estimated bills.

BROKEN METERS

If your bills are very high and you think that something is wrong with your meter, you may ask the utility company to check it. To do this, talk to the accounting department at your utility company. They must test your meter for free, as long as you ask them to do it only once in twelve months. They must give you a report of what they find. If the utility company refuses to test your meter, complain to the BPU. You may also ask the BPU to test your meter, but if they do and do not find anything wrong with it, they may charge you a fee.

DIVERSION OF SERVICE

If you are a tenant in a multiunit building, sometimes bills may be high because someone else is stealing from your meter. If something else is connected to your meter, such as the landlord's hall lights, hot water heater, or gas furnace, it is called *diversion* or *theft of service*. If you suspect this is the case, go to your utility company's office and ask for a form called "Request for Diversion of Service Investigation." Once you fill in the written request, the utility company must, by law, go to your building and investigate. If the utility company tells you that this is a landlord-tenant problem or refuses to get involved, complain to the BPU.

The utility company must inspect your basement and see what is connected to your meter. The company must then send you a written report. If a diversion of service is found, the company will figure out the dollar amount wrongfully run up on your meter. They should tell the landlord to fix the wires and try to get the party who has been diverting services to pay. The amount of service which you did not use will then be subtracted from your bill and added to the other party's bill.

TELEPHONE BILL DISPUTES

In New Jersey, telephone companies are also regulated by the BPU. The BPU has authority over local telephone service and long-distance calls made within the state of New Jersey. Calls made to another state (interstate calls) are governed by the Federal Communications Commission (FCC).

If you have a dispute over a telephone charge that you can't settle with the telephone company, you can request that the BPU conduct an investigation.

State regulations say that disconnection of service and collection activities shall be stopped for all disputed charges pending the BPU's investigation, provided that all *undisputed* charges are paid by the consumer.

If the investigation concludes that the customer must pay some or all of the disputed charges, the telephone company is required to give at least seven days' written notice prior to disconnection of service. If the consumer advises the telephone company that he or she is unable to make payment, the telephone company is obligated to negotiate in good faith with the consumer in order to enter into a reasonable deferred payment agreement. If the agreement is for longer than two months, it must be in writing. The consumer must continue to pay current, undisputed bills during the repayment period in order to continue to avoid disconnection of service.

Your telephone service cannot be disconnected for failure to pay repair, merchandise, yellow pages, or 900-number charges. If you have a problem with a telephone charge as a result of a call made in New Jersey, telephone the BPU.

5. You and Your Job

The rights of employees are governed by a variety of federal and state laws. This chapter discusses the separate federal and state laws that establish the rights of federal and state government employees, as well as the special laws that apply to children and agricultural workers. In addition the chapter discusses the rights and obligations of people applying for jobs, of employees, and of those whose jobs have ended for any of a variety of reasons.

GETTING HIRED

There are a number of ways in which you can get help in finding a job. Some people in New Jersey may also be eligible for training to help them get into the job market.

EMPLOYMENT AGENCIES. Employment agencies—including placement firms, career counseling services, and resume services—may help you to find a job for a fee. Employment agencies are licensed and regulated by the Bureau of Employment and Personnel Services in the Division of Consumer Affairs in the Department of Law and Public Safety.[1]

Fees. The chief of the bureau must approve an employment agency's schedule of fees, which must be posted in a conspicuous place in the office of the agency. The agency may not charge fees greater than those shown in the schedule of fees. Employment agencies must obtain a good-faith order for employment before collecting any fee from a job seeker.

In addition, an employment agency may not charge you more than 1 percent of the scheduled fee for each day worked if you are fired without cause from the job found for you, or if you quit for just cause. However, the employment agency can charge you up to 30 percent of the scheduled fee if you fail to report for duty after accepting employment or if you quit without just cause within thirty days.

Employment agencies are prohibited from publishing any misleading notice or advertisement and from making deceptive or misleading representations to job seekers or employers.

CONSULTING FIRMS. These firms, which are also regulated by the Bureau of Employment and Personnel Services, are compensated for their services by payments from employers only. They appraise, refer, or recommend individuals to be considered for employment. They may not (1) publish false, deceptive, or misleading advertisements or representations about the services they provide to job seekers; *or* (2) give a job seeker information about a job which they have reason to know does not exist or was not listed by the employer, or for which the job seeker is not qualified.

Employment agencies and consulting firms cannot discriminate against any job seeker because of age, race, creed, national origin, ancestry, sex, marital status, or physical or mental handicap. (See this chapter's section entitled "Employment Discrimination.")

JOB TRAINING. Training may be available through the Job Training Partnership Act.[2] Under this law, the federal government gives money to New Jersey's Department of Labor, which in turn transfers it to the different counties. Through Private Industry Councils (PICs), the counties decide what kinds of jobs are most likely to be open in their areas. Training is then offered for these jobs.

Job training is available to

- People who are economically disadvantaged, disabled, or non–English-speaking.
- People who are out of a job and unable to find work in their fields.
- People older than fifty-five who have no or low income.
- Young people between the ages of fourteen and twenty-one who are from low-income homes (Job Corps).

To find out how to enroll in a program offered under the Job Training Partnership Act, call your local Division of Employment Services office. You can do this by looking in the phone book under New Jersey Department of Labor.

WAGES AND HOURS

Both federal and state laws set rules governing how much and how workers are paid.

MINIMUM WAGE AND OVERTIME LAWS. Under both the federal Fair Labor Standards Act (FLSA)[3] and New Jersey law, most employers must pay their employees a minimum wage of $5.15 per hour. Employers must also pay overtime at the rate of one and one-half times their regular hourly wage for each hour that they work over forty hours per week. The right to receive a minimum wage and overtime cannot be waived by either a union contract or grievance decision.

Exclusion from Laws. Both the FLSA and New Jersey law exclude certain classes of employees from these wage and hour requirements. The FLSA excludes executive, administrative, and professional employees; employees of most retail or service establishments; many agricultural employees; and casual employees, such as baby-sitters or home companions. New Jersey law excludes

- Full-time students working at the school they attend (but they must earn at least 85 percent of the minimum wage).
- Car salespersons.
- Traveling salespersons.
- Part-time employees taking care of children in the employer's home.
- Minors, unless they work in a hotel, motel, or restaurant, or canning or packing farm products.
- Persons working in a summer camp or religious retreat in the summer months.
- Handicapped persons employed with a special permit.
- Persons employed as apprentices under a special permit.

Special rules apply to restaurant and hotel workers who receive tips or room and board as part of their job.

In addition to the exclusions already listed, New Jersey law does not require overtime pay for bus drivers, farmworkers, executives, administrators, or professionals.

Violation of the Law. If your employer is breaking the law, you can file a complaint with the U.S. Department of Labor, Employment Standards Administration, Wage and Hour Division, or the New Jersey Department of Labor, Office of Wage and Hour Compliance.

These agencies can investigate your claim and file suit to force your employer to pay you what you are owed. Or you can file your own suit against your employer. You must file suit within two years of the violation. Under federal law, you have three years to sue if you can prove that the employer's violation was *willful*. Willful means that the employer knew or should have known that his or her conduct was against the law.

Under both the FLSA and New Jersey law, you can get your back pay or overtime and attorneys' fees. However, your employer may be able to avoid paying you if he or she acted in good faith, relying on a rule, practice, or policy of the federal or state Department of Labor. Under the FLSA, you can also collect *liquidated damages* in an amount equal to your unpaid back pay or overtime, unless the employer can demonstrate that he or she acted in good faith.

An employer cannot fire you for filing a complaint, or otherwise exercising your rights under New Jersey law.[4] If you are fired for using this law, you are entitled to be reinstated to your job with back pay. To enforce your rights, you can either file a complaint with the federal or state agency or file suit in court. If you win, you will be able to get attorneys' fees.

GETTING PAID. Specific laws state how you are to be paid. Your employer must post a summary of these laws in the workplace. Your employer must pay you your wages at least twice a month on regular paydays which are set in advance, unless you are an executive or supervisor, in which case your employer must pay you at least once a month. Your employer does not have to pay you up to and including payday, but he or she cannot be more than ten days behind.

If you quit, are fired, or are on strike, your employer must pay you your regular wages (or an estimate of them if you work on a commission basis) on the next payday following the date when you stopped working. Your employer has ten more days to pay you if you and the employees who make up the payroll are on strike.

Your employer must pay you either in cash or by giving you a check drawn on a bank which will cash the check for you. Your employer cannot pay you in merchandise. If you agree, your employer can pay you by opening a bank account in your name and putting your wages in the account.

If you die, your employer can pay your wages to (in the following order)

- Your spouse.
- Your children if they are over age eighteen, or their guardian if they are under age eighteen.
- Your parents.
- Your sisters and brothers.
- The person who paid your funeral expenses.

The person seeking to collect your wages must show proof that he or she is related to you or has paid your funeral expenses. Once your wages are paid to this person, your employer does not need to pay your wages again if there is a dispute later on.

PAYROLL DEDUCTIONS. Your employer can withhold money from your wages only if you authorize deductions in writing; if your union contract provides for contributions to medical, pension, or other plans; for union dues; or as otherwise allowed by federal or state law.[5] Under federal and state law, your employer can deduct income taxes, Social Security, and unemployment and disability insurance. Your employer can also deduct from your wages if they are being *garnished* to satisfy a judgment against you or pursuant to a *wage or income execution order* issued by a county probation office for late alimony, maintenance, or child support payments. If money is being deducted from your wages under a garnishment or an income execution order, your employer is entitled to keep a small amount of money for bookkeeping expenses. Your employer must give you a statement of all wage deductions in each pay period.

If your employer violates any aspect of this law, you should file a complaint with the New Jersey Department of Labor's Office of Wage and Hour Compliance.

FAMILY LEAVE

FAMILY LEAVE LAW. Under the New Jersey Family Leave Law,[6] eligible employees in New Jersey with newborn or newly adopted children or seriously ill family members are entitled to a family leave of twelve weeks in any twenty-four-month period with job security guaranteed during the leave. An employer must provide to an employee on family leave any employee benefits that are generally required under the employer's personnel policy concerning leaves of absence. In addition, an employer must maintain any health benefits at the same level and under the same conditions that coverage would have been provided if the employee had not taken leave. An employee is eligible for family leave if he or she has been employed by the same employer in New Jersey for at least twelve months and worked at least 1,000 regular hours during the twelve-month period before going on family leave. The family leave may be paid, unpaid, or a combination of paid and unpaid leave. The protections of this law apply to all businesses with fifty or more employees.

An employee who takes family leave to take care of his or her newborn child or newly adopted child is entitled to twelve consecutive weeks of leave. The employee must give the employer thirty days' notice unless there are emergency circumstances. An employee whose family member has a serious health condition is entitled to twelve weeks of family leave on a consecutive or nonconsecutive basis. The employer always has the right to ask an employee to support the request for family leave with an appropriate medical certificate.

Senior employees may be denied family leave if

- The denial of family leave is necessary to prevent substantial and grievous economic harm to the employer's business,
  and
- The employer notifies the employee of the employer's intent to deny the family leave as soon as the employer decides that the denial is necessary.

After family leave, an employee will be entitled to be restored to the position held when the leave commenced or to an equivalent position. However, if the employer had a reduction in force or a layoff and the employee would have lost his or her position, the employee will not be entitled to be reinstated.

Any period of leave granted because an employee is unable to perform his or her work, including any period during which the employee is collecting disability benefits under the Temporary Disabilities Benefits Law, is separate from and in addition to family leave under the Family Leave Law.

The Family Leave Law says specifically that it does not prohibit a collective bargaining agreement from providing more generous leave policies than the Family Leave Law itself.

FAMILY AND MEDICAL LEAVE ACT. In 1993, the federal government enacted the Family and Medical Leave Act.[7] This act affords employees the same protection given by New Jersey's Family Leave Law. However, the federal law provides that employees are entitled to family leave and medical leave of up to twelve weeks during any twelve-month period. Moreover, it applies to all public agencies, regardless of number of employees, including state, local, and federal employers, as well as schools. In order to be eligible for leave, an employee must have been employed by the same employer for at least twelve months and have worked at least 1,250 hours during the twelve-month period prior to taking leave.

UNIONS

Under federal law, workers have the right to organize, to form unions, to bargain with their employer through a union, and to engage in "concerted activities for the purpose of . . . mutual aid or protection." *Concerted activities* are actions that you take along with other employees or, in some circumstances, by yourself, to improve the terms of employment. The Labor Management Relations Act (LMRA)[8] is a federal law that sets out the rights and obligations of unions and employers. The National Labor Relations Board (NLRB), composed of five people appointed by the president, enforces this law. The LMRA does not cover supervisors, independent contractors, or agricultural workers. It also excludes federal, state, and local government employees; their rights are discussed later in this chapter.

New Jersey's constitution allows *all* employees to organize and to bargain with an employer.[9] Therefore, even if you are not covered by the LMRA, you still have the right to form a union. If your rights to form a union or bargain collectively are denied, you can file an *unfair labor practice* charge with the regional office of the NLRB. If you are a nongovernmental employee who is not covered by the National Labor Relations Act, you may be able to file a lawsuit in New Jersey Superior Court, Chancery Division.

GETTING UNION REPRESENTATION. Workers can secure union representation in dealing with their employer in three ways: (1) The employer can agree to recognize a union that represents the majority of the employees; (2) the union can win an election held by the NLRB to determine if the union has majority support; *or* (3) in the extreme instances in which the employer has flagrantly interfered with the workers' legal right to organize a union, the NLRB and the federal courts sometimes compel the employer to bargain with the union.

The most common way for workers to win union representation is through an NLRB election. The NLRB will hold an election if 30 percent of the employees sign cards indicating their desire for union representation. A majority of the workers voting must cast their ballots for the union if the union is to be considered the employees' "exclusive bargaining representative." If a group of workers vote to be represented by a union, the employer must bargain "in good faith" with the union about wages, benefits, and working conditions.

If the workers subsequently decide that they no longer want the union, they may petition the NLRB to hold a *decertification election* in which employees may vote to leave the union. The law specifies certain times during the life of a contract when a decertification election may be held.

JOINING THE UNION. If your employer signs a union contract which calls for a *union shop,* you must join the union and pay a reasonable initiation fee and union dues within thirty days. Although you have to pay fees and dues to keep your job, you do not have to go to union meetings or vote in elections.

If your employer and union contract to have an *agency shop,* you do not have to join the union although you do have to pay the equivalent of dues, called *agency fees.* Even in a union shop, you do not have to join the union if you belong to a religious group that is against joining or giving money to unions. Instead of paying dues, you may have to pay the money you would pay in dues to a charity. In these circumstances, if you ask your union to pursue a *grievance*, the union may charge you for the service.

A union can spend your dues on all things that it does as your representative to your employer. However, it cannot spend your money on political causes that you do not support. If you tell your union that you object to the money it is spending on political causes, it must refund the amount of your dues which it spent on these causes and reduce your future dues accordingly.

THE COLLECTIVE BARGAINING AGREEMENT. The union's contract with your employer is called a *collective bargaining agreement.* This is generally the most important source of your job-related rights. Employees covered by a collective bargaining agreement are likely to have substantially greater enforceable rights than are otherwise provided by the law. Typically, the agreement establishes a grievance procedure and an arbitration system for resolving disputes. Usually, the courts and the NLRB will look to the agreement and to the grievance-arbitration system to help determine whether you can show any violation of law. The grievance system may have specific time limits or other procedural requirements. It is important that you carefully study your collective bargaining agreement. Upon request to the union's secretary or principal officer, each member is entitled to a copy of any agreement that directly affects him or her.

UNION BILL OF RIGHTS. The Landrum-Griffin Labor Reform Act[10] created a bill of rights for union members. This law protects union members against discrimination by the union for their activity or criticism of the union. As a union member, you have the right to attend membership meetings and to express your views on union matters freely, both at union meetings and otherwise. You also have the right to participate equally with other members in union affairs. This includes equal rights to speak, nominate candidates, run for office, and vote in elections and on other union business. It is unlawful for union officials to prevent you from exercising these rights, no matter how strongly they disagree with you.

The union has the right to set up reasonable rules for participation. If the union violates your rights, you can file internal union charges. The procedures for doing so will be set forth in your union constitution. After you complete all internal complaint procedures, if these procedures fail to meet certain requirements you then have the right to sue your union.

You also have the right to certain protections before the union can discipline you. Before the union fines, suspends, or expels you, it must

- Give you a written copy of the charges against you,
- Give you time to prepare a defense,
  and
- Give you a fair hearing.

DUTY OF FAIR REPRESENTATION. Your union has a duty to represent all employees fairly even if they are not members of the union. The union must represent you in good faith, without discrimination, and in a nonarbitrary way. For example, if you seek to have the union file a grievance on your behalf and the union arbitrarily ignores your grievance without making a good-faith evaluation of its merits, you may have a valid *duty-of-fair-representation* claim. On the other hand, if the union does go through the motions of handling your grievance—however perfunctorily—it probably will be found to have fulfilled its duty. If your union violates the duty of fair representation, you can either file a claim with the NLRB or sue in federal or state court. If the union has an internal appeals procedure that could provide the remedy you seek, you must first exhaust that process. You must do this within six months of the date on which the union's actions occurred.

UNFAIR LABOR PRACTICES. An *unfair labor practice* occurs when an employer or a union violates a provision of the LMRA. An employer commits an unfair labor practice if it interferes with employees' rights to organize to improve working conditions or threatens or discharges employees for engaging in protected *concerted activities*. It is also an unfair labor practice to discriminate against union activists, refuse to bargain with the union, or discipline employees for filing charges with or giving testimony before the NLRB.

A union commits an unfair labor practice if it interferes with the exercise of a member's rights. A union cannot retaliate against a member for filing board charges, interfere with a member's job opportunities, or breach its duty of fair representation. Unions must also bargain with the employer in good faith.

An employee or union can file an unfair labor practice charge against the employer. An employee or employer can file a charge against the union. The charge must be filed at the NLRB's regional office responsible for the area where the employer is located.

The regional NLRB will investigate the charges. If it finds that the charges are valid, it will issue a complaint. If the board does not issue a complaint, the complainant may appeal by letter to the NLRB general counsel in Washington, D.C. However, such appeals rarely succeed. If a complaint is issued, a hearing will be held before an administrative law judge (ALJ). Parties will be allowed to present witnesses and arguments and examine witnesses for the other side. The ALJ will then issue a decision that can be appealed by any party to the full NLRB in Washington, D.C. Enforcement or appeal can then be sought in the federal court of appeals in Washington, D.C., in your region of the country, or in any region where the company does business.

RIGHT TO BE REPRESENTED BY THE UNION AGAINST AN EMPLOYER. If your employer is considering disciplining you, you have the right to union representation at any meeting with the employer concerning your situation. If your employer does not let your representative appear, you have the right to refuse to answer questions or to make a statement. The law does not provide this right of representation for meetings in which the employer has already decided on discipline and is merely advising you of it.

Grievance and Arbitration. If you are having problems on the job, the first thing that you should do is try speaking to your employer. If that does not work, you can file a *grievance* against the employer. Your union contract will explain the time limits and procedures for filing a grievance. Your union representative will usually take charge of processing your grievance. The last step of the grievance procedure is generally *arbitration*. Your union is not required to take your grievance to arbitration if it does not think it worthwhile.

If you do go to arbitration, your union and your employer will pick an arbitrator. He or she will hold a hearing and issue a decision. If the losing party does not comply with the decision, the winning party can have it enforced in court. A court will enforce the decision unless it violates the law, ignores the union contract language, or was obtained as the result of fraud or misconduct on the part of the arbitrator.

JOB SAFETY

Federal and state laws set job safety standards and provide employees with access to information about unsafe conditions.

YOUR RIGHT TO A SAFE WORK ENVIRONMENT. The Occupational Safety and Health Act (OSHA)[11] is a federal law which sets job safety standards covering employees in the private sector. This law does not govern state or local government employees—covered by a separate New Jersey law through the Public Employee Safety Program operated by the state Department of Labor—or federal employees. In general, however, all employees have a right to a safe work environment. Under OSHA, your employer must meet minimum standards for a safe work environment free of known hazards. OSHA standards cover toxic chemicals, noise, radiation, walking and working surfaces, sanitation, fire prevention, and other hazards. OSHA also requires that an employer label known hazardous substances to show the physical or health hazards they pose.

The federal Occupational Safety and Health Administration enforces the act's requirements. However, the law is not always enforced aggressively. One of the best ways of protecting your right to a safe work environment is to bargain for specific safety provisions in your union contract.

Filing a Complaint. If you believe that your employer is violating OSHA and not providing you with a safe work environment, you can file a complaint with the local Occupational Safety and Health Administration office. You can file a complaint anonymously or request that your name remain confidential. If your complaint represents an emergency matter, you should telephone the local Occupational Safety and Health Administration office.

Federal employees have no specific office to which they can complain. Many agencies have their own safety and health departments or have adopted regulations; if an office exists, complaints should be directed there. Your union, the Occupational Safety and Health Administration, or an attorney may be helpful in directing you to the proper place for pursuing a safety problem within the federal government.

State and local governmental employees are covered by the New Jersey Public Employees' Occupational Safety and Health Act (PEOSHA).[12] Under PEOSHA, enforcement is divided between two agencies—the New Jersey Department of Labor and the New Jersey Department of Health—depending upon whether the particular complaint is safety related or health related. If in doubt as to whether your complaint is safety or health related, call either office.

Although there are differences between the various regulatory schemes, the other programs are generally similar to OSHA and you have the same basic rights. It is always best, however, to seek guidance from your union, the particular regulatory agency involved, or a lawyer in pursuing a remedy for any job safety problem. Simply filing a complaint, however, is a protected activity under all of the schemes.

Your complaint should give as much information as possible about the conditions at your workplace. You do not have to be certain that the law is being violated to file a complaint. It is good enough if you suspect that there may be violations. The Occupational Safety and Health Administration must, within twenty-four hours, investigate serious complaints that pose an immediate threat of death or physical harm.[13] For other complaints, the inspection should be done within two weeks of the date the Occupational Safety and Health Administration received your complaint. If the Occupational Safety and Health Administration decides not to inspect, it must notify you in writing with its reasons. If it does inspect, your employer and an employee representative can accompany the inspector on his or her inspection. If there is a union, the union will choose someone to walk around with the inspector.

If the inspector finds violations of any OSHA requirements, a *citation* will be issued to the employer. The citation will describe the violation and give the employer a reasonable time to correct it. Your employer must post the citation near the violation. If the violation is not corrected, your employer may be fined. The amount of the fine will depend on how serious the violation is.

Your employer can appeal all aspects of the citation. Employees may appeal only the length of time that the employer is given to correct a violation. You must file your appeal with the local Occupational Safety and Health Administration office within fifteen days of the day your employer gets the citation. If there is an appeal, a hearing will be held before an ALJ. The ALJ's decision can be appealed to the Occupational Safety and Health Review Commission. That decision can then be appealed to the federal court of appeals.

Your Right to Be Protected When Exercising Your Rights under OSHA.[14] You cannot be disciplined or fired for exercising your rights under OSHA, such as

- Complaining to the employer, the union, the Occupational Safety and Health Administration, or any other government agency about job safety.
- Filing grievances concerning health and safety.
- Participating in an Occupational Safety and Health Administration inspection or case.

If you have been penalized for using these rights, you or your union should complain to the Occupational Safety and Health Administration within thirty days. If the Occupational Safety and Health Administration finds, after investigation, that your rights have been violated, it will sue your employer for you. If the suit is successful, you can be reinstated to your job with back pay.

Other Sources of Protection from Retaliation. In addition to your OSHA rights, you may also have protection from retaliation under other laws. These include common-law, whistle-blower protection; the New Jersey Conscientious Employee Protection Act (discussed elsewhere in this chapter); and, if your safety complaints were a group effort, the LMRA (also discussed elsewhere in this chapter).

Your Right to Stop Working If Your Job Is Unsafe. Under federal law, you have the right to stop working if the conditions at your job are very dangerous. But you will have to show that

- You complained to your supervisor before refusing to work.
- Because of the urgency of the situation, the condition could not be remedied by filing a grievance while you continued to work.
- You reasonably believed that the work posed a serious danger of death or serious bodily harm.

If you are disciplined or fired for refusing to do unsafe work, you can file a complaint with the Occupational Safety and Health Administration. You must file within thirty days of the disciplinary action.

If your union contract provides for specific safety standards that are not met or the contract forbids your employer from requiring you to do unsafe work, your union may be able to file a grievance against the employer. Under some circumstances, you also can file a complaint with the NLRB based on the employer's violation of the LMRA. The LMRA protects employees when they engage in concerted activities to improve working conditions or protect their rights. It also protects employees from working under "abnormally dangerous conditions."

In any circumstance in which you refuse to do work due to unsafe conditions, the burden will be on you to prove that the conditions were sufficiently severe to justify the work stoppage. Accordingly, you should make every effort to document the actual conditions and to locate corroborative witnesses promptly. An employee who refuses to work when fellow employees are willing to take the risk often has an extremely hard time proving that the refusal was justified. Group action, therefore, is preferable when there is to be a refusal to work. Moreover, your supervisor should be notified of your unwillingness to work under the unsafe conditions as far in advance as possible. Employees should bring cameras, tape recorders, notebooks, and even air-sampling devices in order to document the unsafe conditions.

YOUR RIGHT TO KNOW ABOUT HAZARDOUS SUBSTANCES IN THE WORKPLACE.
Both OSHA and New Jersey law require employers to give employees and the public certain information about hazardous substances in the workplace. In general, OSHA regulates private employment within the manufacturing sector and New Jersey law regulates other types of employment. For initial

enforcement of your rights you need not be concerned as to which statute applies; you should simply ask your employer for fact sheets regarding substances in the workplace and for appropriate training in the handling of all potentially dangerous substances. If your employer refuses this information and you complain to the wrong agency, that agency will refer you to the proper agency.

OSHA. OSHA regulates approximately 2,300 of the many thousands of toxic substances to which workers are exposed. Employers in the private sector are required to label these toxic substances in the workplace, explaining what health or physical hazards they present to the employees. They must also provide employees with training and certain information about working with these substances.

Under OSHA, employers must keep fact sheets, known as *material safety data sheets* (MSDSs), concerning all regulated toxic substances in the workplace. An MSDS states the scientific or chemical name of a toxic substance, how exposure can occur, the hazards presented by the substance, signs and symptoms of exposure, permissible exposure limits, whether it causes cancer, and precautions that should be taken for safe handling. Employees have the right to see the MSDS for all toxic substances in their workplace. In addition, employees have the right to see any records concerning their exposure to toxic substances and their personal medical records. An employee must make a written request to review these records; the employer must let the employee see them within fifteen days of a request. Any member of the public can also request to see records concerning an employer's monitoring of exposure, injuries, illnesses or accidents, and compliance records.

New Jersey Law. New Jersey also has a toxic substance law called the Worker and Community Right to Know Act.[15] This law regulates many additional toxic substances not regulated by OSHA. It requires that certain employers label toxic as well as nontoxic substances and provide training and information to employees.

Under the law, employers must keep records of any hazardous substances in their workplace, along with fact sheets on each substance present. If an employee requests this information, the employer must provide it within five days. The Department of Environmental Protection and Energy (DEPE) must also keep records of all environmentally hazardous substances in each place of employment, as well as fact sheets concerning the substances. The Department of Health (DOH) must keep records and fact sheets on both environmentally hazardous substances and other workplace hazards. Any person can request copies of this information from either the DEPE or DOH. These agencies must provide the copies within thirty days.

If you believe that the New Jersey right to know law is not being followed, you can sue your employer, the state DOH, or the state DEPE to force them to comply with the law. You can file suit in New Jersey Superior Court.

You are protected from being fired or discriminated against for exercising your rights under both of these laws. As discussed earlier, if your rights are violated under OSHA, you must file a complaint with the Occupational Safety and Health Administration within thirty days. If your rights are violated under New Jersey's right to know law, you must file a complaint with the commissioner of the Department of Labor within thirty days of the employer's violation, or within thirty days of the time you learned of the violation. Within thirty days of receiving a complaint, the commissioner must conduct an investigation. If, after an investigation, your complaint appears valid, your case will be referred to the Office of Administrative Law for a hearing before an ALJ. The ALJ will make recommendations to the commissioner, who will then issue a final decision. That decision can be appealed to the superior court, Appellate Division.

EMPLOYMENT DISCRIMINATION

The law concerning employment discrimination is extremely complex. If you think that you have been discriminated against, it is advisable that you consult an attorney with experience in this area.

Discrimination occurs when an employer treats one employee or a group of employees differently from other employees for a reason which has to do not with ability but with a trait of the employee(s), such as race, age, or sex. Discrimination also occurs when an employer uses hiring or promotion criteria, such as tests that have a negative effect upon a group of people protected by the law.

Discrimination is unlawful only when the basis for the discrimination is prohibited by statute. Thus, for example, an employer *may* discriminate against a person on the basis that he or she is right-handed since this is not a type of discrimination prohibited by statute.

It is against the law for employers to discriminate when they hire, fire, promote, transfer, or pay employees. It is illegal for labor unions to discriminate when they admit, suspend, or expel members. It is also illegal for employment agencies to discriminate when they refer people for jobs. This section discusses employers but it also applies to unions and employment agencies.

An employer who is accused of discrimination can defend against such a claim by showing that he or she hired, fired, or promoted you or someone else for a valid reason that had nothing to do with race, age, sex, or religion. An employer who is accused of discrimination in hiring can also defend against the claim by showing that sex, age, national origin, or religion—but not race—is a *bona fide occupational qualification*. A bona fide occupational qualification is present when an employer can establish that a certain trait is essential for a job.

112

Your employer can neither make you waive your rights under federal law nor retaliate against you for exercising your rights. However, if you charge your employer with discrimination, he or she can settle with you for a sum of money in exchange for your giving up your right to sue under the discrimination laws.

FEDERAL LAW. A number of federal laws prohibit different types of discrimination.

Title VII. The most widely known federal employment discrimination law is Title VII of the Civil Rights Act of 1964,[16] which prohibits discrimination because of race, color, religion, sex, or national origin. Title VII covers employers with more than fifteen employees, employment agencies, and unions that have hiring halls of more than fifteen members and are the employees' exclusive bargaining representative. Under the Immigration Reform and Control Act of 1986, employers with four to fourteen employees may not treat an individual differently because of that person's ancestry or country of birth, or because the person has physical, cultural, or linguistic characteristics of a national-origin group.[17]

Just as every employee has a right to a safe work environment under OSHA (discussed earlier), every employee has a right to a work environment that is free of sexual harassment. To a victim of sexual harassment and intimidation, the harasser's acts often create an unsafe environment and result in a feeling of danger.

Sexual harassment can be defined as a pervasive pattern of verbal or physical conduct of a sexual nature—including unwelcome sexual advances and requests for sexual favors—that conflicts with the terms and conditions of employment.[18]

The Division on Civil Rights (DCR) directs employers to post notices regarding anti-sexual-harassment policies indicating the employer's stern objection to such behavior in the workplace.[19] The following are recommendations offered by the DCR to victims of sexual harassment:

- Document the specifics of the occurrence (e.g., journals), including the comments and actions of the harasser, dates, times, places, and the victim's reaction to the incident.
- Talk to someone about the problem. (Later he or she can testify that you said something about the incident near the time of occurrence.)
- Notify management (preferably in written form) of the occurrence. Include a demand for corrective action.
- Do not quit the job. The employer is required to take corrective action.
- In the event that corrective action is not taken, file a complaint with the DCR.[20]

The prohibition against discrimination on the basis of religion requires employers to make reasonable accommodations to an employee's religious beliefs. However, an employer does not have to give an employee a four-day workweek to accommodate religious beliefs.

Age Discrimination in Employment Act. The Age Discrimination in Employment Act (ADEA)[21] prohibits discrimination against persons who are at least forty years of age. It covers employers with more than twenty employees, employment agencies, and labor unions with hiring halls of more than twenty-five members. ADEA specifically requires that an employer give employees and their spouses between the ages of sixty-five and sixty-nine the same health care coverage as employees under the age of sixty-five. It also prevents an employer from making an employee retire before the age of seventy unless the employee is sixty-five, is a high-ranking employee, and will get at least $44,000 in pension benefits.

Discrimination against the Disabled. Several federal laws also protect people with disabilities (persons with physical or mental impairments— see Chapter 15, "The Rights of the Disabled").

Under one law, all federal agencies must develop affirmative action plans for hiring, placing, and promoting disabled people.[22] Anyone who believes that he or she has been discriminated against by a federal agency can file an administrative complaint and sue as allowed under Title VII. Also, programs receiving federal aid are prohibited from discriminating against people with disabilities.[23] Individuals who have been discriminated against by a recipient of federal assistance may file an action in federal district court or pursue an administrative remedy.

Another law requires an employer who has a contract for more than $10,000 with the U.S. government to take affirmative steps to hire people with disabilities.[24] If you have been discriminated against under this law, you cannot sue but you can file a complaint with the U.S. Department of Labor, Office of Federal Contract Compliance, Employment Standards Administration. The Department of Labor will investigate your complaint and take whatever actions are necessary to enforce compliance with the law.

NEW JERSEY LAW. New Jersey law prohibits discrimination by all employers, labor organizations, and employment agencies on the basis of age, race, creed, color, national origin, ancestry, sex, marital status, liability for service in the U.S. Armed Forces, or nationality. The law also prohibits discrimination against any person with a physical or mental handicap unless the handicap prevents the person from doing the particular job. Since 1996 the law has also prohibited discrimination based upon "genetic information" or the refusal of an employee to submit to a genetic test or to make the results of a genetic test available to an employer.

FILING A CLAIM. In some cases, you can file discrimination claims under federal law, New Jersey law, or both. However, some forms of discrimination are prohibited by only one and not the other. For example, only New Jersey's law prohibits discrimination because of marital status. If you suffer discrimination for this reason, you must file a claim under New Jersey's law.

Filing a Claim under Title VII. The Equal Employment Opportunity Commission (EEOC) enforces the federal law against employment discrimination.

If New Jersey law also covers your claim of discrimination, the EEOC will *not* handle your case until the DCR has had the case for sixty days. In New Jersey, the EEOC and the DCR have a work-sharing agreement. This means that if you file a claim with one agency, you have automatically filed a claim with both agencies. Thus, you can file a claim with the EEOC and the EEOC will send it to the DCR. At the end of sixty days, the EEOC should assume control over your complaint. It is advisable that you maintain contact with the EEOC to make sure that it does so. If your claim exists only under federal law, you must file a complaint with the EEOC within 180 days of the discriminatory act. You can file a charge with the EEOC either by filling out a form at the EEOC office or by sending the EEOC a notarized letter.

Once the EEOC assumes jurisdiction over your complaint, it will investigate and try to settle your case. If it cannot resolve your complaint, it can file a suit in federal court. If the EEOC thinks your charge is baseless or decides not to file suit, it will send you a *right-to-sue letter.* You can then file suit yourself. You *must* file a suit within ninety days of getting the letter.

If the EEOC does not act on your case within 180 days, you can request that they give you a right-to-sue letter.

Filing a Claim under ADEA.[25] Claims under the ADEA are filed in the same way as Title VII claims. However, the time limits for filing a court action are different. With ADEA claims, you can file suit sixty days after you file a charge with the EEOC if the EEOC does not file suit on your behalf. If the EEOC notifies you that it has completed processing your case, you must file a lawsuit within ninety days of such notification.

Filing a Claim in New Jersey. If you have a claim under New Jersey law, you can either file a claim with the DCR in the office of the attorney general, the agency which enforces New Jersey's Law Against Discrimination (LAD, *N.J.S.A.* 10:5-1 *et seq.*), or file a lawsuit in superior court, Law Division.

If you choose to file a claim with the DCR, you must do so within 180 days of the act of discrimination. The DCR will then conduct an investigation to determine whether or not there is probable cause to believe that discrimination occurred. If the DCR does not find merit to your claim, it will dismiss your claim.

You can file an appeal of the dismissal with the superior court, Appellate Division. If the DCR decides that there is merit to your claim, it will hold a conference and try to settle the case. If that is unsuccessful, it will ask for a hearing before the Office of Administrative Law. If the DCR does not act within 180 days after you file your complaint, you can ask to have the case transferred directly to the Office of Administrative Law for a hearing. A hearing then will be held before an ALJ who will issue a recommended decision. That decision will be sent to the director of the DCR, who will render a final decision. The final decision can be appealed to New Jersey Superior Court, Appellate Division.

If you choose to file a lawsuit in superior court, Law Division, instead, you have two years from the time of the discrimination to file your suit. Some lower courts have permitted such lawsuits to be filed up to six years after the occurrence of discrimination. However, until the supreme court or the legislature clears up the matter, it is advisable to file in superior court within two years.

A lawsuit under the New Jersey law against discrimination filed directly in court will afford much broader rights and remedies than are available in the DCR, including the right to a jury trial and compensatory and punitive damages.

REMEDIES. You may be able to get some of what you want if the EEOC or the DCR settles your case. If you sue or have a hearing and win, your remedies will depend on what statute you used.

If you sue under Title VII, you can get reinstated, hired, or promoted. You can also get back pay for up to two years retroactive to the date you filed a complaint. The amount of back pay will not be lowered by any unemployment benefits you got. However, it will be lowered by the amount of money you earned or could have earned. You can have a jury trial and collect compensatory and punitive damages up to $300,000.

If you sue under ADEA, you can get back pay. You can also get additional liquidated damages in an amount equal to your back pay if the violation was willful. If you sue under ADEA, you can have a jury trial. If you prevail under Title VII, LAD, or ADEA, the employer will have to pay your attorneys' fees and costs, including the costs of your expert witness(es)' fees.

If you file a claim under New Jersey law and have a hearing, you can get everything you could get under Title VII plus damages for pain and suffering. If you sue under New Jersey's law, you can have a jury trial.

EQUAL PAY. Title VII and New Jersey law both say that employers cannot discriminate in the amount that they pay employees. If the minimum-wage law covers your employer, the federal Equal Pay Act[26] requires that he or she pay employees of one sex the same wage as employees of the opposite sex who are performing similar jobs. This applies if the employees' jobs require equal skill, effort, and responsibility and are performed under similar working conditions.

If you think you have been discriminated against under this law, you can either file a complaint with the EEOC or sue your employer. However, if the EEOC files suit, you cannot sue the employer yourself. If you think you have

116

been discriminated against, you must sue your employer within two years, unless, as with the ADEA, your employer's violation was willful, in which case you have three years. You can get back wages and liquidated damages in an amount equal to your back pay, unless your employer shows that he or she acted in good faith and did not believe he or she was discriminating. You can also get attorneys' fees. Your employer can win if he or she can show that the difference in pay resulted from a seniority system, a merit system, or another factor that did not have to do with sex. Your employer cannot reduce the pay on the higher-paying job if you show that you should have been paid more for your lower-paying job.

New Jersey law also provides that an employer cannot discriminate because of sex in the amount he or she pays.[27] If you are paid less than someone of the opposite sex for performing similar work, you can sue or the commissioner of New Jersey's Department of Labor can sue for you. You can get your full salary, up to the same amount as liquidated damages, and attorneys' fees. Your employer cannot discriminate against you for exercising your rights under this law.

DISCHARGES

Virtually every union contract provides that employees can only be fired for *just cause*, or good reason. If you are covered by a union contract and are fired, you can file a contractual grievance against the employer. It is illegal for an employer to fire you for union activities. Even if there is no union, you may have a contract with your employer prohibiting termination without just cause. An oral promise or statement in a personnel manual that all employees whose work is satisfactory will be able to keep their jobs may constitute an implied contract not to fire without good cause. In the absence of such explicit or implicit contractual promises, however, your employer may be able to fire you *at will,* meaning without a specific, good reason.

Sometimes an employer who wants to fire you will give you a choice of quitting or being fired. The advantage of quitting is that you will not have to tell a future employer that you were fired. However, it may be harder to get unemployment benefits if you quit, unless you can show that you did not quit voluntarily.

If you are fired, you will still get your last paycheck, payment for any unused vacation time, and your contributions to any pension fund. Also, under federal law, your employer must offer you a chance to continue your medical coverage for up to eighteen months, at your own expense.

WHISTLE-BLOWER PROTECTION

Whistle-blowers are individuals who reveal their employers' illegal conduct to an appropriate public body. The law protects them from retaliation by their employer. In New Jersey, there are both common-law and statutory protections for whistle-blowing. The New Jersey Conscientious Employee Protection Act (CEPA)[28] generally parallels the common law but provides better remedies and a somewhat easier burden of proof for the whistle-blower.

CEPA applies to state, local government, and private employment. It protects employees who report their employer's violation of federal or state laws from disciplinary action. Employees are protected if they disclose or threaten to disclose any activity, policy, or practice that the employee reasonably believes violates a statute or administrative rule. Employers may not retaliate against an employee who assists or participates in a governmental investigation. Additionally, employers may not retaliate against an employee who refuses to participate in an activity, policy, or practice that the employee reasonably believes to be a violation of a statute or administrative rule, or that the employee reasonably believes to be fraudulent, criminal, or incompatible with a clear mandate of public policy concerning public health, safety, or the protection of the environment.

PROTECTION AGAINST OTHER EMPLOYERS. You are protected by CEPA not only if you complain about your own employer but also if your employer disciplines you for complaining about other employers who enjoy a business relationship with your employer. But in all cases you are protected by CEPA only if you had a reasonable basis for believing that the illegal activity was taking place. Thus, employees may disclose improper employer activity to public bodies—a category that does *not* include newspapers—and may even refuse work in appropriate circumstances and claim protection from retaliation under CEPA. Retaliation is broadly defined, including not only termination and suspension but also any adverse action in terms and conditions of employment.

In the absence of an emergency, an employee must notify his or her employer in writing of any alleged violations and give the employer an opportunity to correct the problem, before "blowing the whistle" in public. In the absence of such notice, CEPA provides no protection.

FORMER EMPLOYERS. An employee may file suit against a former employer for a CEPA violation within one year of the violation.[29] Both the employer and the employee have a right to trial by jury. An employee who prevails in a suit under CEPA can obtain reinstatement with full back pay, full fringe benefits and seniority rights, an injunction against further violations, an award of attorneys' fees and costs, all remedies available in common-law tort actions, and punitive damages. In addition, the court can impose a civil fine upon the employer. An employee who brings a suit *without basis in law or fact,* however, can be forced to pay the employer's attorneys' fees and costs.

EMPLOYER NOTIFICATION. CEPA requires employers to post notices "of its employees' protections and obligations under this act." The notices must

118

include the name of the appropriate person designated by management to receive written notices of allegedly improper employer activity.

CEPA supplements other remedies, such as those that may be available under a union contract or a particular statute such as OSHA. However, CEPA requires an employee to choose among available remedies by deeming the filing of a court suit under CEPA to be a waiver of contractual or administrative rights.

WORKERS' COMPENSATION

New Jersey's workers' compensation program[30] is an insurance program which pays benefits to workers who are unable to work because of a work-related injury or illness. It also pays their medical bills.

Before New Jersey passed a workers' compensation law, if you were hurt on the job you had to sue your employer for negligence. The court would not require your employer to pay you at all if your employer could show that you or another worker were at fault. Moreover, even if you won, you had to wait until the case was resolved before you could collect any money. Under the workers' compensation program that exists today, if you cannot work because of a job-related injury or illness, you are entitled to benefits right away. You do not have to sue for them.

All employers must either carry workers' compensation insurance or be self-insured. Your employer must post a notice where you work stating that you are covered by workers' compensation and telling you which insurance company covers you.

All workers are covered, even if they work only part-time, with the exception of independent contractors and casual employees (such as baby-sitters). Workers' compensation covers work-related accidents and occupational diseases.

ELIGIBILITY. You may be able to collect workers' compensation if you have a work-related accident or an occupational disease. Recovery is limited to injuries "arising out of" and "in the course of" employment. Both conditions must be met before you can receive compensation for an injury or occupational disease. Your accident will *not* be covered if

- You hurt yourself on purpose.
- You were hurt as a result of your being under the influence of alcohol or drugs.
- You were hurt because you did not use a safety device provided to you (under certain circumstances).
- You were hurt doing something recreational at work.

As a general rule, you are not covered for accidents which occur on your commute to and from work, but there are some exceptions particularly when you perform a job-related errand on the way.

119

Workers' compensation also covers *occupational diseases* or diseases which are caused by your work. Some examples of occupational diseases are *asbestosis* (resulting from exposure to asbestos on the job) and hearing loss (resulting from exposure to excessive noise on the job).

If you can get workers' compensation, this is generally your only remedy for job-related injuries or diseases, even when another worker hurts you. You cannot privately sue your employer or another worker unless your injury was caused by an *intentional wrong*. This is a difficult standard to meet. However, you may be able to sue and recover from others who are responsible for an accident. For example, if a machine injured you, you can sue the person who built or designed the machine. If you win your lawsuit and have collected workers' compensation, you may have to give some of your recovery to the employer. Even undocumented aliens cannot be denied benefits if they are otherwise eligible under the worker's compensation law.[31]

NOTIFICATION TO YOUR EMPLOYER. It is important to let your employer know about an injury or illness when it happens. If you have an accident, you must notify your employer in writing within fourteen days. If you have a reasonable excuse for failing to give your employer notice within this time period, you may have up to ninety days to provide notice. If you have an occupational disease, you must tell your employer in writing within ninety days from the date you knew or should have known that your disease was related to your employment. Alternatively, you may tell your employer within five months after you stopped being in contact with whatever was causing the disease. If you do not notify your employer and your employer does not have actual notice of your disease, you will not be eligible for benefits.

TYPES OF BENEFITS. Under the workers' compensation law, you can get *medical* benefits, *temporary disability* benefits, *total permanent disability* benefits, and *partial permanent disability* benefits. If you die, your dependents can get dependents' benefits and money for funeral expenses.

Medical Benefits. Your employer must pay for all necessary medical expenses, including a hospital room. You must ask your employer to provide you with medical treatment unless you are unable to because there is an emergency, or you can show that there was no point in asking. Your employer can select the doctor or hospital. If you go to a doctor without first asking your employer for treatment and you do not come within the exceptions, you may have to pay the bill. But if you ask and your employer refuses, you can still get the medical treatment you need and your employer will have to pay the bill. You can also file a motion with the Division of Workers' Compensation to make your employer pay your medical bills.

Temporary Disability Benefits. If you cannot work for more than seven days *and* your employer's doctor says that you cannot work, you can get temporary disability benefits under the workers' compensation law. You can get 70 percent of your weekly wage, subject to a certain maximum, for up to 400 weeks.

Total Permanent Disability Benefits. If you are totally disabled and your condition will not improve, you can get permanent disability benefits. You will get the same amount of money as for temporary disability benefits, but for a longer time period. Initially, you can get permanent disability benefits for up to 450 weeks. After 450 weeks, if it is determined that you cannot be rehabilitated, you will be paid benefits for the rest of your life. If you work, your benefits will be reduced by the amount you earn.

Partial Permanent Disability Benefits. You can get partial permanent disability benefits if you are not totally disabled but some part of your body (such as your hand or foot) is permanently disabled. The length of time for which you will be eligible and the amount you will receive depend on the type and degree of injury. The workers' compensation law has a schedule that sets compensation for different time periods depending on the type of bodily injury. Each week you are eligible, you will receive a percentage of the statewide average weekly wage equal to the percentage of your disability. For example, the law says that if a thumb is 100 percent disabled, you will get 75 weeks of compensation. If your thumb is 50 percent disabled, you will get 37$\frac{1}{2}$ weeks of disability.

Dependents' Benefits. If you die from a work-related injury or disease, your dependents, such as your spouse or children, are entitled to receive a percentage of your wages. Your children will get benefits until they turn eighteen. Your spouse will get benefits until he or she remarries. After 450 weeks, your spouse's benefits will be lowered by the amount he or she earns. Your dependents will also get $3,500 for your funeral and money for your last medical bills. Your medical bills will be paid even if you have no dependents.

If you die from something unrelated to work while you are receiving workers' compensation benefits, your dependents will get the rest of the workers' compensation benefits that you would have received. However, they will not get dependents' benefits.

Minors. If a minor employed in violation of the Child Labor Law becomes disabled because of a job injury or illness, benefits under the Workers' Compensation Act may be double the amount ordinarily received.

FILING A CLAIM. If you and your employer are able to agree about compensation, you will not need to file a formal claim. Instead, you will simply file your agreement with the Division of Workers' Compensation. The agreement will not be binding unless approved by the division. The division may not approve the agreement if it does not provide for adequate compensation.

Generally, you will have to file a *formal claim petition* to get your benefits. You can get a claim petition from the Division of Workers' Compensation or from any local office of the division.

You must file a petition for a claim arising out of an accident (1) within two years of the date of the accident, *or* (2) if you and your employer have agreed on compensation, within two years of your employer's failure to pay benefits under the agreement (or if your employer paid only partial compensation, within two years of the last payment of compensation, including provisions for medical treatment).

If your exposure to the cause of your occupational disease stopped after January 1, 1980, the time limit on filing a claim does not begin until the date you found out about the disease and learned how it related to your job. Once you *do* know about your job-related disease, you then have two years to file a claim.

After you file the petition you will wait for a hearing to be scheduled. At the hearing, you will have to demonstrate your eligibility for workers' compensation benefits. The compensation judge will then decide whether or not compensation should be awarded. This decision may be appealed by any party to the superior court, Appellate Division.

If you hire a lawyer to file a workers' compensation claim, you will not have to pay the lawyer any money unless you win your case. If you win, the judge will set the amount of attorneys' fees. Your lawyer can get a fee of up to 20 percent of the award. Generally, payment of the fee award will be allocated between you and your employer. Witness fees can be awarded as well.

An award can be reopened if your disability has either increased or decreased. To reopen an award, you must file a petition within two years of your last payment.

You cannot be fired for filing a workers' compensation claim. If you are fired, you can sue your employer. The New Jersey commissioner of the Department of Labor can also sue to have you reinstated to your job.

TEMPORARY DISABILITY BENEFITS

If you are disabled but not covered by workers' compensation, you may be able to get temporary disability benefits through a separate state or private employer program.[32]

ELIGIBILITY. You can get temporary disability benefits if (1) you can no longer work because of an accident or illness that is not work related; *or* (2) you cannot work because of an accident or sickness that relates to your job but does not make you eligible for workers' compensation.

You must be working or unemployed for less than two weeks at the time you became disabled.

STATE PLAN AND PRIVATE PLANS. You must be covered either under the state plan or under a private plan that your employer can set up. Your employer's plan cannot make it harder for you to get benefits than it would be under the state plan. It must also give you at least the same amount of benefits.

To be eligible for benefits under the state plan

- You must have earned a certain amount of money in the last year.
- You must be disabled for more than a week.
- You must be under the care of a doctor.
- You must not be receiving pay for work.
- You must not be a state worker with accumulated sick leave.
- You must not have injured yourself intentionally or sustained an injury while committing a crime.
- You must not be getting more money with temporary disability and money from your employer than you were paid when you were working.
- You must not be disqualified from unemployment because of a labor dispute.

AMOUNT OF BENEFITS. You can get up to two-thirds of your average weekly wage, up to a set amount, for up to twenty-six weeks. If you get benefits for more than three weeks, you will be paid for the first week of your disability. Otherwise, you will not be paid for the first week. You do not have to pay taxes on temporary disability benefits.

You cannot get temporary disability and unemployment benefits at the same time. Nor can you get workers' compensation and temporary disability for the same accident. If you get temporary disability benefits and are later awarded workers' compensation temporary disability benefits, the amount you received for temporary disability benefits will be taken out of your award. Also if you are getting a pension, you may not be able to receive temporary disability benefits.

FILING A CLAIM. You will have to find out if you are covered under the state plan or under a private plan. There are no general rules on how to file a claim under a private plan; you will have to get this information from your employer. Under the state plan, you have thirty days from the date of disability to file a claim. The time limit can be extended if you can show a good reason for not filing in time. If you make a mistake and file with the wrong plan, your claim will be considered timely as long as it would have been on time had it been filed with the right plan. Your employer is supposed to send you the forms you need. If your employer does not send you the forms, you can get them by calling the unemployment benefits claims office in your area. You, your doctor, and your employer must fill out parts of the form for you to get temporary disability benefits. If your employer will not fill out the form, you can send it in anyway and the Division of Unemployment and Disability Insurance of the New Jersey Department of Labor will try to get the information.

There is no deadline for processing your claim. If you are eligible for benefits, your temporary disability check will be mailed to you. If the division asks you to, you must see a doctor who works for the division, or you will lose your benefits. Your employer may ask you to see a doctor whom he or she selects, but you cannot be required to go to that doctor more than once per week.

APPEALS FROM CLAIM DENIAL. If your claim is denied by a private plan, your employer must give you notice telling you why you cannot get benefits and how to appeal the decision. You must appeal within one year of the decision to the Division of Unemployment and Disability Insurance. If you appeal, you will have the right to an administrative hearing. If you are dissatisfied with the hearing officer's decision, you can appeal to the superior court, Law Division.

If your claim is denied under the state plan, you are entitled to a hearing as provided in unemployment compensation cases.

CHILDREN AND EMPLOYMENT

Both the federal FLSA and New Jersey law[33] set limits on the type of work *minors* (children under the age of eighteen) can do. Limits are also placed on the number of hours they can work. There are special rules for children who work in particular areas, including theater, agriculture, newspaper delivery, and street vending.

Minors have to get employment certificates or *working papers* before they can work at most jobs. Your child can get working papers from an *issuing officer* who is an employee of the child's school district. The principal at your child's school should know who the local issuing officer is. To get working papers, your child must bring the issuing officer

- A promise of employment signed by the child's future employer, stating what he or she will pay the child and what hours the child will work.
- Proof of age, such as a birth or baptismal certificate.
- A statement of physical fitness signed by a doctor.
- A school record signed by the child's principal.

An employer can ask someone between the ages of eighteen and twenty-one to provide an age certificate. The local issuing officer can also prepare an age certificate.

A minor must be paid the minimum wage and overtime if the child is working in a job covered by the FLSA. (See this chapter's section entitled "Wages and Hours.") However, many jobs that minors have (for example, delivering newspapers) are exempt from this protection. If the FLSA does not cover the job, under New Jersey law a minor does not have to be paid the minimum wage or overtime unless the minor is working in a hotel, motel, or restaurant, or is processing farm products.

If these laws are violated, you can file a complaint with either the federal or state Wage and Hour Compliance offices.

RIGHTS OF AGRICULTURAL WORKERS

A number of federal and state laws and regulations protect farmworkers.

RIGHT TO WRITTEN INFORMATION. Before you begin to work on a farm, the employer or the person who got you the job must inform you—in writing in a language you understand—of the following:

- Where you will work,
- How much you will be paid,
- What kind of work you will be doing,
- How long you will work,
- Whether you will receive housing and transportation and what you will be charged for such,
- Whether there is a strike going on,
  and
- Whether the owner will get a commission from sales to you by local businesses.

If you are a seasonal worker and do not live on the farm, you are entitled to this information only if you ask for it. The rights of seasonal workers are governed by New Jersey's Seasonal Farm Labor Act.[34]

WAGES. You must be paid at least the minimum wage, $5.15 per hour, even if you are paid *per hamper* or per piece. Generally, you will be paid for overtime. Each time you are paid, the person who pays you must tell you in writing

- The hourly wage rate or per-piece rate,
- The number of piece-work units,
- The number of hours you worked,
- Your total pay,
- What has been withheld and why,
- Your net pay,
  and
- Your employer's name, address, and tax identification number.

WORKING CONDITIONS AND RIGHTS. All employers must provide drinking water, toilets, and handwashing facilities close to the work site.

All farmworkers have the right to be visited by anyone they choose, including employees of federal, state, and local agencies and members of the press. They also have the right to organize and join a union.

125

If your employer provides you with housing, it must meet certain federal standards, which include providing running water and a toilet. If you are fired, your employer must give you time to find other housing and must use court procedures to evict you. (See the section entitled "Evictions" in Chapter 2.)

PESTICIDES. Under New Jersey law, you cannot enter a field which has been sprayed with pesticide until the spray has dried or the dust has settled. For some pesticides, a *reentry time*—the amount of time you should wait before going back into a field that has been sprayed—has been set by the DEPE. The reentry time is based on how toxic or dangerous the pesticide is. Other pesticides have reentry times listed on their labels.

If a pesticide with a reentry time of more than twenty-four hours is used, the employer must inform all the workers. A map should also be posted, marking the field that is going to be sprayed. If a pesticide with a reentry time of seven days or more is sprayed, signs in English and any other language spoken by the workers must be posted.

The Pesticide Control Program within the DEPE has a pamphlet written in English and Spanish which explains your rights. It also has a bilingual investigator. If you have a complaint, you can contact the DEPE Bureau of Pesticide Compliance.

UNEMPLOYMENT. Some particular rules about unemployment benefits apply to farmworkers. (See Chapter 17, "Public Benefits Programs.") In addition to the usual time and earning requirements for unemployment benefits, a farmworker can get unemployment if he or she worked 770 hours at a farm in the year before becoming unemployed. Agricultural employers are subject to the unemployment laws if they either paid $20,000 to employees in the current or preceding year or hired ten people for a day or part of a day for twenty weeks in the current or preceding year. Farmworkers can be disqualified from receiving benefits for refusing an offer to continue to work for an employer after finishing the minimum period of work required under an employment contract. They can also be disqualified for refusing work if they are offered the same or better wages and working conditions as they had in the past year and the employer agrees to pay for transportation no matter how far it is from their home.

Legal assistance for farmworkers is available from Camden Regional Legal Services.

FEDERAL AND STATE EMPLOYEES

FEDERAL EMPLOYEES. The federal civil service law[35] covers appointees of the executive, judicial, and legislative branches of the federal government, except those employed by any branch of the armed forces. Certain federal employees are considered *unclassified* and are not covered by many of the laws discussed in this section. Other employees are called *competitive-service* employees. Veterans and their families are also protected under many of the civil service laws. Before you can get a permanent job in the competitive service, you must serve a probationary period.

Rights before Discipline. Permanent federal employees in the competitive service and veterans are entitled to certain protections before they can be discharged, suspended for more than fourteen days, demoted in job level, or given a salary cut. Before any such action can be taken, the employee must receive thirty days' notice with reasons for the action and be given at least seven days to respond. The employee has the right to be represented by an attorney or other representative and to receive a written decision as soon as possible. A government agency may choose to provide a hearing. The agency's decision can be appealed to the Merit Systems Protection Board (MSPB). The MSPB will hold a hearing and issue a decision. If it determines that an employee was wrongfully fired or suspended, it can award back pay and attorneys' fees. The MSPB's decision can be appealed to a federal court of appeals. Employees who are covered by a union contract that provides protection against discipline can choose to file a grievance instead of using the civil service hearing procedure. That decision can also be appealed to the federal court of appeals.

Additionally, a permanent employee in the competitive service cannot be suspended for less than fourteen days without notice, an opportunity to answer any charge, the right to an attorney, and a written decision.

Unions. Under the federal labor-management and employee relations law,[36] most federal employees have the right to organize, join a union, and bargain about working conditions. They are also entitled to have union representation at any interview with the employer that may result in discipline. However, they do not have the right to strike.

Federal employers must bargain with a union that has been selected by a majority of the employees about work assignments and conditions and procedures for disciplining employees. The union must represent all employees fairly, even if they do not belong to the union.

Unfair Labor Practices. As with private employment, federal law prohibits employers and unions from committing *unfair labor practices.* Basically, unfair labor practices are actions that interfere with an employee's exercise of his or her rights to organize a union or to work to improve working conditions.

Unfair labor practice charges can be filed with the Federal Labor Relations Authority (FLRA), which oversees federal employer-employee relations.

An unfair labor practice charge generally must be filed within six months of the act that gave rise to the complaint. However, this time may be extended if an employee was prevented from filing a charge on time or if the unfair labor practice was hidden from him or her.

Benefits. There is no federal temporary disability program. Federal employees are covered under a workers' compensation program for disability or death resulting from an occupational disease or an accident sustained while working. The law does not cover disability or death if the employee was committing willful misconduct, trying to hurt himself or herself or someone else, or intoxicated. If you have an injury or occupational disease, you generally must give your supervisor written notice within thirty days of the injury.

Under the federal workers' compensation program, you can get medical, disability, and dependents' benefits. You must file a claim petition within three years, although there are special rules for occupational disease. Also, you can file a claim later if you gave written notice within thirty days or your supervisor knew about the disease or injury.

You can ask for a hearing. If you do not prevail at the hearing, you can then appeal to the Employees' Compensation Appeals Board.

Discrimination. Federal employees are covered by Title VII, although different rules on filing discrimination claims apply to them. If you are a federal employee, you must file a charge with your agency's Equal Employment Opportunity (EEO) counselor within thirty days of the discriminatory act. The EEO counselor will conduct an investigation and try to settle the dispute.

If the EEO counselor does not resolve your dispute, you can request an agency hearing. You can then appeal to the EEOC. If you are dissatisfied with the EEOC's decision, you can file a lawsuit in federal court within thirty days of the agency's final decision. You can also file suit if the EEOC does not act within 180 days of receiving your claim.

Federal employees are also covered by the ADEA, the Equal Pay Act, and protections for the handicapped.

Political Activity. The Hatch Act[37] prohibits federal employees from taking an active role in partisan politics. This does not include voting or discussing political issues. However, it does prohibit an employee from being active in any political campaign. This law is enforced by the MSPB. If it finds, after notice and a hearing, that the law has been violated, it can suspend or fire an employee. This law also applies to state employees whose jobs are funded by the federal government.

STATE EMPLOYEES. Special rules and protections cover state employees whose jobs come under the New Jersey Civil Service Act.[38]

New Jersey's civil service law applies to state employees as well as to local government employees in all counties and municipalities that have adopted the civil service laws. Civil service workers are divided between *classified* and *unclassified* jobs. Those in classified service have greater job protections.

Unclassified positions include elected officers, department heads, employees of the governor, legislative officers and employees, state military or naval employees, judges, and teachers. Veterans and their families also have special rights under the civil service law. (See Chapter 16, "Your Rights as a Veteran.")

The Hiring Process. If you want to apply for a civil service job, generally you will be required to take a civil service test. After a civil service test is given, a list is issued ranking the test takers by score. Job vacancies must then be filled from the top three candidates. If you are one of the top three candidates and someone other than one of the three is hired for a civil service job, you can challenge this with the New Jersey Merit System Board.

Job Protection. Classified civil service employees must serve a *probationary period* (also called a *working test period*) before they become permanent employees. For state employees, this period is from four to six months. For local government employees it is three months. After that, classified employees cannot be discharged without just cause. Just cause includes neglect of duties, incompetence, insubordination, intoxication at work, and willful violation of the civil service law or regulations.

Right to a Hearing. In almost all cases, permanent employees and employees in their working test period have the right to a departmental hearing before they can be disciplined or discharged. Before any action can be taken, the employee is entitled to written notice of the charges. A departmental hearing will then be held within thirty days of the notice, unless waived by the employee. A decision must be made within twenty days of the hearing.

That decision can be appealed to the New Jersey Merit System Board. However, a suspension of five days or less can be appealed only in certain instances. An appeal must be filed within twenty days after the employee receives the department's decision. Or, if the employee does not receive an initial decision from his or her department, he or she can appeal directly to the Merit System Board. Either the Merit System Board or an ALJ assigned by the Office of Administrative Law will conduct a hearing. The Merit System Board will then make a final decision. It can order reinstatement and back pay. Its decision can be appealed to the superior court, Appellate Division.

Unions. The New Jersey Employer-Employee Relations Act[39] covers all state, county, and municipal employees except elected officials, high-level employees, and *confidential employees.* This law gives employees the right to organize unions, bargain, and engage in activities to improve working conditions. However, they cannot strike. This law is enforced by the Public Employment Relations Commission (PERC).

A union may be designated to represent a group of employees if the employer finds that the union has been chosen by a majority of the employees. If the employer does not recognize the union or there is a dispute among several unions, an election will be held by PERC. The employees or any union seeking to represent them must file a petition for union certification with PERC.

Once a union is selected by a majority of employees, the employer and the union must bargain concerning working conditions and terms of employment. They must also establish grievance and disciplinary review procedures.

Employees are protected in their exercise of any rights under the Employer-Employee Relations Act. Employers are prohibited from interfering, discriminating, or retaliating against employees for using their rights. Any violations of this law are considered *unfair practices.* If your employer has interfered with your rights, you can file a complaint with PERC. You must file a complaint within six months of the unfair practice unless you can show that you were prevented from filing. PERC can then file a complaint against the employer charged with violating the law and hold a hearing. PERC can order the employer to stop committing an unfair practice and can award back pay. PERC's decision can be appealed to the superior court, Appellate Division or PERC can apply to the Appellate Division to have its order enforced. Similarly, if a union denies you any of your rights under this law, you can file a complaint with PERC.

Employees cannot be forced to join a union. Those who do not belong to the union have the right to pay a representation fee instead of union dues. This allows them to pay only for the services they receive and not for political or legislative activities of the union that are unrelated to their rights as workers. The fee cannot be more than 85 percent of regular union dues.

Benefits. A state employee who is injured on the job can apply to his or her employer for sick-leave-injury benefits. The employee is entitled to receive his or her full salary and can appeal a denial of benefits to the Merit System Board.

State employees are eligible for temporary disability benefits. County and municipal employees are eligible only if their employers have chosen to be covered by this law. Both state and local employees are covered by workers' compensation.

Discrimination. State employees are covered by Title VII, the Equal Pay Act, the ADEA, and New Jersey's Law Against Discrimination. If you are a state employee, you can follow the complaint procedure discussed in this chapter in the section entitled "Employment Discrimination." Or you can file a complaint under the New Jersey Civil Service Law, which prohibits discrimination on the basis of sex, race, creed, color, national origin, ancestry, or political or religious opinions. The Civil Service Commission has a special procedure for discrimination appeals that includes a decision—but not a hearing—by the Merit System Board. Discrimination claims that arise in certain situations, including discharge, suspension, or demotion, will not be resolved through this procedure but in the regular course of civil service disciplinary hearings.

    Political Activity. State employees cannot engage in political activity during work hours or at any other time if it will interfere with their employment; if their employment is financed in part by federal funds, they cannot be a candidate for public office in a partisan election.[40]

6. Protecting You as a Consumer

This chapter begins with a brief description of some of the more common consumer problems that require legal protection, including advertising gimmicks, 900 telephone numbers, advance-free loan scams, and rent-to-own deals. The discussion then proceeds to some key areas of consumer law, such as store refund policies, door-to-door sales, and mail order.

COMMON CONSUMER PROBLEMS, SCAMS, AND RIP-OFFS

Some of the more common consumer complaints—and ways to avoid them—are described in the sections that follow.

FLY-BY-NIGHT HOME REPAIR CONTRACTORS. Many consumers have problems with home repair contractors. Sometimes contractors take a deposit, never to be seen again. Other times, consumers suffer with shoddy workmanship or jobs left unfinished. Often homeowners are "pressured" to sign documents that they do not understand. The best way to protect yourself from a fly-by-night contractor is to get references from the contractor and check them out. Don't trust just anyone who shows up at your door. Also, you should call the Division of Consumer Affairs Action Line to see if any complaints have been registered against the person or company you want to hire.

CAR PROBLEMS. Beware of false advertising schemes and trickery used to get you to buy or lease a new or used car. Also beware of tricks used by auto body and repair shops. Some consumers have paid for costly repairs that were not needed.

TELEPHONE SOLICITATIONS, TELEMARKETING, AND 900 NUMBER SCAMS. Beware of all types of telephone solicitations. Using the telephone to con people has become a multibillion-dollar industry in the past several years. This includes people who call you on the phone asking for your credit card number to purchase magazines or to receive prizes they say you have already won. Usually, you just end up with an unwanted charge on your credit card. Federal and state laws have recently been enacted to help combat this type of fraud. Also, beware of free gifts; high-profit, no-risk offers; and 700, 900, or 976 numbers. You may end up with a huge telephone bill. Instead of buying something over the phone from a stranger, ask the caller to send you written information or a brochure and find out how much you'll have to pay in total before you agree to buy anything. If you do decide to buy goods, avoid paying cash or sending payment by overnight express. *Never* give credit card information to strangers who have called you on the telephone. There are also things you can do to limit the number of telemarketing calls you receive.

FURNITURE DELIVERY DELAYS. When buying furniture, always ask for a specific delivery date and make sure it is written on your order form. Otherwise, you may be kept waiting indefinitely. Don't accept "ASAP" as a delivery date.

FREE VACATION OFFERS. Beware of the free vacation offer that appears on a postcard asking you to call an 800 number to receive your vacation. Frequently, you are then told to call a 900 number and asked to "verify" your credit card number in order to receive the vacation. The end result is an unwanted credit card charge, a large phone bill, and no free vacation.

BAIT-AND-SWITCH SELLING TACTICS. This is the common practice of advertising items for sale as part of a scheme not to sell those items but to sell others that are more expensive. Don't fall for this trick. If you arrive at a store in response to an advertised special, insist on seeing the advertised item and see for yourself if you want to buy it. If a salesperson refuses to show it to you, do your shopping elsewhere. You can also call the Division of Consumer Affairs at (800) 242-5846 to report the seller.

MAIL ORDER RIP-OFFS. Be especially wary of buying items through the mail that sound too good to be true. They usually are. One consumer ordered a chart of what she thought was her family tree, advertised at $49.95. What she received was a list of U.S. citizens with the same last name.

WORK-AT-HOME SCHEMES. Beware of the ads that say, "Earn money at home in your spare time." Usually these gimmicks require you to send in a "start-up fee" of fifteen to twenty dollars and all you get is a kit that tells you how to rip off other unsuspecting consumers.

CONTRACT COOLING-OFF PERIODS. Many consumers enter into contracts with warranties and guaranties on cars they're not sure they want because they believe they have a three-day right to cancel every contract. This is not true. The three-day "cooling-off" period is only available for certain contracts. If you are not given a notice that says you have three days to cancel, you probably don't, and you shouldn't automatically assume you can cancel anyway. If a salesperson tells you that you have the right to cancel, ask him or her to show you where it is written in the contract. If he or she cannot, you should take your business elsewhere.

RENT-TO-OWN. Rent-to-own merchants advertise that they offer products, such as furniture or home appliances, for rent at low weekly payments. If you make every required payment, you keep the product. But if you miss even one payment, the rent-to-own store may take away the product. This is true even if you have already paid for most of the cost of the item. Also, even if you make all of the payments, you may end up paying three to four times as much as it would have cost to buy the product. For example, you may end up paying $1,000 for a nineteen-inch TV that usually only costs a couple of hundred dollars. Interest rates of 75 percent to 300 percent have been found in some stores. Normal interest rates range from 6 percent to 30 percent.

ADVANCE-FEE LOAN SCAMS. An advance-fee loan is one in which a company promises to give you a loan if you pay a fee in advance. The fee may range from one hundred to several hundred dollars. Usually the con artist gets your money and disappear, and you never get your loan. This scam should not be confused with the practice of banks and legitimate lending institutions that charge a fee to process your application. Those lenders will not *promise* to give you a loan but will review your application and credit history first. The advance-fee scam artist, on the other hand, will usually not only promise you a loan, but also say that bad credit is not a problem. They frequently use 800 and 900 telephone numbers. Before you apply for a loan, check out the company. Call the Office of Consumer Protection and the Better Business Bureau in your area and ask about the company.

"FIXING" OR "REPAIRING" BAD CREDIT HISTORY. Many consumers are misled by phony companies that offer to "fix" or "repair" your credit history for a fee. Chapter 7 explains in detail how consumers can review their credit histories and make sure that accurate information is being reported about them. But remember that you cannot "fix" your credit history. That is, you cannot require the credit reporting company to omit from your credit report a late payment or the fact that you filed for bankruptcy, if that is true. This type of adverse information usually stays on your credit report for seven years (bankruptcy stays on for ten years). Don't be fooled by con artists who say they can repair your credit history—they cannot and you would be throwing your money away.

HEALTH SPA MEMBERSHIPS. Health spas frequently use high-pressure sales tactics to get you to sign a membership contract. However, they do not always reveal the terms of your membership clearly before you sign up. Be sure to look over the facilities before you agree to become a member. Read the membership contract carefully and make sure all promises made to you by salespeople are in writing. Do not sign a contract that has any blanks and be sure to get your copy of the contract as soon as you sign it. (This is good advice for all contracts.) New Jersey law does give you three days to cancel a health spa membership contract.

134

TIME-SHARE LURES. Time-shares have also been a problem for consumers. Sometimes you are lured to a site expecting a free gift. When you arrive, the sales pitch is very high pressure and you are made to feel guilty for accepting the gift without purchasing. It is especially important to have all promises in time-share contracts in writing, especially if the site is not completed. Before signing one of these contracts, you should review it with a lawyer.

SOCIAL SECURITY CARDS AND INFORMATION. A recent scam has led some consumers to pay for information and documents that they can obtain for free. Do not send money in answer to advertisements for information on your Social Security earnings or for a Social Security card. The Social Security Administration provides this information free of charge.

FILING BANKRUPTCY TO STOP EVICTIONS. Some con artists send flyers to consumers who are about to be evicted from their homes and say that for a fee, the eviction can be stopped. Frequently, the con artist will file an "expedited" bankruptcy petition, charge the consumer a large fee, and do nothing else. The bankruptcy petition will stop the eviction for a while, but not for long. If the remainder of the petition is not filed, the court will dismiss the bankruptcy and the consumer will be right back where he or she started, facing an eviction and worse off overall because of the large fee paid to the con artist. If you are considering filing bankruptcy or need help to stop an eviction, get an attorney.

"NOTARIOS." Another frequent scam is one by travel agents and "notarios" who claim to be able to help recent immigrants with their immigration problems. Frequently they charge a fee to fill out immigration documents but are essentially practicing law without a license. Unsuspecting immigrants are truly at a disadvantage because usually "notarios" attract those immigrants who do not speak English. If you need help with an immigration problem or are filing an application with the Immigration and Naturalization Service (INS), you should seek the advice of an immigration lawyer.

CONSUMER LAW IN GENERAL

Many federal and state laws protect consumers' rights. Consumer laws protect your rights when you buy goods and services for personal, family, or household use; mortgage or refinance your home; sign up for a credit or charge card; buy or lease a new or used car; buy furniture; and even use utilities like water, gas, and electricity.

There are many old, and some new, advertising schemes and gimmicks of which you should be aware. Many of these advertising gimmicks and other commercial practices are illegal and are covered by a law called the New Jersey Consumer Fraud Act. See the section on the Consumer Fraud Act later in this chapter. This law protects consumers from dishonest sellers.

Knowing the laws that protect you can help you in at least two very important ways. First, knowing your rights will help to ensure that you are treated fairly. Second, although it is not always necessary, it is sometimes helpful to make reference to laws in complaint letters, law-suits, or in court.

CONTRACTS

You enter into some type of *contract* when you buy, lease, or rent goods or services; borrow money; or use credit cards. A contract is a legal document. It is usually between two people (called *parties*). In a *consumer* contract, the person buying the goods or services is the consumer. The other party can be a person, a business, a bank, a corporation, a retail store, or another entity. In a valid legal contract, each party promises to do something that benefits the other party.

Each party to a contract can be made to do what he or she promised to do or, if not, to pay money (called *damages*). Before you sign any contract or loan agreement, assume that it is legally enforceable and make sure you agree to all of its terms. Although most verbal (spoken) contracts are valid and can be enforced, putting things in writing is very important because you can more easily prove who agreed to do what.

Before signing any contract

- Read the contract thoroughly—including the fine print. Don't be afraid to read the contract. Don't feel you are being rude if you take time to read what you are signing. Because valid contracts are legally enforce-able, you should always read the contract carefully and fully and make sure you understand it before you "sign on the dotted line." This includes the "fine print" sometimes found at the bottom of the page. If you don't understand something, ask what it means. New Jersey law requires that consumer contracts be written in simple, clear words that are easy to understand. Do not sign the contract unless you understand and agree with everything it says.
- Bring someone with you. If you feel you may need help understanding a contract, bring someone with you, such as a family member or friend. If after reading it you still have questions, there are places you can go and people you can talk to about the contract. For example, you can call your town or county Division of Consumer Affairs, Home Extension Services, Office on Aging, or a Legal Services office if you qualify. They can give you advice to help you avoid having problems later. Remember, call

before you sign the contract and do not be pressured by a pushy salesperson to sign anything.

- Make sure everything is in writing. Make sure all promises that the other person made verbally are written into the contract. If something was left out, write it in yourself and put your initials and the date beside it. Have the other party put his or her initials and the date by the change also, so it is clear that the person agreed to it.
- Don't sign a contract unless you are completely satisfied. Don't sign the contract if you aren't satisfied with any part of it. Ask the salesperson to cross out those parts of the contract you don't like. If he or she won't change it, you may want to take your business elsewhere.
- Don't sign anything saying that repairs are completed and are satisfactory if they are not.
- Don't sign anything saying that a delivery was satisfactory until after you have examined the goods.
- Shop around, compare prices and credit terms, and read over any warranties or guaranties *before* you decide where to do business.
- Make sure the contract tells you exactly what the credit charges are. This information is required in all contracts when you borrow money or pay for something in installments.
- Know how much interest you are paying. Compare interest rates with other lenders or stores before you sign. Make sure you include the *points,* if any, when you are comparing interest rates. Points are additional interest that you pay up front when you get a loan. Usually, a point equals 1 percent of the loan amount. For example, if you are getting a loan for $15,000, one point would be $1,500, two points would be $3,000, and so on. Points add to the interest rate. In order to make a good comparison between loans, you must compare the annual percentage rate (APR) of the loans. The APR includes the points you will be charged along with the interest rate. The loan with the lower APR is usually a better deal. (See Chapter 7, "Credit, Debt, and Banking," for more information on credit.)
- Know how much the monthly payments are and make sure you can afford them.
- Make sure you understand what penalties there are if you fail to pay on time. For example, find out how much of a late fee will be charged if you miss a payment. Does the contract state that you must pay attorneys' fees and/or collection charges if you are sued to collect on the debt?
- Know if you are signing a security agreement. Know whether you are required to put up your property or whatever you are buying as collateral. Does the contract state that if you fail to pay the debt, the creditor can repossess your property or the goods you are buying? If it does, the creditor has a *security interest.*

- Know if you are required to buy insurance. Find out whether the contract requires you to buy credit, life, or health insurance. If you must buy credit insurance, how much does it cost? Is having the insurance worth the extra cost?
- Don't waive your legal rights. Be careful if the contract says you *waive* (give up) your legal rights and defenses. Even if you signed a contract that states that you have waived some of your rights, you may still have the rights under the law. However, it's best not to give up anything in the first place if you can help it.
- Know if you are buying "as is." Don't buy "as is" unless it is absolutely necessary. This is a warning that something may be wrong with the product and that you may be giving up your right to object.
- Know that cosigners are legally responsible for the contracts they sign. If you cosign a loan for someone else, you are making a contract yourself. You will be responsible for paying the debt if the other person doesn't pay. Your credit history will be affected and you can be sued for what the other person doesn't pay. Make sure you get and keep a copy of the "Notice to Cosigner." You should be given this notice when you enter into the cosigner agreement.
- Get and keep copies of everything you sign. Make sure you receive copies of everything you sign as soon as you sign. Be sure to keep these copies, along with any sales receipts and canceled checks. Set up a file and keep copies of all warranties and guaranties you receive. Keep the warranty or guaranty and purchase receipt together. Make sure the date of purchase and name of the store are on the receipt. This will help you later if you have a problem with what you purchased.
- Get the name and address of the seller and his or her representative. If you have a problem with a seller or manufacturer and you talk to someone who claims they will help you, be sure to get that person's name and title. Make sure you have the full name and address of the business they work for. Send the person a letter confirming what he or she promised to do for you.

CONTRACTS FOR SERVICES. Before you sign a contract with someone who will perform a service for you, such as a plumber or electrician, check him or her out first. For some jobs, service providers must pass tests before they get licensed. Other jobs only require that service providers pay a fee; their ability (or lack of ability) is not considered in licensing. The New Jersey Division of Consumer Affairs supervises the work of twenty-seven licensing boards and advisory committees that regulate over fifty professions and occupations in New Jersey. Before you sign a contract for services, call the Division of Consumer Affairs Action Line to see if any complaints have been filed against the person or company. You should also check with your local municipal office, the Division of Consumer Affairs' county office, and the Better Business Bureau. Call the Action Line to get the information you need about any of the licensing boards. If you are having a problem, a representative will determine what can be done and who might best help you.

Some professions and occupations may be regulated by state government divisions other than the Division of Consumer Affairs. If a profession is not licensed, there may be a trade association that can help mediate complaints. On the other hand, if an occupation, industry, or enterprise is new (for example, 900-number businesses) or if a business has just opened, there will not have been time for any complaints to have been filed. If this is the case, you must be even more careful and remember to think before you act.

CONSUMER PRIVACY RIGHTS

One question frequently asked by consumers is, "How can I limit the mail and telephone solicitations that I receive—usually at odd hours or during dinner time?" Here are some suggestions:

- You can sign up for a free service operated by the Direct Marketing Association that will inform its mail-marketing members to take you off their mailing lists.
- You can sign up with a similar service to limit telephone solicitations. Write to the Telephone Preference Service.
- You have the right under federal law to tell a telemarketing company not to contact you by phone or in writing. Once you have done so, the company must keep your name and address on a list and it may not contact you further. Keep a list of the all companies to whom you make such a request, including the name, address, and date of your request. If the company contacts you again, file a complaint with the Federal Communications Commission (FCC) in Washington, D.C.
- You have the right to ask all manufacturers, mail order catalogs, or magazine companies with whom you have done business not to sell your name to promoters of mailing lists.
- Mailing lists are developed in many ways from information obtained from loan applications, warranty cards, checks, and credit cards, to name a few. To help guard your privacy, don't put your credit card numbers on checks; don't release your Social Security number unless you know there is a legitimate purpose for having it, such as a request from an employer, credit bureau, or lender; and don't fill out any

optionalorunnecessaryinformationonwarrantyorothermanufacturer's information cards, including information cards for seller's "suggestion boxes."

- You also have the right to review files that contain information about you. For example, you may contact credit bureaus that keep records about your credit history. (See Chapter 7, "Credit, Debt, and Banking.").

THE CONSUMER FRAUD ACT

The Consumer Fraud Act (*N.J.S.A.* 56:8-1 *et seq.*) protects you against dishonest sellers and from being ripped off when you buy goods or services. There are also many regulations that interpret the Consumer Fraud Act and protect consumers. These regulations are found in the *New Jersey Administrative Code* (*N.J.A.C.*) Section 13:45A, and are issued by the New Jersey Division of Consumer Affairs. They cover home improvement contracts, advertising, mail order sales, car sales, car advertising and repairs, home appliances and repairs, and many other consumer transactions. The Consumer Fraud Act allows the court to charge fines of up to $7,500 for the first violation and up to $15,000 for further violations. As a consumer, you have the right to take a business to court. You can sue a business or seller for three times the amount of your *damages* (what the deceptive act has cost you), plus court costs and attorneys' fees. Court cases have determined that if you win a case under the Consumer Fraud Act the business must pay for the lawsuit you filed. This includes paying for your attorney.

ADVERTISEMENTS AND SELLING PRACTICES. The Consumer Fraud Act tries to make sure that consumers are not unfairly misled by advertisements. The act requires that a seller of goods or services meet the following requirements for advertisements:

- Ads that offer specific items for sale must include the retail selling price of the item and how long the sale price will last.
- Ads that offer items over $100 for sale at reduced prices must also tell you the advertiser's or their competitors' usual selling price or price range for identical or comparable merchandise.
- Ads must state which items have special or limiting factors relating to price, quality, conditions, or availability. An advertisement must tell you if the goods are damaged, floor models, discontinued, or one of a kind.
- Sale ads for home appliances must tell you the manufacturer's name or trade name, the model or series number, and any other information necessary to inform consumers of what is being advertised.
- Sale ads that offer you a percentage discount range, such as 20 to 25 percent off, must not mislead you to think that the larger discount

always applies. For example, if an ad tells you that you can save 10 to 40 percent, "10 percent" must not be printed smaller or lighter or be less noticeable than "40 percent."

- Ads cannot say prices are *at or below* wholesale or cost, unless the price is equal to or less than what the store paid for it.
- Ads cannot tell you that the advertiser is a factory outlet, warehouse, discounter, clearance center, liquidator, or other similar name, unless it's true.
- A store must have enough of each advertised item to meet reasonable consumer demand for the time period stated in the ad. Unless the ad says there's a limited supply, the store must have enough to last for at least three days.
- The store must post notices of advertised items. The notices should be posted where you can easily see them, such as near the advertised items or at all store entrances.
- Stores do not *have* to give you a rain check if they run out of advertised items. But if they do, they must give rain checks to everyone who wants one and the store must honor them for sixty days. If you have a rain check for an item that costs more than $15, the store must tell you when the item becomes available and must hold it for you.

The Consumer Fraud Act says that certain advertising practices are deceptive; those practices are illegal. It is illegal for a merchant to

- Sell goods without clearly marked prices. (Any item offered for sale at a retail store *must* have the selling price *clearly* marked with a stamp, tag, label, or sign *on or near* the item.)
- Tell you that you have won a prize, but require that you buy something or listen to a sales pitch in order to get the prize.
- Advertise or show pictures of assembled goods when the goods are sold unassembled. (The advertisement must state if an item is sold *unas-sembled*.)
- Falsely lead you to believe that the business is a charity or a nonprofit corporation.
- Advertise a "going out of business sale" for more than ninety days, or have more than one such sale in a year.
- Mislead you about the type of food sold at a restaurant (for example, the menu says steak, but you get ground turkey).
- Pretend to be a government agency or use the words "public notice" or "public sale" where such sale is not required by court order or conducted by an auctioneer for a nonbusiness entity.
- Have you sign any paper with legal significance without giving you a copy at the time of the sale.
- Do anything else that involves lying, trickery, or unfairness to you, the buyer.

Bait and Switch. *Bait and switch*, which is illegal under the Consumer Fraud Act, is a common advertising gimmick often used by sellers. The common bait-and-switch scam is an advertisement for a consumer item at a *very low price* to lure consumers into the store. When the consumer arrives at the store to purchase the advertised item, the consumer is told that the seller is sold out or out of stock. Then, the seller tries to get the consumer to buy another item for more money.

If you think you have been a victim of a bait-and-switch scam, contact the Division of Consumer Affairs immediately. Make sure you keep copies of the advertisement and write down the salesperson's name.

900 Numbers. Businesses involving the use of 900 telephone numbers have recently become a big problem for consumers. For this reason Congress passed a law—the Telephone Disclosure and Dispute Act—to help stop abuses involving 900 numbers. These laws are changing frequently because 900 numbers are an issue of great importance to consumers. If you have a problem with a 900 number, call the Division of Consumer Affairs office nearest you for the most up-to-date information. The Consumer Fraud Act also covers 900 numbers. In New Jersey, phone scams have been largely targeted at senior citizens and children. In some scams, you are asked to call an 800 number (which is free) and the operator then tells you to call a 900 number, for which you will be charged. Another scam gives you an 800 number to call—frequently to claim a fictitious prize—and the scam artist then gets your phone number, using caller ID, and calls you back collect.

Federal laws and the New Jersey Consumer Fraud Act regulate the way 900-number businesses must advertise. A person or business that advertises or sells an information service by a 900 telephone number must, in all of its advertisements, clearly give you

- A truthful and accurate description of the service.
- The total price of the service. (Where the charges are based on time, the rate per unit of time must be stated, e.g., $3 per minute.)
- Any other charge or cost for the service (e.g., $5 per call, $3 per minute).
- The legal name and street address of the information service provider.
- Instructions to minors to get their parents' consent before calling.

Callers must also be given time to hang up *before* they are charged for the service; an additional warning to hang up must be given to minors at the beginning of the call if the call is likely to cost more than $5, unless they have their parents' permission. This will give minors a chance to hang up without being charged for the call.

If calls to 900 numbers show up on your phone bill, you should first determine whether anyone in your household (such as minor children or their friends) made the calls. If not, you should notify the telephone company, in writing, that you are disputing the bill.

If you have minor children, you may want to have the phone company "block out" 900 numbers from your home phone, which you can do by simply calling your phone company.

Telephone companies cannot disconnect your phone because of unpaid 900-number bills. It is the responsibility of the 900-number business to collect its charge, *not* the phone company.

If you have a problem with your phone company as a result of a 900 number, you should contact the New Jersey Board of Public Utilities (BPU).

REFUNDS. New Jersey law says that stores do not have to give refunds. However, retail stores are required to put up signs that tell you about their refund policies. For example, if the store does not want to give refunds, there must be a sign that says "No refunds given." These signs can be posted

- On the item,
- On the cash register where you pay for the item (or visible from there),
  or
- At each store entrance.

Note: If the store has a policy of giving refunds up to twenty days after purchase, no sign is required.

The refund must be in cash if you paid in cash. If you paid on credit, you may receive a credit to your account or a cash refund.

If the store *does* give refunds, the sign must tell you if it applies to items on sale. The sign must also tell you

- If you need a receipt,
- How long you have to return the item,
  and
- If the store gives cash refunds or a store credit only.

You will be given the current price only if you can provide proof that you paid the original price for the item. This is why it is so important to keep your receipt.

If the store does not give you the information on its refund policy, you automatically have the right to a cash refund or a credit, up to twenty days from the date of your purchase. You can choose whether you want a cash refund or credit. You must have proof of purchase and return the merchandise unused and undamaged. You may also have the right to $200 in damages if the store refuses to accept return of the goods. You can bring an action by filing a complaint with the municipal court where the store is located.

Note: The law on refunds *does not* apply to sales of motor vehicles, perishables (such as food products), custom-ordered or -finished merchandise, and other merchandise which is not returnable by law.

DOOR-TO-DOOR SALES: BUYING CONSUMER PRODUCTS AT HOME. There are many ways to buy products at home, including buying from a door-to-door salesperson. Door-to-door sales include sales made at your home, at another's home (for example, houseware parties), or anywhere that is not the regular place of business of the seller. In these types of sales, there are laws that protect you from high-pressure salespeople.

Both federal and state laws protect you when you buy goods or services costing more than $25 from a door-to-door salesperson. State law says that the contract for goods or services must be more than $25 and paid in two or more installments. Under federal law, you are also given the right to cancel for leased goods, under certain conditions.

Your receipt for a door-to-door sale should contain the following information:

- The name and place of business of the seller,
- A description of the goods or services you bought,
- The amount of money you paid or the value of any goods delivered to you,
- A notice of your right to cancel the contract within three business days, *and*
- A notice of how you should cancel if you choose to do so.

Both federal and state laws give you a "cooling-off" period of three days to change your mind after a door-to-door sale. This means you can change your mind and cancel the sale for any reason within the three days.

The door-to-door salesperson *must* tell you of this right to cancel. He or she must also give you two copies of a "Notice of Cancellation" form. This form should be filled in by the salesperson. It should tell you that you have three days to cancel and should give you the date by which you have to return the notice in order to cancel the sale. If the sale, advertisement, or agreement is made in a language other than English, the salesperson must also give you a copy of the receipt and the notice of your right to cancel in the other language. Make sure the *correct date* is on the notice and the contract. Unscrupulous salespersons have been known to put the wrong date on a contract and notice of cancellation, making it appear that the three days have already expired.

To cancel, sign and date the seller's notice. Keep one copy of the notice and send the other to the seller before 5 P.M. of the third business day after the contract date.

Note: Federal and state law calculate the cancellation time differently. Both allow until the third business day to cancel. However, federal law counts Saturday as a business day and allows until midnight. Your receipt should tell you the date by which you must cancel. To be safe, postmark your cancellation by 5 P.M. Send it by certified mail, return receipt requested, and keep the receipt.

After you cancel the contract, both you and the salesperson have obligations. Within ten days after you cancel, the *salesperson* must

- Refund any money you paid,
- Return any goods or trade-in you gave to him or her,
  and
- Cancel and return any contract you signed.

You must also do some things within the ten days after you cancel. You must let the salesperson pick up any goods left in your home. If the salesperson tells you that you may return the goods at his or her expense, through the mail for example, you can do that.

The law protects you from pushy, high-pressure salespersons. It allows you to cancel a contract, but you must meet your obligations. If you do not make the goods available to the seller or do not return them within the ten days and the salesperson has met her or his obligations, *you will be responsible for all of the payments on the contract.*

If you have a problem with a door-to-door salesperson, contact the New Jersey Office of Consumer Protection. The Federal Trade Commission (FTC) in Washington, D.C., may also investigate if it receives enough complaints about the same door-to-door salesperson.

The laws giving you three days to cancel apply only to *some* door-to-door sales and leases. These laws do not apply to sales under $25, mail order sales, telephone sales, or catalog sales.

Note: You may have the right to cancel under other laws. For example, the Truth-in-Lending Act (TILA) also gives you three days to cancel a contract when you give a security interest in your home that is not a first mortgage to buy or build the house. You may also have the right to cancel some real estate contracts and health club memberships.

If you do not see the three-day right to cancel provision in your contract, ask the salesperson about it. You may be signing a contract that does not give you the right to cancel, or the salesperson may be leaving it out on purpose.

BUYING BY MAIL OR BY TELEPHONE. Products sold by mail or over the phone are covered by an FTC trade practice rule called the Mail or Telephone Order Merchandise Rule. Products sold over the telephone are covered by the federal Consumer Fraud and Abuse Prevention Act (15 *U.S.C.* Section 6101 *et seq.*) and the Telemarketing Sales Rule (16 *C.F.R.* Section 310). The laws tell you how long you can be kept waiting for your merchandise and what to do if you receive something you didn't order.

Under the FTC rule, a mail or telephone order seller must deliver or mail the goods you ordered within the time stated in the seller's advertisement. If no time was stated, your order must be delivered or mailed within thirty days (unless you applied for credit to pay for your order, in which case the seller has fifty days to deliver). If the seller cannot deliver the goods in 30 days, the seller must send you a letter telling you when delivery is expected. If you do not want to wait for the goods, the seller must offer to refund your money within one week. Under New Jersey law, a mail order business has six weeks to deliver your merchandise.

If you have not heard from the seller after thirty days and the advertisement did not say delivery would take longer, you should write to find out what happened. If you do not hear anything, call the New Jersey Office of Consumer Protection. If you have already paid for the item by credit card, use the credit protection rights described in Chapter 7. If you order something from a mail order company outside of New Jersey and have a problem, contact the FTC in New York. You can also file a complaint with the U.S. Postal Inspection Service.

Note: These mail order requirements do not apply if you order items (such as magazines) that have not yet been manufactured when you order them.

You can reject or demand a refund for an item substituted by the company for the one you ordered. If the mail order company sends you a substitute item, it must also send you a letter with the substitute. The letter must say that you can return the substitute within fourteen days at the company's expense and get a full refund. The company must also send you a postage-paid card or letter that you can return if you want a refund or credit. Your refund or credit should be received within fourteen days.

When a seller gives a post office box address on order forms or advertisements, the company's legal name and street address must also be included. Keep a copy of any order forms or advertisements in case you have any problems with delivery and need to contact the company later. Be careful of mail order companies that only give a post office box number. Check out the company with the U.S. Postal Inspection Service, the New Jersey Office of Consumer Protection, and the Better Business Bureau.

It is a violation of the Postal Service Law and the Federal Trade Commission Act to send unordered goods through the mail unless they are (1) clearly marked "free sample," *or* (2) an item mailed by a charity (such as Easter Seals) asking for a contribution.

You do not have to pay for anything you receive that you have not ordered. Tell your local postmaster if you receive a bill for something you did not order. Billing for unordered goods may be mail fraud, which is a federal crime and may be investigated by U.S. postal investigators. Sellers who are found guilty of mail fraud may be fined or even jailed under federal criminal law. You can also sue the seller if you have been a victim of mail fraud. If you are harassed to pay for something that you did not order, you should also contact the New Jersey Office of Consumer Protection and the FTC.

TELEMARKETING. The federal Telephone Consumer Protection Act of 1991 (47 *U.S.C.* Section 227) provides certain protections for consumers against companies that sell products over the phone (*telemarketing*). FCC regulations under the law forbid telephone solicitations before 8 A.M. and after 9 P.M. (*your* time). Telemarketers must disclose to you the name of the seller, that the purpose of the call is to sell you goods or services, and what these goods are. If they are calling about a contest, they must tell you the odds of winning and how the odds will be calculated, that you need not buy anything in order to win, and how you can enter by either giving you an 800 number or disclosing how to enter without making a purchase. You must be told whether a refund, exchange, or cancellation is allowed.

The laws forbid a telemarketer from collecting a fee from you in advance if you were promised a high likelihood of obtaining credit or a loan. If you were promised that your credit report would be fixed, the telemarketer must first wait six months and then send you a corrected report before it can request payment.

All of these disclosures are required before a telemarketer can arrange for a courier pickup of your payment. You have the right not to be harassed or threatened over the phone, and the telemarketer must stop calling you as soon as you say so.

If you suspect telemarketing fraud, call the National Fraud Information Center. This organization may be able to tell you if a deal seems fraudulent and may file a complaint with the FBI, the FTC, and other organizations on your behalf. If fraud is found, you can recover your actual money damages, or up to $500 per violation, and a court may award treble damages (three times the amount you are determined to be owed).

To help reduce the number of telemarketing calls you receive, send your name, address, and telephone number to the Telephone Preference Service.

ADVANCE-FEE LOANS

An example of an advance-fee loan is a situation in which a company promises to give you a loan if you pay a fee in advance; these companies usually advertise that "bad" credit is no problem. The fee may range from one to several hundred dollars. Usually, the con artist gets your money and disappears, and you never get your loan.

You should not confuse advance-fee loan scams with offers of credit from legitimate banks, mortgage brokers, savings and loan institutions, or credit unions. These credit grantors may charge fees to process your loan application (*application fee*), but they will not *guarantee* that you will qualify for a loan.

The FTC has investigated complaints about companies that guarantee loans and has developed the following suggestions on how to protect yourself:

- Be wary of advertising claiming that bad credit will not prevent you from getting a loan. If you can't get a loan through a traditional lending institution (such as a bank, savings and loan, or mortgage broker), it is unlikely that you can get it elsewhere.
- Be cautious of lenders who use 800 or 900 numbers. If you call an 800 number which then directs you to dial a 900 number, remember that you must pay for 900-number calls and the charges can be high.
- Check out the company *before* you apply for the loan. Call the Division of Consumer Affairs, the local Chamber of Commerce, and the Better Business Bureau for starters. Ask them how long the company has been in business and to send you copies of its licenses.
- Be careful about making loan agreements over the phone.
- Don't give your credit card, Social Security, or checking account number to *anyone* over the phone, unless you know the company and are familiar with its operations.
- Review and understand all loan offers *in writing* before you go ahead with the deal.

RENT-TO-OWN

Rent-to-own businesses use *rental contracts* or *lease agreements* requiring you to make weekly payments over a period of time. Often, rent-to-own businesses do not tell you what the price of the item would be if you paid cash for it or the total amount of "rent" you must pay before you own it. It is very difficult to see how bad a deal it is because you are not told how much you will have paid at the end of the lease. Recently, a New Jersey Superior Court judge determined that the way some rent-to-own dealers do business in New Jersey is in violation of several laws, including the New Jersey Consumer Fraud Act.

Many consumers are tempted by rent-to-own dealers who advertise the following: "No credit check!" "No down payment!" "Low weekly payments!" "No obligation to buy!" or "No repair bills!" Contrary to the sound of these advertisements, rent-to-own agreements are often the most expensive way to buy a TV, stereo, appliance, or furniture! Under rent-to-own, if you make every payment over a period of time, you can keep the item. But if you miss even *one* payment, the item may be taken away. Also, under rent-to-own, you often pay two to three times *more* for an item than consumers who pay for the same item with cash, on layaway, or with a credit installment plan.

Unless you pay cash or agree to a layaway plan, the total cost of the item includes some interest. The interest that you pay under a rent-to-own contract is much higher than it is under a credit installment sale.

Under a rent-to-own contract, an appliance may be several years old and may have been rented by other people. Rent-to-own businesses often claim that they are not responsible for repairing or replacing the item if it breaks or is stolen.

A rent-to-own business often repossesses an item as soon as one payment is missed. Even if you pay late, you can lose the appliance and all the money you paid toward owning it. Worse, the rent-to-own business may not refund any of your money, even if the missed payment is the very last payment.

Instead of renting to own, you can

- Wait, and put the money aside as if you were making weekly payments. Pay cash with the money you saved. (This may be difficult because you may have to wait a while before you can have the item.)
- Find a store which offers a layaway plan.
- Apply for credit to buy the item.
- Apply for a short-term loan from a finance company.
- Buy a used item at a yard sale, through the classified ads, or at a second-hand store or repair shop.

If you are convinced that you must rent to own, you should at least do the following:

- Ask whether the item is new or used.
- Ask whether the store will repair or replace an item that breaks or is stolen (many will not, and you may be stuck paying for an item that doesn't work or isn't there).
- Ask what the store's policy is on missed or late payments. (Some rent-to-own stores will take back the item and keep all your money if you are late or miss a payment, even if it is your last payment.)
- Ask what the price of the item would be if you paid cash for it. Then compare how much it costs in other stores or on layaway.
- Ask how much the item will cost you after you have made all the payments.

When the rent-to-own store answers the above questions for you, ask them to show you where in the contract it says what they have told you. If they have made promises that aren't in the contract, ask them to write the promises in and initial where they wrote. Keep a copy of any contract you sign. If they refuse, take your business elsewhere.

WARRANTIES

A *warranty* is a promise to fix a product that doesn't work, give you a new one, or give you your money back. There are different kinds of warranties. Before you buy anything, find out what warranties come with it. A warranty is either *full* or *limited,* depending on what it covers. A warranty can be written, verbal, or implied by law.

A full warranty means that the product will be repaired within a reasonable time without charge, replaced for free, or your money will be refunded if there is a problem with the product. "Fully guaranteed or your money back" is an example of a full warranty. Full warranties are rare, especially on expensive items.

A limited warranty gives less protection than a full warranty. A limited warranty covers only certain things that might go wrong, covers only certain repair charges, or requires you to meet certain conditions first. Read the limited warranty carefully to find out what it covers and what it doesn't. Some limited warranties are not worth very much. "This is a limited warranty. The company will replace parts during the first year after purchase. Customer will pay for all labor and shipping costs," is an example of a limited warranty. Usually both full and limited warranties only last for a specific length of time (the *warranty period*).

A warranty may be either *express* or *implied,* depending on what you are told when you buy the product.

EXPRESS WARRANTIES. When a seller states a fact or makes a promise about a product or sells by model or sample, it is an express warranty. An express warranty can be written or verbal. For instance, an owner's manual may state or a salesperson may tell you, "This tire is guaranteed to last two years." That is an express warranty. The company promises that the tire will last two years. If it doesn't, you have certain warranty rights. For example, the seller may say, "I'm going to sell you a toaster exactly like this one." The salesperson shows you a blue toaster that can toast hamburger buns. When you get it home, you realize you got a green toaster and hamburger buns don't fit. You were given an express warranty by sample. Note, however, that a salesperson's or advertisement's view or *opinion* about the quality or value of a product is *not* a warranty. For instance, the seller may say, "I think you'll love these tires." This is the salesperson's opinion, not a fact or promise to you and therefore not a warranty.

Note: It may be hard to prove a verbal warranty was even made. It's always best to get it in writing.

No law requires that sellers or manufacturers give you an expressed, written warranty. However, the federal Magnuson-Moss Warranty Act (15 U.S.C. Sections 2301–2312) says that if a seller *chooses* to give you a written warranty on a product that costs $15 or more, the seller has to be able to show you what the warranty is *before* you buy the product. The Magnuson-Moss Warranty Act also says that the warranty should be clear and easy to understand; that the company giving the warranty (usually the manufacturer) must honor the warranty within a reasonable period of time; and that the company can't require you to do anything hard or expensive (except in very rare cases) to get the company to make good on the warranty.

IMPLIED WARRANTIES. Some warranties *automatically* come with most products purchased from a dealer. They are not written or verbal statements about a product but are created by law. These types of warranties are called *implied* warranties. There are two types of implied warranties: the warranty of merchantability and the warranty of fitness for a particular purpose.

Warranty of Merchantability. The *warranty of merchantability* covers a seller who regularly sells a product. It means that products sold by such a seller must be good for the purpose for which people usually buy the products. For example, an appliance store selling a toaster must sell you something that can make toast, not just a metal box without heating coils; a car dealer selling a thing that looks like a car must sell you something that can get you from place to place, not just a shiny thing without an engine.

Warranty of Fitness for a Particular Purpose. The *warranty of fitness for a particular purpose* means that you have told the seller that you have a certain need and you're relying on the seller's skill or judgment to sell you an item that fits your need. For example, if you tell the seller you need a toaster big enough for hamburger buns and the seller says, "Here you go, buy this," that product is warranted to toast hamburger buns. You have remedies if it doesn't.

Disclaiming the Warranty. A merchant may try to arrange a sale in which the buyer doesn't get a warranty. This is called *disclaiming the warranty.* A merchant may not disclaim a warranty if the disclaimer is made after the consumer agrees to buy the item. The consumer must have a chance to refuse to buy the item *after* the merchant disclaims the warranty.

In most cases, an express warranty cannot be disclaimed. The merchant cannot tell a buyer that "Yes, there is one," and "No, there is not" at the same time. However, a verbal warranty can be disclaimed by the seller if the disclaimer is in writing. For example, a salesperson tells you that the toaster you bought is fully guaranteed. Yet the sales receipt that you sign says that the toaster is being sold "as is" and without any warranties. In such a case, you should refuse to go through with the purchase.

Sometimes sellers also try to disclaim implied warranties. Remember, there are two different types of implied warranties. An implied warranty of fitness for a particular purpose can be disclaimed if the disclaimer is in writing and is conspicuous. An implied warranty of merchantability (for example, a

151

toaster that can make toast) can be disclaimed verbally or in writing. However, in order to do so the merchant must use the term "merchantability" or specific words which make it plain to you that there is no implied warranty. Words such as "as is" or "with all faults" generally will disclaim the implied warranties. A disclaimer in a written warranty or contract must stand out in the contract. It can't be hidden in fine print. "As is" is a red flag that something—maybe lots of things—are wrong with the goods (for instance, an ad saying, "Toaster for sale, $5.00, as is"). If a consumer buys the toaster and it doesn't make toast, he or she has no claim against the seller for the $5.00 because it was sold "as is."

If a manufacturer or seller does not honor his or her warranty, you may want to take them to court. You will first have to show that a warranty existed at the time of the sale. You will also have to show that the defect in the product existed at the time of the sale or during the warranty period, and that you complained to the proper party, i.e., to the store about the store's warranty or to the manufacturer about the manufacturer's warranty. If the product or the seller fails to meet the promises made in the warranty and the failure caused you *damages* (cost you money), you may be able to sue for *breach* of the warranty.

Contact a lawyer if the item is worth more than $1,500. The seller may be sued for a replacement or a refund and damages, including expenses, court costs, and attorneys' fees. If the item cost less than $1,500, you can sue in small-claims court without a lawyer.

ENFORCING WARRANTIES. If you buy an item from a dealer or retail seller and the item is broken or doesn't work as the dealer promised it would, you have the following options:

- Refuse delivery. Don't accept the item, even if the seller promises to fix it later.
- If you discover a defect after delivery, notify the store or dealer where you bought it right away. If the warrantor is the manufacturer, the store or dealer may work out the problem or just take the item back.
- Keep a list of all dates, names, and phone numbers of everyone you contact to fix the item.
- Contact the manufacturer in writing, if the store's response is unsatisfactory. Contacting the manufacturer is especially important if the warranty is due to run out.
- If you bought something using a store credit card and you cannot get them to fix the problem, refuse to pay the bill. Follow the directions for billing error disputes found on your monthly statement.
- If you bought something using a credit card (such as a Visa or Master-Card), you can still refuse to pay the bill if the item cost more than $50 and was purchased within 100 miles of your home or in your home state,

and you have done your best to solve the problem with the store. Follow the billing-error-dispute instructions as soon as the charge appears on your credit card statement.

- Settle through the warrantor's informal settlement dispute program, if it has one. (See "Complain to the Manufacturer" in this chapter.)
- Contact your local county or municipal Division of Consumer Affairs office or the New Jersey Office of Consumer Protection. The New Jersey Division of Consumer Affairs provides information on filing a complaint for violations of New Jersey's consumer protection statutes or regulations. You may also contact the Better Business Bureau, but they do not have any enforcement power.
- Sue to get your money back.

As of July 3, 1996, New Jersey law also provides *statutory warranties* on new and used cars. You also have federal warranty protection on some new mobile homes. Information on these laws may be found in Chapters 2 and 10.

Note: No warranty is any better than the company that gives it. Stores or manufacturers can go out of business. A "lifetime warranty" from a company with an out-of-state post office box address may be no warranty at all. The best protection is your own care in choosing what and from whom you buy.

HOME APPLIANCES AND REPAIRS

Home appliances include clothes washers, dishwashers, dryers, televisions, refrigerators, radios, fans, air conditioners, and other electrical, mechanical, or thermal articles used in the home.

The New Jersey Consumer Fraud Act says that when you buy a home appliance, the seller must give you a written copy of

- Any manufacturer's warranties. (If the appliance costs more than $15, the federal Magnuson-Moss Warranty Act says that the warranty must be available for you to read before the purchase.)
- Any dealer's warranties.
- The dealer's service contract if the dealer offers one.

You are paying for repair services in advance when you buy a dealer's *service contract*. The written service contract must explain any charges you will have to pay for the service contract. The charges may include any fees to see what is wrong with the appliance. The written contract must also tell you how the dealer will figure the costs for parts and labor.

The New Jersey Consumer Fraud Act regulation on buying home appliances also protects you when you have a home appliance repaired. Before beginning any work, the appliance repair shop must

- Tell you how much it will cost to find out what the problem is with the appliance.
- Tell you how the total charge (including parts and labor) will be figured.
- Give you a written or verbal estimate of the parts and labor and get your written or verbal approval before beginning work.
- Give you a copy of the written estimate and any other papers that you sign.
- Offer to return any replaced parts, unless the parts are too heavy or large.
- Not mislead you in order to influence your choice of repair shop.
- Not charge you more than the estimated repair price, unless you give the repair shop permission to do extra work.

Contact the Office of Consumer Protection if you have a problem with a home appliance repair shop or warranty.

BUYING FURNITURE

Regulations under the Consumer Fraud Act cover the sale and delivery of household furnishings, including furniture, major electrical or gas appliances, and such items as carpets and draperies. You have the right to delivery at the promised time.

When you order household furniture, the sales contract must tell you (in large, bold type):

The merchandise you ordered is promised for delivery to you on or before
_____.

(The blank should be filled in with a date, or length of time agreed upon, e.g., "August 6, 1998, or six weeks from the date of the order.") Make sure the blank is filled in with specific time limits when you order furniture. Do not let the store write "as soon as possible." Be sure to save your copy of the order in case of slow or no delivery.

The sales contract should also state in large, bold type:

If the merchandise ordered by you is not delivered by the promised date, the seller must offer you the choice of (1) canceling your order with a prompt, full refund of any payments you have made, or (2) accepting delivery at a specific later date.

When the promised delivery date arrives, you should either (1) receive your household furnishings, or (2) receive a notice that the seller cannot deliver the furnishings on time. The notice must tell you that you can cancel your order and receive a prompt and full refund or accept a later, specific delivery date. If you are unable to work out delivery problems with the seller, you should complain to the New Jersey Office of Consumer Protection.

154

HOW TO COMPLAIN ABOUT PROBLEMS
WITH PRODUCTS OR SERVICES

Even the best consumers run into problems with products and services. That is why it is important to know your rights and how to protect yourself. But you must also know how to complain. Knowing how to complain may help get your problem solved. If your problem is not solved, you may have to take other action, such as going to court. This section provides some helpful suggestions about what to do when you have a dispute with a seller. First, you should complain to the seller or manufacturer. If your problem is not resolved, you may want to consider arbitration or mediation. Both are explained below. You can also complain to governmental agencies, such as the New Jersey Division of Consumer Affairs or the FTC. If you are still not satisfied, you may have to go to court. This section also explains how to go to small-claims court.

COMPLAIN TO THE SELLER. If you have a problem with defective products or poor repair service, try to work it out with the person who sold you the item or performed the service. Bring copies of your sales receipt, warranty, and/or repair order. Tell the salesperson or service provider what the problem is and what you want him or her to do about it: repair it, replace it, or refund your money. Ask to speak to the supervisor or manager if the first person you speak to does not help you. Note the name of the person to whom you spoke, the date, and his or her comments. If you complain in person, it's a good idea to bring someone with you. You may need to have a witness later on. If you still don't receive satisfaction, send a letter to the owner of the company stating what your complaints are, what you want, and that you have not received any satisfaction. Be sure to keep a copy of this letter. Send it certified mail, return receipt requested, and keep the green receipt card when it is returned so that you will have proof that it was received.

COMPLAIN TO THE MANUFACTURER. If you are having a problem with a defect in the merchandise and you can't work out the problem with the seller, write to the manufacturer and complain. Your letter should include

- Your name, address, and telephone number.
- The name and address of the store or dealer from whom you purchased the item or service.
- The make, model, and serial number of the item and the date of purchase.
- Copies (*not* originals) of the sales receipt, warranty, repair order, etc.
- A clear, brief statement of the facts.
- A statement of what you want: repair, replacement, or a refund of your money.

Keep a copy of the letter you send and any replies you receive. It's best to mail your letter by certified mail, return receipt requested, especially if the dispute involves a lot of money. Also, be sure to keep the defective merchandise in its defective condition. Don't throw it away or attempt to make repairs yourself; if you do, you may jeopardize your rights under the warranty.

ARBITRATION AND MEDIATION. If the seller or manufacturer does not resolve your problem, there are still other alternatives. You can take your case to court but before you decide to do so, you might want to consider *arbitration*. In arbitration, the arbitrator or decision maker is someone who does not represent either party in the dispute. Instead, an arbitrator listens to both sides of the problem and then decides what to do.

Before you agree to any kind of arbitration, find out whether it is binding or nonbinding. *Binding arbitration* means that you agree in advance to accept whatever the arbitrator decides. You may not be satisfied with his or her decision; however, you are stuck with it. You do not get another chance to go to court. In *nonbinding arbitration,* you can reject the decision if you are not satisfied with it and all you have lost is your time and trouble. You can then bring your case to court. Generally, you should always choose nonbinding arbitration and not give up your right to go to court unless the amount in dispute is small or you think it's not worth your time and effort to go to court.

Mediation is different from arbitration. In *mediation,* the mediator talks to both parties and suggests a solution or a compromise. A mediator does not decide what to do. A mediator helps the parties to communicate with each other and avoid going to court. Mediation will not work if one party won't agree to try it.

In New Jersey, the Division of Consumer Affairs offers an Alternative Dispute Resolution (ADR) unit which can provide mediation. The ADR unit has trained, impartial volunteer mediators to help disputing parties reach an agreement that both can accept.

If you use the Division of Consumer Affairs' ADR unit and the mediation does not help, you can still sue the party in court. ADR is not used for cases involving the Lemon Law (problems with cars) nor for cases in which there is obvious fraud. If the problem is serious, you may want to discuss it with an attorney before presenting it for arbitration or mediation. An attorney can also give you advice for getting the best results at the mediation.

COMPLAIN TO THE NEW JERSEY DIVISION OF CONSUMER AFFAIRS. The New Jersey Division of Consumer Affairs Local Assistance Network has county offices and some municipal offices to help buyers work out problems with sellers and manufacturers. If you can't work out the problem with the seller or manufacturer, call your city or town hall to see if your city or town has a consumer affairs officer. If there is no consumer affairs officer where you live, contact the Consumer Affairs Office where the business or businessperson about whom you are asking or complaining is located, *not* where *you* live. The people in these offices help residents resolve consumer problems by contacting the business directly and trying to work out a solution. They may refer your problem to law enforcement officials or the state Division of Consumer Affairs for legal action. They are not lawyers themselves and cannot take your case to court.

OFFICE OF CONSUMER PROTECTION. The New Jersey Division of Consumer Affairs, Office of Consumer Protection investigates complaints of fraud and deceptive acts if there is a potential violation of the Consumer Fraud Act, and can sue on behalf of consumers. Unlike the county offices, the state Office of Consumer Protection may bring consumers' cases to court if there is a pattern of fraud or abuse by the seller, manufacturer, or service provider, and especially if the fraud or abuse is very clear. There are two locations for the Office of Consumer Protection: in Newark and in Camden.

The Division of Consumer Affairs also operates special offices for particular kinds of problems:

- *Lemon Law Unit.* If you have a problem with a new car or motorcycle, you can contact the Lemon Law Unit.
- *Charities.* If you have a problem with an organization that solicits over $10,000 in contributions in New Jersey, you can contact the charities registration section.
- *Employment and personnel services.* If you have a problem with an athletic or booking agency, career consulting or outplacement organization, career counseling service, consulting firm (headhunter), temporary health agency, nursing registry, home health agency, prepaid computer job-matching service, resume service, temporary-help firm, employment agency, job-listing service, or modeling and talent agency, you can contact the New Jersey Division of Consumer Affairs Regulated Businesses Section in Newark.
- *Legalized games of chance.* If you have a problem with bingo or raffle games in New Jersey, you can contact the Office of Legalized Games of Chance in Newark.
- *Securities.* If you have a problem with financial securities sold in New Jersey or with people or firms that sell securities or give investment advice in New Jersey, you can contact the New Jersey Bureau of Securities in Newark.

SMALL-CLAIMS COURT

If you've tried but haven't been able to work out your problems with a creditor or seller, you may decide to sue in small-claims court. The small-claims section of superior court provides a fast, inexpensive way of suing someone for small amounts of money. You will have to use the small-claims court in the county in which the person you are suing lives or where the business you are suing is located. You cannot sue in the county where you live, unless the seller also lives there. In small-claims court there is a dollar limit, which occasionally increases, on how much you can recover.

Generally, you do not need a lawyer in small-claims court. This is because the rules in small-claims court are less complicated than in other New Jersey courts and many people are not represented by a lawyer. But if your case is very complicated or if the other side has a lawyer, it might be a good idea for you to get a lawyer also.

To sue for recovery in small-claims court, go to the county courthouse building of the county where the person you are suing lives or where the business you are suing is located. Look for the clerk's office of the Special Civil Part. Tell the clerk you want to start a small-claims suit. Or you can call the clerk for information.

FILING A SUIT. To start a suit, you have to file a complaint with the court clerk, who will have a complaint form you can fill out. When you fill out the complaint form, you should give

- A short, clear statement that explains the facts of your case and why you are suing (this can be as short as one or two sentences),
- The amount of money for which you are suing,
- Your name and address (you are the *plaintiff*), *and*
- The name and address of the person you are suing (he or she is the *defendant*).

Be sure to spell the person's name correctly and use the full, correct name if you are suing a business. The name of a business is not necessarily the corporate name. You can find out the corporate name and address of a business by calling the secretary of state in Trenton or, for unincorporated businesses, by checking with the county clerk.

If you are suing regarding a contract, you should attach a photocopy (*not* the original) of the contract to the court papers.

You also have to fill out a *summons*. A summons is a document that will be sent to the person you are suing. It notifies the defendant that you are suing and that he or she *must* show up in court.

Ask the court clerk for help if you have questions about filling in the complaint or the summons. You should also ask the court clerk to check that your papers are filled out properly. You must pay a filing fee. When you complete the complaint, make sure you give the clerk the correct amount.

Your case can be heard if it is within the dollar limit and concerns

- A contract or agreement. (The agreement doesn't need to be in writing.) Generally, you have six years to bring these claims.
- Damage to property caused by someone's negligence (for example, driving of a motor vehicle). However, medical, malpractice, probate, and tax matters are *excluded.*
- A landlord-tenant dispute for rent, money damages, or return of security deposit. This does not include a *judgment for possession,* which is brought in the Landlord-Tenant Section of the Special Civil Part.

Find out from the court clerk the date and time your case will be heard. Also find out the *docket number* (case number). Before the court date, gather all the information you need to prove your side of the story, such as the contract, canceled checks, and receipts. If you are suing about a small item such as a radio, plan to bring that to court. If the object is something too large to bring (such as a car or a sofa), take pictures and bring them with you. This will help the judge understand your problem. You might also want to get a witness, such as a car mechanic if your case involves a car, to come to court with you to explain the problem and the cost of repair.

SETTLING OUT OF COURT. Before the court date, the person you are suing may make you an offer to settle out of court. He or she will probably offer you less than the amount you are asking for. You can accept a settlement if you decide to do so. Any agreed upon settlement should be in writing and signed by all the parties. All aspects of what you agreed upon should be put down in writing. Be sure not to leave anything out. However, you should know that once you settle, you cannot sue the same person again for the same problem to get more of your money.

If you decide to settle, write to the court clerk before the court date or call if you do not have enough time to write. Tell the clerk that the case has been settled and that you are dropping your lawsuit. Make sure you receive the settlement money *before* you cancel the court date. If the defendant pays by check, it's a good idea to make sure the check clears the bank before you drop your suit.

GOING TO COURT. On the court date, bring all the evidence you have that you feel will help prove your case. This includes the contract, canceled checks, photos, receipts, and witnesses. If you are going to ask a witness to testify on your behalf, spend a few minutes reviewing what he or she is going to say before you go to court.

At the hearing, both you and the person you are suing will each get a chance to tell your side of the story. Generally, the plaintiff goes first. As the plaintiff, you have the *burden of proof* to show the judge that you are right.

This means that you have to provide the judge with enough evidence (contracts, witnesses, pictures, etc.) so that he or she will decide in your favor. After you finish, the defendant then tells his or her side of the story and brings in his or her own evidence. The judge will listen to the facts and make a decision.

In the superior court, Law Division, all corporations and businesses— except a person who owns his or her business—must be represented by an attorney. However, any corporation officer or employee may represent a business in small-claims court; an attorney is not required by court rule.

If the defendant does not show up for the court date, you have to sign an affidavit stating that your complaint was true and that the defendant does owe you the money sued for. You still have to show the judge your evidence. If the judge decides you are entitled to an award, you will be given a *default judgment* because the defendant is in *default* for not appearing in court.

THE JUDGE'S DECISION. If the judge decides in your favor, he or she will enter a judgment for you telling you the amount you have won. However, the judge does not order the defendant to pay you. Fortunately, some people pay voluntarily after a judge renders a decision.

If the defendant was not in court, contact that person and let him or her know that the judge decided in your favor. Ask the defendant to pay you the amount of money the judge ordered. Once you get your money, you have to *release* the defendant from the judgment. This means the defendant is no longer responsible for the judgment. Do not sign anything releasing the defendant from liability (such as a *release form, satisfaction of judgment,* or *settlement of judgment amount*) unless you are paid with cash, a certified check, or a money order.

COLLECTING THE JUDGMENT. If the defendant refuses to pay a judgment, you will have to go back to court and have the court enforce its own judgment. You cannot sue the defendant to pay on your own. Go to the clerk at small-claims court and explain the situation. The court clerk will tell you how to collect the money owed to you. It might be necessary for the constable of the Special Civil Part to collect the money for you. You will have to pay a small fee plus the constable's mileage costs for this service. However, you first must find out where the defendant's money is. One easy way is to locate the defendant's bank. If you paid the defendant by check at the time of purchase or service, the name of the defendant's bank will be stamped on the back of the check when it is returned to you. Also, if you find out where the defendant works, his or her salary can be *garnished.*

Collecting a small-claims-court judgment from a reluctant defendant can be a complicated process. If the defendant owns a house, there is a procedure for placing a lien on the house, although this is not the best way to collect your money because it can take a long time. Your judgment begins to collect interest from the day it is entered. When you collect your judgment, be sure to include all of the interest to which you are entitled. The small-claims-court clerk can usually help you to figure out how much you are owed. You may want to hire an attorney to collect your judgment, depending on the amount of money the judge has awarded you.

If you are owed more than the dollar limit of small-claims court and do not want to give up the amount over that limit, you will have to sue in superior court, either in the Special Civil Part or the Law Division, depending on the amount involved. The rules in these courts can be complicated and make it more difficult for you to represent yourself. If you have to go to the superior court, Law Division, you should see a lawyer.

IF YOU ARE SUED. If you are sued, you will receive a summons and complaint; you are the *defendant.* The summons will tell you how long you have to respond to the complaint. DO NOT IGNORE a complaint, even if you just received it in the mail. Failure to respond can lead to a default judgment being entered against you. If you lose the case, the judgment will be entered against you for a certain amount of money. If you do not pay the judgment, interest will be added to the amount. The judgment can be enforced through a wage execution (*garnishment*) or a property execution. You should also be aware that a judgment entered against you, or another judgment that gets docketed, in superior court becomes a lien on real estate that you own and is valid for thirty years.

If you lose your case you have the right to appeal if you think you are correct. Appealing the case can be difficult, so you should see a lawyer if you want to appeal. You have only forty-five days after the date the judgment against you was entered to appeal.

7. Credit, Debt, and Banking

This chapter identifies some common terms associated with credit and borrowing money. It also discusses your rights and responsibilities as a credit user. When you buy something on credit or borrow money, you are protected by several consumer laws, some federal and some state. In some cases, you will have the protection of more than one law.

Before delivering into specific consumer laws, you should first understand terms involving borrowed money or credit. If you want to buy a car but don't have enough money to pay cash, you may decide to borrow money and buy the car on credit. This means that rather than pay all at once at the time of sale, you will pay the price of the car plus credit charges over a period of time. The person to whom you owe money is called the *creditor.* You are a *debtor,* since you're in debt for the money. You will sign an agreement (or *contract*). You may also be asked to sign a *loan note* or *promissory note.*

If the creditor gives you credit and one of the terms of the credit agreement is that the creditor can *repossess* (take back) the car (or some other goods you are buying) if you fail to pay, the creditor is *secured.* If the creditor cannot repossess, he or she is an *unsecured creditor.*

There are three different types of creditors; all three can be either secured or unsecured.

1. *Seller-lender.* Sometimes the seller gives credit. For example, if you have a charge account in a store, you deal directly with the seller, paying off your credit (and interest) to the store.
2. *Third-party lender.* Sometimes the seller doesn't want to give credit and wants a cash payment instead. For instance, if you are buying a used car, the seller might tell you to arrange your own financing. You might apply to a bank for a used-car loan. The bank would be a *third-party lender.*
3. *Assignee.* If you buy a car and the car dealer gives you credit, you will sign a contract promising to pay the dealer the balance due (after a down payment) plus interest and other charges in installments over a period of time. Up to this point, this is just like the seller-lender arrangement. The seller then *assigns* (or sells) the contract to a bank, finance company, or an independent company such as the General Motors Acceptance Corporation (GMAC). This company is the *assignee.* The assignee then has the right to collect whatever money you owe. The seller must let you know that your contract is being assigned.

If you buy something on credit and fall behind on your payments, the person or company assigned to collect the debt from you for the creditor is

162

called a *debt collector.* The debt collector may work for the creditor or for a *debt collection agency.*

APPLYING FOR CREDIT

There is no law which requires a creditor to give you credit. However, the federal Equal Credit Opportunity Act (ECOA) says it is illegal to discriminate against you when you apply for credit because of your race, color, religion, national origin, sex, marital status, or age. ECOA also says it is illegal to discriminate against you if your income is from a public assistance program (such as welfare or Social Security) or because you exercise your consumer rights.

The bank or finance company that lends you money is called a *creditor.* To be sure that you can pay the money back, a creditor might ask questions about your income, expenses, debts, and credit history. A creditor will also consider how well you have paid your bills in the past. A creditor must use this information fairly and without discrimination in deciding whether to give you a loan or credit card. The creditor can get a copy of your *consumer credit report* from a *credit bureau* to check your credit history. In addition to this information, the creditor must also consider any information you give to show that a reported credit history is unfair, inaccurate, or incomplete. If a creditor usually considers joint accounts, all accounts you hold jointly with your spouse and accounts that both you and your spouse are permitted to use must be considered. However, the creditor is *not* supposed to consider any past account that you shared with a spouse if it does not correctly show your current willingness or ability to repay. This situation frequently arises as the result of a divorce.

It is illegal for a creditor to

- Count only part of your income because of your sex or marital status.
- Assume that you will stop working to have children.
- Refuse to count all of your income from part-time work, pensions, or retirement funds. (However, the creditor may consider how long this income will last.)

Except in limited circumstances, when you apply for credit the creditor is *not* supposed to ask you

- Your race, color, religion, or national origin. A creditor may ask these questions if you are applying for a mortgage loan or a special-purpose credit program.
- Your plans to have children or your birth-control practices.
- Whether you receive alimony, child support, or separate maintenance payments, unless you want to count this income to get credit. (The creditor *can* ask whether *you pay* alimony or support.)

A creditor cannot use any of this information to discourage you from applying for credit, refuse to give you credit if you qualify, or give you credit on different terms than those given to another person with similar income, expenses, credit history, and collateral.

Whether a creditor can ask for your sex and marital status depends on the type of loan for which you are applying. For example, if you are applying for a joint account held by husband and wife, the creditor may ask for your marital status.

The creditor *can* ask for your immigration status. This is because it is thought that a consumer's ties to his or her country or community relate to the consumer's ability to pay back the creditor.

The creditor cannot ask you for your spouse's signature if you are applying for credit *in your own name*. But a creditor may need a spouse's or other co-owner's signature for a mortgage on property that is owned by both spouses or co-owners.

A creditor *may not* require you to reapply for credit, change the terms of your account, or close your account, unless (1) you have shown the creditor you are unable or unwilling to repay what you owe, *or* (2) you relied on your spouse's income when you first applied for credit, have since changed your marital status, and your income alone is not enough to pay for the same amount of credit.

It is unlawful for a creditor to discriminate against you because you receive public assistance, including Social Security, unemployment compensation, or other government benefits. This means that a creditor cannot have a blanket policy to refuse credit to everyone who receives public assistance; the creditor *must* treat this the same as income from any other source. However, in deciding whether to grant you credit, a creditor may ask questions about how long you have been receiving the public assistance and other questions which relate to how long you are likely to continue receiving it, such as the age of your dependents or how long you intend to remain living within the state in which you are receiving benefits.

A creditor is allowed to take into account the fact that you have filed for bankruptcy in the past. (Bankruptcies stay on your credit report for ten years.) Some creditors will refuse to give you credit while others will not care that you filed for bankruptcy.

After you have filled out an application for credit, a creditor will look at your income, debts, and credit history to decide whether to give you credit. In most cases, a creditor must let you know whether your credit is approved within thirty days after receiving your application. If credit is denied, the creditor must send you a written notice that states the following:

- That you were denied credit.
- The name and address of the creditor which denied you credit.

164

- A statement recognizing that ECOA prohibits creditors from discriminating against applicants on the basis of race, color, religion, national origin, sex, marital status, or age.
- Either the specific reasons why you were turned down or your right to request the specific reasons.

If you are told only of your right to *request* the reasons, you must *also* be told that you may request the reasons within sixty days after you received the denial. The creditor has thirty days to respond to your request for the reasons for denial with the name of any credit bureau that was used by the creditor and the name and address of the federal agency which has enforcement authority over the transaction.

If you are denied credit, find out why. According to the federal Fair Credit Reporting Act (FCRA) (15 *U.S.C.* Section 1681–1681(t)), if the creditor has denied you credit based on information in a credit report, you are entitled to a *free* copy of the credit report. The creditor may have made a decision based on an incorrect credit report that you should correct.

If you are turned down for a loan due to problems with your financial ability to repay, you may be able to work something out with the lender, such as making a larger down payment or borrowing for a longer period of time.

If you apply for credit and do not get an answer within thirty days, write to the company or store. Tell them they are required by law to send you a written notice. You can also send a complaint to the Federal Trade Commission (FTC) in New York City.

If you think you have been denied credit because of discrimination, you may want to see a lawyer. If you can prove the creditor discriminated against you because of your age, sex, national origin, or any of the other prohibited reasons, you may sue the creditor under ECOA for *actual damages* (what the discrimination has cost you) and up to $10,000 (*punitive damages*), plus attorneys' fees and court costs.

CONSUMER REPORTING AGENCIES

Consumer reporting agencies, also called *credit bureaus,* prepare reports about how we pay our bills. Credit bureaus collect information about consumers and sell these reports to creditors, insurance companies, landlords, state or local government agencies, and even a few employers. An incorrect report could keep you from getting a loan or a job. In order to protect consumers from the harmful effects of unfair or incorrect reports about credit, Congress passed the FCRA. To strengthen the act, Congress adopted the Consumer Credit Reporting Reform Act of 1996. The purpose of these laws is to protect consumers from unfair credit reporting and make sure that credit reports are correct and are used properly.

A credit report includes basic information, such as your name (and any former names), spouse's name, past and present addresses, Social Security number, birth date, job, and salary. In addition, a report may include other information, such as your marriages, divorces, and home ownership; lawsuits to which you are a party; records of arrest; and liens. A credit report can be either written or verbal. The information in the report is supposed to show whether you are a good or bad credit risk. It may include a history of the credit you have obtained in the past and whether you paid the credit back on time. Late payments may show up on the report.

A copy of your credit report can be given only to specific persons for specific reasons. For example, credit reports may *not* be given to news reporters, curiosity seekers, or police. Credit reports can be given only to the following persons for the following reasons:

- To you, at your written request,
- To a lender, to make a decision about giving credit or collecting on an account,
- To an employer, to make an employment decision,
- To an insurance company, to make a decision about insurance,
- To a government agency, to determine your eligibility for a license or other government benefit if your financial responsibility or status must be considered,
  or
- To a businessperson who has a legitimate need for the information in a business transaction involving you.

In addition, a credit report can be given to someone who is *not* on this list, but only in response to a court order. Effective September 30, 1997, credit reports for child support enforcement purposes may be provided to government agencies and/or officials in two specific situations:

- An agency administering a state plan may obtain a credit report to set an initial child support award or to modify it subsequently.
- A state or local agency may also obtain a credit report for child support enforcement purposes even if it is not the agency administering the state plan. However, in order to obtain a copy of a given report, a state or local official must first certify to a reporting agency the following four things: (1) the report is needed to determine the capacity to make or the level of child support payments; (2) paternity has been established or acknowledged by the consumer; (3) the consumer has been provided at least ten days' notice that the report will be requested, by certified or registered mail to the consumer's last known address; *and* (4) the report will be kept confidential and will not be used in connection with any other purpose, including other civil, administrative, or criminal proceedings.

On the other hand, unfavorable information, such as a late payment, cannot be reported if it is more than seven years old. The FCRA says how long certain unfavorable information can remain on your credit report. The following is a list of information that would be considered unfavorable by a creditor and the length of time it may appear on your record:

- Bankruptcies—ten years.
- Lawsuits—seven years from the date of filing or until the governing statute of limitations has expired, whichever is longer.
- Judgments—seven years from the date judgment was rendered, including "paid" judgments, or until the governing statute of limitations has expired, whichever is longer.
- Paid tax liens—seven years.
- Accounts placed for collection or charged off—seven years.
- Records of arrest, indictment, or conviction—seven years from the date of disposition, release, parole, or dismissal.

Note: In addition, a credit report *can* contain the above information beyond the time period listed *only if* you are being considered for a job that pays more than $75,000 a year or for a loan or life insurance involving more than $150,000.

PUBLIC INFORMATION AND INVESTIGATIVE REPORTS. A credit bureau may give employers credit reports containing information of public record. For example, papers filed with courts about any civil or criminal case (such as arrests, convictions, or judgments) are considered to be *public record.* However, effective September 30, 1997, a credit bureau may not release a report for employment purposes without certification by a given employer that

- The employer has notified the consumer that a credit report may be obtained for employment purposes
  and
- The consumer has authorized in writing the procurement of the report.

In addition, effective September 30, 1997, the employer must also certify that, prior to taking adverse action based in full or in part on a credit report, the employer has given the consumer a copy of the report along with a Summary of Consumer Rights as prescribed by the Federal Trade Commission.

On the other hand, an *investigative report* can be part of a credit report if you have applied for a job or insurance and the employer or insurance company requests it. It includes information about your character, general reputation, personal characteristics, and lifestyle. This information is obtained through interviews with your neighbors, people you know, or anyone who may have information about you.

As with regular reports for employment purposes, you must be notified in writing that someone has ordered an investigative report about you. You must be notified within three days of the request. Ordinarily, this will mean that you will receive the notice before the investigation has been completed, but not necessarily before it has started. The notice must explain your right to know what information is being requested. If you want to find out what information about you was requested, write to the company or person who requested it. The user of the information *must* send you a written explanation within five days.

If someone denies you a job, credit, a government benefit, or insurance, or increases the cost of getting credit or insurance because of negative information in a credit report, that person must tell you the name and address of the credit bureau that furnished the report. You are entitled to a *free* copy of your credit report from the credit bureau if you request it within sixty days of the notice denying your credit. If you ask, the credit bureau must give you

- All information (except medical) in its file about you,
- Sources of information (except sources used solely for investigative consumer reports),
  and
- Names of the people who have received your report for employment reasons in the past two years and the people who have received it for other reasons in the past six months.

When a lender denies you credit or increases its charge for credit because of information from a source other than a credit bureau, it must tell you. If you write to the lender within sixty days of an unfavorable decision, the lender must tell you the source of the information it relied upon when it denied you credit.

CORRECTING YOUR CREDIT REPORT

Credit bureaus are required by law to assure the "maximum possible accuracy" of the information they report. But many credit reports contain mistakes.

Report any mistake you find on your credit report to the credit bureau *immediately, in writing*. You should send copies of any documents showing that the report is in error (copies of paid bills or canceled checks, for example). Keep a copy of your letter and documents. After you report the mistake

- The credit bureau *must* look into your complaint and promptly take incorrect, inaccurate, or obsolete information out of your file under the Consumer Credit Reporting Reform Act of 1996. Reinvestigations must be completed within thirty days of receipt of your written complaint, with one fifteen-day extension allowed.

168

- Notice of the results of the reinvestigation must be provided to you within five business days of the completion of the reinvestigation. Within the same five-day period, the bureau must also give you a statement that the reinvestigation has been completed; a revised credit report; a notice that, upon request, the bureau will provide a description of procedures used to determine the accuracy and completeness of information; a notice of the right to add a brief statement of dispute (which may be limited to 100 words) to the file; a notice of the right to require the bureau to notify previous users of disputed information.
- If the credit bureau's investigation does not solve the problem, remember that you have a right to file a short statement that explains your side of the story. The credit bureau *must* include this statement in your file, as part of your credit report. To maximize the impact of this statement, however, you will have to file it with every credit bureau whose file contains the same inaccuracy. You should also note that, at your request, the bureau will show your statement or a summary of your statement to anyone who recently received a copy of the old report.
- The credit bureau will notify past recipients, at your request, that the disputed information was removed from your file. No charge may be levied if you respond within 30 days. After that, there may be a reasonable charge.

Credit bureaus *do not* have to take out information about you that is *true,* even if it may be bad for your credit. Beware of credit bureaus or advertisements that ask you to pay money to "fix" or "repair" your bad credit (see Chapter 6, "Protecting You as a Consumer"). These are usually con artists who take your money and provide no service. For very little cost, you usually can take care of getting inaccurate information off your credit report yourself. There is no legal way to force a credit reporting agency to remove accurate information from your credit report, even if it is harmful to your credit. The only way to "repair" a bad credit history is to establish a record of good credit practices over a period of time.

If you are damaged by a credit report which is untrue, you can file a lawsuit against the credit bureau. If you believe you have been damaged by a violation of the FCRA, you should see a lawyer. You can sue for actual damages and reasonable attorneys' fees and costs. However, FCRA does not create liability merely for inaccurate credit reports. To establish liability you *must show* that the credit bureau was negligent in failing to follow reasonable procedures to assure the "maximum possible accuracy" of the reported information. On the other hand, if you do show in addition that a violation by a credit bureau was *willful,* you can also be awarded statutory damages, ranging from $100 to $1,000, and punitive damages. Generally,

169

you have only two years from the date of the violation to file your lawsuit. There is an exception for willful and material misrepresentations. In the latter case, your lawsuit may be brought within two years after discovery of the misrepresentation.

BILLING ERRORS ON CREDIT AND CHARGE CARD ACCOUNTS

The federal Fair Credit Billing Act (FCBA), which is part of the Truth-in-Lending Act (TILA), explains how billing disputes on charge or credit card accounts are settled. Your bill should give an address where you can write if you think there has been a mistake. (The address is generally not the same place where you send your payments.)

If you think there is a mistake on your credit card bill, write a letter to the creditor within sixty days after the date of your bill. Do not telephone because a phone call will *not* protect your rights. Send the letter by certified mail, return receipt requested. Keep a copy of the letter and keep the green receipt card when it is returned to you. Include in your letter your name, account number, the amount of the charge you question, and the reason why you think there is a mistake. Send photocopies (*not* originals) of sales receipts or other proof to back up your claim that there is a mistake. The creditor must answer your letter within thirty days.

After you send the letter, the creditor must, within two billing cycles or ninety days (whichever is sooner), (1) correct the mistake, credit your account for the amount of the incorrect charge, and report the correction to any credit bureau that was notified of a delinquency, *or* (2) send a letter to you explaining why the creditor does not think there is a mistake.

You do not immediately have to pay the amount that you think is a mistake. You are still responsible, however, for the other *correct* charges that appear on your bill. Also, until the billing mistake is settled, the creditor may not try to collect the disputed amount and you don't have to worry about a bad credit report. Until the matter is resolved, the creditor is not allowed to do the following three things:

1. Make or threaten to make a bad report about your credit standing to anyone,
2. Report that your account or the disputed amount is overdue,
   or
3. Close your account for nonpayment.

If the creditor decides there is no mistake on your bill, the creditor must write you a letter and tell you why it believes there is no mistake. If you still think there is a mistake, write another letter within *ten days* after you receive the creditor's letter. As with your first letter, send copies of sales receipts to prove your claim. Ask the creditor for copies of receipts that show why the creditor thinks there is no mistake.

At this point, the creditor may tell credit bureaus that your account is overdue. However, if you sent your letter in time and explained that you are *not* paying your bill because you think there is a mistake, the creditor *must* tell the credit bureaus your reason for not paying. The creditor *must* also let you know to which credit bureau(s) you were reported and *must* tell them when the problem is settled.

If you use a bank credit card, such as Visa or MasterCard, to buy something and there is a problem with it, federal law (part of TILA) gives you the right to withhold payment to the bank credit card company for the amount of the purchase, but *only if*

- You first try to settle the problem with the seller,
- The item costs more than $50,
  and
- The purchase was made in your state or, if outside your state, within 100 miles from where you live. (If you buy goods on your credit card from a store in another state that is more than 100 miles from your home, you must first pay the credit card company and then try to get your money back from the seller.)

If your credit card is stolen, report the theft immediately to your credit card company. If you do, the most you will be responsible for is the amount charged or $50, whichever is less.

CREDIT INSURANCE

When you take out a loan or buy something on credit, some creditors try to get you to buy credit life, health, or involuntary unemployment insurance. This insurance is supposed to pay your bill if you die, get sick, or become involuntarily unemployed. It is usually very costly. You have the right to refuse to buy this expensive insurance. If you buy credit insurance because the creditor requires it as additional collateral, it counts as interest under TILA and the cost must be included on the truth-in-lending statement as part of the finance charge. It is not counted as interest if it is listed on a separate line in the contract and is voluntary. If you buy insurance voluntarily, you must sign a statement that no one is forcing you to buy it. Either way, credit insurance can add to the cost of your debt. These policies will pay only the portion of the balance you owe on the day you die, become disabled, or are involuntarily unemployed. If you fall behind in your payments before that day, the in-surance will not cover that part of the debt. The problem with credit insurance is that it is extremely expensive and you may pay extra interest to finance the insurance.

BUYING INSURANCE ON CREDIT

If you need insurance but cannot afford to pay for it in cash, you may borrow money to buy it. You can *finance* all types of insurance, including credit insurance, as discussed above. State and national banks sell insurance and finance the premiums. The New Jersey Premium Finance Company Act (*N.J.S.A.* 17:160-1) regulates companies that offer insurance paid for with borrowed money. These premium finance companies must be licensed by the New Jersey Department of Banking.

Insurance premium financing is very expensive. Some insurance brokers convince people to borrow money to buy insurance because the brokers receive an extra commission if a person buys on credit, even though the person can pay cash.

Not only is insurance premium financing expensive, it can be very confusing. If the insurance company decides to raise your premium or if you decide to cancel the insurance, your loan must be readjusted with the finance company. Cancellation of insurance can cause delays and you may be charged prepayment penalties. Instead of buying insurance on credit

- Try to pay cash.
- Ask the insurance company if it accepts installment payments. Most companies do not require payment of the whole premium in advance. Many companies offer a "40-30-30" plan: You pay 40 percent of the premium in advance, 30 percent three months later, and 30 percent three months after that.
- Get your own loan to pay for the insurance. You may get a loan at a lower interest rate and without all of the extra charges.

If you do decide to take out insurance premium financing, a written agreement between you and the finance company is often arranged by insurance agents or brokers. The finance company pays your insurance premiums, and you pay the finance company in installments for the premiums and finance charges.

In addition to the credit information required by TILA, the agreement should state the name and address of the insurance agent or broker, identify the insurance policy being financed, and notify you to read the agreement and not to sign it if there are any blanks in it. You are entitled to a copy of this agreement when you sign it. You should keep a copy of the agreement at least until the loan is repaid.

BORROWING MONEY AND PAYING FOR CREDIT

When you borrow money to make a purchase, you end up paying much more for the item than if you were paying cash because you are buying two

172

things. First, you are buying the item you want; second, you are buying a loan. For this reason, you should think very carefully before you borrow money. Be certain that you can afford to repay the loan and that you really need the item.

TRUTH-IN-LENDING ACT. TILA requires creditors to tell you how much they will charge for credit. The purpose of this law is to help consumers compare credit terms offered by different creditors. Once you have this information, you are able to shop around for the best terms. In general, the law applies whenever a person borrows money, buys something on credit, or uses a credit card. There are some exceptions. For example, TILA does *not* apply if the loan or credit is more than $25,000 and the loan is *not* secured by real property or personal property to be used as a dwelling, such as a mobile home. Most student loans are also not covered by TILA. (For example, all loans guaranteed by the Higher Education Assistance Act are *not* covered by TILA.)

TILA requires creditors to tell consumers in words easy to understand how much the credit will cost and to make the finance charge and the annual percentage rate (APR) very clear before the contract is signed. In order to shop around, you must know and compare the APR and the finance charges. You should also know what your total payments will be. TILA requires creditors to give you this information. Make sure that you are not seeing these percentages and amounts for the first time *as* you are signing the contract.

Under TILA, creditors must give information to consumers about the following terms:

- *Finance charge.* The finance charge is the total dollar amount of the interest plus other charges you pay to borrow money or buy goods on credit.
- *Amount financed.* The amount financed is the dollar amount that you borrow including the loan principal or the financed cost of goods. The amount financed may also include legitimate charges which the creditor pays to third parties, such as appraisal fees. Credit insurance is included in the amount financed only if you agree to buy it.
- *Total of payments.* The total of payments is the sum of all of your monthly payments. The total of payments should equal the amount financed *plus* the finance charge.
- *Annual percentage rate.* The APR is the cost of credit as a yearly interest rate, for example an APR of 12 percent.

Use the APR yardstick to see which loans cost less. How will you know what the APR is? The best method is to call ahead and ask the creditor for the APR *before* you apply for a loan. Then, call other lenders to compare rates.

In general, the lower the APR, the better the deal. But you should remember that if you finance something for a very long time, you will pay more interest. For example, if you pay off short-term credit card debts with a twenty-year home equity loan, you will pay much greater amounts of interest and a lot more money in the long run. Many people check the monthly payment to see if they can afford the loan. But look also at the finance charge and the total number of payments to see how much in total you will have to pay off.

TILA also requires lenders to give you information about any charges connected with the loan and to make sure you can read it. The information usually appears on a form that includes a box stating (1) the APR, (2) the finance charge, (3) the amount financed, *and* (4) the total of payments.

Generally, there are two different types of credit transactions under TILA: *open end* and *closed end.*

Open-End Credit. Open-end credit is an account to which new charges can be added. Most credit cards and charge accounts in stores, under which finance charges are usually added on to the unpaid amounts each month, are open-end credit accounts.

You have the right to buy different things or borrow new amounts with an open-end credit account. The finance charges on an open-end credit account depend on how much is charged and when and how much of the debt is paid back. You must pay special attention to the APR to know what open-end credit really costs.

TILA says that when you begin an open-end credit account (or before you make your first purchase), the creditor must give you a *disclosure statement.* The disclosure statement includes information about credit charges. The statement must be in clear, easy-to-understand language and you must receive a copy.

Closed-End Credit. Closed-end credit is credit for a specific amount of money which must be paid back by a specific date. Borrowing money from a finance company to buy a car and most mortgages are examples of closed-end credit. Creditors offering closed-end credit must also give you a disclosure statement before you sign the credit contract.

Violations of the Law. If you think a creditor has violated TILA, you may want to see a lawyer. You can collect up to $2,000 for some closed-end transactions ($1,000 for others plus attorneys' fees) for a TILA violation. You have one year from the time of the violation to sue. If the creditor takes you to court because you have not paid, you can use the creditor's TILA violations as a defense for not paying the creditor. The one-year time limit does not apply if you are *raising a defense* to paying. (This means that if you are sued for not paying the debt, you can raise a TILA violation as a defense even if more than one year has passed.) This is called a *recoupment.*

SECURITY INTERESTS. Some credit contracts or loans require that you give a mortgage or security interest in your home as collateral for the loan. Please see the discussion of these loans in Chapter 3, "About Your Home."

An FTC regulation protects you if you received credit on or after March 1, 1985, from a seller or finance company. Under the FTC regulation

- A finance company cannot take a security interest in household furnishings (except for certain luxury items and antiques) on a loan for money.
- Borrowers cannot *waive* (give up) their right to be heard in court.
- No *waivers of exemption rights* are allowed (i.e., you cannot give up your right to keep exempt property). However, the actual goods bought from the seller are not protected.
- Cosigners must be given a notice that they will have to pay the debt if the primary debtor doesn't pay.
- If you pay late for just one month, the finance company cannot claim that you are late or charge you late fees for the following months.

RETAIL INSTALLMENT SALES ACT. The New Jersey Retail Installment Sales Act (RISA) (*N.J.S.A.* 17:16C-1) may give you some protections for installment purchases. RISA covers the sale of goods or services up to a specified amount, but only if it is for household or personal use and you pay for it in two or more installments. Store charge accounts are covered under RISA. Many car purchases, however, are not covered because many cars cost more than the $10,000 limit of the law. RISA does not apply to home repair agreements or insurance premium finance agreements. Home repair agreements are covered by other laws.

RISA says that each retail installment sales contract must tell you (1) the cost of credit, (2) that you should not sign the contract if it is blank, *and* (3) that you have the right to a copy of the contract when you sign it.

Perhaps more important, the law says what a RISA contract should *not* contain

- Blank spaces when you sign it, except where serial numbers of the goods should go.
- An agreement that you waive your legal rights if the seller illegally tries to collect payments or repossess the goods.
- A *power of attorney* (language that gives the creditor the legal right to contract on your behalf).
- A *confession of judgment* (language that lets the creditor obtain a judgment against you without giving you a chance to tell the court your side of the story).
- A provision that *garnishes* your wages (turns over your wages or salary to the seller) without making the seller go to court first.
- A release of the seller from any claims you may have under the contract or account.
- A mortgage on real estate.
- A balloon payment.

Do *not* sign an installment sales contract that contains any of the above.

A seller may *assign* (sell) your retail installment sales contract to a bank or finance company. If this happens, you will make your payments to the bank or finance company instead of to the seller. You should make sure that the amount charged is correct. Under federal regulations, you still have the same rights that you have with the seller.

A retail seller may require that you buy insurance on the goods, but only if the seller keeps title to or takes a lien on the goods that you are buying. You have the right to choose your own insurance company. The insurance has to protect your interest in the goods—not just the seller's—unless you are unable to find insurance to protect your interest.

If you buy a car in installments and the seller requires you to pay for insurance on the car, find out what that insurance covers. The sales contract must say if the insurance does not cover bodily injury or property damage.

If you make installment payments in cash, the seller must give you a written receipt that includes the date of the payment, your account number, and the amount you paid. If the seller does not give you regular statements, you have the right to request a statement showing your payments and the balance due. The seller must send this statement, at no charge, twice a year if you request it, within ten days of your written request.

If you buy different items at different times from the same store, the store must apply your payment to your earliest purchase first. If you miss a payment on the last item you bought, the store cannot repossess everything you bought there.

If you are ten days late in making a payment, the seller can charge you a late fee of not more than $10. The late fee can be collected from you *only* if the charge is provided for in your contract. The late charge may be collected by the creditor or added to your contract account. If the seller adds the charge to your account, it must be added within thirty-five days from the date that you defaulted and the seller must notify you in writing of the charge within five days.

If the seller hires an attorney to collect your debt, attorneys' fees can be added. However, attorneys' fees cannot be more than 20 percent of the first $500 you owe, plus 10 percent of any amount over $500. If you can prove you did not miss payments or that you have a legal reason for not paying, you cannot be charged attorneys' fees.

Unless the contract provides for late charges and attorneys' fees, you cannot be charged for them.

If you have problems with a retail installment seller and suspect the seller has violated RISA, you should see a lawyer. If you were billed for charges that the law does not allow, the store may lose its right to collect finance charges or other added costs. Some RISA violations also give consumers rights under the Consumer Fraud Act.

FINANCING SMALL LOANS. In the past, finance companies gave only small loans of up to $5,000. The loans offered today by finance companies may be as much as $15,000. Under a New Jersey law called the Consumer Loan Act (*N.J.S.A.* 17:10-1), finance companies that give loans for $15,000 or less are required to be licensed. Licenses must be posted where they can easily be seen by customers. Most finance companies are also licensed to give secondary mortgage loans and other loans that are secured by a home. They also give open-end credit, such as a credit card account. The maximum interest rate currently allowed in New Jersey is 30 percent. Most finance companies charge close to this amount.

Under the Consumer Loan Act, closed-end loans can be *variable-rate loans* (have a variation in the interest rate). This means the loan companies may raise or lower the interest rate *after* you have taken out a variable-rate loan. The amount of the interest charged can vary by as much as 6 percent over the life of the loan and by as much as 3 percent in one year. A loan that starts at 18 percent could cost you as much as 24 percent a few years later, resulting in much higher monthly payments. Because they are so un-predictable, variable-rate loans are often not as good a deal as fixed-rate loans at a higher interest rate. Variable-rate loans can *never* go over the 30 percent limit on interest set by law.

The Consumer Loan Act says that finance companies must give you a statement when the loan is made. The statement must include

- The amount of the loan,
- The date of the loan,
- The date that the loan is due to be completely paid off,
- The security (*collateral*) is, if any,
- The payment schedule (payments should be for equal amounts and due at about equal intervals),
  and
- The APR and the total amount of interest.

Note: TILA also applies to small-loan companies and requires the dis-closures already discussed.

Small-loan companies cannot by law

- Make false or misleading statements about the terms of their loans,
- Take a lien on real estate you own (unless they have a license to make second mortgages),
- Ask you to sign a *power of attorney* or *confession of judgment,*
- Ask you to sign a note, loan agreement, or other paper that contains blank spaces,
- Do business at any place other than a licensed office or under any name other than a licensed name,
  or

- Add on any charges except interest, insurance, or certain legal costs if you fail to repay your loan.

You may (but are not obligated to) agree to get life, health, and unemployment credit insurance in order to receive your loan. If you do so, the law gives you some protections. The company must explain the insurance policy to you in clear language. It also must tell you the benefits and limitations of the insurance. The company may not *require* you to buy property insurance on the loan collateral (for example, the company cannot force you to buy fire insurance on furniture or collision insurance on a car).

If you miss a payment on your consumer loan, the lender can declare you in default and sue you for the full amount due on the loan. If you pay late, a consumer loan company can charge you extra interest. If that happens, you will end up paying more for the loan than the total of the payments shown on the loan document because more of your next payment will pay for interest and less will pay off the loan principal. The difference in interest can add up by the end of the loan, even if you have been just a little late with payments now and then.

When you have paid the loan, the loan company must mark every loan agreement that you signed with the word "paid" or "canceled" in *ink*. The company must return anything you gave as *security* (collateral) and any proof that you owed the company money (i.e., *loan documentation*).

The law provides for very strong penalties for violations by consumer loan companies. For some violations of the law, the loan becomes *void*. This means that the lender has no right to collect any money owed by you. If you think there has been a violation concerning your loan, see a lawyer to protect your rights. A company can also lose its license and be prosecuted under criminal law for some violations. You should also complain to the New Jersey Department of Banking.

Consumer loan companies are also regulated by the FTC. If you are having problems with a consumer loan company, you may want to complain to the FTC.

ABOUT YOUR DEBTS

After you take out a loan or buy something on credit, the lender or store will want to be sure that you pay back the debt. Most written consumer contracts state the creditor's rights if the buyer fails to pay. In the United States, no one can be sent to jail for not paying his or her debts, except (sometimes) people who disobey orders to pay child support.

A contract will often say that when you miss a payment, the creditor can declare the entire debt in default and the entire amount that is still owed on the contract becomes immediately due. This is called *accelerating* the debt.

However, if a credit contract is ended early because the creditor accelerated the debt, you do not have to pay the full total-of-payments amount because part of the interest has not yet been earned.

Once a debt is accelerated, the creditor can go ahead with the default remedies that it has under the law or under the contract. These remedies can differ widely. The actions that are available to a creditor after a default depend mostly on whether or not the creditor has taken a security interest in the property that was sold to you (or, sometimes, in other goods you own). *Secured debts* exist when the creditor has a security interest in the goods; an *unsecured debt* is a debt under which the creditor does not have a security interest.

SECURED DEBTS. A security interest gives the creditor the right to *repossess* (take back) the property if you fail to pay on time. Usually, the property that can be repossessed is the property that you purchased on credit. A car loan is a common example of a secured debt. If you fail to make payments, the creditor can repossess your car. A mortgage is another example of a secured debt since the creditor has a security interest and can foreclose on your home if you don't pay.

Repossession. For a repossession to be lawful, it must meet certain requirements. First, the creditor must have a valid security interest in the property that is specified in the sales contract. For the security interest to be valid, it must be in writing, specify the property, and be signed by the consumer. If there is no valid security interest, there can be no repossession.

Second, there must be a *default,* which is some specific reason that allows the creditor to repossess. The sales contract must authorize repossession for the specific default that has occurred. The usual repossession case involves a buyer who has failed to make payments, but other circumstances can lead to repossession, such as the failure to keep insurance on a car.

Third, if the contract allows repossession, the repossession must be performed lawfully. A creditor can repossess secured property without telling you first and without first getting court permission, but *only* if it can be done without a *breach of the peace.*

In New Jersey, it is a breach of the peace for someone to enter your house without your permission, whether or not anyone is home. Entering your garage or place of business without your permission is also a breach of the peace. However, repossession from a street or even from a driveway is not *by itself* a breach of the peace. Some courts have said that trickery or sneakiness may be a breach of the peace. It is also a breach of the peace when the repossessor

- Is accompanied by a sheriff or police officer without court authorization.
- Pretends to be an officer or flashes a badge.
- Takes a car and promises to repair and return it but repossesses it instead.

In some cases, creditors violate criminal laws during repossession. If the creditor breaks into a house or pushes or hits someone during the repossession, that creditor could also be liable for money damages for an illegal repossession.

After the property is repossessed, the creditor must first notify you (see below) and then will probably sell the property at either a public or a private sale. If the creditor does not get enough money from the sale to pay off the debt, the creditor may sue you for the difference between what the property sold for and what you still owe the creditor. This is called the *deficiency.* A repossession and deficiency suit means that you still pay the deficiency, even though the creditor took the goods back.

In a deficiency suit involving a car, the auto dealer will also sue you for repossession costs, storage, and attorneys' fees, which can add on a great deal more money.

The creditor cannot sue you for the deficiency unless two requirements are met: (1) you received proper legal notice, *and* (2) the sale was held in a commercially reasonable manner.

What amounts to proper legal notice will depend upon the type of sale conducted. In a public sale, the creditor must send you a notice of the time, date, and place of sale. In a private sale, the notice must state the date after which a private sale will be held. For example, the notice might say, "A private sale of your repossessed car will be take place after January 5, 1998." The notice must allow you a reasonable time to respond. What is meant by a "reasonable time" may differ from case to case. In one case involving the repossession of a car by a bank, a New Jersey court said that three days' notice of a private sale was not reasonable. A notice is invalid if

- The notice was not sent.
- It did not contain the correct information about the time and place of the sale.
- It was not sent at the right time (that is, it did not allow a reasonable time to respond).

The purpose of giving you notice of the planned sale of the repossessed property is to allow you to do any of the following:

- Protect your property by paying the debt before the sale.
- Find a buyer for the property and pay off the debt before the sale.
- Attend the sale and bid on the property or have others attend the sale and bid on the property. This may help push up the price and therefore reduce your potential liability for deficiency.

Getting the Property Back. Unless you and the creditor agreed otherwise in writing *after* default, you have a right to get your property back before it is sold. You must pay the creditor the full amount you owe plus any money the creditor spent getting the property ready for resale (towing, cleaning, storage, etc.).

If you have paid at least 60 percent of the cash price of the property or 60 percent of the loan, strict foreclosure is not allowed. Unless you give up this right by signing a written statement after default, the creditor must sell the collateral within 90 days of taking possession and may not retain the collateral.

If you have paid less than 60 percent, the creditor must send you a notice if he or she wants to keep the repossessed property to satisfy the debt. If you do not want the creditor to keep the property and say so in writing within twenty-one days, the creditor must sell it.

Commercial Reasonableness. All aspects of the repossession and resale of the goods must be *commercially reasonable.* A very unfair resale price may be evidence that the resale was not commercially reasonable. There are several ways you can check to see if the price was fair. If the property was a car, you can look up the average selling price for the year and make of your car. The auto dealers' *Blue Book* lists this information. It is available at public libraries. Check to see if the sale was advertised. Check to see if anyone came to bid. Find out who bought your car and how much was paid.

The creditor who repossesses property and sells it in a public or private sale must prove that the sale price was fair and reasonable if the creditor wants to collect a *deficiency judgment.* Otherwise, the presumption is that the fair value of the goods is equal to the balance of the debt and the creditor cannot collect a deficiency.

Generally, the creditor can choose to have either a public sale or a private sale. If the creditor chooses a public sale, it must be some kind of auction, advertised in a way to attract bidders. A creditor may also have a duty to clean, wash, or repair the item before offering it for sale.

If the creditor does not give proper notice of the sale or if any part of the repossession and resale is not commercially reasonable, you may sue the creditor for all of the interest or finance charges plus 10 percent of the cash price of the goods (or 10 percent of the original loan amount). Also, some courts hold that a creditor that violates any of these repossession laws may not win a deficiency suit.

Although logically and legally repossessions should give money back to the consumer after subtracting the loan balance and other costs, they almost never do. Creditors usually sell repossessed cars to other dealers at auctions for below the wholesale costs. The creditor is also allowed to deduct reasonable expenses of retaking and preparing for the sale (and, if allowed in the sales contract, reasonable attorneys' fees and legal expenses). After subtracting those expenses from the resale price, the difference must be given to you. This is called a *surplus* and is *very* rare.

UNSECURED DEBTS. A debt is *unsecured* when the creditor cannot take back the property to pay the debt. The creditor must try to get the money by taking you to court, winning the case, and getting a judgment. Then the creditor must try to collect the judgment by either *garnishing your salary* (taking money from your weekly paycheck) or *executing* on some of your assets, such as your bank account or car. There are legal restrictions on how much the creditor can take from your wages and on the property that can be taken.

Creditors know that going to court to collect debts is expensive and takes time. Often it is not worth the trouble because many debtors have no property that the creditor can take or sell after winning in court. Often creditors try to collect the debt without going to court by using debt collectors, such as collection agencies.

GARNISHMENTS ON WAGES AND BANK ACCOUNTS. A *garnishment,* or wage execution, is a court order that requires your employer to hold a part of your wages and pay it to a creditor, or allows money to be taken from your bank account.

Unless all of the funds in your bank account are exempt from garnishment, a creditor is allowed to garnish money from your bank account. The rules for how this is done are very specific. A creditor who has a judgment against you must ask the sheriff or constable to *levy* on (collect from) your bank account. The creditor can't just do it alone. The sheriff or constable must go to the bank with the court documents showing that the creditor is entitled to levy. You must receive notice of the levy and be given the opportunity to go to court to ask that the money not be taken. You have the right to claim a $1,000 state exemption (this $1,000 is in addition to the other exemptions or income listed below) in your bank account.

A creditor cannot ask an employer to withhold your wages without a court order. The creditor must first take you to court for failing to pay your debt, get a judgment against you, and then go back to court for a court order to get the wage garnishment. The creditor must also give you notice before getting the court order for wage garnishment. Your employer can withhold your wages only after *all* of these conditions have been met.

In general, a creditor can garnish only 10 percent of your weekly salary and only one creditor can garnish your wages at a time. If you earn more than $7,500 a year, a greater percentage can be taken but this is generally not done unless your wages are being garnished for child support or alimony.

A federal law also protects you from excessive garnishments. The federal Consumer Credit Protection Act says that garnishments on your wages have to be the lesser of 25 percent of your weekly *net disposable income* (your salary after federal and state taxes and other deductions), or the amount by which your net weekly disposable income (after taxes) exceeds thirty times the federal minimum hourly wage (as of September 1, 1997, $154.50). For some part-time workers who have wages lower than that amount, paychecks may not be garnished at all.

Your employer is allowed to take a $1 deduction from your paycheck each time part of your check is deducted to pay the creditor. This is not to penalize you; it is to pay for the employer's time to deduct the amount and pay the creditor. An employer can take no more than $1 from each check.

Both federal and New Jersey law prohibits an employer from firing you or taking any disciplinary action against you because there is, or has been, a wage garnishment against you.

Some income is protected from garnishments. None of the following income can be garnished:

- Welfare (county or municipal);
- Workers' compensation benefits;
- New Jersey disability insurance;
- New Jersey unemployment insurance;
- Certain types of insurance benefits (examples: health or disability benefits, group life or health policy or proceeds);
- Social Security payments;
- Supplemental Security Income benefits;
- Veterans' pensions;
- Railroad Retirement Act pensions;
  and
- Certain other types of pensions (examples: ERISA-qualified benefits, and pensions for public employees, street and water department employees, teachers, school district employees, and county employees).

These benefits are protected from garnishment even if the money is in a bank account. But you must be able to prove that the money in the account is entirely from a federal or state benefit program. Therefore, if you receive any of the above benefits and have concerns about garnishment, you should keep them in a separate account.

DEBT COLLECTION HARASSMENT. The Fair Debt Collection Practices Act (FDCPA) is a federal law that protects consumers against abusive practices by debt collectors. The law generally applies to debt collectors and other persons who regularly attempt to collect debts owed to someone else. It applies to collection agencies, attorneys who regularly handle collection cases (collecting on behalf of their clients), some other third parties (such as someone who buys the original debt if it is in default at the time it is bought), and even a creditor who uses a different name when collecting a debt. This law does not apply to creditors who, on their own, collect on debts owed to them.

When debt collectors contact you to collect the debt, they must use words such as, "This is an attempt to collect a debt. Any information obtained will be used for that purpose." Also, the first time or within five days of when they communicate with you about paying a debt, the debt collector *must* send you a written notice that tells you the amount of the debt and the name of the creditor. The notice must also state

- That unless you dispute the validity of the debt or any portion thereof within thirty days after receipt of the notice, the debt will be assumed to be valid by the debt collector.
- That if you notify the debt collector in writing within the thirty-day period that the debt (or any portion thereof) is disputed, the debt collector will obtain verification of the debt or a copy of a judgment against you and will mail you a copy of such verification or judgment.
- That, upon your written request within the thirty-day period, the debt collector will provide you with the name and address of the original creditor, if different from the current creditor.

The FDCPA gives you the (very helpful) right to stop the debt collector from contacting you. You can send the debt collector a letter stating that you do not want the collection agency to contact you anymore. Send your letter by certified mail, return receipt requested. Keep a copy of the letter so that you have proof it was sent. Keep the green receipt card when it comes back so that you have proof that it was received.

After you send a letter telling the debt collector to stop contacting you, the FDCPA says that the debt collector cannot bother you, except to advise you that the debt collector's efforts are being terminated or to notify you of specific steps the debt collector intends to take.

If a debt collector knows that an attorney is representing you in connection with a debt, the collector must contact that lawyer—not you or any of your friends or neighbors. A debt collector who continues to call or send you letters is in violation of the federal law.

If you are unsure about what you are being asked to pay or if you know that it is not right, you can request that the debt collector check the debt. You must make this request in writing. This means that the debt collector must send you information about the debt they are asking you to pay. During the time the debt is being *verified* (checked), the collector may not try to obtain payment from you.

A debt collector may contact a person other than you, such as a neighbor or friend, but *only* to find out or verify where you are. In doing so, the collector must

- Give his or her name and state that he or she is confirming or correcting information to locate you. The collector may say that he or she is a debt collector and identify his or her employer but only if your friend or neighbor asks.

- Not state that you owe a debt.
- Not give or mail anything to anyone other than you suggesting that you owe a debt.
- Not communicate with the friend or neighbor more than once unless reasonably necessary.

If you have *not* sent the debt collector a letter telling him or her to stop calling you, the debt collector may continue to contact you, following certain rules. But a debt collector may *not* contact you

- At an inconvenient or unusual time (between 8 A.M. and 9 P.M. is considered to be convenient),
- At an inconvenient place,
- At your work if it is known that your employer prohibits such contact,
- If you have a lawyer and have told the debt collection agency who your lawyer is (the agency should contact your lawyer instead),
  or
- If you have written to them and told them to stop contacting you.

The law prohibits the debt collector from engaging in harassing, oppressing, or abusive conduct while trying to collect a debt. The law says that a debt collector may not

- Use or threaten violence or harm to you, your reputation, or your property.
- Use obscene, profane, or abusive language.
- Publicize the debt of particular consumers, except to a consumer reporting agency.
- Place annoying, anonymous, or repetitive telephone calls.

Additionally, the law prohibits false, deceptive, or misleading conduct by debt collectors, such as

- False, deceptive, or misleading representations of the collector's identity (for example, pretending to be an attorney or a sheriff when he or she is not).
- False representations of the amount or status of the debt and the consequences of nonpayment (e.g., falsely representing that the consumer has been sued in court and that the consumer's car will be taken away).
- Failure to disclose adequately the reasons for contacting you. In any communication that a debt collector has with you, he or she must say or write: "This is an attempt to collect a debt and any information obtained will be used for that purpose."
- Collecting an additional fee not authorized by law or the terms of the debt agreement.

185

- Misrepresenting the involvement of an attorney in collecting a debt.

The debt collector is also prohibited from using unfair or unconscionable means to collect any debt. Unfair or unconscionable conduct includes

- Threatening or taking actions to seize property when there is no right or no intention of doing so (for example, the debt collector for a hospital bill threatening to repossess a consumer's car).
- Accepting a check postdated by more than five days, except under specified written conditions.
- Charging the debtor with collect calls or telegram fees.
- Communicating by postcard.
- Collecting any amount greater than your debt, unless allowed by law.

You may sue any debt collector who breaks this law. You may be entitled to your actual damages plus $1,000 additional damages, as allowed by a court. You can also sue the collector for court costs and reasonable attorneys' fees. You have only one year from the date of the violation to file your lawsuit.

Remember, the Fair Debt Collection Practices Act is a strict liability statute. Thus the degree of the defendant's (for example, the collection agency's) culpability is relevant only in computing actual damages, not in determining liability.

On the other hand, the FDCPA does not apply to stores, banks, finance companies, or law firms that are collecting debts owed to them. Unfortunately, many people are harassed by retail stores who collect their debts owed. New Jersey does have a criminal law against harassment that may apply in serious cases. In New Jersey, intentional harassment of any kind is a crime. The law says that no person may purposely harass another by

- Making (or having someone else make) a communication during which the person making the communication (phone call or visit) fails to say who he or she is.
- Calling at extremely inconvenient hours.
- Using obscene or threatening language.
- Causing the other person annoyance or fear.
- Hitting, kicking, shoving, or other offensive touching of a person or threatening to do so.
- Engaging in any other course of alarming conduct or repeatedly acting with the purpose of alarming or seriously annoying the other person.

Intentional harassment is a petty disorderly persons offense. If you are subject to this type of harassment you can make a complaint in municipal court. Also, if you are being harassed by a creditor, you can contact the New Jersey Office of Consumer Protection. You may also want to see a lawyer. If the harassment is intentional and outrageous or if it invades your privacy, there may be grounds to sue.

BANKRUPTCY

Bankruptcy is a legal proceeding in federal bankruptcy court by means of which a person who has more debts than he or she can handle seeks relief from those debts. The federal laws regarding bankruptcy are found at 11 *U.S.C.* Section 101 *et seq.* The purpose of declaring bankruptcy is to give a debtor a fresh start in life, free of most of his or her past debts. When you file a bankruptcy petition, you bring to life an instrument of awesome breadth and power: the "automatic stay" of the Bankruptcy Code. Few other legal steps that may be taken on behalf of a consumer can bring about relief so simply, so effectively, and so dramatically. The stay halts almost all forms of civil legal actions. Among the many types of actions and proceedings affected by the stay are

- Attachments,
- Garnishments,
- Executions,
- Repossessions,
- Utility shut-offs,
- Evictions,
- Foreclosures,
- Debt collection harassment,
  and
- Almost all family-related court proceedings, including custody, divorce, and some support cases.

In addition, administrative proceedings—such as those to revoke driver's licenses, to intercept tax refunds, and to determine and collect overpayments of public benefits—are also stayed.

Notwithstanding, sometimes there are alternatives to filing a bankruptcy petition. A lawyer may be able to help you with creditors and collection agencies and try to get them to agree to a repayment plan. A consumer credit counseling service can contact your creditors and arrange for you to send them regular, affordable payments. Creditors do not have to accept the payment plan, though many do. If these alternatives are not helpful, bankruptcy is available to get you a "fresh start" if you need it.

You declare bankruptcy by filing a *petition* in U.S. Bankruptcy Court. Bankruptcy forms and pleadings can be obtained at these locations or bought at office supply stores where legal forms are sold. Once the forms have been filled out, they are filed in federal bankruptcy court. The fees for filing these documents are $175 to file a Chapter 7 straight bankruptcy and $160 to file a

Chapter 13 wage earner plan. The court may allow you to pay this filing fee in installments if you file for an application and meet certain eligibility tests. The form for this application is provided in Official Form 3. This application may not be filed, however, if you are represented by an attorney. Once you have filed your petition, you will automatically be legally protected against lawsuits, foreclosure of your home, and garnishment of your wages for a period of time. Also, creditors must stop all direct contact with you. As you already know, this is referred to as an *automatic stay.*

The bankruptcy process usually begins at a lawyer's office, but it is not necessary to have a lawyer in order to file bankruptcy. However, it is a good idea to get a lawyer to explain the basic steps of a Chapter 7 straight bankruptcy and a Chapter 13 wage earner plan, the advantages and possible disadvantages of a bankruptcy filing, and the conditions under which bankruptcy may be the wrong solution for you. It is also a good idea to see a lawyer who specializes in bankruptcy practice.

The bankruptcy law does not set the minimum amount of debts a person must have before he or she can file for bankruptcy. But there are maximum amounts set for Chapter 13 bankruptcies (for example, unsecured debts of less than $250,000 and secured debts of less than $750,000). Debtors usually decide with the help of an attorney whether bankruptcy is really necessary. Even though the law does not have minimums, many lawyers do not advise filing for bankruptcy unless the person has debts of at least $5,000. If the person owes less than $5,000, a repayment plan or plans can probably be worked out without filing for bankruptcy.

An unemployed person who does not own a home may want to wait until he or she is working before filing bankruptcy. Until you are working, creditors are unable to *garnish* your wages (take part of your wages to repay debts).

There are two ways to file for personal bankruptcy—Chapter 7 and Chapter 13 of the federal Bankruptcy Code.

CHAPTER 7. Chapter 7 (also called a *regular* or *straight bankruptcy*) is the most common type of bankruptcy proceeding. A Chapter 7 bankruptcy proceeding results in a court sale, administered by a court-appointed trustee, of all of the debtor's *nonexempt property,* with the proceeds being distributed among the creditors. However, in consumer cases this rarely occurs. All parties involved usually recognize that when such nonexempt property is of limited value the simplest method of disposition is to sell it back to the debtor, who may purchase it with exempt assets or postpetition income. On the other hand, you should note that most individuals contemplating Chapter 7 bankruptcy have only exempted property and, therefore, have no assets available to be sold to pay creditors. This circumstance does not affect the bankruptcy process or the discharge. The result of a successful Chapter 7 proceeding is a *discharge* (legal forgiveness) of bankruptcy, under which most debts will be wiped out. However, some debts—such as taxes, alimony, maintenance, and support—are not dischargeable. This means that even if you file for a Chapter 7 bankruptcy, there will be some debts you will have to continue to pay after the bankruptcy is over. You can file a Chapter 7 bankruptcy only once every six years.

CHAPTER 13. Chapter 13, also referred to as a *wage-earner plan,* is a special kind of bankruptcy available to individuals with "regular income" whose secured and unsecured debts do not exceed certain dollar limits. For bankruptcy purposes, "regular income" includes

- Wages,
- Pensions,
- Unemployment benefits,
- Disability benefits,
- Workers' compensation,
- Alimony,
  and
- Welfare.

A Chapter 13 proceeding allows you to propose a feasible repayment plan, subject to court approval. This plan sets out how you wish to reorganize your financial situation. Generally, you will agree to pay back your *secured creditors.* You will also agree to pay back your *unsecured priority creditors* (for example, claims for administrative expenses, such as attorneys' fees or trustees' fees, tax claims, alimony, maintenance, or support). You will also agree to pay your unsecured creditors as much as they would have been entitled to in a Chapter 7 bankruptcy proceeding. Needless to say, you may end up paying only twenty cents on every dollar that you owe. You generally have three years to complete the repayment plan, but never more than five. To get your repayment plan approved, your schedules' property and budget figures must show sufficient income or other financial resources to meet the payments proposed.

EXEMPTIONS. One way in which bankruptcy works to provide you with a fresh start is through the property exemptions provided in the Bankruptcy Code. The Code allows you to exempt—that is, *take out and keep*—certain property interests. However, in some instances, the Bankruptcy Code does not exempt the total value of the property in question. Instead, the Code exempts the money value (*equity*) of your property after adjustments have been made. This difference will be very important in deciding whether or not you should file for bankruptcy and in selecting which type of bankruptcy (Chapter 7 or Chapter 13) you should file.

Assuming that $15,000 is the allowable federal bankruptcy exemption for a home, let's consider the following example:

Debtor A lives in a beautiful four-bedroom, two-and-a-half-bath home with a fair market value of $100,000. He owes $85,000 in mortgages and liens on his home. Debtor B, on the other hand, owns a modest one-bedroom apartment with a fair market value of $40,000. There are no mortgages or liens on Debtor B's property. Each debtor files a Chapter 7 bankruptcy petition, and each uses the allowed $15,000 homestead exemption. Since it is only the equity (money value after adjustments) that can be exempted, Debtor A can exempt the entire amount of the equity in his house, and his home cannot be taken because he has only $15,000 in equity ($100,000 – $85,000 = $15,000). Debtor B, however, can exempt only $15,000 of the $40,000 value of his home because he has no debts against it ($40,000 – $0 = $40,000), leaving $25,000 outstanding.

One of two things would happen if Debtor B decided to file Chapter 7 bankruptcy. Either he would make an offer to the trustee in the amount of $25,000 to buy back his apartment, or the trustee would take the apartment, sell it, pay off the debtor's $15,000 exemption, and then retain the $25,000 for ultimate distribution to creditors. Given these facts, Debtor B would be better off filing for Chapter 13 bankruptcy.

Effective October 22, 1994, the Bankruptcy Reform Act of 1994 doubled the dollar amounts provided in the exemptions for the first time since 1978. In addition, effective April 1, 1998, these dollar amounts will be adjusted every three years to reflect changes in the cost of living.

The federal exemption provisions which can be claimed are as follows:

- *Homestead.* You may exempt up to $15,000 of equity in real or personal property. The exemption applies to your equity in the property, but it does not guarantee continued possession. Real property includes not only a house or apartment but also mobile homes, houseboats, condominiums, and cooperatives. You may also apply any unused amount of this exemption up to $7,500 to any other property of your choosing.
- *Motor vehicles.* You may exempt up to $2,400 of equity in one motor vehicle, including any car, truck, motorcycle, van, or moped titled to you.
- *Household furnishings.* The furnishings provision allows you to exempt up to $400 of equity in any item of household furnishings, household goods, wearing apparel, appliances, books, animals, crops, or musical instruments held for personal, family, or household use. There is an $8,000 cap on the total value of all of the individual items that you can claim as exempt under this provision. Examples of household furnishings would include linens, dinnerware, utensils, pots and pans, and small electronic equipment such as radios.
- *Jewelry.* The jewelry provision allows you to exempt up to $1,000 of equity in jewelry held for personal, family, or household use. Jewelry

includes items created for personal adornment, such as a watch. It also includes wedding and engagement rings.

- *Wild card.* The wild card provision allows you to exempt any kind of property you wish up to a value of $800. In addition, if you have not claimed the full homestead exemption, you may, to the extent of the unused amount, exempt any kind of property up to $7,500. Thus, if you do not own a home and do not claim the $15,000 homestead exemption, you may instead claim $7,500, plus $800 worth of any other property.

- *Tools of the trade.* This provision allows you to exempt up to $1,500 equity in professional books, implements, or tools of the trade.

- *Unmatured life insurance.* This provision allows the exemption of any unmatured life contract, other than a credit life insurance contract. This provision is specifically designed for those interests in life insurance owned by you that do not have a cash or loan value. Therefore, any interest in term insurance can be exempted. In addition, unmatured life insurance can be exempted, regardless of dollar value.

- *Life insurance policy.* Unlike the exemption provision presented above, this provision applies to interests in life insurance policies that do have a cash value. You may exempt up to $8,000 of the interest earned from, or the loan value of, any unmatured life insurance policy. In other words, this provision simply exempts the first $8,000 of loan value or accrued dividends in a given policy. Thus, a trustee can borrow the loan value of the policy or accrued dividends in excess of $8,000.

- *Health aids.* This provision allows you to exempt any professionally prescribed health aids for yourself or your dependents, such as wheelchairs, crutches, hearing aids, prosthetic devices, automobile modifications to accommodate a disabled person, or artificial limbs.

- *Pensions miscellaneous and public benefits.* This provision allows an individual debtor to exempt the right to receive
  —Social Security benefits, unemployment compensation, or a local public assistance benefit, regardless of dollar value.
  —Veterans' benefits, regardless of dollar value.
  —Disability, illness, or unemployment benefits, regardless of dollar value.
  —Alimony, support, or separate maintenance, to the extent the debtor and/or a dependent of the debtor reasonably needs them for support.
  —Payments under most pension plans and any payments under stock bonus plans or annuities payable on the basis of illness, disability, death, age, or length of service, to the extent the debtor and/or any dependent of the debtor reasonably needs them for support.

- *Personal insurance and public compensation.* This provision allows an individual debtor to continue to receive property or money that has been awarded because of various types of injuries or losses. Injuries or losses include

—Crime-victim reparation awards, regardless of dollar value.

—Payments on account of the wrongful death of an individual of whom the debtor was a dependent, to the extent the debtor and/or any dependent of the debtor reasonably needs them for support.

—A payment under a life insurance contract that insured the life of an individual of whom the debtor was a dependent, to the extent the debtor reasonably needs it for support.

—A payment, limited to $15,000, on account of a personal bodily injury, not including pain and suffering or compensation for actual monetary loss of the debtor or an individual of whom the debtor is a dependent.

—A payment in compensation for loss of future earnings of the debtor or an individual of whom the debtor is or was a dependent, to the extent reasonably necessary for support.

In joint cases of husbands and wives, the above amounts are doubled. In other words, each debtor is entitled to the full dollar value of his or her exempt property. By way of example, a married couple would exempt up to $30,000 on their marital residence. And each one would be allowed to exempt up to $2,400 ($2,400 + $2,400 = $4,800) of equity in one motor vehicle.

In New Jersey, where the choice between federal and state exemptions still exists, debtors are allowed to choose between a state and a federal exemption standard. However, in most New Jersey cases, the federal exemptions will be preferable to the state exemptions. Remember: New Jersey law provides no homestead exemption. There are no wild card or tools of the trade exemptions, either. Worse yet, furniture, household goods, and other personal property (except clothing) may only be exempted up to $1,000. However, in some cases the state exemptions may be preferable to the federal.

If goods were sold to you on credit with a *security interest,* you are only a partial owner of the goods even if bankruptcy is declared. Although you may not have to pay the debt, you could be forced to return the goods to the creditor. You have several choices as to what to do about this:

- In Chapter 7 proceedings, you can *redeem* the goods by paying the creditor the fair market value of the goods (that is, pay the creditor the amount the goods would sell for now).
- If you are not behind in payments, you can continue to make the payments.
- You can *reaffirm* the debt by signing a new contract promising to pay this secured debt even after the bankruptcy case is over. Nevertheless, the debt in question should not be reaffirmed in an amount exceeding the value of the collateral.
- You can give the goods back (and walk away from the debt).
- In Chapter 13 repayment plans, you can propose new payment terms.

192

If you do not take one of the above steps, the creditor may ask the court to make you give the goods back. (These remedies for goods purchased on credit should not be confused with a loan from a finance company which took the furniture you already own as collateral for the loan. These finance company loans are not secured and can be wiped out in bankruptcy court.)

If you are behind on a home mortgage or on property taxes, there is a danger of a *foreclosure* suit to take the house away from you. Filing a Chapter 13 bankruptcy can help you keep your house. If you have enough income, you can catch up on the mortgage *arrears* (late payments) through the repayment plan while making current mortgage repayments. See a lawyer at the first sign of trouble if you are in danger of losing your home.

Also, you may be able to keep your home if you file Chapter 7 bankruptcy and certain conditions are met. For example, a husband and wife who own a home may be able to file for bankruptcy without losing their house—assuming mortgage payments are made—by filing *jointly* (together) and taking the federal homestead exemption. As noted earlier, the couple will be able to exempt $30,000 worth of *equity* in their home (that part of the house for which the owner has already paid).

AFTER THE PETITION IS FILED. Once the bankruptcy petition has been filed in federal bankruptcy court, your creditors must stop calling you and must stop trying to collect what you owe. They must begin to work through the court system. The bankruptcy court will appoint a trustee. The trustee's job is to gather all your assets and all your debts and figure out whether your creditors can be paid anything. The trustee will collect everything you own that is *not* exempt.

A *Chapter 13* wage earner plan is commenced by the filing of a two-page petition. In addition to the petition, you are also required to file schedules (Official Form 6), a statement of financial affairs (Official Form 7), a disclosure of attorneys' fees, and a Chapter 13 plan. If these documents are not filed with your two-page petition, they must be filed within 15 days afterward. Once the petition has been filed, the trustee will call a first meeting of creditors perhaps twenty to fifty days after the filing. The primary purpose of this meeting will be to examine you and determine the feasibility of the plan proposed.

If no one objects to the proposed plan, in another thirty to forty days you will go before the bankruptcy judge for approval of the plan. After the judge approves the repayment plan, you can ask for permission to change the plan to increase or decrease the amount of money paid on certain debts. The procedure to change an approved plan is the same as the one used to get a plan approved.

After your plan has been completed successfully, you are no longer legally responsible for paying your discharged debts.

A *Chapter 7* straight bankruptcy proceeding commences with the filing of a two-page petition. As with Chapter 13, a number of other forms must also be filed either concurrently with the petition or within 15 days afterward. These forms include the debtor's statement of financial affairs, schedules, a disclosure of attorney's fees, and a statement of intentions. Once the petition is filed, the trustee will call a meeting of creditors (called the "341 meeting of creditors") to be held within thirty to forty-five days after filing of the petition. If no one objects, you will be asked questions by the trustee, such as why you declared bankruptcy. You may also be asked other questions about your bankruptcy petition. Your creditors will be allowed to come to this meeting, but generally they do not. About four to six months later, you will receive notice of your discharge in the mail. Once the discharge is granted, you are no longer legally responsible for the discharged debts.

However, you should note that Chapter 7 bankruptcy will *not* cancel

- Certain state and federal taxes.
- Debts you obtained by means of fraud, false pretenses, or false financial statements.
- Alimony, maintenance, and child support.
- Marital property settlement debts that you can afford to pay.
- Criminal fines and traffic tickets.
- Certain student loans (less than seven years after the student repayment period began, unless there would be undue hardship).
- Debts you forgot to include in your bankruptcy papers.
- Debts incurred through drunk driving judgments.
- Possibly Division of Motor Vehicles (DMV) surcharges (at least one bankruptcy judge in New Jersey has declared DMV debts to be nondischargeable).

Once you file a bankruptcy case, you should expect difficulty in getting credit for some time afterward. However, by the time of filing bankruptcy, most people already have "bad" credit because they have not made payments that are due. Even if you repay a debt in full, if you made any payments late that fact can remain in your credit history for seven years. Remember that no one has to lend you money and bankruptcy would be a good enough reason to reject you for a loan or mortgage. While other negative information remains in your credit file for seven years, bankruptcy may appear in your credit report for ten years. Bankruptcies more than ten years old are not allowed by law to be in your credit report. If you apply for credit and are turned down, get a copy of your credit report to verify that an old bankruptcy is no longer in your file.

After you have filed for bankruptcy, if you do get credit from someone you dealt with before you filed, make sure you are not agreeing to pay back the same debts you had discharged. This is called *reaffirmation*. Some creditors may try to get you to agree to pay them back even though your bankruptcy erased those debts.

ABOUT BANKING SERVICES

Most people need banks to conduct consumer transactions. Whether it is to cash a check, pay for an item by check, or save money safely, banks are an essential part of everyday life.

Before you agree to do business with a particular bank, you should shop around and compare terms. You should also make certain that the bank is federally insured. Generally, a bank or other financial institution that is federally insured will cover an individual for up to $100,000 in deposits if the institution fails.

CHECKS. Personal checks are called *negotiable instruments.* That means that after you write them, checks can be passed from one person to another for payment of money or something else of value. If you give a check to someone to pay for goods or services and that person then transfers it to a third person without any specific knowledge of your original transaction, the third person becomes a *holder in due course.* The holder in due course is not responsible for any claims you may have against the original seller for defective goods or services. You can still assert these claims against the original seller, but you will not be able to tell your bank to refuse to pay the check that is now in the hands of the holder in due course.

When you write a check on a bank checking account, your bank must pay that check on demand if

- There is money in the account to pay it.
- It bears a valid signature by you or your authorized representative.
- There is proper identification of the person presenting the check for payment.

If a check is made out to you or *endorsed* to you and you sign (endorse) it with your own name, you are then liable on the check to any party to whom the check is later *negotiated* (transferred for value).

Writing a check that you *know* will not be honored (cashed) by the bank can be a criminal offense in New Jersey. The severity of the offense depends on the amount of the check. So, before you make out a check, make sure you have enough money in your bank account to cover it.

Every bank is required to tell you about its policies regarding the availability of funds after you deposit them into your account. The bank must tell you when you will be able to withdraw money from your account, which will usually depend upon the type of check deposited.

Under federal law, banks are required to cash most checks in not more than ten business days.

The New Jersey Check Cashing Privacy Act took effect in March 1992. This law limits a seller's use of credit card information when accepting a check to purchase merchandise. The seller can request that you display a credit card or charge card as identification, but can record only the type of credit card or charge card and the expiration date. In other words, they cannot require that you place your credit card account number on the check.

Sometimes you may want to write a money order or cashier's check instead of a regular check. You do not need to have your own checking account with a bank in order to do so. Generally, a money order is better. You can trace it easily if it's lost or falls into the wrong hands, and you are better protected under state law.

CHECK-CASHING SERVICES. Check-cashing companies are required by law to be licensed and there are limits on what you can be charged to cash your check. Check-cashing companies cannot charge more than 2 percent of the value of the check if the check is drawn on a New Jersey bank or other state institution. If you are a recipient of welfare, you can only be charged 1 percent of the check; if you receive SSI, you can be charged 1$\frac{1}{2}$ percent of the check.

Note: Since any amount of money deducted from your check is important, using a consumer checking account in a bank is better than using a check-cashing service. With a consumer checking account, cashing a check will not cost you anything. (However, there may be other fees involved in maintaining a checking account.)

Every time you cash a check, you should be given a receipt which shows the amount of your check, the amount of the fee you were charged, and the amount given back to you. Make sure you get a copy of this receipt. Finally, if you are treated unfairly by a check-cashing company, call the Department of Banking.

ELECTRONIC FUND TRANSFERS. Modern technology allows consumers to get instant cash twenty-four hours a day from their savings or checking account. You can do this through the use of *automated teller machines* (ATMs) as long as you have a savings or checking account.

ATMs use a plastic card called a *debit card* or electronic fund transfer (EFT) card, which looks similar to a credit card. Each card has a personal code. The code is your personal number, which no one other than you and your bank is supposed to know. This code is commonly called a *personal identification number* or PIN.

The use of ATMs and EFT cards has greatly reduced the need for writing checks. You can use the EFT card to obtain money directly from your bank account. You can also use it to pay for purchases at a store. This is called a *point-of-sale* (POS) transaction. In the common POS transaction, you are transferring funds from your bank account to the merchant's account. No money or checks change hands. Everything is done completely electronically. You will be given a receipt to record your transaction. It is very important to keep track of your ATM transactions, especially withdrawals. It is easy to lose track of the number and amount of transactions, especially if you use the EFT card regularly. Remember, since the transaction is a direct withdrawal from your account, the money you wish to use must be in your account and must be available in order for the transaction to take place.

A federal law called the Electronic Fund Transfer Act (15 *U.S.C.* Section 1693 *et seq.*) provides some protections for consumers who use ATMs. Also, New Jersey's Electronic Fund Transfer Privacy Act (*N.J.S.A.* 17:16K-1 *et seq.*) contains some added privacy and security protections for consumers.

The law requires that an ATM issue a receipt each time a consumer completes a transaction. The receipt shows the date, amount of the transfer, and other information.

Your bank statement must also show all EFTs into and out of your account. It should show the date and the party to whom payment was made. The statement should include any fees that were charged for the EFT transaction. The fees charged must be disclosed to you when you open your account or when you contract for the EFT service.

As with credit cards, the law provides consumers with the right to ask banks to investigate and correct any errors with EFT. If you think there is an error on your statement from an EFT, you should do the following:

- Write to the bank where you have your account as soon as you discover the error, *but no later than* sixty days from the date the statement that has the error in it was mailed to you. Your letter should include your name, address, and account number. You should explain why you think there is an error, how much the error is, and the date it occurred. You may also call the bank or inform it of the error in person, but writing is always better in order to protect your rights.
- Within ten days, the bank must investigate and resolve the error. If it takes longer than ten days, the bank must put the money back into your account until it finishes its investigation. In any event, the bank must complete its investigation within forty-five days.
- If the bank says there is no mistake, it must explain to you in writing why it thinks there is no mistake. It must tell you if it has deducted any amount recredited to your account and that you are entitled to copies of all documents the bank relied on during the investigation.

Under New Jersey law, your bank or financial institution can disclose information about your EFT only for certain reasons:

- If you give your written permission.
- If the information is needed to resolve a dispute or complete the transfer.
- To verify the account, such as to a credit bureau.
- If it is requested by a regulatory or government agency such as the Department of Banking.
- To verify income or assets if you are applying for public assistance.

197

8. Law and the Family

This chapter discusses legal issues concerning families, beginning with a discussion of parental duties, termination of parental rights, marriage, and divorce. Other issues covered include the laws dealing with domestic violence and name changes.

New Jersey, like all states, has a large number of laws specifically affecting people as members of a family. Most laws governing family rights and responsibilities are made at the state level, rather than by the federal government. When people move from state to state, significant questions can arise as to which state's laws apply. In general, in family matters the governing law is that of the state where family members currently live. However, court orders and judgments of another state, as well as the laws of another state defining the significance of prior acts that occurred there, normally will be given full effect (called *full faith and credit*).

Most family cases described in this chapter are filed in the Family Part of the superior court; every county has at least one Family Part judge to hear cases.

RIGHTS AND RESPONSIBILITIES OF PARENTS AND CHILDREN

Parents have certain responsibilities to take care of and financially support their children. Children have only limited rights to undertake certain actions on their own until they reach majority.

CARE AND SUPPORT. When a child is born, the mother and father, regardless of whether or not they are married, are equally responsible for providing care and support. They are obligated to provide their children with food, shelter, clothing, education, and medical care. They may even be required to contribute to their children's college education. Children generally are not required to support their parents.

Parents may exercise broad discretion in raising their children, and their rights as parents will be protected as long as they are not found to harm their children. (See this chapter's section entitled "Termination of Parental Rights.") Parents have a legal responsibility to supervise and control their minor children and may be held responsible if a child willfully causes harm to another person or property.[1] Parents may also be held liable for any damage to school property caused by their minor child.[2] If a parent willfully fails to supervise his or her child, the child may sue the parent for any injuries sustained as a result. However, because the courts are reluctant to interfere with the right of parents to raise their children as they see fit, a parent cannot be held liable for injuries to a child that result from only negligent supervision of the child.

Parents' obligations to care for and support their children extend until a child is emancipated. Although *emancipation* ordinarily occurs when a child reaches majority at age eighteen, this is not automatic.[3] It can also be found to occur when the child moves permanently out of the family home, becomes employed on a full-time basis, enlists in the military service, marries, or graduates from college or graduate school.

RIGHTS OF MINORS. Under New Jersey law, children are considered minors until age eighteen.[4] A number of activities are barred to children before they reach majority. These include the rights to vote, enlist in the military, serve on a jury, marry without parental consent, adopt children, become an agent or director of a corporation, sell alcohol, consent to medical treatment, execute a will, buy or sell real property, and gamble. A minor cannot sue or be sued or inherit property except through a guardian. Although a minor can sign a contract, he or she can refuse to honor it at any time while still a minor. However, the minor must pay for any benefit received from the contract. If the minor does not void the contract, it will become enforceable when he or she reaches age eighteen.

Different age limits apply to several other activities. A driver's license cannot be obtained in New Jersey until age seventeen. The legal drinking age in New Jersey is twenty-one. A minor's right to work is also limited to certain types of work and number of hours. (See the section "Children and Employment," in Chapter 5, "You and Your Job.") When a child does work, the child's earnings belong to his or her parents.

CHILD WELFARE

Parents' rights to care for and retain custody and control of their children are fundamental constitutional rights protected by law. However, the New Jersey Division of Youth and Family Services (DYFS) may temporarily or permanently remove children from their parents under certain circumstances to protect the children. DYFS also has an obligation to provide services to families to prevent family separation and to help families reunite after separation to the extent possible. When parental rights are terminated, children can be placed for adoption.

TEMPORARY PLACEMENT OF CHILDREN. If children have been or are at risk of being abused or neglected,[5] DYFS may seek to have them placed in foster care or other out-of-home placements by requesting a court order for temporary placement out of the home[6] or accepting a *voluntary placement agreement* from the parents. When parents sign voluntary placement agreements—also called *foster home placement agreements* or *informed consent documents*—DYFS does not have to get a court order to remove the children.

By signing these agreements, parents give DYFS temporary custody of their children without any decision by the court that they have abused or neglected them. When children enter foster care through voluntary placement agreements, parents and children do not get free legal representation as they do in court-ordered placements. Nor do they have regular court reviews of their cases. Both of these can be a significant disadvantage as cases may languish and the family usually has no assistance in advocating for what they need.

If parents refuse to sign a voluntary placement agreement or if DYFS chooses not to use its voluntary placement procedure, DYFS must obtain a court order to remove the children. In emergency situations, DYFS may remove the children first and then apply for a court order the same day or the next day. DYFS must demonstrate that the children have been or are at risk of being abused or neglected in order to place or keep the children in foster care. Whenever DYFS seeks a court order to remove children from their parents, both children and parents—if they are indigent—are entitled to be represented by lawyers without charge through the Office of the Public Defender.

The court becomes involved with the foster placement of children even if the children enter foster care by voluntary agreements. Within five days of the children's out-of-home placement by DYFS under a voluntary placement agreement, DYFS must file a notice with the court explaining why the placement is necessary and what efforts were made to prevent placement.

Within fifteen days of the time DYFS files its notice, the court must either

- Approve the placement,
- Return the children to their parents,
- Ask for more information,
  or
- Set a date for a hearing.

Parents have a right to request a hearing before the judge makes a decision. Within forty-five days of the child's placement, either through court order or voluntary placement, the Child Placement Review Board (CPRB) must review each case. CPRBs are groups of private citizens that function as arms of the family court by reviewing all cases of children placed out of their homes by DYFS and making recommendations to the court. Within ten days of completing this review, the CPRB must send a written report to the judge recommending one of three things:

- Return of the children to the parents,
- Continued placement until the case goal is met,
  or
- Continued placement pending additional information from DYFS.

Case goals of the CPRB are

- Return to the parents,
- Adoption,
- Long-term foster care,
- Independent living,
  or
- Institutionalization.

Parents can *revoke* (cancel) voluntary placement agreements and ask that their children be returned to them, but revoking the agreement does not mean that they automatically get their children back. If DYFS believes that the children need to remain in foster care, it must file a court complaint within five days of the parent's cancellation of the agreement. If a parent revokes his or her agreement and DYFS brings an action against him or her to keep custody of the children because of abuse or neglect, the parent will, if indigent, have the right to an attorney.

RIGHTS UNDER FOSTER CARE. Parents with children in foster care have other rights as well:

- The right to visit with their children soon after they have been placed and on a regular basis, as long as the children are in foster care, including the right to transportation to the visits if they cannot afford it.
- The right to services to help correct the problems that are preventing them from getting their children returned.
- The right to have DYFS place the children in the most homelike environment available near the parents.
- The right to have the children placed with relatives if possible.
- The right to participate in developing a plan for the children.
- The right to be informed about the progress of the children and any change in living arrangements while they are in foster care.
- The right to be told in advance when the court or the CPRB is reviewing the case, to give information to the court or the board concerning the children, and attend any hearing concerning the children.

DYFS is required to look for family members who may be able to help care for children as soon as it places them in foster care or assumes some other type of care for them.[7] The search for relatives must start within thirty days of the DYFS placement of the child. DYFS must complete an assessment of each interested relative's ability to care for or assume custody of the child. If DYFS determines that a relative is unwilling or unable to care for the child, it must inform the relative in writing of

- The reason for the decision.

- The responsibility of the relative to inform DYFS if there is a change in the circumstances upon which the decision was made.
- The possibility that parental rights may be terminated if the child remains in foster care for more than six months.
- The right to seek review of the DYFS decision.

SERVICES TO HELP FAMILIES. DYFS is supposed to make "reasonable or diligent efforts" to keep families together. This means that DYFS must provide services to help families remain intact and to prevent foster care placement if possible. DYFS must also provide services to help families reunite in cases in which foster care placement has become necessary. In addition to providing services to help the family correct the problems that keep the children and parents apart, DYFS must help parents and children visit with each other. Children also have the right to visit with their siblings and to be placed as close to their home as possible.[8] Unfortunately, DYFS lacks the resources to perform this important function in any meaningful way.

TERMINATION OF PARENTAL RIGHTS. In certain cases, DYFS may seek to permanently terminate the rights of birth parents by filing a *guardianship petition* in the Family Part of superior court. The law governing termination of parental rights in cases involving DYFS includes some requirements about what DYFS must do for families before trying to permanently end parents' rights to their children.[9] (There are separate laws that govern termination of parental rights when children are placed privately or through an adoption agency and DYFS is not involved.) DYFS may decide to pursue the termination of parental rights on the following four grounds:

1. A parent or guardian has been convicted of abuse, abandonment, neglect, or cruelty under New Jersey's child abuse and neglect laws.
2. It is in the *best interests of the child.* This means that
   —The child's health and development have been harmed by the parental relationship and will continue to be harmed by it,
   —The parent cannot or will not fix the harm or provide a safe home for the child and it will be harmful for the child to wait longer (such harm may include evidence that separating the child from his or her foster parents would cause serious and enduring emotional or psychological harm to the child),
   —DYFS has made *diligent efforts* to provide services to help the parent, and the court has considered alternatives to termination of parental rights (such as additional services, placement of the child with a relative, or continuing foster care placement without ending the parents' rights to have contact with the child),
   and

—Terminating parental rights will not do more harm than good. (This requires the court to ensure that if a parent's rights are terminated there will be a permanent home for the child.)

3. The child has been in placement for one year and the parent has failed to change the situation that led to placement although physically and financially able to do so. The court must also find that DYFS made diligent efforts to help the parent or guardian.

4. The child has been *abandoned.* A child is deemed abandoned if the court finds that (a) the parent, although able, has not had contact either with the child, with the child's foster parents, or with DYFS for a period of six months or more and the parent's whereabouts are unknown even after diligent efforts by DYFS to locate him or her; *or* (b) the parent's identity is unknown even after DYFS has exhausted all reasonable methods of attempting identification.

Diligent efforts are those DYFS must make to help the family get back together. This means helping a parent correct the circumstances and conditions that led to placing the child in foster care, including

- Working with the parent to develop a plan to provide services to help the family reunite,
- Providing services agreed to by the family,
- Informing the parent of the child's progress, development, and health, *and*
- Providing appropriate visitation.

A petition to terminate parental rights must be filed in the Chancery Division of the superior court in the county where the child resides at the time of the petition. Unless parents surrender their parental rights voluntarily, the court will conduct a trial to determine whether or not to terminate parental rights. An attorney will be assigned to represent the children. Parents who are indigent are entitled to have counsel assigned to represent them as well. If a court determines that parental rights should be terminated, the parents will have no further responsibilities for their children and the children may be placed for adoption.

ADOPTION. *Adoption* is the creation of a new parent-child relationship. An adoptive parent must be at least eighteen years old and ten years older than the child to be adopted, unless the court finds reason to dispense with this requirement. If the adoptive parent is married and living with his or her spouse, the spouse must consent to the adoption. Before a child can be adopted, the rights of the birth parents must be terminated. There are three basic ways in which an adoption can occur: (1) after termination of parental rights by DYFS, (2) after a child has been placed for adoption privately, *or* (3) after a child has been placed for adoption by an adoption agency.

Adoptions through DYFS Child Placement. If the adoptive parents have received the child from DYFS and parental rights have been terminated, the adoption procedure is fairly simple. The adoptive parents must file a complaint in the Family Part of superior court and a hearing will be held. Unless DYFS objects to the adoptive parents, the court will usually approve the adoption.

In cases in which the birth parents place a child with an approved adoption agency, they will sign a surrender of their rights.[10] The surrender will in most cases be irrevocable. The adoptive parents must usually wait six months to file a complaint for adoption. The court will then hold a hearing between ten and thirty days from the filing of the complaint, after having received a report from the adoption agency. If the agency approves the adoption and the judge finds adoption to be in the child's best interests, the adoption will be granted.

Private Adoptions. In cases in which a party seeks to adopt a child placed privately by the birth parents, the adoption proceeding may be more complicated.[11] In this case, the rights of the child's birth parents' must be terminated. The adoptive parents must generally file a complaint within forty-five days of receiving the child in the Family Part of superior court. Birth parents are entitled to notice of the action and may object to the adoption, unless their rights have already been terminated, surrendered, or waived as set forth in the statute.[12] In this type of adoption proceeding, the court will set a preliminary hearing between two and three months from the time the complaint is filed. An agency will be appointed to investigate the parties and issue a report to the court. If the court determines at the preliminary hearing that the birth parents' rights should be terminated and approves the adoptive parents, it may terminate the birth parents' rights and set a date for a final hearing. To terminate parental rights, the court must find that the parents substantially failed to provide care and support for the child although the parents were capable of doing so, or that the parents are unable to care for the child and are unlikely to change in the immediate future.

A final hearing will then be held between six and nine months later. During this time, the investigating adoption agency will continue to observe the adoptive family and make a final recommendation to the court. If the agency recommends adoption, the final hearing can be dispensed with and an order of adoption entered. If the recommendation is not favorable, a guardian will be appointed to represent the child's interests and a hearing will be held.

In cases in which the adoptive parent is a stepparent, no investigation need take place prior to the hearing. Also, a final hearing is unnecessary when the adoptive parent is a sibling, grandparent, aunt, uncle, natural father, foster parent, or person who has had custody of the child for at least two years. Recent New Jersey court decisions[13] liberally interpreting the New Jersey stepparent exception have permitted adoptions by same-sex cohabitants to proceed, so long as the best interests of the child are promoted.

Generally after adoption, the birth parents have no right to maintain contact with the child and may only do so with the adoptive parents' permission. In some cases, birth parents have tried to arrange what is called an *open adoption,* in which the parent and child retain the right to maintain contact after adoption. Although New Jersey's adoption statute does not authorize this type of arrangement, New Jersey courts have granted ongoing contact between the child and the birth family in some cases based on the child's best interests.[14]

GUARDIANSHIP. In many instances, *guardians* must be appointed to care or make decisions for or represent children who have no parents or whose parents have abandoned them. When a guardian other than the parent is appointed, some of the rights of the natural parents are terminated.

An action for appointment as guardian of a child should be started in surrogates court. If a contest arises, it will be heard by the superior court. A guardianship application must set forth the child's age and residence and the names and residences of all close relatives or other persons who take care of the child, including the persons with whom the child lives. The court will then appoint as guardian the interested party who is best able to care for the child.

The guardian of a minor has the powers and obligations of a parent except that the guardian is not legally required to support the minor from his or her own funds. Any money received by the guardian for the minor must be used for the minor's needs for support, care, and education. The guardian must exercise care in using the minor's funds and conserve any excess funds to provide for the minor's future needs. A guardian for a minor is entitled to compensation in the same manner as a guardian of an incompetent person.

STANDBY GUARDIANSHIP. The New Jersey Standby Guardianship Law[15] was enacted in 1995 to help parents who suffer from serious illnesses, such as cancer or AIDS, prepare for their children's future when they cannot. Under this law, a parent may appoint a standby guardian—someone to "stand by" to care for the children once the parent becomes too ill or dies. A parent can do this while still able to care for his or her children and without giving up the rights as parent or custodian. The parent may also specify the situations in which the standby guardian should begin to act. The parent will still be able to have his or her children returned if he or she becomes able to care for them again. The parent's proposed guardian may also apply to be approved under this law.

There are two ways to name a standby guardian: (1) by filing a court petition, *or* (2) by filling out and signing a designation.

Court Petition. With a court petition, there is an initial court proceeding to approve the petition and a second procedure for the surrogate to confirm that the standby guardian has assumed his or her duties. A key advantage to a court petition is that an initial judicial hearing on the appointment can take place while the parent is still able to participate. Standby guardianships may be challenged in court by others with legal rights to the children. A court petition must be filed in surrogates court in the county in which the applicant lives and must state the following:

- The name, address, and qualifications of the proposed standby guardian.
- That there is a significant risk that the parent or custodian will die, become incapacitated, or debilitated as a result of a chronic condition or a fatal illness.
- Under what situation the standby guardian will act. This is known as the *triggering event* (death, mental incapacity, or debilitation) after which the guardian will begin to care for the children.

If the court finds that the proposed standby guardian will protect the children's interests, the court will appoint the standby guardian. If, however, the choice of guardian is challenged, the court will look to whether the other persons filing a challenge will be good caretakers for the children and will make its best decision.

Within sixty days after the triggering event, the proposed standby guardian begins to act as guardian of the children. The standby guardian must petition the court for confirmation. The proposed guardian is required to submit a medical determination or a death certificate for the parent. The determination, generally provided by a doctor caring for the parent, should state his or her opinion about the parent's medical condition.

If a parent changes his or her mind about the choice of a standby guardian, he or she can undo it by filing a written revocation with the court and notifying the standby guardian.

Designation. The parent or custodian may also use a designation instead of a court petition. A disadvantage to a designation is that if the parent's choice of standby guardian is challenged when he or she is not available to appear in court, that choice may not be followed. Designations are also temporary and expire after six months unless a petition is filed with the court.

A written designation form must identify the parent or legal custodian, the child, and the triggering event. It may also name an alternative guardian in case the first person named cannot act as guardian for any reason. A designation form is provided in the statute. Designations must be signed in front of two witnesses, who must also sign the designation. If the parent is physically unable to sign his or her name, he or she may ask someone else to sign for him or her.

A designation form is valid for six months from the date it is signed. In order for it to stay in effect longer, the parent must file a court petition as discussed above. If the proposed standby guardian has not begun to act as guardian, a new designation form may be signed.

206

The Standby Guardianship Law does not apply to children under the supervision of DYFS. If your children are residing in a placement by DYFS as a result of a voluntary agreement or a court order, this law does not apply to you.

GUARDIAN *AD LITEM*. In any court action, an infant or incompetent person who sues or is sued must be represented by a guardian. If there is no guardian, the court will appoint a temporary guardian or *guardian ad litem* to protect the infant's or incompetent person's interests.

Generally a child's parent(s) will act as a guardian *ad litem* merely by filing a certificate stating the parental relationship, the child's age and status, the parent's consent to act, and that there is no conflict of interest between parent and child. A petition may also be filed proposing that the court appoint a particular person as guardian *ad litem*. The proposed guardian *ad litem* will have to submit a statement to the court that he or she will act with undivided loyalty on behalf of the infant or incompetent person. Unless there is a good reason not to, the court will appoint the proposed guardian. In the absence of a parent or other proposed guardian, the court may appoint any appropriate person to serve as guardian.

A guardian *ad litem* may apply for counsel fees. The court can order one or both parties to the proceedings to pay counsel fees or can arrange for the court to pay the costs.

In addition, in all cases in which issues about child custody or visitation are involved, the judge may appoint a lawyer and/or a guardian *ad litem* for the child.[16]

MARRIAGE

A marriage contract must meet certain requirements to be valid. A valid marriage contract gives rise to certain rights and responsibilities between spouses.

MARRIAGE CONTRACTS. In New Jersey, a marriage contract is recognized only between

- A man and a woman over the age of eighteen, or under eighteen with parental consent (if a child is under sixteen, court approval must also be obtained).
- Parties who are not related by any prohibited degree, such as siblings or first cousins.
- Parties who are capable of consenting to the marriage (they cannot be under the influence of drugs or alcohol or mentally or emotionally incapable of consenting).
- People who are not already married.

In order to get a marriage license, both parties must have blood tests performed to show that they have no communicable venereal diseases. A marriage license must then be obtained in the municipality where the woman lives or, if she does not reside in New Jersey, in the municipality where the man resides. If neither party lives in the state, the license must be obtained in the municipality where the marriage will take place. The marriage license must set forth the name, age, race, birthplace, residence, and marital status (single, widowed, or divorced) of each spouse and their parents' names and counties of birth. Generally, there is a seventy-two-hour waiting period to get a license, which is then good for thirty days. A valid marriage can be performed by most judges and magistrates; by the mayor, village president, or township committee chair for any municipality in the state; or by any minister of any religion. The marriage must be witnessed by two people who must sign the marriage certificate that accompanies the license.

RIGHTS AND RESPONSIBILITIES OF MARRIED COUPLES. Once married, both parties are obligated to support each other financially. With certain exceptions, property acquired by either or both parties together during the marriage becomes the property of both spouses. If the marriage is later dissolved, any such property can be divided in an action for *equitable distribution*. Marriage also allows both spouses to receive certain benefits, such as medical, Social Security, and pension benefits previously belonging to only one of the parties. Spouses can be held liable to one another for any injuries one sustains as the result of the other's negligence or for any direct acts of domestic violence. (See the section in this chapter entitled "Domestic Violence.")

Privilege Protecting Confidential Communications. In court proceedings, spouses have certain protections from testifying. In a criminal case, the spouse of a defendant cannot testify—except to prove the existence of the marriage—unless both spouses consent or the defendant is charged with an offense against the spouse or a child of either spouse. In civil actions, spouses cannot testify about any confidential communication between them unless both consent to disclosure or the communication relates to an issue in a case between them. Communications made during the marriage are protected even after separation or divorce. However, there is no privilege for communications made *after* separation or divorce.

Ownership of Real Property. When a husband and wife own real property together, they generally own it as *tenants by the entirety*. This means that they hold the entire property jointly, and if one spouse dies, the other automatically owns the entire property. If the parties divorce, their property owned by entirety will be converted to a *tenancy in common*.

Spouses can choose to hold their property as tenants in common by specifying this in the deed. This form of ownership means that each spouse owns a one-half undivided interest in the property and the property will *not* automatically belong to one upon the death of the other. Instead, it will be distributed as required by the deceased spouse's will or the laws of *intestacy*. (See the discussion on wills in Chapter 9.)

COMMON-LAW MARRIAGE. *Common-law marriage* was abolished in New Jersey in 1939. Couples who live together in New Jersey without marrying do not take on the rights and responsibilities of marriage. On the other hand, many other states still do recognize common-law marriages. If two people have lived together in another state long enough for their relationship to be recognized as a common-law marriage in that state, the marriage will also be recognized in New Jersey.

In some cases, an unmarried couple may enter a specific agreement which obligates them to share resources or provide for one another. In cases in which both parties benefit from the agreement, the courts generally have recognized an enforceable contract at the time of separation. For example, in cases in which a man agrees to support a woman for life in exchange for her providing a home for him, courts have awarded support—or *palimony*—at the termination of the relationship.

PRENUPTIAL AGREEMENTS. Before marriage, prospective spouses may enter a *prenuptial agreement* to govern certain matters during their marriage and in the event of divorce or death. Such agreements most commonly provide for living-expense arrangements during the marriage, the distribution of property in case of death or divorce, and *alimony*.

Other issues that the parties want to agree upon prior to marriage can be included in these agreements as well. Prenuptial agreements generally are enforceable as long as they do not encourage divorce.

Prenuptial agreements are often attractive to persons who have been married before and wish to make certain their property will pass to their children from the previous marriage via living-expense arrangements and estate planning.

ENDING THE MARRIAGE

Marriages can be ended through either divorce or annulment proceedings. Often, the first step toward divorce or annulment is separation.

SEPARATION. At the time of separation, it is important for each spouse to assess his or her legal and financial situation, determine his or her needs, and take the proper steps to settle the most pressing problems as quickly as possible. Ideally, both spouses should consult lawyers to protect their rights and meet their responsibilities after separation. If spouses are able to resolve issues between themselves without litigation, their attorneys can draw up an agreement which later may become part of their divorce judgment. A judge in a later divorce proceeding is free to make a new decision on any of the issues in the agreement and is bound by the settlement agreement. However, if an agreement has been entered voluntarily by both parties and appears generally fair, it will usually be accepted by the court.

The most common pressing legal problems people face prior to divorce are temporary support and *child custody*. Both support and custody can be decided by the court on a temporary basis prior to the divorce, and later on a permanent basis.

DIVORCE. A divorce is a legal procedure to dissolve a marriage. To get a divorce in New Jersey, one party must have been a resident of the state for at least one year before the divorce is started. After the divorce is started, either party may leave the state and the divorce can proceed, as long as the parties are present for the trial date.

When a divorce is sought on grounds of adultery, the one-year residency requirement is waived. However, the plaintiff must live in New Jersey from the time he or she discovers the adultery until the divorce is commenced. Many of the grounds for divorce in New Jersey have waiting periods before a divorce complaint can be filed.

The grounds for divorce in New Jersey are as follows:

Fault Grounds
- *Adultery*—no waiting period.
- *Willful and continuous desertion* (for twelve or more months).
- *Extreme cruelty*—three months' waiting period. This includes any physical or mental cruelty that endangers the safety or health of the plaintiff or makes it improper or unreasonable to expect the plaintiff to continue living with the defendant.
- *Habitual drunkenness or voluntary addiction to any narcotic drug* (for twelve or more consecutive months after the marriage).
- *Institutionalization for mental illness* (for twenty-four or more consecutive months following the marriage).
- *Imprisonment* of the defendant for eighteen or more consecutive months after the marriage, provided that there was no reconciliation if the defendant was released before the complaint was filed.
- *Deviant sexual conduct*—no waiting period. This must be voluntarily performed by the defendant without the plaintiff's consent.

No-Fault Grounds
- *Separation.* The parties must have lived apart and in different residences for at least eighteen consecutive months with no reasonable prospect of reconciliation. Neither party argues that the other is at fault for the breakup of the marriage.

210

Filing for Divorce. To get a divorce, you must file a complaint with the Family Part of the New Jersey Superior Court. The complaint will have to state specific information, including

- The names and addresses of the parties.
- The *legal residence* of the plaintiff. (You need state only your county of residence if you are a victim of domestic violence and you want to keep an abuser from finding out where you live.)
- A statement that the parties were married, as well as where, when, and by whom.
- The specific ground(s) for divorce and a statement that any requirements for that ground have been met and that any waiting period has passed.
- The names, birth dates, and residences of any children.
- A request for custody of the children, if desired, or a request for visitation.
- A specific request for equitable distribution of all property and allocation of debts or a statement that the parties have agreed to the division of property.
- The docket numbers of any other matrimonial actions previously brought by the parties regarding divorce, custody, child support, alimony, visitation, or any other matter related to the marriage, including restraining orders under the Prevention of Domestic Violence Act.

If you have no children and no assets or debts, you may be able to handle your own divorce without a lawyer. In some counties, the county judicial Assignment or Family Part clerk's office may have forms or otherwise be willing to help you handle the paperwork. Any person involved in a divorce who has children, assets, debts, or other complex issues should seek the advice of a lawyer.

A party must bring all claims and lawsuits against the other spouse before, or at the same time, as the divorce action. Failure to do so will prevent the spouse with a claim from raising it later.

Once the complaint has been filed with the court and is returned to the plaintiff with a docket number, the defendant must be served with a copy of the complaint and a summons to appear in court or answer the complaint. The defendant has twenty days to provide a written answer to the complaint (thirty-five if he or she is out of state) and declare that he or she is contesting the case. If the defendant does not respond in writing within the time specified on the summons, the case is considered uncontested and the court may enter a default judgment against the defendant. (A *contested* divorce is one in which the defendant has chosen to defend the action and the parties have not reached a settlement.) Even if the matter is uncontested, the plaintiff must appear in court to obtain a final judgment of divorce. If the plaintiff seeks equitable distribution of marital assets or debts and no agreement has been entered, a notice must be served on the defendant with a list of the assets and/or debts to be divided and a proposed hearing date on the issue of property distribution.

211

If the case is contested, a trial will be held. At the trial, the plaintiff will have to prove the claims made in the complaint. The plaintiff will have to show that there are valid grounds for a divorce. The parties will also have to testify about the other issues to be decided by the judge including alimony, *child support*, child custody, and equitable distribution.

The Divorce Judgment. After the trial, the judge will make a final judgment on divorce, custody, support, distribution of property, and any other issues raised. At the time of the divorce, a woman who has assumed her husband's name may resume her previous name or any prior name used by her as long as she is not changing her name for fraudulent purposes.

Child support, child custody, and spousal-support decisions are never final, in the sense that they may be reopened and modified should circumstances change. However, decisions regarding equitable distribution are final at the time of divorce. If equitable distribution and alimony claims are not raised by the date of trial, they are usually considered waived and cannot be reopened.

In order to enforce a final judgment of divorce, you must have a *certified copy* of the judgment, which carries the state seal and a certification by the court clerk stating that it is a true copy. You can get this from the Family Part clerk. You will need this copy for a name change with the Social Security Administration, the Division of Motor Vehicles (DMV), and the county Board of Social Services if you are receiving any public assistance. It is an important document and should be kept in a safe place.

Out-of-State or Foreign Divorces. Before honoring another state's divorce decree, the reviewing court must evaluate whether the state granting the divorce had the power to do so. To grant a valid divorce, a court must have *jurisdiction* over the parties. This usually means that one of the parties must have lived in the state for a certain period of time. For example, in New Jersey, one party must reside in the state for one year before a divorce can be granted. A "quickie" divorce, in which one spouse travels to another state just to obtain a divorce and then returns to New Jersey, can be challenged in a New Jersey court. An out-of-state divorce may also be challenged if the party against whom the action was filed is not properly served with papers. Once a New Jersey court decides that an out-of-state divorce is invalid, the divorce decree is no longer recognized.

Sometimes divorces are obtained in foreign countries. These are not recognized as readily as other states' divorce decrees. New Jersey courts will consider not only whether the foreign court had jurisdiction to grant the divorce but also whether recognizing the foreign divorce is against New Jersey public policy. In deciding whether or not a foreign divorce runs counter to public policy, a court will look at such factors as the opportunity for the parties to be heard in the foreign proceeding and the parties' citizenship.

ANNULMENT. Contrary to common belief, an annulment is *not* a quick divorce. In order to obtain a divorce, one must show that facts and circumstances which occurred after the marriage make it improper and unreasonable to continue the marriage. In order to get an annulment, however, one must show that facts and circumstances which occurred *before* the marriage make the marriage itself invalid.

Grounds for annulment are

- *Prior marriage (bigamy).* One party had another spouse living at the time of the marriage.
- *Related parties.* The parties are related to each other to a degree prohibited by law, such as siblings or first cousins.
- *Impotence.* Either party to the marriage is unable to engage in sexual intercourse, and the other party had no knowledge of this at the time of the marriage.
- *Incapacity to consent, duress, or fraud.* Either party lacked the capacity to understand what he or she was doing because of a mental condition or the influence of alcohol or drugs, or there was a lack of mutual consent to the marriage, duress, or fraud as to matters basic to the marriage. An annulment will not be granted if the complaining party continues to live with the other party after learning of the ground for annulment.
- *Under legal age.* Either party was under eighteen years of age at the time of the marriage.
- *General equity.* An important matter, such as the intent not to have children or drug addiction, was concealed by one of the parties.

Children of parents who obtain annulments are protected under the law and are considered legitimate children. Support may be awarded to either party in an annulment. However, there is no equitable distribution of property in an annulment proceeding. In the case of real estate, the annulment complaint should request partition of that property. Residency requirements for annulments are the same as for divorces.

COUNSEL FEES. In family cases, the judge may require one party to pay all or part of the other party's counsel fees. Fees can be awarded in any action for divorce, annulment, support, alimony, custody, visitation, equitable distribution, separate maintenance, and enforcement of agreements between spouses regarding family matters. A party may be required to pay fees even if he or she was the successful party in the case. The court can make a final award of counsel fees at the end of the case or can make an award at the beginning to enable a spouse without funds to retain an attorney. This fee will be based on an analysis of the services needed.

EQUITABLE DISTRIBUTION, ALIMONY, AND CHILD SUPPORT

In a divorce proceeding, parties may be awarded property or assume debts on the basis of equitable distribution, as well as spousal and child support. The tax consequences of spousal and child support should be considered in structuring any such awards. Child support may also be awarded in a separate support proceeding against the noncustodial parent of the child whether or not the couple was married.

EQUITABLE DISTRIBUTION. *Equitable distribution* is the division of real and personal property acquired during a marriage that takes place in a divorce proceeding. It is also the division of marital debts acquired during the marriage. Division is not necessarily done on an equal basis. Instead, each case is decided individually, based on what is fair under the particular circumstances. A number of factors are considered, including the contribution of each spouse to the marriage—financially and otherwise—and the length of the marriage.

ALIMONY. Alimony or spousal support is an allowance for living expenses that one divorced spouse is ordered to pay to the other. It may be permanent, temporary, or rehabilitative, allowing the nonworking spouse the opportunity for training or education to enable him or her to be financially self-sufficient. Typically, the husband is obligated to pay alimony to his former wife. However, alimony can be awarded to the husband, also.

The court looks at several factors in deciding how much alimony to award. These include

- How much money the person requesting alimony needs for living expenses,
- How much alimony the ex-spouse can afford to pay,
- How long the marriage lasted,
- The health of the parties and their education, training, and prior work experiences,
  and
- What arrangements, if any, have already been made by the parties.

The court may also consider why the parties are getting divorced. This cannot be used to deny alimony. However, it can be used to lower the award received. For example, if a party gets a divorce based on the other party's adultery, the court may award the adulterous party less alimony than if he or she were free from fault.

Alimony generally stops when the ex-husband or ex-wife dies, the spouse receiving alimony remarries, or the claim for alimony is dropped or eliminated by court order. A payor spouse can be ordered to maintain life insurance to benefit the former spouse or, in some circumstances, to create a trust fund so that alimony can continue until the receiving spouse's death.

CHILD SUPPORT. Both parents have a legal obligation to support their children. The parent with custody of the child or children can request child support in a divorce action or file a separate complaint for child support. New Jersey has statewide Child Support Guidelines that determine each parent's proportional share of the support obligation based on the income of each.[17] A judge cannot set support at any amount he or she chooses. The judge must look at the parents' income, the number of children, and other factors listed in the guidelines and then set the amount of support based on the formula in the guidelines. In cases in which the judge finds that it would be unfair to use the guidelines, the judge must give a good reason for not using them.

Temporary Support. If married parents are separating and unable to agree about support at the time of separation, the parent with custody will need to file for temporary support so that he or she will have money for the children while waiting to get a divorce. The amount of temporary support awarded is very important because it will often be the basis upon which a judge decides the amount of permanent support at the time of divorce.

Before going to court to ask for support, the parent seeking support should draw up a record of his or her finances, including a list of all sources of income available and a complete list of expenses. It is important to gather as much documentation of expenses as possible, including receipts or canceled checks for all recurring expenses.

All child support orders are supposed to be enforced right away by wage withholding. This means that the child support is collected out of the paycheck of the parent owing child support. The support order will be paid by wage withholding unless (1) both parties agree to an alternative arrangement, *or* (2) the judge finds good cause to order an alternative arrangement.

In cases in which the order is not paid by wage withholding, the county probation office must begin a wage withholding when the payor falls fourteen days behind in support payments. Failure to pay child support may result in the interception of federal and state tax refunds; revocation, suspension, or denial of professional or driver's licenses; and even incarceration.

Modification of Child Support. Support orders must be reviewed and updated at least every three years to make sure they still comply with the Child Support Guidelines. If they differ by 20 percent or more from the guidelines, the order will be modified. However, child support cannot be modified retroactively except to the date a motion for modification was filed. Anyone with an order more than three years old can ask the New Jersey Office of Child Support to review their order. Their address is as follows: New Jersey Office of Child Support, CN 716, Trenton, NJ 08625. You may also be able to get your order changed by the court if your circumstances have changed.[18] For example, if you earn less money or your child's other parent earns more, you can file a motion in court for increased child support. If you are going to file for increased support because your income decreased, you should apply as soon as the decrease happens because reductions will *not* be retroactive to the date of the decrease in income, but only to the date you filed a motion for increased support.

TAX CONSEQUENCES OF DIVORCE. Alimony payments can be included in the gross income of the receiving spouse and deducted from the paying spouse's gross income. To be considered taxable alimony, payments must be legally required, periodic payments for spousal support made pursuant to a court order or a written agreement.

Child support payments, on the other hand, are *not* taxable. They are neither counted as part of the receiving spouse's income nor deducted from the paying spouse's income. In order to be tax free, the payments must be specifically designated as child support, either in a court order or other written agreement, and the support must be for children under age twenty-one.

CHILD CUSTODY, VISITATION, AND ABDUCTION

When parents decide not to live together, one of the most important decisions that must be made is who will have custody of the children. Also, visitation arrangements must be made for the parent who does not get custody. A number of laws protect custodial parents from having their children abducted by the noncustodial parent.

CHILD CUSTODY. Sometimes parents are able to agree about who gets custody of their children. However, the court is not bound by an agreement between the parties if is not in the child's best interests. If the parties are unable to agree or the court rejects their agreement, a custody decision must be made by a court. Permanent custody decisions are made at the time of divorce or in a separate custody proceeding. The court can also make a temporary custody award at the time of separation.

Both parents, whether married or not, have equal rights to child custody. Custody decisions are based on the best interests of the child and can be changed if circumstances change. Factors to be considered in a custody award include[19]

- The warmth, love, and affection each parent has for the child.
- Which parent can best provide the child with a stable and wholesome environment.
- The interests and values of the parents.
- The financial circumstances of the parents, especially if one party cannot meet the child's basic needs, such as food and clothing.
- The parents' history of caring for the child and any improper behavior toward the child.
- The history of domestic abuse, if any.
- The safety of the child and the safety of either parent from physical abuse by the other parent.

If a child is old enough to have an opinion, the child's preference will be taken into consideration as well.

Most of the time, the court gives custody to the parent who was the primary caretaker—the parent who actually dressed, fed, nursed, and otherwise cared for the child before the separation. Children under one year old are usually left with the mother if the mother has been the primary caretaker and has not been found to have abused or neglected the children. However, in many cases the child has been left with grandparents, the natural father, or even total strangers, and the court has allowed the child to remain where he or she was, until the court gathered enough facts to decide the case.

Temporary Custody. Temporary custody may be granted as an emergency measure, after a full hearing with both parents present. To protect the children, the court generally will try to prevent unnecessary changes until a permanent custody decision is reached. If the children are in school, the court will try to make a temporary award that allows them to stay in the same school.

Permanent Custody. Permanent custody is decided in a divorce proceeding or in a separate complaint for custody. Custody generally is decided in the county in which the child lives so that the court can have ready access to information about the child. This includes information on where the child lives, school records, other family members, and medical histories. The court will order the county probation department to conduct an investigation of the living arrangements of both parties to a custody dispute. If one party lives out of state, that state's agency will carry out a similar investigation there at the request of the New Jersey county's probation department.

If one parent claims that the other is unfit to have custody, that parent must prove that the other parent's misconduct has a direct and harmful effect on the child. The court must then decide whether the conduct complained of injured the child directly. Although some custody awards say they are "permanent," all custody awards can be changed if the circumstances of the family substantially change.

Joint Custody. Courts will sometimes divide custody between the two parents, giving *joint custody*. This works well only in certain situations.

Factors to be considered in awarding joint custody include

- Whether the children have a close relationship with both parents so that the children will benefit more from joint custody than they would from the usual custody and visitation arrangement.
- Whether both parents are physically *and* psychologically able to fulfill the role of parent and are willing to accept custody.
- The financial status of the parents, the proximity of their homes, the demands of their jobs, and the ages and number of children.
- Whether the parents can cooperate with one another.
- The children's preference, if they are old enough.

As with all custody awards, joint custody decisions can be changed if the circumstances of the family substantially change.

Interference with Custody. In some cases, parents who have lost custody of a child, or other adults who want custody of a child, have abducted the child and taken him or her to another state to either avoid or modify an existing custody order. A number of laws have been enacted to protect against interstate custody disputes. These laws require states to cooperate with each other in enforcing custody awards and promoting the best interests of children.

The Uniform Child Custody Jurisdiction Act (UCCJA),[20] which has been enacted by most states, establishes standards governing which state should decide a custody issue. Before this law was enacted, a state court would generally decide child custody cases if the child was present in the state or one parent lived in the state. That allowed for new custody decisions to be made whenever a child was taken from one state to another. Under the UCCJA, it is the child's home state or the state with the strongest connection to the child that must decide custody. A state is usually considered the child's home state if the child has lived there for the last six months. Another state can act only under emergency circumstances. Child abduction is also deterred by the federal Parental Kidnapping Prevention Act.[21] This law does several things: It requires every state to enforce proper out-of-state custody orders, it establishes a federal system to assist in locating abducted children, and it makes interstate child abduction a federal crime. A number of New Jersey's criminal laws also make parental kidnapping illegal.

VISITATION. A child has the right to know and spend time with both parents. This is called *visitation*. Because of the child's right to have both parents, visitation is rarely denied to the noncustodial parent. If it is proven that the child would be harmed or at risk in some way, visitation may be allowed only with supervision. Payment of child support and visitation are not related, and visitation privileges cannot be denied because of the failure to make support payments.

In New Jersey, grandparents and siblings have independent rights to visitation with children in certain cases.[22] A grandparent or sibling seeking visits with a child may apply to the superior court and must show that visits are in the child's best interests.

DOMESTIC VIOLENCE

The New Jersey Prevention of Domestic Violence Act[23] offers legal remedies and protections to victims of domestic abuse. The Prevention of Domestic Violence Act was written so that victims can do everything themselves, without lawyers. However, it may be important to consult a lawyer, especially if there are children or if there are issues regarding property.

The Prevention of Domestic Violence Act applies if

- The victim and the abuser presently live together or have lived together in the past (this includes lesbian and gay couples and elderly persons abused by an unrelated caretaker);
- The victim and the abuser together are the parents of one or more children or the victim is pregnant with the abuser's child, regardless of whether they have ever lived together;
  or
- The victim and the abuser had a dating relationship.

OBLIGATIONS OF THE POLICE. Under the Prevention of Domestic Violence Act, it is the primary duty of the police officer who responds to a domestic violence call to enforce the law and to protect the victim. When domestic violence occurs, a victim should immediately call the police. The victim should tell the dispatcher what has happened and *stress the emergency nature* of the situation. The police must also be told whether anyone is armed or injured.

The police are required to give victims a written notice in English and Spanish of their rights under the Prevention of Domestic Violence Act. Victims have a right to file a court complaint requesting an order restraining the attacker from further abuse and requiring the attacker to leave the household. Victims also have a right to file a criminal complaint.

The Prevention of Domestic Violence Act *requires* the police to make an arrest if a victim shows signs of injury from domestic violence or if there is probable cause to believe that the attacker has used a weapon or has violated a current restraining order. The police may also arrest a suspected abuser if there is a good reason to believe an act of domestic violence has been committed.

GETTING TEMPORARY AND FINAL RESTRAINING ORDERS. If a person has been abused, is in immediate danger, and fits into one of the categories covered by the law, he or she should be able to get a *temporary restraining order* (TRO). This is a temporary court order which may provide for one or more of the following:

- That the abuser is temporarily forbidden from entering the shared home or the victim's home.
- That the abuser is forbidden from having contact with the victim or the victim's family.
- That the victim is to have temporary possession of a car, a key, a checkbook, or other necessary items.
- That the abuser is to pay support for the children and/or emergency rental payments.
- That the victim is to have temporary custody of the children.

- That the abuser's contact with the children is to be restricted until an evaluation is done to assess the risk to the children.
- That the abuser is to repay the victim for any losses, such as moving expenses, attorneys' fees, or money spent to repair damage to the property.
- That the abuser is to pay for the victim's pain and suffering.
- That the abuser is to receive psychological counseling.
- That the abuser is temporarily forbidden from possessing a weapon.

To get a TRO, the victim may file a complaint at the Family Part of the superior court. A municipal judge must also be assigned to issue TROs on an emergency basis on weekends, holidays, and other times when the courts are closed. The police should be able to help with the emergency procedure. Normally, however, an intake worker with the court will help with the forms. In order to get a TRO, the victim must state that a specific act of domestic violence has been committed. Some of the more common examples of acts of domestic violence which qualify for a restraining order are

- *Assault.* An assault occurs when one person causes or attempts to cause bodily injury to another person (e.g., strikes, kicks, or throws something at the other person).
- *Criminal mischief.* Criminal mischief occurs when one person intentionally damages property belonging to another person (e.g., breaks down an apartment door, throws a rock through a window, or slashes car tires).
- *Harassment.* Harassment occurs when one person repeatedly contacts another at extremely inconvenient hours, in offensive language, or in another manner likely to cause alarm.

Other acts of domestic violence include homicide, kidnapping, criminal restraint, false imprisonment, sexual assault, criminal sexual contact, lewdness, terroristic threats, stalking, and burglary. If any of these crimes have been committed against a person with one of the previously described relationships to the abuser, the victim can apply for a TRO.

Within ten days after a complaint is filed, a hearing date must be scheduled. If the judge did not grant a TRO, he or she will decide whether to issue a restraining order after the hearing. If the judge *did* issue a TRO, a hearing will be held to decide whether the temporary order should become permanent. Both a TRO and a final order are enforceable throughout the state of New Jersey.

Issues of support and custody may also be decided at the time of the hearing, but often the judge will set another date for these matters. Under the law preventing domestic violence, the court will presume that the child is best off with the parent who is not abusive. If the victim has no income, that fact should be made clear to the judge with a request that support be decided at that time. (The judge cannot grant a divorce in these proceedings.)

If the abuser does not obey the terms of an order, the police should be called immediately. The abuser can be arrested and put in jail. Recent amendments to the domestic violence law also require that an abuser who violates a TRO be charged with criminal contempt of court. If an abuser is found guilty of contempt for a second violation of an order, he or she must serve a mandatory thirty days in jail.

CRIMINAL CHARGES. A criminal complaint involves charging the abuser with a crime. Once a criminal complaint has been filed, the person charged can be arrested. A criminal charge may result in the abuser being jailed and having a criminal record. The procedure for filing criminal charges varies according to the crime and sometimes from county to county. The police, court clerks, and prosecutors will be able to explain the procedures.

If criminal charges are filed, the abuser may be released from custody on *bail* or on his or her own word (*own recognizance*). The court which releases the abuser on bail may require him of her to follow certain rules. These rules are listed in a *bail order,* which, like the civil restraining order, is a legally enforceable document. The rules on the bail order may include requiring the defendant not to have any contact with the victim.

EMERGENCY SHELTERS. Many counties offer free emergency shelters for victims who feel they must leave home to be safe from abuse. Most local shelters keep their location confidential so residents will be safe from pursuit by their abusers. Over the past few years, many agencies have developed counseling services for batterers as well.

To get more information about shelters or batterers' services in your area, call either of the agencies below:

New Jersey Coalition for Battered Women
2620 Whitehorse-Hamilton Square Road
Trenton, New Jersey 08690
(609) 584-8107

New Jersey Division on Women
379 West State Street
CN 801
Trenton, New Jersey 08625
Statewide Domestic Violence Hotline: (800) 572-SAFE

NAME CHANGES

Anyone who wishes to may change his or her name simply by adopting a new name, without a legal proceeding. However, a legal name change proceeding is often advisable so that you can change your name on all of your official pieces of identification, such as your birth certificate and driver's license.

If you live in New Jersey and wish to change your name, you may file a complaint in the superior court.[24] The complaint must be accompanied by a sworn affidavit containing the following:

- Your name.
- Your date of birth.
- Your Social Security number.
- A statement that you are not changing your name to avoid or obstruct criminal prosecution, avoid paying money owed, or perpetrate a fraud.
- Whether or not you have ever been convicted of a crime or have any charges pending against you. If convictions or pending charges exist, you must provide details.

Usually, name changes are granted. As long as the judge who hears your case feels certain that no fraud is involved and that the proposed name is not ridiculous or harmful, there will not be a problem. Often, for example, a person wishes a legal name change because the person has come to be known by a name that is not on his or her birth certificate. This should be granted easily.

Sometimes, parents may wish to change the names of their minor children. If so, the parent(s) with custody can sign and file the papers on the children's behalf. It is a good idea to state why the change is desired. Many parents do this so that their children's last name will be the same as theirs. A decision about the name change will be based on the children's best interests.

HOW TO CHANGE A NAME. Once you prepare your complaint and affidavit, you must file them with the court. If criminal charges are pending, you must serve a copy of the complaint and affidavit on the state or county authority prosecuting the charges. Knowingly giving false information constitutes a crime of the fourth degree. If a child's name change is involved, the court may require that a parent who does not have custody be sent notice of the complaint at his or her last known address.

After you file your complaint, a judge will sign an order fixing a hearing date not less than thirty days after the date of the order. This order must then be published in the legal section of a newspaper of general circulation in your county at least two weeks before the hearing date. This is to allow anyone who might object to your choice of a new name to have a chance to challenge it, although such a challenge is unusual.

On the date set for the hearing, the judge will look at your papers and see if there are any objections to the change. If there are no objections and the judge thinks that the name change is reasonable, he or she will sign the order allowing you to assume the new name in not less than thirty days after the date of the hearing. Otherwise, the judge may hear testimony from you to answer any questions or objections raised. If your name change is granted, make sure to get a certified copy of the order before you leave the court. The court will forward a copy of the order to the state Bureau of Identification if you have been convicted of a crime or if there are criminal charges pending against you.

As soon as the date on the judge's order is reached, you should be known only by your new name and by no other name. Within twenty days after the judge's decision is made, a copy of the order must be published in a newspaper of general circulation in the county where you live. Within forty-five days, a copy of the order and an affidavit stating that the order was published must be filed with the deputy clerk of the superior court in the county in which the name change proceedings were heard. A certified copy of the order should also be filed with the secretary of state. You should also take a copy of your order to Social Security, the DMV, your bank, and any other agencies with which you are involved in order to obtain new identification or to have your new name put on your records. If you receive welfare, it is very important to take a copy of the order to the welfare office. You should change your will, insurance policies, and other important papers, too. In order to continue voting, you must reregister to vote. You may also need to show the order to any professional licensing board under which you are licensed, to have your new name substituted on your license.

If your name has been changed by a court, you may obtain a new birth certificate or marriage certificate by taking a certified copy of the judgment to the state registrar's office and paying a small fee.

OTHER WAYS TO CHANGE A NAME. New Jersey law provides for several other ways to change a name. If you seek to reassume your maiden name or any prior name upon divorce, that can be done in the context of your divorce action. However, while a divorced spouse's name may be changed to a maiden name or any prior name by a judgment of divorce, you *must* change a child's name in a legal name-change proceeding as outlined above. Legal name-change proceedings are also required if a divorced spouse wishes to assume a name not previously used. If a child is adopted, he or she will be known by the name proposed in the adoption complaint. If a child is born out of wedlock and his or her parents later marry, the child's last name may be changed by presenting proof of the marriage to the state registrar's office.

A person who becomes a U.S. citizen can assume a new name by proposing the new name in the Petition for Naturalization. If the judge allows the change, a decree will be issued changing the name and the Certificate of Naturalization that makes a person a citizen will be issued in the new name.

9. Securing the Future for Senior Citizens and Their Families

This chapter discusses federal and state laws of special interest to senior citizens. It provides an overview of public retirement systems and private retirement plans as well as Social Security and Supplemental Security Income (SSI) retirement benefits. It also discusses a variety of legal arrangements that can allow important decisions to be made on your behalf if you lose the capacity to make them for yourself. The chapter concludes with an outline of New Jersey law on wills and estates, topics of great importance to people of all ages, not just to senior citizens.

SUPPLEMENTAL SECURITY INCOME

SSI is a federally funded program run by the Social Security Administration to provide monthly cash benefits to low-income U.S. citizens who are sixty-five years of age or older, blind, or disabled. Most aliens are also eligible under various circumstances. The federal government runs the program and pays most of the benefits. New Jersey adds a supplemental benefit, which is included in the monthly SSI check that recipients receive. If you are eligible for SSI, you are automatically eligible for Medicaid (see the section on Medicaid in Chapter 14, "Your Right to Health Care").

ELIGIBILITY REQUIREMENTS. To qualify for SSI, you must be at least sixty-five years old, blind, or disabled. (How you may qualify for SSI on the basis of your disability is discussed in Chapter 15, "The Rights of the Disabled.")

Income. A limit is placed on the amount of income you may earn and still be eligible for SSI. You must have less countable income than the benefit amount that you would receive.

When an eligible person lives in the same household with an ineligible spouse, parent, or stepparent, the income of the ineligible person may be counted in determining the eligibility of the SSI-eligible person. Every dollar of income after deductions and exclusions reduces the SSI benefit by one dollar.

Resources. You must also show that you do not have resources in excess of certain set limits. In 1998, counted resources may not exceed $2,000 for an individual or $3,000 for a couple.

Certain resources are *exempt* or not counted toward the limit. These include the home in which you live and household goods and personal effects up to a value of $2,000.

THE APPLICATION PROCESS. Any person has the right to apply for SSI by filing an application at any Social Security office. Generally, you will complete and sign a required form. In some cases, a written statement other than the required form will be treated as an application if you later fill out the required form. In other cases, the date on which you asked about SSI will serve as an application date if you later complete the required application form. If you are physically unable to go to a Social Security office, you can apply by mail. This is done by sending Social Security a letter saying that you want to apply for SSI.

Although you may get help in filling out the application, you must sign it yourself unless you are incompetent. In that case, an authorized representative can sign the form for you. An authorized representative can be a relative, close friend, guardian, lawyer, paralegal, or institution.

At least one personal interview is always required, except if (1) you are already receiving other Social Security benefits and the Social Security office is satisfied as to your existence and identity, *or* (2) you are filing as a *representative payee* for the claimant and the Social Security office has no reason to doubt the existence or identity of the claimant.

Proof of Eligibility. When you apply, you must present information to prove that you are eligible. This may include your Social Security card, birth certificate, or citizenship papers. But if these documents are not immediately available, do not delay in filling out your application. Proof may always be submitted later, but benefits are only retroactively payable to the month of application. If evidence is not provided within thirty days of a written request for it by Social Security, the application may be denied.

There is no time limit within which the Social Security Administration must process applications. In New Jersey, the process can take up to a year.

Representative Payees. If you cannot handle your own funds, you may have your checks sent to a *representative payee.* A representative payee may be an institution (such as a social service organization), a friend, or a relative. This person must use the money to support the named recipient or in payment of his or her bills. Social Security guidelines require that (1) representative payees be "interested in or concerned with the welfare of the individual," *and* (2) their appointment be in the "best interest" of the recipient.

BENEFITS UNDER SSI. The basic SSI benefits are monthly cash benefits. In 1998, a single individual in New Jersey with no other income could receive a maximum of $515.25 per month. A couple with no other income could receive a maximum of $751.36 per month. These rates change each year. The payment recipients in New Jersey receive is higher than the federal maximum because the state supplements the federal benefit levels with a small amount of money each month. Some factors reduce benefit amounts. For example, if you live in a household with other people who pay for some or all of your living costs, your benefits could be reduced significantly unless you can prove that you intend to pay this back.

RIGHTS AND OBLIGATIONS OF SSI RECIPIENTS.   SSI recipients have certain rights and obligations under the program.

Changes in Eligibility. You must report any change in your situation to the Social Security Administration. Prompt reporting of changes may avoid overpayment or underpayment problems.

Overpayments. An overpayment occurs when a person receives payments for which he or she is ineligible or that are larger than they should be. Overpayments generally occur when a change in status or increase in resources or income is reported too late to adjust the benefit amount of the next check.

The Social Security Administration will generally try to recover overpayments. It can do this by asking you to agree to repay the money, deducting the amount of the overpayment from future payments, or suing you. It cannot recoup more than 10 percent of your countable income each month.

In certain cases, you have the right to *not* repay an overpayment. This is called a *waiver of recovery of the overpayment.* In order to get a waiver of recovery, you must be *without fault.* This means that you must not have been overpaid as a result of misinforming Social Security about your eligibility. In addition to your being without fault, one of the following must apply:

- Recovery would defeat the purpose of the SSI program,
- Recovery would be against equity or good conscience,
  or
- The amount of the overpayment is so small that its recovery would not be efficient.

If you offer to repay an overpayment, Social Security must explain your waiver rights before it allows you to make any repayment.

Social Security cannot take any action to collect an overpayment until it has first notified you in writing of the total amount due, the action being taken by Social Security, and the time allowed for bringing an appeal.

Underpayments. A change in circumstances could entitle you to more benefits. If this happens and Social Security does not increase the amount of your check as soon as a change occurs, it would owe you all benefits that should have been paid.

When you receive a smaller check than you should, bring that to the attention of a claims representative. Proper documentation of the status change must be shown in order to raise benefit levels. There is no time limit on the retroactivity of benefits when an underpayment is discovered.

APPEALING AN SSI DECISION. The procedure for appealing SSI decisions is the same as that for appealing Social Security decisions in general. See the section entitled "Appealing Disability Determinations" in Chapter 15, "The Rights of the Disabled."

SOCIAL SECURITY

Social Security is a federal program that provides benefits to workers who are disabled or who have reached retirement age, as well as to certain of their dependents and survivors. (How you, your family members, and/or your survivors may qualify for Social Security on the basis of your or their disability is discussed in Chapter 15.) Social Security benefits are financed by deductions from employees' paychecks and by employer contributions required by law.

GENERAL ELIGIBILITY REQUIREMENTS. To be eligible for Social Security benefits, you must work and pay taxes into Social Security. The maximum amount of taxable earnings in 1998 is $68,400. (Some people get benefits as a dependent or survivor on another person's Social Security record.)

As you work and pay taxes, you earn Social Security *credits*. Almost everybody who works earns four credits per year. In 1998, specifically, you will have earned one credit for each $700 in income—however, four credits is the maximum that can be earned in one year. (The amount of income needed to earn one credit goes up every year.)

How many credits you need to qualify for Social Security depends on your age and the kind of benefit for which you might be eligible. Most people need forty credits (ten years of work) to qualify for benefits. (Younger people need fewer credits to be eligible for disability benefits, or for their family members to be eligible for survivors' benefits if they should die.)

RETIREMENT BENEFITS. You must be at least age sixty-two to qualify for retirement benefits. You can get full benefits at age sixty-five. Starting with people born in 1938, the normal retirement age will gradually increase from age sixty-five to sixty-seven. The normal retirement age for people born between 1943 and 1954 will be sixty-six. People born after 1959 will get full benefits at age sixty-seven. If you start getting benefits before age sixty-five, your benefit rate will be lower to take account of the longer time you will be receiving them. The size of the reduction in benefits depends on the number of months you receive checks before you reach age sixty-five. For each month that you put off retirement past the normal retirement age, your benefit amount will be increased.

When the increase in retirement age is fully effective, a worker retiring at age sixty-two will get a benefit equal to 70 percent of the benefit amount that he or she would receive if he or she retired at age sixty-seven.

If you apply for early-retirement benefits, your checks can start no earlier than the month you apply. If you wait until after you are sixty-five to apply, you can generally receive back payments for up to six months, but not before the month you turn sixty-five.

Applying for Benefits. You should apply for your Social Security retirement checks at least two to three months before you turn sixty-five. This way, your benefits will start promptly. You can apply at any Social Security office.

When you apply for Social Security, you will need to present the following documents: (1) proof of your date of birth *and* (2) your W-2 (Wage and Tax Statement) for the past two years.

If you are self-employed, Social Security will ask you for copies of your tax returns to verify your income and as proof that you have filed tax returns for the past two years. Sometimes you may need to show a marriage certificate. If you were married before, you will need to provide information about the duration of the previous marriage. If you have eligible unmarried children, you should submit their birth certificates and a record of their Social Security numbers, if available.

In some situations, other documents may be needed, but those listed here will be enough in most cases. If you do not have the required documents, call your Social Security office to find out what other documents are acceptable.

Medicare. Even if you do not plan to retire, it is important for you to contact Social Security two to three months before you or your spouse reaches age sixty-five to arrange for your Medicare health insurance to start promptly at age sixty-five. (See the discussion on Medicare in Chapter 14, "Your Right to Health Care.") If you wait until the month you reach sixty-five or later, you will lose one month or more of Medicare medical insurance.

This is important because many private and nonprofit health insurance plans adjust their coverage when a person reaches age sixty-five to take account of Medicare coverage. You may want to get in touch with your insurance agent or the office where you pay health insurance premiums to discuss your health insurance needs in relation to Medicare protection. This is particularly important if you have dependents who are covered under your present policy. Be sure, however, not to cancel any health insurance you now have until the month your Medicare coverage begins.

Amount of Benefits. When you apply for retirement benefits, Social Security will check your Social Security record, which shows all of your earnings covered by Social Security. Social Security will then calculate your exact benefit rate. Your rate will depend on your age and amount of earnings. The higher your earnings over the years, the higher your benefit rate will be. Social Security can make mistakes; if you believe their calculations are in error, you have the right to request an audit of your record. You should file a "Request for Earnings and Benefit Estimate Statement" with the form provided for this purpose.

There is no fixed minimum rate. The maximum benefit payable to a retired worker who reaches age sixty-five in 1997 is approximately $1,326 per month. The average is approximately $629. Once you are on the Social Security benefit rolls, your check will increase automatically to keep up with increases in the cost of living.

Working after Retirement. You can continue to work after you become eligible for Social Security benefits. How much you can earn depends on your age. If you are age sixty-five to sixty-nine in 1998, you can earn $14,500 and receive all the benefits you are owed for the year. If you are under age sixty-five in 1998, you can earn $9,120. If you are over age seventy, there is no reduction.

These annual exempt amounts will increase automatically in future years to keep up with increases in average wages. If your earnings exceed the annual exempt amount and you are under age sixty-five, $1 in benefits will be withheld for each $2 of earnings above the exempt amount. For people age sixty-five to sixty-nine, $1 in benefits will be withheld for each $3 of earnings above the annual exempt amount. Starting in the year 2000, the age at which this rate applies will increase as the retirement age increases toward age sixty-seven.

SOCIAL SECURITY PUBLICATIONS. Some of the clearest and best information on Social Security can be found in pamphlets available at your local Social Security office. For descriptions, based on those pamphlets, of who else besides yourself can receive benefits and to how much they are entitled, see the boxes on the following pages.

REPORTING CHANGES TO SOCIAL SECURITY. You must report to Social Security any event that might have an effect on your Social Security (or SSI) benefit checks.

If you are receiving benefits you need to report if

- Your mailing address changes.
- You earn more than the annual limit.
- You leave the United States.
- You work outside the United States.
- You are imprisoned for committing a felony.

If your family is receiving dependents' benefits, you or your family must report any changes in your family situation that may affect your eligibility. Failure to report changes can result in Social Security making an overpayment to you. If you are overpaid, Social Security will take action to recover any benefits you were not owed. (See the discussion of overpayments in this chapter.) Also, if you fail to report changes or make a false statement, you can be fined or charged with the crime of fraud.

DIRECT DEPOSIT OF CHECKS TO YOUR BANK ACCOUNT. You can have your Social Security (or SSI) check deposited directly into a checking or savings

WHO CAN RECEIVE SOCIAL SECURITY BENEFITS

When you start collecting Social Security benefits, other members of your family might also be eligible for payments. For example, benefits can be paid to

- Your husband or wife if he or she is sixty-two years old or older (unless he or she collects a higher Social Security benefit on his or her own record).
- Your husband or wife at any age if he or she is caring for your child (the child must be under sixteen or disabled).
- Your unmarried children, if they are (1) under eighteen, (2) under nineteen but in elementary or secondary school as a full-time student, *or* (3) eighteen or older and disabled (the disability must have started before age twenty-two).

HOW MUCH IN BENEFITS FAMILY MEMBERS CAN RECEIVE. Usually, a family member will be eligible for a monthly benefit that is up to 50 percent of your retirement or disability rate—depending on how many family members are eligible. Your spouse is eligible for a share of the 50 percent rate if he or she is sixty-five or older or if he or she is caring for your minor or disabled child. If your spouse is under sixty-five and is not caring for a minor or disabled child, the rate is reduced by a small percentage for each month before reaching age sixty-five. Currently, the lowest reduced benefit is 37.5 percent at age sixty-two.

MAXIMUM FAMILY BENEFITS. There is a limit to the amount of money that can be paid on each Social Security record. The limit varies but is higher for survivor and retirement cases than for disability cases. If the sum of the benefits payable on your account is greater than the family limit, then the benefits to the family members will be reduced proportionately. *Your* benefit will not be affected.

BENEFITS FOR DIVORCED PEOPLE. If you are divorced (even if you have remarried), your unmarried ex-spouse can be eligible for benefits on your record. Your ex-spouse is also eligible for benefits on your earnings period if he or she has married a person who is receiving benefits as a widow, widower, parent, or disabled child. In order to qualify, your ex-spouse must

- Have been married to you for at least ten years.
- Be at least sixty-two years old.
- Not be eligible for an equal or higher benefit on his or her own Social Security record or on someone else's Social Security record.

If your ex-spouse receives benefits on your account, it does not affect the amount of any benefits payable to you or your other family members.

SOCIAL SECURITY SURVIVORS' BENEFITS

When you die, certain members of your family may be eligible for benefits on your Social Security record if you had earned enough credits while you were working.

The family members who can collect benefits include

- A widow or widower who is sixty years old or older.
- A widow or widower who is fifty or older and disabled.
- A widow or widower at any age if she or he is caring for a child under sixteen or a child who was disabled before age twenty-two.
- Your unmarried children if they are (1) under eighteen, (2) under nineteen but in an elementary or secondary school as a full-time student, *or* (3) eighteen or older and disabled (the disability must have started before age twenty-two).
- Your parents, if they were dependent on you for at least half of their support.

SURVIVORS' BENEFITS TO DIVORCED WIDOWS AND WIDOWERS. If you are divorced (even if you have remarried), your ex-spouse will be eligible for benefits on your record when you die. In order to qualify, your ex-spouse must

- Be at least sixty years old (or fifty if disabled) and have been married to you for at least ten years.
- Be any age if caring for a child who is eligible for benefits on your record.
- Not be eligible for an equal or higher benefit on his or her own record.
- Not be currently married, unless the remarriage occurred after age sixty—or fifty for disabled widows. (In cases of remarriage after the age of sixty, your ex-spouse will be eligible for a widow's or widower's benefit on your record, or a dependent's benefit on the record of his or her new spouse, whichever is higher.)

If your ex-spouse receives benefits on your account, it does not affect the amount of any benefits payable to other survivors on your record.

HOW MUCH IN BENEFITS YOUR SURVIVORS WILL RECEIVE. The amount payable to your survivors is a percentage of your basic Social Security benefit—usually in the range of 75 to 100 percent. There is a limit to the amount of money that can be paid each month to your survivors. The limit varies but is generally equal to about 150 to 180 percent of your benefit rate. If the sum of the benefits payable to your surviving family members is greater than this limit, then the benefits to your family will be reduced proportionately.

account in a bank or credit union. If you want to arrange for direct deposit of your checks, contact the bank or credit union of your choice and ask for a direct deposit form. Once you send this form to the Treasury Department, your Social Security benefits will be electronically transferred to your bank on the third day of each month. Your filling out the form allows deposits to be made into only your account; only you or those allowed by you may make withdrawals. If you want to stop the direct deposit of your check and have it sent to your home or somewhere else instead, notify your Social Security office. As of 1997, new Social Security recipients must have their benefits directly deposited into their bank account. As of January 1, 1999, *all* benefit checks will be directly deposited, although there may be some exceptions.

APPEALING A SOCIAL SECURITY DECISION. The procedure for appealing Social Security decisions is the same as for appealing SSI decisions. See Chapter 15, "The Rights of the Disabled."

PENSIONS AND OTHER RETIREMENT BENEFITS

Many employees are covered by pension, profit-sharing, or other kinds of retirement plans. An employer is not required to have a retirement plan; however, if your employer *does* have one, it is important to understand your rights regarding the plan. These rights are guaranteed under the Employee Retirement Income Security Act of 1974 (ERISA),[1] passed by Congress to establish uniform rules for all retirement plans maintained by private companies. ERISA does *not* cover federal, state, county, or city government retirement plans, which are subject to separate federal and state laws (discussed elsewhere in this chapter). Aside from plans maintained by employers, it may also be useful to understand how an individual retirement account (IRA) might help build retirement security.

RETIREMENT PLANS MAINTAINED BY PRIVATE EMPLOYERS. A number of different factors determine the type and amount of benefits you will collect under your pension plan.

Kinds of Plans. There are several important differences among the various types of retirement plans maintained by private employers. Perhaps the most basic difference is between *defined benefit* plans and *defined contribution* plans.

Under a defined benefit plan (which is often simply called a pension plan), the benefit you receive is based on a formula spelled out in the plan. The formula almost always takes into account the number of years you worked for the company; the formula frequently also recognizes your average earnings with the company, although this usually is not done with pension plans for union employees. Sometimes the formula takes into account the benefits you will receive from Social Security; again this is not common with union plans.

Under a defined contribution plan, the benefit you receive is not based on a formula at all but is based instead on the balance credited to your "account" under the plan. The size of your account will be determined by how much the company puts into the account (you may be able to contribute as well) and by how well the plan's investments perform. The common types of defined contribution plans include profit-sharing plans, money purchase plans, 401(k) plans, and employee stock ownership plans (ESOPs).

Another basic difference is whether the plan requires you to contribute in order to participate (a *contributory* plan), or whether employee contributions are optional or even allowed.

The third basic difference is whether a plan is managed by people appointed by the company alone, or whether it is managed by a board of trustees, half of whom are appointed by company representatives and half appointed by a union. Where there are both company and union representatives running a plan, it is usually a defined benefit plan and the benefit formula is determined by the collective bargaining agreement.

Eligibility. A retirement plan generally will not cover *all* people who work for an employer. However, plans are required to cover employees and provide benefits on a nondiscriminatory basis; that is, a plan cannot be structured in such a way as to discriminate in any manner in favor of highly compensated employees. The plan will have rules as to which employees are eligible to join the plan and—if they work long enough—receive some form of benefits. There are two basic kinds of eligibility rules: age and service requirements, and employee category limits.

Most retirement plans require that you work at least 1,000 hours per year to be considered eligible for the plan at all. All plans must make you eligible to join by the time you reach age twenty-one and have completed one year of service.

Aside from these age and service rules, a plan may also be limited to certain categories of employees. It may cover only employees working for a certain division of the company or only those who work at a particular plant or office. It may also exclude all employees who belong to a union or may cover only employees who *do* belong to a union.

Benefit Accruals and Vesting. For each year you participate in a retirement plan, you will usually earn an additional piece of your ultimate retirement benefit. (The exception would be a profit-sharing plan, in which from year to year the company may or may not make a contribution to the participants' accounts, depending on its financial condition.) The sum of the benefits you have earned up to the present time is called your *accrued benefit*, although with defined contribution plans people usually refer to their "account balances." However, to know what benefit you are actually entitled to, you also have to know whether you have become *vested* in your benefit.

To be vested means that you will receive your accrued benefit when you reach retirement age, even if you leave the company now and go to work for someone else (or stop working entirely). The portion of your accrued benefit that is attributable to your own contributions is fully vested immediately. Accrued benefits attributable to your employer's contributions must be 100 percent vested after five years of service, or within seven years if your plan uses *graded vesting*. Graded vesting means that you become vested over a period of years. Under the least-liberal vesting schedule permitted, 20 percent of accrued benefits must be vested after three years of service, with 20 percent more becoming vested each year until benefits are 100 percent vested after seven years. Some plans use *cliff vesting*, which means that you are not vested at all until you have five years of service with the company; you then become 100 percent vested all at once.

If you work in a small company where the people who own the company have more than 60 percent of the accrued benefits under the plan, the vesting schedule will be much shorter. You must either (1) become 100 percent vested after three years *or* (2) become vested in 20 percent steps from years two through six. This accelerated vesting schedule also applies to "top-heavy plans"; that is, plans in which certain "key employees" hold more than 60 percent of the accrued benefits under the plan.

Employees of large companies become either (1) 100 percent vested after five years *or* (2) 20 percent vested per year from years three through seven.

In all cases, you must become 100 percent vested in your accrued benefits when you reach the plan's retirement age, even if you have only a few years of service.

Collecting Your Benefits. There are two basic points to understand about receiving your vested benefits: *when* and *how*.

When you will get your benefits is determined by the type of plan. Although some defined benefit plans have a policy of paying out benefits within a year after an employee leaves, it is common for *no* benefits to be paid until retirement age, even more if an employee leaves at a much younger age. However, many defined benefit plans provide for early-retirement benefits, which you may receive as long as you have at least ten or fifteen years of service and have reached age fifty-five or sixty. If you take early retirement you will typically receive a lower benefit than normal because the full benefit will not have accrued by your early-retirement date and will have to be paid out over a longer period of time.

With a defined contribution plan, such as a profit-sharing or 401(k) plan, it is much more common for an employee to receive the vested account balance within a year after leaving, regardless of his or her age. However, a defined contribution plan *may* provide that benefits will not be paid until retirement age.

How you will receive your benefits is also usually a function of the type of plan. Under a defined benefit plan, your accrued benefit is an *annuity,* or a right to receive a certain dollar amount each month from retirement age until your death. If you are married, your benefits will be paid as a *joint and survivor annuity,* which means that monthly payments will continue for as long as either you or your spouse is alive. The plan will usually reduce the dollar amount of monthly benefits with a joint and survivor annuity to reflect the fact that benefits are likely to be paid for a longer time. You and your spouse may elect for you to receive an annuity for your life only if you think that will be financially advantageous.

Under some defined benefit plans, particularly in smaller companies, you may elect to receive the value of your accrued annuity benefit in a single lump sum, either when you leave or when you reach retirement age.

With a defined contribution plan, the most common form of benefit is a single lump sum payment equal to your vested account balance. Some plans also offer an installment payment option: You are allowed to withdraw your account balance in roughly equal installments over a number of years. With certain types of defined contribution plans (called *money purchase* and *target benefit* plans), you must be given the option of having the plan use your account to purchase an annuity contract from an insurance company. The annuity contract will pay monthly benefits for your life, or for your and your spouse's life if you are married.

You will have to fill out one or more forms to receive your benefits. These forms may give you an opportunity to select when and/or how your benefits will be paid. They will also deal with the taxes on your benefits (see the next section) and what options you have about paying the taxes.

If you think you are not receiving benefits that you are owed, you should find out from the company what the plan's *claims procedure* is. This will let you know what steps you should follow to file a formal claim for the benefits you believe you should get. There are strict rules under ERISA about how the company must handle your claim, including giving you a written explanation of why benefits are not being paid and allowing you to appeal that decision.

Taxes on Benefits. The benefits you receive under a retirement plan are generally fully subject to income taxes, except to the extent of your own after-tax contributions to the plan. Some states, such as New Jersey, provide a limited exemption for retirement plan benefits. If your benefits are paid to you in a single lump sum, there are very complex rules involving possible use of pre-1987 lump sum tax rules, five-year averaging, and gains on employer stock held by the plan. In addition, a lump sum benefit may be "rolled over" into an IRA to postpone any tax obligation until you start withdrawals from the IRA; this is frequently the best thing to do with a lump sum because of the tax deferral. These rules will be explained in a notice from your employer. You will probably want the help of an accountant or tax lawyer for more information.

Getting Information. The most important source of information about your employer's plan is the *summary plan description* that must be given to each participant within ninety days after entering the plan. This should explain all of the basic information you need to understand how you will earn benefits under the plan and when you will receive them. You should also receive a *summary annual report* each year providing some financial information about the plan. If the company does not automatically distribute an *annual benefit statement,* you may ask the company to tell you what your annual accrued benefit is each year and when you will be vested, if you are not already.

IRAS. An IRA is a personal savings plan to set aside money for your retirement that offers you tax advantages not available for regular savings accounts. You can set up an IRA with several types of organizations. Most banks and similar savings institutions, mutual funds, stock brokerage firms, and insurance companies offer IRAs that meet Internal Revenue Code requirements.

In a traditional IRA, you may be able to deduct contributions to your IRA in whole or in part, depending on your circumstances, so that (generally) amounts in your IRA, including earnings and gains, are not taxed until distributed to you after a certain age. Your ability to deduct your contributions to a traditional IRA depends on your income and whether you pay into a pension plan at work. If you do *not* have a pension plan at work, you can invest up to $2,000 a year in an IRA without paying any taxes on it. If you have a spouse who does not work, you can set up a separate IRA for your nonworking spouse. The combined contribution to the two IRAs cannot exceed $2,250 a year. You can divide the contributions to the two IRAs in any way, provided that no more than $2,000 is paid into either account. You *cannot* set up one IRA that you and your spouse own jointly. Spouses must file a joint return to get a deduction for their contributions. If both you and your spouse work but neither of you has a pension plan at work, you can each invest up to $2,000 in separate, regular IRAs without paying any taxes on the amount contributed. If you are covered by a pension plan, you can get a full or partial deduction only if your adjusted gross income is below a certain amount.

There is also a new kind of IRA called a Roth IRA, which will allow you, if you have income below certain limits, to contribute up to $2,000 annually, whether or not you have a pension plan. Contributions are not tax-deductible, but the earnings will not be taxed until distributed to you if the IRA has been open for at least five years.

FEDERAL AND STATE PENSIONS

ERISA does not cover federal or state pensions. Separate laws indicate who can join, when vesting occurs, and how much in benefits participants can receive. Generally, people covered by federal or state pensions receive more money than those with private pensions who have had equivalent earnings.

FEDERAL PENSIONS. The federal government has a number of different pension programs. This section discusses the two pension systems that cover most full-time civilian employees. The first one covers employees who were hired before January 1, 1984.[2] The second one covers employees hired on or after that date.[3] The reason that there are two systems is that employees hired on or after January 1, 1984, pay into and are covered by Social Security. Also, the old federal pension was the United States' third-largest entitlement program. The new pension program will cost less and give lower benefits.

Hired before January 1, 1984. Eligible employees (permanent full-time employees) are required to contribute 7 percent of their annual pay. Federal employers contribute the same amount. To receive a pension, a federal employee must work in civil service for at least five years.

Generally, federal employees may receive a full pension at

- Age fifty-five, with thirty years of service,
- Age sixty, with twenty years of service,
  or
- Age sixty-two, with five years of service.

However, the rules vary depending on the type of work and the circumstances under which you leave your job. For example, police officers and firefighters can retire at an earlier age with fewer years of service.

A federal employee's pension depends on his or her average pay (the average of his or her highest three years of pay multiplied by a percentage based on years of service). Employees get a 1½ percent credit for each year up to five years; 1¾ percent credit for each year between five and ten years; and 2 percent for each year after ten years. The limit is 80 percent of average pay. An employee on a disability pension receives at least 40 percent of his or her average pay. Employees who retire before the age of fifty-five *and* who receive certain kinds of annuities will have their pensions reduced. A federal employee's pension will be reduced to provide an annuity for a surviving spouse, unless the spouse waives this right in writing. (There are special rules for former spouses and marriages after retirement.) There are also cost of living increases.

A surviving spouse is a person who was married to the federal employee for at least nine months or is the mother or father of the employee's child or children. A child is a person dependent on the employee for support; unmarried; and either age eighteen, between eighteen and twenty-two but a full-time student, or over eighteen but not self-supporting because of a disability that occurred before the child was eighteen. Spouses and children can get 55 percent of the federal employees' benefits. A child's benefits will vary according to the number of children. There is a minimum payment for employees who die with at least eighteen months of service.

Hired on or after January 1, 1984. Employees covered under the old pension program were given until December 31, 1987, to join the new program. Employees covered by the new program contribute less money since they are also paying into Social Security. Federal employers still contribute.

Employees are still eligible for an unreduced pension at age sixty with twenty years of service and at age sixty-two with five years of service. However, the age fifty-five, thirty-year annuity has been gradually increased to begin at age fifty-seven. A supplemental annuity will be paid to employees who retire at age fifty-seven with thirty years of service, age sixty with twenty years of service, and age sixty-two with five years of service, until they are eligible for Social Security. Federal employees who have served eighteen months may still receive a disability pension.

The new pension system calculates the amount of the pension based on average pay multiplied by a percentage determined by years of service: 1 percent until the employee has served at least twenty years and is sixty-two years old; the percentage then increases to 1.1 percent.

The new law created a "thrift savings plan." Federal employees can contribute up to 10 percent of their pay every year. The federal employer will match the employee's contributions in varying amounts up to 5 percent. Members of the old system can contribute up to 5 percent of pay, but the federal employer does not have to match the contributions.

The new pension system lowers a surviving spouse's benefits. A surviving spouse of an employee who served eighteen months receives $15,000 plus 50 percent of the employee's pay. The spouse will receive 50 percent of the employee's annuity only if the employee served at least ten years.

Applying for a Pension. The Office of Personnel Management (OPM) handles federal retirement applications. If the OPM turns down your application, you must first ask the OPM to reconsider its decision. If the OPM reconsiders and still turns down your application, you can file an appeal within twenty days to the Merit Systems Protection Board (MSPB). If the MSPB upholds the OPM's decision, you can then appeal to the court of claims or a federal court of appeals. The federal court will review the decision but in a very limited manner.

Health Insurance. There are two ways of maintaining health insurance after retirement. Employees who retired before 1960 are covered by the Retired Employees Health Benefits Plan. Either the federal government contributes money toward private health insurance or the employee is covered under a special plan. Employees who retired after 1960 can continue their health coverage by permitting the OPM to make deductions from their checks.

NEW JERSEY PENSIONS. New Jersey's state pension programs include statewide retirement systems and county and municipal pension programs. The three largest pension programs are the Public Employees Retirement System (PERS),[4] the Teachers Pension and Annuity Fund (TPAF),[5] and the Police and Firemen Retirement System (PFRS).[6]

The New Jersey law against discrimination forbids the mandatory retirement of most public and private employees. An employer can force an employee to retire only if the employer can show that the retirement age has a strong relation to the type of employment or if the employee cannot do the job. This law applies to tenured teachers. However, it does not apply to police officers or firefighters. State police officers can be forced to retire at age fifty-five. Other PFRS members must retire at age sixty-five.

This section discusses some of the main features of the PERS, the TPAF, and the PFRS. Generally, the TPAF and PERS have the same requirements and give the same benefits; the PFRS has special rules.

Membership and Contributions. Most full-time state employees must join PERS, the PFRS, or the TPAF, depending on which plan covers them. When you begin working for the state, you will fill out a pension application. This is processed by the Division of Pensions, which runs all of these programs.

Each state employee contributes to his or her pension through payroll deductions. The amount you pay depends on your age when you start working for the state. The older you are, the higher the deduction will be. Your employer also contributes to the pension system. Each year, you will get a statement from your employer showing how much you have contributed.

If you leave state employment before you are eligible for a pension, you can ask to receive your contributions back. You will receive interest on your contributions from the TPAF and PERS if you worked for more than three years.

Retirement Pensions. Retirement pensions are based on how long you worked and how much money you earned. You have several options for about deciding when to retire. You can retire from the PERS or the TPAF at age sixty, regardless of how many years you have worked. Both plans have Class A and Class B members, depending on how they contributed to the plan and when they joined. At retirement, Class A members receive a *total allowance* (an annuity as well as a pension) in the amount of one-seventieth of their *final compensation* for each year of service. Class B members receive one-sixtieth of their final compensation for each year of service. Final compensation is defined as the average annual salary for your three highest-earning years.

You can retire with an allowance from the PFRS at age fifty-five. Your total retirement allowance from the PFRS will be the greater of one-sixtieth of your average pay for any three years multiplied by your years of service, or 2 percent of your average pay for each year of work up to thirty years and 1 percent for each additional year.

If you are a member of the PERS or the TPAF with ten years of service, you can leave your job before age sixty and get a deferred pension when you reach retirement age. Ten-year members of the PFRS can do this at age fifty-five. Your pension will be calculated the same way as discussed above. You can leave by your own choice or involuntarily, as long as you were not fired for misconduct.

In the TPAF and PERS, you can retire after you have served twenty-five years and receive a pension immediately. If you have reached the age of fifty-five, your benefits will be calculated the same way as described in the first section above. Otherwise, your benefits will be reduced by ¼ percent for each month that you are short of reaching age fifty-five. The PFRS also has a special retirement program for members with twenty-five years of service. That provides for a retirement allowance of 65 percent of final pay, plus 1 percent of final pay for each year of service between twenty and thirty years. Members who reached thirty years of service before July 1979 also get an additional 1 percent for each year of service over thirty years.

Filing for Benefits. In order to receive benefits, you must file an application. The application must be approved by the board of trustees that runs your plan. About six months before you retire, you should make a "request for estimate." The Division of Pensions will then tell you approximately how much you will receive under the different options discussed below.

The surviving spouse and children of a retired PFRS member automatically receive an annuity equal to a certain percentage of the member's pension. This is not true for survivors of retired PERS or TPAF members. If you are a member of the PERS or the TPAF, you have several options. You can choose a full pension for life, leaving nothing to your survivors when you die, or you can choose to take a lower pension during your life with continued payments to your survivors after you die. If you choose this type of pension, a number of payment options to your survivors are available. If you elect to receive full payment during your lifetime, you will have to sign a form stating that you understand that your survivors will *not* receive benefits after your death. The Division of Pensions will also notify your spouse of your choice.

Health Insurance. All three pension systems let you keep up your health insurance when you retire if you agree to pay monthly payments from your pension check.

Appeals. You can dispute any pension decision made by your program's board of trustees by filing an appeal within forty-five days of the decision. Your case will then be heard by an administrative law judge (ALJ) assigned by the Office of Administrative Law. The ALJ will make recommendation to the board, which will then review its original decision and accept, reject, or modify the ALJ's decision. A final decision of the board of trustees can be appealed to the superior court, Appellate Division.

GUARDIANSHIP

In many instances, *guardians* must be appointed to care and make decisions for, or represent, an incompetent elderly person. (Guardianship for children is discussed in Chapter 8, "Law and the Family"; guardianship for the developmentally disabled is discussed in Chapter 15, "The Rights of the Disabled.")

GUARDIAN OF AN INCOMPETENT PERSON. A person is considered legally incompetent when—due to mental or physical disabilities, chronic alcoholism, drug abuse, or other causes—he or she is unable to manage his or her affairs. New Jersey law states that when an individual is proven to be legally incompetent, the court will appoint a guardian to act on his or her behalf.[7] This differs from a commitment proceeding that may result in the confinement of an individual to an institution for necessary treatment. (See the section entitled "Involuntary Commitment" in Chapter 14, "Your Right to Health Care.")

THE INCOMPETENCY PROCEEDING. Before a guardian can be appointed, a court must make a determination that the person is incompetent. An incompetency proceeding must be started in New Jersey Superior Court, Chancery Division, Probate Part, in the county where the incompetent person lives. The action is usually started by a relative, a friend, or an agency with responsibility for the incompetent person. A complaint must be accompanied by affidavits from two doctors describing the person's condition and stating that the person is unable to take care of himself or herself or manage his or her affairs. The complaint must also contain a description of the person's property and its value. If the papers justify proceeding with an incompetency action, the court will order that notice of a hearing be served on the incompetent person, his or her family, and any other concerned parties. The court will appoint a lawyer to represent the incompetent person. If the court determines that the individual is incompetent, a guardian will then be appointed. Generally, the guardian will be a close relative. However, if there is no one close to the incompetent person willing or able to act as guardian, the court may appoint someone else. One person is usually appointed as guardian of both the person and the estate, although the court may appoint separate guardians for each.

Once a person is adjudicated to be incompetent, he or she loses control over his or her affairs and the guardian can make all personal and financial decisions for the incompetent person (the *ward*). The guardian may decide where the ward will live and gives consent for medical or other professional care. The guardian must also manage the ward's property and use it to provide for the ward's support, maintenance, education, and general use and, if necessary, to support the ward's dependents. Once adjudged to be incompetent, an individual loses the power to make such decisions for himself or herself and other important rights, such as the right to marry and to enter contracts.

A guardian is entitled to be compensated from the ward's estate. He or she may take 6 percent of all income received and a certain percentage of the estate each year. If unusual services are provided, the court may allow additional compensation.

Guardianship continues until the ward regains competency or dies. To regain competency, the ward or someone on his or her behalf must file a complaint in superior court to begin a court proceeding in which the ward must be proven once again capable of managing his or her affairs.

GUARDIAN *AD LITEM*. An incompetent person who sues or is sued and is not represented by a guardian will have a court-appointed temporary guardian (guardian *ad litem*) to protect the incompetent person's interest. A guardian *ad litem* may be appointed for a person who is alleged to be incompetent without medical evidence of incompetency or an incompetency proceeding.

A petition may be filed proposing that the court appoint a particular person as guardian *ad litem*. The proposed guardian *ad litem* will have to submit a statement to the court that he or she will act with undivided loyalty on behalf of the incompetent person. Unless there is a good reason not to, the court will appoint the proposed guardian. In the absence of a proposed guardian, the court may appoint any appropriate person to serve as guardian.

A guardian *ad litem* may apply for counsel fees. The court can order one or both parties to the proceedings to pay counsel fees or can arrange for the court to pay the costs.

PUBLIC GUARDIAN. New Jersey has a public guardian who can be appointed to serve as guardian for people over age sixty who have no family members or friends willing or able to serve as their guardian.[8] Any person or agency with responsibility for the elderly person may petition the court to have the public guardian appointed. The public guardian may be given broad or only limited powers to act on behalf of the elderly adult.

CONSERVATORSHIP

A person who has not been found incompetent by a court but who— because of age, illness, or physical infirmity—cannot manage his or her affairs may have a *conservator* appointed to manage his or her property.[9] A conservatorship is a voluntary arrangement and cannot be imposed if the conservatee objects to it. It is a much less restrictive form of substitute decision making than a guardianship. A conservatorship proceeding is filed in superior court by the person in need of a conservator (the *conservatee*) or by a relative, a friend, a local social services agency, or the head of an institution that services the conservatee. The complaint must state the conservatee's age and residence; the names and addresses of all relatives; and the nature, location, and value of all property of the conservatee. Notice of a conservatorship proceeding must be served on the conservatee (unless he or she files the action); the conservatee's spouse, adult children, or closest relative; and the person with whom the conservatee lives. A hearing will then be held. The conservatee must be present, unless he or she is physically unable to appear. The court may appoint an attorney to represent the conservatee in this proceeding. Other concerned parties may also testify at the hearing. The conservator can be either an individual or a financial institution. The court must give first priority to the conservatee's choice of appointee.

A conservator is responsible for using the conservatee's estate and income for the conservatee's support, maintenance, education, and general use, as well as for the needs of any dependents and for investing the conservatee's income. These responsibilities can be limited or expanded by the court. The conservator must file annual reports or accountings with both the conservatee and the court.

A conservatorship will end when the conservatee dies, is adjudicated to be incompetent, or upon an application by the conservatee for termination. A conservator receives compensation in the same manner as a guardian of an incompetent person.

ADVANCE DIRECTIVES

The New Jersey Advance Directives for Health Care Act[10] allows you to make advance decisions about health care in the event that you become incapacitated and lose *decision-making capacity.* You lose decision-making capacity if you lose the ability to understand and reach a decision on the benefits and risks of proposed medical treatment (for example, if you become permanently unconscious without any capacity to interact with the environment or other people).

Advance decisions can include the decision to accept or reject life-sustaining treatment. Thus, while still competent, you can direct that you be allowed to die and that life-sustaining treatment that would otherwise keep you alive in a vegetative state should be withdrawn.

TYPES OF ADVANCE DIRECTIVES. There are three types of advance directives that you can give: (1) a proxy directive, (2) an instruction directive, *or* (3) a combined directive.

In a *proxy directive,* you name a health care representative to make medical care decisions for you in the event that you lose decision-making capacity. Any competent adult can serve as your health care representative, except a person who works at the health care institution where you are a patient, unless that person is related to you.

In an *instruction directive,* you give written instructions directing the type of treatment that you want if you lose decision-making capacity.

In a *combined directive,* you name a health care representative and at the same time give written directions to that person.

Your advance directive must be signed and dated in the presence of two adult witnesses or signed before a notary public or an attorney. Your advance directive may be changed by written notification or by a subsequent directive. This subsequent document must also be signed in the presence of two adult witnesses or before either a notary public or an attorney. A directive can be canceled at any time. You can do this by telling your health care representative,

243

physician, nurse, or other health care professional verbally, in writing, or by any other act that shows your intent to cancel the directive.

An advance directive takes effect when it is given to your attending physician or health care institution or when it is determined that you lack the ability to make a health care decision.

The determination that you lack the ability to make a decision must be made by your attending physician. It must then be confirmed by a second physician.

You may direct life-sustaining treatment to be withdrawn. Life-sustaining treatment is defined as any medical device or procedure—including artificially provided fluids and nutrition, drugs, surgery, or therapy—that uses mechanical or other artificial means to sustain, restore, or supplant a vital bodily function, thereby prolonging your life.

If you so direct, life-sustaining treatment may be withdrawn under the following circumstances:

- When you are permanently unconscious according to your own and a second, qualified physician.
- When you are in a terminal condition according to your own and a second, qualified physician.
- When your treatment is experimental and not a proven therapy, or is likely to merely prolong an imminent dying process.
- If none of the above applies, when you have a serious irreversible illness and the likely benefit from the medical treatment that is to be withdrawn is outweighed by the harm of the treatment, or if the treatment on an unwilling patient would be inhumane.

WILLS

Even if you have no property or assets, it may be a good idea to have a will. The *executor* you designate will oversee your estate, pay your bills, and make funeral arrangements. You can state in your will that your executor may serve without buying a bond. This can save money from your estate. You can also name a guardian for small children or appoint a trustee for money left to them. But you should be aware that naming a guardian in your will does not supersede the parental rights of a surviving parent. (See Chapter 8, "Law and the Family.")

PROBATE PROPERTY AND NONPROBATE PROPERTY. Not all of your property can be disposed of by a will. *Probate* property can be disposed of by a will but *nonprobate* property cannot. Life insurance and the proceeds of retirement plans are common forms of nonprobate property. When you die, these assets will go to the beneficiary you have designated in the policy or plan, regardless of whether or not you have a will and what the will directs.

244

Real estate, bank accounts, and securities held as joint tenants with right of survivorship will go to the survivor, regardless of what the will says. In New Jersey, a husband and wife usually own their home jointly as *tenants by the entirety.* This means that when one spouse dies, the home goes to the other.

Real estate, bank accounts, and securities *held in your name alone* are examples of probate property.

PREPARING TO MAKE A WILL. Before you prepare your will, you should review your assets and liabilities to know approximately what your estate is worth. You should then decide how you want to divide your property. Generally, specific pieces of property or amounts of money are given to named family members, friends, or institutions, and then the remainder of the estate is given to a designated person or group of people. However, you may choose not to include minor items of personal property in your will. Instead, these can be listed in a *letter of instructions* to the executor. This will avoid your having to change your will later if you happen to change your mind about someone to whom you were leaving a piece of personal property, or if you decide to sell a piece of property listed in the letter of instructions.

The executor named in your will is responsible for ensuring that your assets are properly disposed of and that all taxes are paid and other legal requirements are met. Whether it is a relative, a friend, or your lawyer, the executor should be a person you feel can carry out the task responsibly and who is likely to be available at the time of your death. Because handling the estate requires time, you should consider naming someone who lives near you. A family member or close friend probably can handle a simple estate easily enough. A will should also name a substitute executor so that you will not have to rewrite your will if something happens to the person named as executor.

WILL REQUIREMENTS. Anyone who is eighteen years of age or older and of sound mind may make his or her own will. There is no requirement that an attorney write a will (you can write your own in your own handwriting); however, it is a good idea to have a lawyer prepare the document if your estate is large and if tax advice is necessary. A person not licensed as an attorney is *not* allowed to prepare a will for another person.

You and at least two witnesses must sign the will. Witnesses must be over the age of eighteen and *competent* (of sound mind). You must sign the will with the witnesses watching and then the witnesses must sign. If you cannot sign your name, you may mark it with an X or have someone else sign it for you in your presence; however, the witnesses must state on the document that even though you could not sign your name, they saw you sign an X or someone held your hand while you signed.

The purpose of having witnesses is so that they can testify that the will was properly prepared and signed when it is *probated.* When a will is probated, it is filed with the surrogates court. The surrogates court determines whether or not the will is genuine and legally acceptable.

To avoid the need for witnesses to come and testify later about the validity of your will, you should make your will *self-proving*. To make a will self-proving, the person making the will (the *testator*) and the witnesses must each sign a self-proving affidavit that the testator is over eighteen, of sound mind, and voluntarily making the will. These statements must be signed before a notary public or an attorney. A will can be made self-proving either at the time it is written or any time after it is prepared.

If you handwrite your own will, it need not meet all the formal requirements for a will. This is called a *holographic* will. Although you do not need witnesses, it is a good idea to have two witnesses to make your document more credible. You may want to make this type of will if there is an emergency and you need to have a will prepared quickly. Otherwise, it is important that your will be properly prepared and signed. If it is not done as required by law, it will not be valid and your property will be distributed as if you did not have a will.

AFTER YOUR WILL IS WRITTEN. Your attorney, if you have one, and your executor should each be given a copy of your will. You should keep the original in a safe place where it can be found upon your death. Your safe deposit box is a very good place to keep the original, or you may ask your executor to keep the original in his or her own safe deposit box so it will be easy to find after your death.

You can change or cancel your will in several different ways. A will can be canceled by being destroyed or torn up. A will can also be canceled if you write a new will that is different from the first. The most recent will is the one that controls how the property is distributed.

You can change your will without writing a new one by adding a *codicil* to your existing will. This is a provision stating the changes you want to make in the original will without including all the provisions that are still in effect. A codicil must be signed and witnessed in the same way as the will, although the witnesses can be different people. It should then be kept with the will. Merely writing changes on the margins will not cause the changes to be made and may, in fact, invalidate part or all of the will. Do not write on the will or remove any of the staples or the binder holding the will together.

Under New Jersey law, children born or adopted after a will is written who are not provided for under the will, will receive the share of the property that they would get if there were no will at all.

If someone receiving property under your will dies before you do, the property he or she would have inherited may go to his or her descendants, unless you provide otherwise in the will. If there are no descendants, the property passes to the *residuary legatee*, the person named in the will who is to inherit the rest of the property after all the other heirs receive their specific

246

legacies. If there is no such person named, the leftover property will be divided up as though there had not been a will.

YOUR SPOUSE'S RIGHT TO YOUR PROPERTY. Your surviving spouse has the right to take one-third of your *augmented estate* regardless of what your will stipulates. The rules on what is included and what is excluded in this augmented estate are complicated, and you will probably need legal advice to figure it out. For example, property you give away within a certain time period *before* your death may be considered as part of your augmented estate.

If you do not provide for your spouse in your will or leave less than one-third of your augmented estate to your spouse, he or she can elect instead to take a one-third share of the augmented estate. This is true even if you intended to leave your spouse out of your will or if you transferred property to your spouse instead of providing for him or her in the will. Your spouse will not be eligible for this *elective share*, however, if you are separated at the time you die.

If you are divorced or your marriage is annulled, any provisions of your will giving property to your former spouse are automatically canceled.

DYING WITHOUT A WILL. If you die without a will, your probate property will be distributed under New Jersey's laws of *intestacy* and automatically pass to your spouse, your descendants, or your parents—persons you may or may not have chosen, in shares you may or may not have chosen.

ESTATES

If you have a will, your executor must apply to the surrogates court for probate of the will. Your executor is then required to distribute your estate to those people named in your will. If you die without a will, an application must be made to the surrogates court for letters of administration. The surrogates court will appoint an administrator to distribute your property as required by New Jersey's laws of intestacy.

SURROGATES COURT. The surrogates court consists of a surrogate who is elected by the voters of the county for a five-year term, a special deputy surrogate, special probate clerks, and other employees who assist the surrogate.

The application for probate of a will or for letters of administration is filed with the surrogates court of the county in which the *decedent* (dead person) was living at the time of death, unless the person was not living in New Jersey in which case the application is filed in the surrogates court of any county where the decedent had property. The surrogates court may only perform routine and nonadversarial administrative functions. The surrogates court cannot act if there is any dispute. In cases in which the surrogates court may *not* act (contesting a will, cases of doubt, and the like), the New Jersey Superior Court, Chancery Division, Probate Part, will resolve the matter. Any interested person must file a complaint with the New Jersey Superior Court, Chancery Division, Probate Part, by filing it with the surrogate in his or her capacity as deputy clerk of the Chancery Division, Probate Part.

If the surrogates court has already probated a will or issued letters of administration, any person adversely affected may file a complaint with the Chancery Division, Probate Part, seeking review of the surrogates court's action.

PROBATING A WILL. Under New Jersey law, a will cannot be probated until ten full days after death. The executor of the will is not required to post a bond with the surrogates court if the will states that no bond is required. The executor is required to sign an affidavit saying that he or she will administer the estate according to law. The executor must also give the surrogate a *power of attorney.* This allows the surrogate to accept court papers if someone sues the estate and personal service upon the executor is not made. The surrogates court then mails a copy of the papers to the executor at the address given in the power of attorney.

An executor serving under a will can sue and be sued as a personal representative of the decedent. If the decedent's death was wrongfully caused by someone else, the executor can sue that other person.

Sometimes a trustee is named in a will or the will makes it necessary to appoint a trustee (for example, if money is left in trust for minor children with delivery of the money to be made when the children reach maturity). In such a case, the potential trustee must file a sworn, written acceptance of the trusteeship. The trustee must also give a power of attorney to the surrogate.

After all the necessary steps have been completed, the surrogates court admits the will to probate and gives the executor documents known as *letters testamentary,* which authorize the executor to administer the estate.

PROCEDURES AFTER THE WILL IS PROBATED. Within sixty days from the date that the will has been probated, the executor must mail all beneficiaries a copy of the will. The executor must also mail all beneficiaries, the decedent's spouse, heirs, and next of kin, a notice that the will has been probated and the date and place of probate. If the will gives property to a charity, a similar notice and copy of the will must also be sent to the attorney general of New Jersey.

The executor is under an immediate duty to collect the property of the estate. The executor must also learn what the debts of the estate are and pay the decedent's debts out of the estate. Funeral expenses and *administration expenses* take precedence over all other debts. Administration expenses include lawyers' fees and all costs reasonably incurred by the executor in administering the estate.

248

In order to find out how much debt the estate has and to settle the estate as soon as possible, the executor may get an order to *limit* creditors of the estate. This requires the executor to publish a notice to creditors in the local newspapers that they must present their claims to the executor within six months of the date of the order. The order must also be mailed to each creditor of the estate known to or ascertainable by the executor. A creditor's claim must specify the amount claimed and the reason for the claim. If a claim is not presented within six months, the executor will not be liable to the creditor if there are insufficient assets to cover the claim.

It is also the duty of the executor to prepare and file the last income tax return for the decedent. This return is due at the same time the decedent would have had to file had he or she lived. Generally, a joint return may be filed in the case of a married decedent for the year of his or her death.

ADMINISTERING ESTATES WHEN THERE IS NO WILL. In some counties an application for administration of someone's estate without a will (*intestate*) may be made at any time after death. In others, application may not be made until five full days after death.

There is no need to wait the ten days required for proceedings involving a will.

If the decedent was married, the spouse has first right to apply to surrogates court for *letters of administration,* which authorize an administrator to administer the estate. If there is no surviving spouse, the right to administer the estate then goes to the next of kin in order of degree.

A person applying to administer the estate must ensure that no other competent adult with an equal or greater right to administer the estate seeks letters of administration. It is enough to prove that sufficient notice of the application was given to all such persons.

If none of the heirs is willing to serve, then any other person may apply to become administrator. If no one files for administration within forty days after the death of the intestate person, the court may grant letters of administration to any fit person. Sometimes that person is the funeral director or other creditor.

The application in an intestacy proceeding is almost identical to the application that is filed in a proceeding with a will. It is also necessary for an administrator to file a power of attorney with the surrogates court.

Before letters of administration will be given, an administrator is required to sign an affidavit saying that he or she will perform the duties of administrator. The administrator is also required to give a bond as security for the benefit of creditors and relatives. The amount of the bond, in most cases, must cover all personal property. Thus, the amount or value of cash, jewelry, bank accounts, stocks, bonds, cars, etc., are considered in fixing the size of the bond.

The procedures for distributing assets and terminating an estate when no will was left are essentially like those involving a will, except that the distribution of property is made according to New Jersey's laws of intestacy. There are some special rules for small estates.

ESTATES OF LIMITED VALUE. If the total of all the real and personal property of an intestate person does not exceed $10,000 and there is a surviving spouse, the spouse is entitled to all the assets free from the decedent's debts, up to $5,000. In such a case, the spouse does not need to file for letters of administration. Instead, an affidavit may be filed in surrogates court stating that the person is the surviving spouse and that the real and personal assets are not worth more than $10,000. The surviving spouse will then have all the rights, powers, and duties of an administrator. The affidavit must also specifically identify all of the individual pieces of property, stating where they can be found and their value. It must also say where the decedent resided at the time of his or her death. The spouse is entitled to take only the property listed. If additional property is discovered later and if the total exceeds $10,000, an application for letters of administration must then be made.

If there is no surviving spouse and the estate is worth $5,000 or less, the next of kin may follow this same procedure. However, in this case the decedent's assets are distributed to all next of kin and creditors.

TAXES. Both federal estate taxes and state inheritance taxes may be payable from an estate.

Federal Estate Taxes. The federal estate tax is a tax that is based on the value of the estate of a decedent at the time of death. The property that is taxed includes not only real and personal property but can also include legal rights a decedent had with respect to property. The value of property up to $600,000 is exempt from federal estate tax.

In most cases there will be no tax due nor will a federal estate tax return need to be filed. Various deductions and credits may reduce the taxable estate below the level at which a tax must be paid.

State Inheritance Taxes. The New Jersey Transfer Inheritance Tax is imposed on the transfer of real and personal property valued at more than $500. Unlike federal estate tax, the New Jersey inheritance tax is imposed on the value of the property transferred, not on the value of the estate. This tax applies to property transferred at death by will or under the laws of intestacy and, under certain circumstances, may also apply to property transferred by the decedent by deed, sale, or gift within three years *before* the decedent's death. The amount of the inheritance tax depends upon the value of the property transferred and the relationship of the property's *transferee* (recipient) to the decedent. Transfer to Class A beneficiaries, including spouses, children, parents, grandparents, and grandchildren are tax exempt. Transfers to other beneficiaries are taxed at rates from 11 to 16 percent.

10. You and Your Car

This chapter discusses your rights and responsibilities as a car owner and driver. It will also help you decide what to do if you buy a defective car or need car repairs.

BUYING A CAR

You should find out as much as possible about the car you are interested in before you buy it. It is a good idea to take a mechanic or someone who knows about cars with you when you shop for a car. Both federal and state laws protect you in buying new or used cars.

ADVERTISING. A car dealer is not supposed to mislead you about the cars he or she has for sale. One common trick is the *bait and switch,* in which the dealer advertises one car and then tries to sell another or to sell a car at a higher price than advertised. Bait and switch practices are illegal. If the dealer does not deliver the car you ordered, you can refuse to accept it. (See Chapter 6, "Protecting You as a Consumer.")

ODOMETERS (MILEAGE). Federal law[1] gives you the right to know how many miles a used car has been driven. It is against the law for car dealers and private sellers to turn back the odometer to make it look as if the car has less mileage on it than it really does.

A used-car seller must give you a signed certification telling you the mileage on the car and whether he or she knows if the mileage is incorrect. If the odometer has passed 99,999 miles, the dealer must state this on the form.

A repaired or replaced odometer that cannot be adjusted to show the true mileage must be set to zero. The dealer must attach to the left door frame a sticker giving the true mileage before repair or replacement, and the date of the repair or replacement of the odometer.

If a used-car seller has turned back the odometer and hidden the true mileage, you may be able to sue the seller for three times the amount of damages, or $1,500, whichever is greater, plus attorneys' fees and court costs. There are also criminal penalties and fines for violating this law.

You can check the real mileage by asking for copies of each Certificate of Title on the car from the Division of Motor Vehicles (DMV). Every time the car is sold, the mileage must be recorded.

DEFECTIVE CARS. You have several options if you buy a defective car.

Rejection and Revocation. If you buy a car and the seller delivers a car other than the one you ordered or a car with major defects, you have the right to reject it. You should immediately tell the seller that you will not accept the car, and demand your money back. If you accept the car, drive it away, and later discover that it has a major defect, you have a right to *revoke acceptance.* If you revoke acceptance within a reasonable time after you discover the defect (a few days is likely to be considered a reasonable time), the effect is the same as a rejection. If you return the car, the dealer is obligated to return your money. It is usually a good idea to consult a lawyer if you decide to revoke acceptance. (See Chapter 6, "Protecting You as a Consumer.")

If the car you purchased is new, it will be covered by New Jersey's Lemon Law for two years after delivery, or the first 18,000 miles, whichever comes first.

Warranties. A *warranty* is a promise or agreement that an item will work well for a specific period of time. (See the discussion on warranties and defective products in Chapter 6, "Protecting You as a Consumer.") There are two types of warranties: those written and those implied by law. Even if you don't get a written warranty in your contract, the law also gives you an *implied* warranty (i.e., the dealer who sold you the car makes an implied promise that the car will run).

Different warranties may apply, depending on whether you buy a new or used car. For example, a new car usually will have a written warranty covering at least the first 12,000 miles or the first twelve months you own the car, whichever comes first. Some new-car manufacturers give warranties for a longer period. Anything covered by the warranty that fails to work must be repaired for free during the warranty period.

When you buy a used car, the dealer may give you a written warranty. A dealer's written warranty must tell you

- How long the warranty lasts.
- Whether it includes service or labor charges.
- What parts are included in the warranty.
- Whether parts will be replaced or repaired or the cost refunded to you, and whether it's up to the dealer to decide which to do.

Under New Jersey law,[2] a dealer must also guarantee that a used car will pass inspection. However, you are responsible for taking the car through inspection. If the car fails inspection, the dealer must make repairs for free or give you your money back.

A sales contract for a used car may try to avoid this dealer obligation by saying that the dealer does not guarantee that the car will pass inspection. If you sign a contract containing such a statement, you are giving up your rights and the car may require major repairs (at your expense) before it will pass inspection.

The law does not require a private person who sells you a car to fix it if it fails inspection. There are no implied warranties in car sales made by private individuals. You are buying the car "as is," unless you get a written warranty. A written warranty should say exactly what the seller promises to do, and for how long.

Before you buy a used car, the dealer must put a window sticker called a *buyer's guide* on the car. This sticker will tell you if there is a written warranty or if the car is sold *as is*. Any warranty terms must be described, and it is illegal for the dealer to tell you that there is a warranty when there is none. In addition, if a dealer knew of defects in the car before the sale but did not tell you about them or lied about the car's condition, the dealer may be guilty of fraud. However, if the car has defects, the dealer does not have to *write them down* even if he or she knows what they are.

The words "as is" are a dealer's attempt to get you to give up your warranty rights, and you should not agree to them. But if you get stuck buying a car "as is," see a lawyer. You may be able to avoid the effect of the "as is" clause. You may still be able to revoke acceptance, for example.

A written warranty from the dealer or manufacturer is a contract that you can enforce. If something goes wrong after you accept the car, notify the dealer right away. If the dealer fails to fix it after a reasonable number of attempts, you can sue the dealer under the warranty.

New Jersey's Lemon Law. New Jersey's Lemon Law gives consumers certain rights in relation to defective new cars and motorcycles, whether leased or sold.[3] The Lemon Law covers vehicles purchased or leased in New Jersey, regardless of where the vehicle is registered. The Lemon Law requires the *manufacturer* (not the dealer) of a new car to repair all defects that substantially impair the car's use, value, or safety, if reported within the first 18,000 miles of operation, or within two years of delivery, whichever is earlier. You must pay for the repairs if they are made after one year, or 12,000 miles—whichever is earlier—unless they are covered by a manufacturer's warranty. However, you may recover these costs if you win in a subsequent action under the Lemon Law.

If the manufacturer (or a dealer on its behalf) is unable to repair a defect within a reasonable time, you are entitled to a refund of the full purchase price you paid plus other charges and fees. However, you may, if you wish, accept a manufacturer's offer of a replacement car. You should keep all repair receipts and a complete record of all contacts with the manufacturer and dealer. Also, send all mail certified, return receipt requested, and keep the original documents.

Under the Lemon Law, a new car is presumed to be a "lemon" if it has a defect that still exists after three repair attempts or after it has been out of service for twenty calendar days. That is, there is a legal presumption that the manufacturer cannot fix your car if there are three unsuccessful repair attempts (or twenty days in all out of service) within the first 18,000 miles of operation, or during the two-year period from delivery, whichever is earlier.

You are entitled to a statement from the dealer or lessor acknowledging your rights under the Lemon Law. If you have a dispute with a manufacturer, you may (1) use the manufacturer's informal dispute settlement procedure, (2) submit the dispute to administrative proceedings at the Division of Consumer Affairs, *or* (3) file an action in superior court.

Administrative proceedings under the Lemon Law are very speedy. Disputes submitted to the Division of Consumer Affairs for resolution are referred to the Office of Administrative Law for a hearing before an administrative law judge (ALJ). The hearing will be held within twenty days of the date your application was accepted; the ALJ will submit his or her recommended decision to the Division of Consumer Affairs within fifteen days of the hearing. This recommended decision will be deemed to be the final decision of the Division of Consumer Affairs unless the division accepts, rejects, or modifies the ALJ's recommended decision within ten days. (The division has recently proposed legislation which would give it more than ten days to accept, modify, or reject the ALJ's decision.) The manufacturer will be liable for penalties of $5,000 per day if it does not comply with the final decision of the Division of Consumer Affairs. Both the manufacturer and the consumer may appeal a final decision to the Appellate Division of the superior court.

A consumer who prevails in any action in the Division of Consumer Affairs or superior court will be awarded reasonable attorneys' fees and costs. If you ask for and win a full refund of the purchase price of your car, the refund will include any credit for your used car, the cost of options installed on the new car within thirty days of delivery, sales tax, license and registration fees, finance charges, and reimbursement for towing and rental of a substitute car, minus an allowance to the manufacturer for your use of the new car.

If a car is returned to a manufacturer because it is defective, the manufacturer can resell the car but only under certain conditions. Consumers who later buy the car must be told in writing that it was defective. On a separate piece of paper, the consumer must be given the following notice:

> This vehicle was returned to the manufacturer because it did not conform to the manufacturer's warranty and the nonconformity (defect) was not corrected (fixed) within a reasonable time as provided by law.

The Lemon Law also requires that any vehicle that is returned to the manufacturer because it is defective must say so on the Certificate of Title. This statement must be clear and easily readable and must remain on the Certificate of Title each time the vehicle is sold or transferred. If you think you have bought a defective car, you can telephone the Lemon Law Unit for a recorded message on how to proceed. You can also write to the Division of Consumer Affairs, Office of Consumer Protection.

The Used-Car Lemon Law covers passenger motor vehicles that are transferred from the original buyer. It does not cover commercial vehicles, motorcycles, motor homes, or off-road vehicles.

It is illegal for a used-car dealer to

- Misrepresent the mechanical condition of a used car (in other words, tell you it runs great when it does not).
- State that the car is free from mechanical defects unless the dealer has a reasonable basis for believing this statement.
- Fail to tell you about the existence of any written warranty, service contract, or repair insurance, before you agree to buy the car.
- Misrepresent the terms of any written warranty, service contract, or repair insurance.
- Misrepresent that a used car is being sold with a warranty when, in fact, it is not.
- Fail to give you a clear written explanation of what "as is" means before selling you a used car "as is."

The law states that a used-car dealer must provide you with specific warranties for *certain* used cars. However, the law also excludes other categories of used cars sold by dealers for which the dealer is *not* required to give you a warranty. These latter categories include used cars that

- Are sold for less than $3,000.
- Are more than seven years old.
- Have more than 100,000 miles.
- Have been declared a total loss (commonly referred to as "totaled") by an insurance company, *if* the consumer has been told that the car has been totaled.

Any warranty required to be given under the Used-Car Lemon Law must be given to you at or before the time of the sale. However, even if the dealer fails to give you a written warranty, the dealer will nevertheless be deemed to have given you one, unless you have signed a waiver.

Provided that a used car is covered under the Used-Car Lemon Law, the warranty period shall be extended to include the time for the dealer or his agent to begin or complete repairs of a covered defect.

If the dealer does not repair the defect during the warranty period after having a reasonable opportunity to do so (i.e., three times for the same defect or a total of twenty days), the dealer must give the consumer a refund. The refund will be the full purchase price excluding sales taxes, title or registration fees, or any other similar charges. The dealer will also be entitled to subtract from the refunded purchase price a reasonable allowance for excess wear and tear plus a deduction for personal use (the mileage you put on the car).

CAR REPAIRS

When you buy a car, you may want to purchase a service contract to cover future repairs. You should also know your rights with regard to car repairs.

SERVICE CONTRACTS AND EXTENDED WARRANTIES. Sometimes a car dealer will try to sell you a service contract or an extended warranty. Whereas most warranties are part of the sale and come with the car, extended warranties cost extra. Whether they are worth the extra cost depends on how much they cost and how much you get.

Some of the problems people have with service contracts are as follows:

- These contracts sometimes cost hundreds of dollars. Ask how likely it is that the repairs on your car would cost that much during the service contract period.
- Some service contracts cover only repairs to certain parts of the car. Make sure you understand which parts are covered and which are not before you decide to buy a service contract.
- Even if the needed repair *is* covered, some contracts require you to pay a deductible cost. If the repair costs less than the deductible, the contract does not pay anything.
- Some contracts may require you to have all work done by a certain shop, such as the dealer's. If their work is poor or their hours or location are inconvenient, you are stuck with them.
- Some contracts duplicate free protection you already have under a manufacturer's or dealer's warranty.

GETTING MECHANICAL REPAIRS DONE. New Jersey law requires that repair shops post visible notices telling you about your rights.[4] You have the right to be honestly informed of what work needs to be done. The repair shop is required to give you copies of all papers you sign. Remember to get them and hold on to them in case you have any problems.

The repair shop must write a work order, which you must sign before work can be started. The work order should describe the problem or the work to be done. The repair shop must also give you one of the following types of written estimate, unless you waive your right to receive one:

- A written estimate of the maximum the repairs may cost.
- A written estimate of the parts and labor needed to fix the car and their separate costs. (You may be charged for labor to find out what the problem is, if you agree in advance to pay that charge.)
- A written estimate to do a specific repair.

You should not waive your right to get a written estimate.

If you bring the car in outside of normal working hours, the repair shop can get your verbal permission to fix the car. It must be noted on the authorization form that you gave verbal permission. The repair shop must get your permission before starting any work that was not included in the estimate (*N.J.A.C.* 13:21-21.11). Make sure you find out how much any additional work will cost *before* giving approval.

The repair shop cannot charge you more than the original estimate for any additional work done without your permission. You should be given a clear copy of the invoice for all work done. The invoice must list all work done and the costs for all parts and labor. If any parts were replaced, the invoice must say whether they were new, rebuilt, used, or reconditioned.

If any of the parts are guaranteed, the repair shop must give you a written warranty or guaranty that explains exactly what parts are covered and for how long. Any repair shop that does not do so is violating the New Jersey Consumer Fraud Act.[5] If you have problems with a car repair shop, call the New Jersey Office of Consumer Protection.

If you do not pay a car repair bill, an auto repair shop can take a *non-possessory lien* on your car.[6] If an auto repair shop keeps your car or says it will sell your car if you do not pay your bill, you should see a lawyer. The auto repair shop has no right to take your car before giving you an opportunity to have your case heard by a judge.

AUTO BODY SHOPS. Auto body shops are licensed by the state. Any auto body shop not licensed is breaking the law and can be fined or shut down. A body shop convicted of fraud or padding a bill could lose its license and be fined. Each body shop must post a notice advising customers of their rights to file a complaint with the New Jersey Department of Insurance.

Auto body shops are required to give consumers written estimates. Estimates must list the parts necessary for each repair, with the approximate cost for each part, and indicate which are not new parts. An estimate must also contain the labor charge for each repair and a promised date of delivery, plus the terms and limits of any guaranty for the repair work done.

STATE MOTOR VEHICLE LAWS

State laws and regulations govern who can drive, and set rules that drivers must obey.

DRIVER'S LICENSES. Most of New Jersey's drivers have the choice of either a photo driver's license or a paper license without a photograph. Both must be renewed every four years. Photo licenses are required for drivers aged seventeen to twenty-one and persons obtaining their first New Jersey driver's license. The charge for a photo license is $18. The paper license costs $16.

MOTOR VEHICLE VIOLATIONS. The privilege of driving carries with it an obligation to comply with a variety of driving laws. Infractions of motor vehicle laws
may result in different types of penalties.

The Point System. If you violate a motor vehicle law, you may get a
ticket or a summons from a police officer. The summons will direct you either
to plead guilty and pay a fine or to contest the charge in municipal court. If
you go to court to challenge the ticket, you and the police officer who gave
you the ticket will each have an opportunity to present your side of the story.
The judge will then make a decision as to whether you must pay the fine. If
you have to go to court to answer a summons, you should bring any witnesses
who can support your side of the story. Depending on the charges against you,
you may want to talk with a lawyer.

The DMV adds *points* to your driving record when you are convicted of
a moving violation. The more serious the violation, the more points you are
given. (You can receive a complete list of the points given for violations from
the DMV.)

When you receive six or more points on your driving record, you will get
a written notice warning that you are approaching the twelve-point limit. If
you receive twelve or more points, you will be notified that your license will
be suspended. The length of the suspension will depend on the number of
points you have accumulated. The shortest suspension period is thirty days.

Up to three points will be subtracted from your point total for every year
that you go without a violation or suspension.

Motorists who incur six or more points in a period of three years or less
are also subject to an insurance *surcharge* of $100 for six points, plus $25 for
each additional point. This surcharge is payable for three years. The surcharge
remains in effect as long as a motorist has six or more points on his or her
record for the immediate past three-year period. Failure to pay results in
indefinite suspension of all driving privileges.

Point reductions granted under the point system are not considered in
reviewing the three-year record for insurance surcharge purposes.

You may be allowed to attend a DMV driver improvement course in place
of all or part of a suspension. You must attend each session of the program. If
you fail to successfully complete the program, your license will be suspended
for the time period in the notice of proposed suspension. If your license has
been suspended, you may be required to attend and successfully complete a
DMV driver improvement program in order to have your driver's license
restored. There is a fee of $100 for attendance at a driver improvement
program.

The DMV can require any person who is licensed to attend a probationary driver program whenever the driver accumulates two or more violations.
If the probationary driver program is not successfully completed, the driver's
license can be suspended. This program also has a fee of $100.

258

If your license is restored after a suspension and you break any state motor vehicle laws within a year, your driving privileges will be suspended again. The length of suspension will depend on how soon the violation occurs after restoration.

If you drive during a suspension, your loss of driving privileges may be extended for six months or for a period decided by the DMV. If the DMV discovers, after your license is restored, that you drove during the suspension, your license may be revoked or suspended for six months. The DMV may also suspend your vehicle registration for driving during a suspension. Some motor vehicle convictions also result in fines or annual surcharges to the driver.

Appealing Fines, Suspensions, and Surcharges. If you think the DMV has made a mistake in calculating your points or surcharge, you can appeal. The DMV must refer the case to the Office of Administrative Law, which will schedule it for a hearing before an ALJ. You have a choice of either appearing before an ALJ for a hearing, or asking that the judge decide your appeal by reviewing the written record and documents. The record can include such things as a person's driving record and evidence of motor vehicle convictions or suspensions. The appeal has to be based on the way the surcharge was calculated or on the accuracy of the driving record; you cannot challenge the original moving violation conviction at this time.

The director of the DMV has the final authority to overturn or modify an ALJ's ruling. If the director of the DMV ultimately rules against you, you can then appeal your case to the Appellate Division in superior court. You must file your appeal within forty-five days.

Penalties for Drunk Driving. If you are found guilty of driving under the influence of alcohol or drugs, you can lose your license, be fined, or even face a jail sentence. You can also lose your license or be fined if you refuse to take a chemical test after being stopped for driving under the influence.

Breath tests measure a driver's blood-alcohol content on a machine called a Breathalyzer. A driver arrested for drunken driving has no legal right to refuse to take a breath test. Your refusal to take a test can be used as evidence that you knew you would have failed the test. A driver who refuses to take a breath test can still be convicted for drunken driving based on other evidence. For example, many police departments make videotapes of an arrested driver doing simple tests, such as finger-to-nose touching and walking heel to toe.

In addition to the court-imposed fines and penalties, anyone arrested and convicted of *driving while intoxicated* (DWI) who refuses to take a chemical test is subject to an insurance surcharge of $1,000 a year for three years for a first and second violation. A surcharge of $1,500 for three years will be imposed if a third and subsequent violation occurs within three years of the first violation. If a drunk-driving conviction and a conviction for refusal to take a test arise out of the same arrest, only one of the convictions is sur-charged.

Failure to pay the surcharge will result in indefinite suspension of all driving privileges. The surcharge will be imposed regardless of whether the offense occurs in New Jersey or some other state.

Out-of-State Convictions. Out-of-state convictions, suspensions, and revocations are given full effect in New Jersey. Two points are added to your driving record for any moving violation committed in another state. New Jersey regularly exchanges information with other states.

Seat Belt Law. New Jersey drivers and front-seat passengers who do not buckle their seat belts can be fined $40 plus court costs. The police cannot stop you solely on the basis of suspected seat belt violations; you must be stopped for some other suspected violation in order to be charged with the secondary offense of failing to wear seat belts.

The law does not apply to cars built before July 1, 1966, or to taxicabs, buses, trucks, or cargo-carrying vans. The law also does not apply to people with a doctor's note stating that they are unable to wear a seat belt for physical or medical reasons.

There are special safety requirements for children under five years of age. A child under eighteen months old must be placed in a restraint system similar to an infant car seat held in place by seat belts. A child eighteen months to five years old must sit in a rear seat wearing a seat belt. If a rear seat is not available, the child must use a restraint system in the front seat. If you violate this law, you can be fined up to $42.

Unpaid Parking Tickets. If you have many unpaid parking tickets, you could lose your driver's license or face other penalties. Municipal court judges can enter a default judgment against anyone who fails to pay a fine or appear at a court hearing for traffic or parking violations. The judgment must be entered within three years of the date the ticket was issued. Once the judge has acted, local parking officials can proceed to collect any unpaid fines from a person's paychecks, bank accounts, or other financial holdings.

BUYING CAR INSURANCE

Most insurance companies require you to submit a written application for insurance. Often, insurance companies check information given in applications by getting copies of driving records from the DMV. Make sure you carefully read any application or coverage selection form before signing it.

Your car insurance policy is a legal contract between you and your insurance company. It states the rights and responsibilities of both you and the insurance company. Do not wait until you have a claim to learn what your policy covers. If you have any questions, call your company, agent, or broker.

If you still need help, write to the New Jersey Department of Insurance, Division of Enforcement and Consumer Protection.

Your insurance company will issue you an insurance identification card that you must carry in your car at all times. If you are in an accident and do not have the card, you may be subject to a fine.

Every vehicle registered in New Jersey must have auto liability and no-fault insurance, called *personal-injury protection* (PIP) coverage.[7] If you are caught driving a car without insurance, you can be fined up to $300 and be sentenced to community service. You will also lose your license.

Liability insurance covers the cost of injury and property damages you may cause in an accident. The minimum coverages you must have are

- $15,000 for injury to or death of one person in any one accident.
- $30,000 for injury to or death of more than one person in any one accident.
- $5,000 for damage to property in any one accident.

How much more liability insurance you actually need depends on how much money you make and how much property you own. If you injure someone in a car accident and a court awards an amount higher than what your insurance covers, the injured party can collect against your other property.

NO-FAULT INSURANCE. *No-fault* or PIP insurance means that when someone is hurt in an accident, his or her own insurance company must pay him or her benefits, regardless of whose fault the accident was. You and any family members living with you are entitled to PIP coverage if injured while operating or occupying any car. Also covered are people who drive your car with your permission, passengers in your car, and pedestrians struck by your car. If you are injured in an accident with a motor vehicle, even if you were a pedestrian, you must report the accident to your insurance company.

You have the option to select your health-care-coverage provider instead of your car insurance company to pay for your no-fault medical expense claims. (Medicare and Medicaid will not provide primary coverage. Therefore, you cannot choose this option if your health benefits are provided by Medicaid or Medicare.) Although the Department of Insurance requires that health insurance sold in New Jersey cover car-related injuries, you may be covered by a policy sold out of state or by a policy that is not subject to New Jersey law because the employer who provided it to you is self-insured.

New Jersey law requires you to buy *uninsured motorist* coverage. This provides benefits to you, your passengers, and relatives living in your household if an uninsured or underinsured motorist becomes liable for injuries to any of you or to your car.

Collision insurance covers damage to or loss of your car in an accident. You must have collision insurance if you are buying a new car and financing it through a bank. A car with little value does not need collision coverage.

Comprehensive insurance covers noncollision damage or loss in a fire, vandalism, or theft. Some comprehensive policies also include liability and collision coverage. Comprehensive coverage also provides for medical payments to people injured in your car and for protection if you are hit by an uninsured driver.

Both the costs and coverage of comprehensive and collision insurance depend on the value of the car. You are not required by law to have collision or comprehensive coverage.

VERBAL THRESHOLD. Under New Jersey law, you may voluntarily limit your right to sue for *pain and suffering* (noneconomic loss) caused by a car accident. If you do so, you will pay lower insurance premiums. If you make this choice, your spouse and children cannot sue for noneconomic loss unless the injury sustained is on the statutory list[8]:

- Death,
- Dismemberment,
- Significant disfigurement,
- Fracture,
- Loss of a fetus,
- Permanent loss of use of a body organ or member,
- Significant limitation of use of a body function or system, *or*
- A medically determined injury or impairment of a nonpermanent nature that prevents the injured person from performing substantially all of the material acts that constitute the person's usual and customary daily activities for not less than 90 days during the 180 days immediately following the occurrence of the injury or impairment.

AUTO INSURANCE CANCELLATION NOTICES. For a cancellation to be effective, the company must give you two notices. Each performs a different function.

The *notice of intent to cancel* tells you that the company will cancel your auto insurance policy unless you pay within ten days. The notice must be clear so that you fully understand it and know what you have to do to prevent cancellation.

The *notice of cancellation* is sent after you have failed to pay. It tells you that the company has canceled the policy and that you are no longer insured. When it is received, you can no longer prevent cancellation if the notice of intent to cancel was adequate. The law states that the insurance cannot be canceled less than three days after the notice of cancellation has been mailed. This allows time for mail delivery of the notice.

AUTO ACCIDENTS

If you have an accident, the first thing you should do is stop the vehicle as soon as possible. Warn oncoming traffic by putting on your flashing hazard lights. Ask someone to call the police and an ambulance if someone is hurt. Do not move your car until the police arrive.

You must notify the police of accidents in which someone is injured or killed or if there is vehicle or property damage over a few hundred dollars. When the police arrive, you will have to answer questions about what happened. You should get the police officer's name and find out when and where you can go to pick up a copy of the police report.

Get the other driver's name, address, license plate number, driver's license number, and the name and address of his or her insurance company. This information will also be in the police report. Do not discuss whose fault the accident was. If there were any witnesses to the accident, you should get their names and addresses, too.

You must also notify the DMV. If the accident in which you were involved resulted in more than $500 of damage to property or injuries to someone, you must send a written report to DMV within ten days if no police report will be filed. A written report from you is *not* required if a report is filed by the police. You can get a report form from the police.

You must also report any accidents to your own insurance company right away. Give them all the information about the accident. If you fail to notify your insurance company immediately, it may refuse insurance coverage for the accident.

If you are hurt in an accident, you may be able to collect on other insurance policies you may have, depending on what benefits the policies provide. Your other policies might include private or group hospital insurance, accident and health insurance, or union or employment benefits. However, if, because of your injuries, you also receive payments from workers' compensation, temporary disability, or Medicare, these payments will be subtracted from the amount you receive under your PIP coverage.

If your car is damaged in an accident and you do not have collision insurance, you can sue the owner and/or driver of the other car. If you have collision insurance, you can collect for damage to your car even if you accidentally caused it.

For collision and comprehensive coverage claims, your insurance company may inspect the car and must offer you a settlement within a reasonable period of time. The company must also inform you of all estimates it makes of damage to your car, all deductions based on the condition of your car, and the deductible applicable to the settlement figure. If your company required you to provide more than one repair estimate, it must pay the reasonable cost (if any) of all additional estimates.

If you have a complaint or problem that your insurance company will not settle, call the New Jersey Department of Insurance.

11. The Rights and Obligations of Citizenship

Nearly all the chapters in this book explore ways in which the government affects the lives of citizens. This chapter deals with some specific rights and obligations under our governmental systems that are not covered elsewhere in the book. Voting and service on a jury are fundamental attributes of citizenship and the bedrock of our governmental system. This chapter discusses them first.

Public participation is essential to a democratic system of government. However, without access to government information, an individual cannot participate effectively in national, state, or local government nor be aware of governmental abuse. This chapter discusses a number of federal and state laws that ensure public access to government information. Also discussed is the Federal Privacy Act, which protects you against government misuse of information it may have about you. In addition, the Genetic Privacy Act is reviewed. This is a recent New Jersey law governing the use of genetic information.

This chapter also discusses the New Jersey gross income tax. Federal tax law is too broad to discuss in this book. Several other New Jersey taxes are discussed, including the state property tax and a state sales-and-use tax of 6 percent on goods and services. Many goods and services, such as shoes, clothing, rent, restaurant food, school textbooks, fuel, and newspapers are not taxed.

The chapter concludes with a discussion of federal immigration law. Immigration law determines who may be legally admitted to the United States, who may remain here, and under what conditions immigrants who choose to become citizens may do so and become full participants in our complex democracy.

JURY DUTY

Only citizens of the United States may serve on juries. To be eligible for jury duty you must be over eighteen years of age and be able to read and understand the English language. You will not be eligible for jury service if you cannot effectively serve because you are physically or mentally disabled. People who are on probation or parole or who are in prison are also ineligible for jury service.

State jury lists are compiled from voter registration lists, Division of Motor Vehicles (DMV) lists, and lists of New Jersey income tax return filers and filers of applications for homestead rebates. Jury lists for federal courts are compiled from voter registration lists only. If your name is selected for jury duty, you will first receive a questionnaire. Then you will get a summons to report to the courthouse at a specific date and time for jury duty. For New Jersey court trials, you must be a resident of the county in which you are summoned. If you do not answer the questionnaire or show up, you may be punished for contempt of court or you may be liable for a fine not to exceed $500.

EXCUSES FROM JURY DUTY. Several categories of people may be excused from jury duty. The federal district court will exempt you from jury service if you are in active service in the armed forces of the United States. Certain officials in all branches of federal and state government are exempt from federal jury service. So are fire and police department officers. Any citizen summoned for federal jury service may be excused upon a showing of undue hardship or extreme inconvenience. No citizen may be excluded from service on a federal or state jury solely because of his or her race, color, religion, gender, national origin, or economic status.

You may be excused from state jury service if you have served as a juror within the past three years in the county to which you are summoned. People who are over seventy-five years of age are also excused from state jury service. Furthermore, potential jurors who might suffer severe hardship if they serve will be excused. For example, you may be excused if jury service would be a severe financial hardship for you. You may also request to be excused if you must take care of a small child or if you cannot serve for medical reasons.

SERVING ON A JURY. If you serve on a federal court jury, you will get paid $40 per day. You will also receive a travel allowance.[1] Federal and state law protects you against being fired because you served on a federal court jury.[2] A federal court may appoint a lawyer to represent you in proceedings against your employer if you are dismissed from your job because of your service on a federal jury. If you win, your employer will have to give you back pay and reinstate you.

If you serve on a New Jersey court jury, you will get paid $5 per day.[3] If you are employed full-time by any agency or political subdivision of the state, your employer must excuse you for jury duty and must pay you the difference between what you are paid for jury duty and what you are usually paid. Other employers are not required to pay you while you are on jury duty, but many do. If your employer penalizes you for serving on a jury, your employer may be found guilty of a disorderly persons offense; you may also bring a civil action for economic damages and reinstatement.

VOTING RIGHTS

To be eligible to vote in an election, you must be a U.S. citizen and at least eighteen years old. You must also be a resident of New Jersey and the

SOURCES FOR VOTER REGISTRATION FORMS

The following New Jersey public agencies[4] provide voter registration forms at their offices:

✔ The Division of Workers' Compensation.
✔ The Division of Employment Services.
✔ The Division of Unemployment and Disability Insurance
✔ The Division of Taxation.
✔ New Jersey Transit.
✔ Any county or public library.
✔ Any office or commercial establishment where New Jersey licenses or permits are available to the public.
✔ Any recruitment office of the New Jersey National Guard.

county in which you wish to vote for at least thirty days prior to the election. You must be registered to vote in the county in which you reside, prior to the twenty-ninth day before the next ensuing election.

When you register to vote, you must give your address. However, if you are the victim of domestic violence and have obtained a permanent restraining order against the abuser, New Jersey law allows you to register to vote without disclosing your place of residence. In this case, you must provide a mailing address, post office box, or other contact point. You must also attach to the registration form a copy of the permanent restraining order and a note stating your fears about disclosing your street address.

If you have been convicted of certain crimes, you can be denied the right to register to vote. If already registered, your registration and record of voting forms will be transferred to the conviction file until your voting and other citizenship rights are restored or you are pardoned. Upon restoration of your citizenship rights, you are required to register or reregister before being allowed to vote.

According to New Jersey law, you can register to vote in person or by mail. You can register in person at any office designated by the county commissioner of registration that provides and collects registration forms. You can also register by completing a voter registration form while applying for a driver's license at the DMV.

If you do not wish to register in person, you may register by completing and returning to the secretary of state a voter registration form provided by certain public agencies, voter registration agencies, and a variety of other sources (see the boxes above and on the following page).

VOTER REGISTRATION AGENCIES

The following voter registration agencies[5] must provide registration forms and offer to help you register to vote:

✔ Any agency participating in the Special Supplemental Food Program for Women, Infants, and Children (WIC).
✔ Any recruitment office of the armed forces of the United States.
✔ Any county welfare agency or county board of social services.
✔ Any municipal clerk's office.
✔ Any office of the Division of Developmental Disabilities.
✔ Any office of the Division of Vocational Rehabilitation Services.
✔ Any office of the Commission for the Blind and Visually Impaired.

Just because you did not vote in one or more elections, you do not lose your right to vote and you can vote again without reregistering. In addition, if you change your name when you become married or divorced or if your name is changed by the judgment of a court, the law does not require you to reregister. However, you *must* file a written statement notifying the county commissioner of registration of the change.

You *must* reregister to vote if you have moved from an election district in one county to an election district in another county. If you have moved but only within the same election district, you must file a change of address with the office of the commissioner or the municipal clerk.

If you have a voting rights problem or question, the New Jersey Department of State Election Division and the New Jersey branch of the League of Women Voters may be able to help you.

THE RIGHT TO PUBLIC INFORMATION

Informed and concerned citizens are basic to democratic government. Therefore, federal and state laws enable public participation in government by providing citizens with access to information.

Two federal laws, the Government-in-the-Sunshine Act[6] and the Freedom of Information Act (FOIA),[7] allow citizens to get information. Several New Jersey statutes perform similar functions on the state government level. One is the Open Public Meetings Law,[8] which applies to meetings of public bodies. Another is the Right to Know Law (RTKL),[9] which applies to public records and documents. In New Jersey, individuals also have a nonstatutory right of access to some public records under New Jersey common law.

In addition to these special statutes, there are other ways in which you can have access to public records. If you are suing or being sued by a government agency, you may *discover* the records through the litigation process. If government records are relevant to a legal case even though a government agency is not involved, you may be able to subpoena the records.

THE GOVERNMENT-IN-THE-SUNSHINE ACT. The federal "sunshine" law requires agencies of the federal government to publish advance notices of their meetings and to permit members of the public to attend certain meetings. Notices must be published in the *Federal Register,* which is available in most libraries. The law requires that federal agencies conduct their meetings in public. The public can, however, be excluded from portions of a meeting when certain subjects, including the following, are to be discussed:

- National defense and foreign policy.
- Information about or accusations of criminal activity.
- Personal information, if disclosure would unnecessarily invade a person's privacy.
- Law enforcement records.
- Information about stocks, bonds, and other financial transactions, the early disclosure of which would lead to speculation.

THE FREEDOM OF INFORMATION ACT. FOIA allows any person to ask for information from a U.S. government agency, not including Congress or the courts. Using FOIA, you can secure copies of documents prepared by the federal agency, as well as documents it may have received from a state or local agency or private party, provided that the documents are not exempted under the statute. Any federally funded or regulated activity that takes place at the state or local level may require that the state or local agency involved provide the federal regulatory agency with documents concerning its activities. Many documents prepared and kept by state or city agencies are sent to federal government agencies. You can get copies of these documents directly from the federal agency. For example, local public housing authorities must prepare a budget each year describing income and expenses. They are required to send a copy to the U.S. Department of Housing and Urban Development (HUD). A citizen who wishes to inspect the budget can do so at the housing authority's offices, using New Jersey's RTKL, or at the HUD office in Newark, using FOIA.

Before you make a FOIA request, there are two things you should do. First, you should try calling the Federal Information Center in New Jersey to see if the information you want is public. Second, you should try to find out who is in charge of FOIA at the agency to which you are writing. This will save you time. In your letter you should state

- That you are making a FOIA request.
- What information you want.
- That you want an answer within ten days.
- That you will pay for search costs and copying.

Federal agencies are supposed to answer your letter within ten days and tell you whether they will provide the documents, any exemptions they are claiming, and how to appeal if you are dissatisfied with their decision.

You can also file a suit in federal court if the agency refuses to give you the documents you requested or is not processing your request within the time limit set by law. The court will look at the matter and decide whether the agency is required to release the documents. It can also make the agency pay for attorneys' fees and court costs.

THE OPEN PUBLIC MEETINGS LAW. New Jersey's Open Public Meetings Law gives citizens the right to have adequate advance notice of all meetings of public bodies. This law also gives the public the right to attend meetings of public bodies at which any business affecting the public is discussed or acted upon. The public also has a right to copies of the minutes of all meetings.

To be covered by the Open Public Meetings Law, a public body must be organized by law and be collectively empowered as a multimember voting body to spend public funds or affect persons' rights. Therefore, informal or purely advisory bodies with no effective authority are not covered. Neither are groups composed of a public official with subordinates or advisors, such as a mayor or the governor meeting with department heads or cabinet members who are not empowered to act by vote. The law specifically exempts the judiciary, political party organizations, and the New Jersey Commission of Investigation, among others.

The law applies to meetings, whether attended in person or conducted by phone, that meet the following requirements: (1) the meeting must be open to all the public body's members or a committee thereof *and* (2) it must be attended by a majority of the members of that public body. The law specifically prohibits a public body from failing to invite just some of its members.

Members present at the meeting must intend to discuss or act on public business. Therefore, the law does not cover political caucus meetings and chance encounters of members of public bodies. An annual or a forty-eight-hour notice of meetings is adequate advance notice. The public body must give forty-eight hours' notice when it wishes to convene a meeting not scheduled in the annual notice. This notice must include the time, date, location, and, to the extent known, the agenda of the meeting.

Both the annual and the forty-eight-hour notice must be posted in one public place reserved for such announcements. These notices must also be sent by mail to any person upon his or her request. The public body must send the notice to at least two newspapers in time for publication, forty-eight hours in advance of the meeting. Finally, the notice must be filed with the county or municipal clerk or with the secretary of state if the public body has statewide authority.

Public bodies must permit public attendance at meetings. However, the right to *attend* meetings does not entail a right to *participate* in the meetings. The public body may not exclude the public from a meeting, except when the meeting is in *executive session*. Before excluding the public from a closed session, the public body must first adopt a resolution at a prior meeting that is open to the public. The resolution must state what matters in general will be discussed in closed session and when these discussions will be disclosed to the public. The courts have recognized the potential for misuse of the closed-session exceptions by public bodies. In an effort to ensure that public meetings are open in most instances, courts have ruled that closed-session exceptions should be carefully controlled. Under the law, a public body must make and keep reasonably clear and complete minutes of all meetings. Statements must be entered into the minutes at the beginning of each meeting indicating that adequate notice has been provided (specifying the time, date, and manner in which the notice was provided), or that adequate notice was not given and an explanation of the reason. The minutes are to be made promptly available to the public.

A public body may hold an emergency meeting when an urgent and important matter arises and a delay of the meeting for the purpose of providing adequate notice would likely result in substantial harm to the public interest. If an emergency meeting is held without adequate notice, the public body must follow very strict procedural requirements. These include

- An affirmative vote of three-quarters of the members present to hold the meeting.
- Providing notice of the meeting as soon as possible following the calling of such a meeting.
- Inclusion in the minutes of a detailed statement explaining
  —The nature of the urgency,
  —The nature of the substantial harm to the public interest likely to result from a delay in holding the meeting,
  —That the meeting will be limited to those urgent and important matters,
  —The time, place, and manner in which notice of the meeting was provided, *and*
  —Why the need for the meeting could not have been foreseen in time for adequate notice of it to be given or, if the need for the meeting

could have been foreseen, the reason(s) why adequate notice of the meeting was not provided.

Any person may file a lawsuit in New Jersey Superior Court to invalidate any action taken by a public body at a meeting that violates the Open Public Meetings Law. The lawsuit must be brought within forty-five days after the action has been made public. You may also ask the court to issue an injunction or other remedy to ensure compliance with the law.

Another remedy is a complaint to the county prosecutor or the state attorney general about possible violations of the law. These officials may prosecute any person who knowingly violates the law. Violators may be fined $100 for the first offense and between $100 and $500 for any subsequent offenses.

If a public body meets in violation of the law, it may later correct its action by holding another public meeting in conformity with the requirements of the law. At the second meeting, it can again deal with the public business that had previously been discussed and acted upon.

RIGHT TO KNOW LAW. New Jersey's RTKL gives all citizens of New Jersey the right to examine *all* documents defined as public records. Since you also have a common law right of access to certain public records, the legal question often is whether or not you have a right of access to *particular* records on either a statutory or common law basis. (Special rules concerning your rights to see your child's school records are discussed in Chapter 13, "Educating Your Children.")

Under the RTKL, the legal question usually is: Does the law require the records "to be made, maintained, or kept on file"? If so, the documents qualify as *public records* under the RTKL. Once documents are found to be RTKL public records, citizens of New Jersey have an absolute right to inspect, copy, or purchase them, without showing any personal interest in the documents as long as they are not intended to be used for an "inappropriate purpose." Inspection or copying of a public record is subject only to reasonable controls with respect to time, place, and reproduction costs.

However, it is often difficult to get access to public documents under the RTKL. The documents must first be found to be RTKL public records. If they are *not* such public records, then there is no right of access to them under the RTKL. The New Jersey Supreme Court has consistently held that the definition of a public record in the RTKL is narrow and is to be strictly construed. For example, the supreme court has held that there is no right of access to an audiotape of a public meeting, even if the tape was made for the purpose of preparing the minutes. The court reasoned that, although minutes of a public agency are public records under the RTKL because the Open Public Meetings Law requires minutes to be made and kept, no law required the agency to audiotape its meetings. For similar reasons the supreme court has held that computer tapes of municipal tax assessments were not RTKL public records because the defendants were only required by the law to make and maintain a hard copy, not computer tapes as well.

The New Jersey common law definition of a public record is broader than the RTKL definition of a public record. A *common law record* is one that is made by a public official in the exercise of his or her public functions, either because the law required the record to be made or kept or because it was filed in a public office. Therefore, all RTKL documents are common law records as well, but not all common law records are public records under the RTKL.

On the other hand, unlike the right of access to RTKL public records, the right of access to common law records is qualified, not absolute. Under the common law, therefore, the legal question is often: Does the law require that a particular applicant be given access to particular public records? The answer under New Jersey common law is that the right of access depends on three requirements, not always easily met. These are as follows:

1. The records must be common law public documents as defined above.
2. The individual seeking access must "establish an interest in the subject matter of the material."
3. The individual's right of access "must be balanced against the state's interest in preventing disclosure."

THE RIGHT TO PRIVACY

There is growing recognition that private citizens need to be protected against unnecessary invasions of privacy by government agencies.

THE FEDERAL PRIVACY ACT.[10] Congress passed the Federal Privacy Act to set rules on what information agencies can keep, to let individuals see information an agency has about them, and to make sure agencies do not give information about individuals to other people without the individual's consent. The Federal Privacy Act protects citizens and lawful aliens.

Under the Federal Privacy Act, federal records should include only information that is accurate, necessary to agency functions, and, whenever possible, obtained directly from the individual. Agencies should not keep records about how a person exercises his or her First Amendment rights, such as writing or speaking in a public forum. When agencies ask for information, they must tell people what they need the information for and what will happen if they do not get it. Although an agency is not supposed to let others see information about you without your consent, there are many significant exceptions to this rule.

If you want to see your own records, you should write to the person in charge of the Federal Privacy Act at the particular agency that has, or that you think may have, your information. You will have to give some proof of identification. You can do so by including your Social Security number in your letter or by having the letter notarized. You do not have to explain why you want to see the records. In your letter, you should say that

- You want to see the records the agency has concerning you.
- You are making a FOIA and Federal Privacy Act request.
- You will pay search and photocopying fees up to a certain amount.

You can also ask a federal agency to change a record. You can sue in federal district court if the agency will not show you information, will not change your (inaccurate) record, or does not keep accurate information about you. You can be awarded damages only if the agency *willfully* failed to keep accurate information and this failure had an adverse effect on you. The federal district court can order the agency to change your record or let you see it. The court may also order the agency to pay for your attorneys' fees. You should be aware, however, that the Federal Privacy Act has many exceptions. These may free an agency from many of the requirements mentioned here.

THE GENETIC PRIVACY ACT.[11] This New Jersey law requires the *informed consent* of an individual or his or her representative before obtaining or retaining any *genetic information* from an individual or from his or her DNA sample. The law defines genetic information as information about genes, gene products, or inherited characteristics that may derive from an individual or family member. Informed consent is not defined in the statute and regulations doing so have not yet been promulgated. Exceptions to the informed consent requirement include criminal investigations attempting to establish the identity of a person, newborn screening, paternity determination, and determining the identity of a dead person.

THE OBLIGATION TO PAY TAXES

Paying taxes is often perceived as our most onerous obligation to the government. The duty to pay taxes is, nevertheless, the most inescapable of our civic duties. No modern government is possible without a sophisticated and sometimes hard to understand system of taxation. In democratic systems the question of whether the tax burden is equitably shared is constantly debated. How that question is answered reflects the power of different classes and groups. The answers elected officials give may determine the length of their tenure just as much as their decisions about how to spend tax revenues.

Federal taxes are beyond the scope of this book. Each year numerous commercial and governmental publications give detailed guidance on how we may legally meet or avoid our obligation to pay personal federal income taxes, the largest source of tax revenue. There are numerous other federal taxes, including a federal estate tax, which, together with the New Jersey inheritance tax, are very briefly discussed in Chapter 9, "Securing the Future for Senior Citizens and their Families."

TAXES IN NEW JERSEY. The New Jersey Constitution gives the state the authority to tax. New Jersey taxes include those that must be paid annually on real estate, those paid at death, the sales-and-use tax, franchise taxes on business corporations, and the state income tax (discussed below). The Division of Taxation in the Department of the Treasury assesses the personal income tax, sales-and-use taxes, the franchise taxes of business corporations, and other state taxes. The Division of Taxation also supervises the administration of local property tax assessment. Local assessors in each municipality set values on all taxable real property in each tax district. County boards of taxation supervise local tax assessment under the general supervision of the Division of Taxation.

The division must respond to taxpayers' questions within a reasonable time. Notices of taxes and penalties due must clearly identify the purpose of the notice and must tell you how to appeal. New Jersey has established a tax court that has statewide jurisdiction over state tax issues, including the decisions of all state tax officials on state tax matters. The tax court also reviews county board decisions on local property tax matters. The tax court is a trial court, specially staffed with judges who are experts in tax matters. You must usually appeal to the tax court within ninety days. Decisions of the tax court are reviewed by the New Jersey Superior Court, Appellate Division.

NEW JERSEY GROSS INCOME TAX. Every resident of New Jersey is required to file a New Jersey gross income tax return if gross income received during the taxable year is more than $7,500 ($3,750 for a married person filing separately). If a person was a full-year resident in New Jersey and had a gross income of $7,500 or less, he or she is not required to file a tax return except to obtain a refund or to obtain a homestead property tax rebate.

Any person who became a New Jersey resident or moved out of New Jersey during the taxable year is subject to the New Jersey gross income tax only for that portion of the income received while he or she was a resident of New Jersey. Part-year residents must prorate all exemptions, deductions, and credits to reflect the period covered by the return. If they receive income from New Jersey sources as nonresidents, they may also be subject to taxation for the period when they were *not* residing in New Jersey. Both resident and nonresident returns must be filed when a part-year resident received income from New Jersey sources during the period when he or she was not residing in New Jersey.

A return for a taxpayer who died during the year must be filed by the taxpayer's executor, administrator, or surviving spouse. When a person in the armed forces serving in a combat zone dies as a result of wounds, disease, or injury received there, no income tax is due for the taxable year the death occurred or for any earlier years served in the combat zone.

All taxpayers must use the same filing status on their New Jersey returns as they use for federal income tax purposes. The filing categories are: single, married filing jointly, married filing separately, head of household, or qualifying widow or widower. The only exception to this rule is when one spouse was a resident and the other a nonresident for the entire year. In this case, the resident may file a separate return and use the married-filing-separately tax rates.

All income received by a New Jersey resident—even if derived from sources outside New Jersey—is included in gross income except for the items below, which are excluded from gross income and are not taxable:

- Federal Social Security.
- Railroad retirement (Tier I and Tier II) benefits.
- Life insurance proceeds received because of a person's death.
- Employee death benefits.
- Permanent and total disability, including Veterans Administration (VA) disability benefits.
- Temporary disability received from the state of New Jersey or as third-party sick pay.
- Gifts and inheritances.
- Workers' compensation.
- Qualifying scholarship or fellowship grants.
- New Jersey lottery winnings.
- Unemployment compensation.
- Homestead property tax rebates.
- Income tax refunds (federal, New Jersey, and other jurisdictions).
- Employer and employee contributions to 401(k) plans (but not federal thrift savings funds).
- Certain distributions from New Jersey qualified investment funds.
- Direct payments and benefits received under homeless persons' assistance programs.
- Interest from direct federal obligations exempt under law, such as U.S. savings bonds and Treasury bills, notes, and bonds, or from obligations of the state of New Jersey or any of its political subdivisions.
- Welfare benefits.
- Child support payments.
- Some benefits received from certain employer-provided cafeteria plans.

Since these exceptions are exclusions from income, you should not include them when deciding whether you have enough income to be required to file a gross income tax return.

Employer contributions to a cafeteria plan or flexible-benefit plan are included in gross income as wages and are therefore taxable, but only to the extent that the employee can elect to take taxable benefits. Where the terms of the plan require that a portion of the employee's benefit dollars *must* be used to purchase certain nontaxable benefits (e.g., medical, life insurance, long-term disability coverage), the minimum amount required to be used by the plan is not to be considered as wages. Any amount that the employee sets aside into a flexible-spending account *is* taxable as wages.

All interest from savings and loan associations, credit unions, bank deposits, bonds, and other sources received during the taxable year (including interest derived from sources held out of state) is taxable income. However, interest from state of New Jersey or local New Jersey municipal bonds, or from direct federal obligations, such as U.S. savings bonds and Treasury bills, is not taxable.

Payments you receive for personal injury or sickness are not taxable; however,

- The payments must be for wage loss that results from absence due to injury or sickness of the employee,
- The payments must be due and payable under an enforceable contractual obligation,
  and
- The payments must not be related to sick-leave wage continuation.

New Jersey taxpayers are entitled to a number of different *exemptions.* Exemptions are deducted from gross income to arrive at the amount of *net income* you must pay taxes on (taxable income). But in deciding whether you must file an income tax return (that is, whether you have enough gross income for the law to require you to file a gross income tax return), you cannot subtract your exemptions.

A taxpayer may claim exemptions of $1,500 each for himself or herself, and his or her spouse if a joint return is filed. You may claim an additional personal exemption of $1,500 for each dependent under twenty-two years of age who is a full-time student at an accredited college or postsecondary institution. The dependent must be under age twenty-two for the entire tax year and the taxpayer must show that he or she paid one-half or more of the tuition and maintenance cost. Financial aid received by the student is not taken into consideration in determining whether the taxpayer paid one-half of the cost of tuition and maintenance (except for income earned by students in college work-study programs). A full-time student must be enrolled for the number of hours and courses considered by the school to be full-time attendance. The student must spend at least some part of each of five calendar months of the tax year at school.

Other personal exemptions that a taxpayer can claim for children and other qualified dependents apply if the taxpayer or the taxpayer's spouse was sixty-five years of age or older, blind, or disabled at the end of the tax year. Disabled means total and permanent inability to engage in any substantial gainful activity because of any physical or mental impairment, including blindness. A taxpayer may also claim exemptions for other dependents who qualify for federal income tax purposes. Each personal exemption so claimed is a $1,000 exemption.

Taxpayers may deduct or get credit for certain expenses incurred during the tax year. A taxpayer may deduct alimony and separate maintenance payments made by the taxpayer to a spouse or former spouse, but only if they are made under a decree of divorce or separate maintenance. Such a payment, when received by the taxpayer's spouse or former spouse, is taxable income. On the other hand, child support payments made by a taxpayer are not deductible, and income from child support payments is exempt from New Jersey's gross income tax.

Employee business expenses are not deductible from income. All allowances for employee business expenses paid to you by your employer must be reported in full as income. However, reimbursements from your employer for business expenses are not considered income if the reimbursements are for job-related expenses that you have incurred and for which your employer accordingly reimburses you.

Moving expenses are also not deductible. Reimbursements received for moving expenses are not counted as income if they are for (1) the cost of moving your household goods and effects from the old home to the new home *or* (2) the actual expenses incurred by you for traveling, meals, and lodging when moving to your new residence.

Reimbursements for any other moving expenses, however, are considered to be income.

Your or your dependents' medical expenses may be deductible if you were not reimbursed for them. However, you may only deduct medical expenses that were not reimbursed to the extent that the medical expenses exceed 2 percent of your New Jersey gross income. Medical expenses that may be deducted (if not reimbursed) include fees to physicians and dentists, and payments for prescription eyeglasses, hospital care, nursing care, medicines, drugs, prosthetic devices, and X-rays and other diagnostic services. You may also deduct health insurance premiums, including Medicare Part B, and the cost of transportation that was essential for your medical care. Remember, however, that you can only deduct your total medical expenses that exceed 2 percent of your gross income.

If you were a homeowner or a tenant during the taxable year, you may be entitled to a homestead property tax rebate. Your principal residence (whether owned or rented) must be subject to local property taxes that must have been paid on that residence either as actual property taxes or through rent. However, tenants are not eligible for the rebate, unless their dwelling has its own separate kitchen and bath facilities. You are also not eligible for this rebate if your total gross income is more than $100,000. Because of lack of funding, not everyone who is eligible under the law will currently get the rebate. Senior citizens who qualify *will* get the rebate.

In addition to the homestead property tax rebate, as of the 1996 tax year, eligible homeowners and renters who pay local property taxes (either directly or through rent) on their principal residence in New Jersey may receive either a deduction or a refundable tax credit. Your gross income must be at least $7,500, or $3,750 if married and filing separately. For the 1996 tax year, eligible renters and homeowners were allowed to deduct 50 percent of the first $5,000 of property taxes due and paid, or $2,500, whichever was less. For tenants, 18 percent of rent paid during the 1996 tax year was considered property taxes paid. A rented dwelling must, however, be subject to property tax and have its own separate kitchen and bath facilities. Taxpayers living in a rental unit that does not have its own separate kitchen and bathroom will not be allowed any property tax deduction, even if the building is subject to local property tax and the taxpayer's rental payments are used, in part, to pay local property taxes. Taxpayers who are blind or disabled and have a gross income of less than $7,500 ($3,750 if married and filing separately) are, however, eligible for a refundable tax credit.

IMMIGRATION AND ALIEN STATUS

Federal law governs immigration into the United States. Congress passes immigration laws that determine who can be admitted and who can be allowed to remain in the country. Federal immigration law also governs the naturalization of aliens who wish to become citizens of the United States. In addition, federal immigration law governs *removal proceedings*, a new procedure for removing aliens from the United States on the basis that they are inadmissible or deportable.

In removal proceedings, aliens who were not legally admitted to the United States are charged with one or more grounds of *inadmissibility*. Aliens who were legally admitted may be charged in removal proceedings with being *deportable* on one or more grounds.

The Immigration and Naturalization Service (INS)—the federal agency that enforces immigration laws—is part of the U.S. Department of Justice. The INS has offices around the United States that handle applications from people who are not citizens. The INS is also responsible for finding and removing people who are living unlawfully in the United States.

CITIZENSHIP. U.S. citizens have rights and privileges not available to non-citizens. If you are a citizen of the United States you can vote in elections, can be appointed or elected to public office, are eligible for any kind of employment, and may freely enter the United States. You cannot be deported. There are three ways of becoming a citizen of the United States.

First, all persons born in the United States or its possessions (e.g., Puerto Rico) are U.S. citizens with the exception of children of foreign diplomats.

Second, all persons born outside the United States to parents both of whom are U.S. citizens are entitled to U.S. citizenship. Matters are not so straightforward if only one parent is a citizen of the United States. If a child was born after November 14, 1986, outside the United States to one citizen and one alien parent, the citizen parent must have been physically present in the United States for at least five years prior to the child's birth and be over the age of fourteen in order to pass U.S. citizenship to the child. If the parents of a person born outside the United States become naturalized citizens *after* the person was born, the person may acquire *derivative* citizenship.

Third, a person may become a citizen of the United States through naturalization. Under the U.S. Constitution, naturalized citizens may not serve as president or vice president of the United States. There are no other distinctions between citizens who were naturalized and those who were citizens at birth.

In order to be eligible for naturalization, you must be eighteen years of age or older. You must have been a permanent resident for at least five years (three years if married to a citizen); be a person of good moral character; and be able to read, write, and understand ordinary English words or phrases. (There is an exemption from this last requirement for older people who have been permanent residents for a long time.)

IMMIGRANTS. There are two basic ways for aliens to obtain lawful status in the United States. One is through the visa process. The other is through exceptions in federal immigration law. The law responds to certain difficult situations in which people who are noncitizens might find themselves.

OBTAINING A VISA. There are various immigrant visas and nonimmigrant visas for different categories of immigrant aliens and nonimmigrant aliens. Lawful permanent residents are aliens (the legal term for all people who are not U.S. citizens) who have *immigrant visas*. They are aliens who have been given permission to permanently live in the United States ("green card" holders). They may travel freely within and enter and leave the country. They are free to take almost any kind of employment (not including most kinds of employment by the federal government).

Most immigrants who get *permanent resident visas* do so because family members who are already citizens or permanent residents of the United States file petitions on their behalf (see the discussion of relative petitions on the following page). Employers may also file petitions.

Once the INS approves the petition, the alien files an application for a permanent resident visa. An alien must get his or her visa before he or she can be admitted to the United States as a permanent resident. Often, visas are not available for certain categories of immigrants, especially if they are from countries (such as Mexico or the Philippines) with many visa applicants. If so, the alien must wait—in some cases for very long periods *after* their petitions have been approved—before he or she can immigrate to the United States as a permanent resident.

A permanent resident can lose his or her status by *abandoning residence* in the United States. Permanent residents who remain outside the United States for more than one year will be considered to have abandoned their residence and must be able to prove that they have maintained their status. Permanent residents who plan to be outside the United States for more than a year should first obtain a permit to reenter before leaving the country.

U.S. citizens and permanent residents can petition for an immigrant visa for certain relatives. Such petitions are called *relative petitions*. There are four types of family members for whom a U.S. citizen may petition: (1) a spouse, (2) a child (regardless of age or marital status), (3) brothers and sisters (if the U.S. citizen is twenty-one years of age or older), *and* (4) parents.

Permanent residents can petition for only two types of family members: (1) a spouse *and* (2) any unmarried child (regardless of age). Permanent residents cannot petition for their parents, their married sons and daughters, or for their siblings.

Before a person can become a permanent resident because of marriage to another permanent resident or to a U.S. citizen, he or she must first obtain *conditional permanent resident status.* At the end of a two-year period in this status the couple must file a *joint petition* to have the conditional status removed and the spouse granted full permanent resident status. During the two-year period the INS can end the conditional permanent resident status if it discovers that the marriage was annulled, the couple divorced, or the marriage was entered into fraudulently.

As of 1997, all new family-based immigrants must have legally enforceable *affidavits of support.* An affidavit of support is a contract agreeing to provide financial support. The petitioning relative must sign the affidavit of support. This relative is called the *sponsor.* Sponsors must have a certain minimum income in relation to their own family size and the number of people being sponsored.

Aliens can also get *employment-based* immigrant visas. Generally, highly skilled and professional workers will have an easier time getting a visa; unskilled workers will find the process more difficult and lengthier. Immigrants who come to work for a relative must have affidavits of support. Those who come to work for a corporation in which relatives have a significant financial interest must also have affidavits of support.

Besides employment-based visas and visas based on relative petitions, aliens may apply for another kind of immigrant visa called a *diversity visa.*

Diversity visas are intended for people from countries (mostly European and African) that have sent fewer than 50,000 immigrants to the United States in the past five years. Applicants must have the equivalent of a high school education or two years in an occupation that requires two years of training and experience to be qualified for the occupation.

The most important nonimmigrant visas are those for tourists (*B-2 visas*), temporary workers (*H visas*), exchange students (*J visas*), and students (*F-1 visas*).

OBTAINING LEGAL ALIEN STATUS. The INS admits certain aliens and allows them to remain in the United States if they face certain situations in the United States or abroad which immigration law takes into consideration. The following are the most common kinds of legal status granted to aliens under immigration law.

Lawful Temporary Resident. A *lawful temporary resident* is a person who received amnesty under one of the two legalization programs of the Immigration Reform and Control Act of 1986 (IRCA).[12] The two programs are for aliens (often called *amnesty aliens*) who lived unlawfully in the United States since before January 1, 1982, or who worked as agricultural workers for certain times before May 1986. Most lawful temporary residents are now lawful permanent residents.

Family Unity. *Family unity* is an immigration status that provides protection against deportation for spouses and children of aliens who legalized their status under IRCA. To qualify, a person must have been the spouse or child of an amnesty alien as of May 5, 1988, and have been residing in the United States prior to that date.

Registry. Aliens who have lived in the United States since before January 1, 1972, may apply for *registry*. If the INS grants registry, the person becomes a lawful permanent resident. It does not matter whether the alien has been in the United States lawfully or in an undocumented status. Applicants must be of "good moral character."

Asylees. The United States grants *asylum* to persons unable or unwilling to return to their country because of persecution or a well-founded fear of persecution. The feared or actual persecution must be perpetrated by the government or by a group that the government is unable or unwilling to control. Asylum is also available to people with a well-founded fear of being subject to coercive population control measures, such as forced abortion or involuntary sterilization. An application for asylum must usually be filed within one year of the date of the alien's last arrival in the United States.

Refugees. A *refugee* is like an asylee except that a refugee was outside the United States when he or she was given permission to come into the United States because of persecution or a well-founded fear of persecution in his or her own country.

Withholding of Deportation. The United States cannot return a person to a country where he or she would be persecuted. Aliens seeking refugee or asylum status need only prove a reasonable possibility of persecution. However, people seeking *suspension of deportation* must prove that persecution is probable if they were deported to a particular country.

Temporary Protected Status (TPS). TPS is granted to aliens in the United States who are nationals of countries that are subject to armed conflict, natural disaster, or other extraordinary conditions. Countries most recently designated under the TPS program include Bosnia-Herzegovina, Liberia, Somalia, and Rwanda.

Parolees. Some people detained by the INS because they do not seem qualified for admission into the United States are granted *parole.* Parole is temporary permission to remain in the United States without technically being "admitted." If parole is not granted, an alien will be detained during removal proceedings.

Undocumented Aliens. Some aliens come into the United States without being legally admitted (called "entering without inspection by an immigration officer"). Others overstay the time allowed on a nonimmigrant visa, such as a tourist or student visa. It is preferable to refer to such people as *undocumented aliens,* rather than as "illegal" aliens. If the INS finds an undocumented alien living in the United States it may start removal proceedings against him or her. While undocumented aliens have no legal right to stay in the United States, in some cases they are nevertheless allowed to remain.

GROUNDS FOR INADMISSIBILITY. The INS may decide not to let an alien enter the United States after a visa has been approved. Whether they seek to enter the United States at ports of entry, are stopped in international or U.S. waters, or are found in the United States although not admitted, all aliens must be able to prove that they are *admissible.*

The following are the main grounds for finding an alien to be inadmissible under immigration law:

- Health-related reasons, such as being a drug addict or having a communicable disease (e.g., tuberculosis).
- Certain criminal offenses, such as drug offenses or prostitution.
- Reasons of national security, such as spying or terrorist activity.
- Other reasons, such as the conclusion that the alien is likely to become a *public charge* (i.e., he or she is likely to go on welfare), illegal entry, or commission of other immigration violations.

People who might be found inadmissible under immigration law may, however, be able to get waivers. This means that they may be found admissible despite grounds for finding them inadmissible. If you think you may be eligible for a waiver you should consult an immigration lawyer.

In general, aliens present in the United States without being admitted or paroled are considered inadmissible. One exception is for aliens who are victims of domestic violence or have been subject to extreme cruelty. Aliens are also eligible for the exception if their child has been battered or subjected to extreme cruelty. Such aliens must "otherwise qualify for immigrant status."

Aliens seeking to reenter the United States will be barred for three years if they were living unlawfully in the United States for more than 180 days after April 1, 1997. Aliens seeking to reenter the United States will be barred for ten years if they were living unlawfully in the United States for more than one year after April 1, 1997. There are some exceptions to these rules but they are very limited.

12. The Criminal Justice System

This chapter examines your rights relating to the law enforcement process, both when you are charged with a violation of the law and when you are the victim of or witness to a crime. It also explains your rights concerning actions by the police and how you can have a record of an arrest or conviction expunged.

THE LEGAL BASIS OF THE CRIMINAL JUSTICE SYSTEM

Our system of criminal law and procedure has developed from statutory law, constitutional law, and the decisions made by courts (case law).

STATUTORY LAW. The New Jersey legislature gave state courts the power to hear criminal cases. It also passed the code of criminal justice, which defines *crimes.* Crimes are offenses that can result in a jail sentence of six months or more.[1] Murder, conspiracy, and burglary are examples of crimes. Crimes are divided into crimes of the first, second, third, and fourth *degree.* The length of the jail sentence that can be imposed by the court upon conviction of a crime depends on the degree of the crime.

Any offense that carries a sentence of six months or less is not a crime, although it is sometimes considered quasi-criminal. Disorderly persons offenses, petty disorderly persons offenses, and motor vehicle offenses are not crimes. The distinction between crimes and other offenses is important. Whereas most crimes are tried in the Law Division of New Jersey Superior Court, most disorderly persons offenses, petty disorderly persons offenses, and motor vehicle offenses are tried in municipal court. Also, some constitutional rights apply only to crimes.

CONSTITUTIONAL LAW. The Bill of Rights of the U.S. Constitution was adopted to protect citizens against abuses of power by government officials. New Jersey's constitution, which is modeled on the U.S. Constitution, also provides for protections in the criminal law area (see the box on the following page).

CASE LAW. Courts have provided interpretation of some of the general language of the Bill of Rights. In the course of deciding cases, they have defined (for example) the terms "probable cause" and "speedy trial" and forged remedies for violations of constitutional rights. The New Jersey Supreme Court has interpreted some provisions of the New Jersey Constitution to provide greater protection from police actions than the U.S. Supreme Court has found to be guaranteed by the U.S. Constitution. For example, the U.S.

RIGHTS GUARANTEED BY BOTH THE U.S. AND NEW JERSEY CONSTITUTIONS

✔ The right to be free from "unreasonable searches and seizures."
✔ The right to have search warrants and arrest warrants issued only if there is *probable cause.*
✔ The right not to incriminate yourself.
✔ The right to be indicted by a grand jury if you are charged with a crime.
✔ The right to a speedy trial by an impartial jury.
✔ The right to know the charges against you, to confront witnesses against you, and to have witnesses in your favor be subpoenaed.
✔ The right to be represented by a lawyer.
✔ The right not to be tried twice for the same offense.
✔ The right to be free from "cruel and unusual punishment" and the right to a bail that is not excessive.

Supreme Court has ruled that under the U.S. Constitution, a suspect does *not* have to know that he or she could refuse to allow the police to search his or her person or home in order for the police to prove that the suspect consented to the search. By contrast, the New Jersey Supreme Court has ruled that under the New Jersey Constitution, a suspect *does* have to know of his or her right to refuse a search before it can be considered consensual.

THE CRIMINAL COURT SYSTEM

Victims, witnesses, and people charged with crimes all have rights under the criminal justice system.

THE RIGHTS OF CRIME VICTIMS AND WITNESSES. Crime victims and witnesses have the right to be treated with dignity and compassion by the criminal justice system. The law recognizes that protecting the rights of crime victims and witnesses helps make them cooperative. This makes prosecution of dangerous criminals easier and helps ensure that these people will be convicted and sent to prison before they can commit further crimes of violence. Respecting crime victims' rights also helps them to deal with the negative impact of the crime on their lives.

The New Jersey Crime Victims Bill of Rights[2] states that victims and witnesses to crime are entitled to

- The right to be free from intimidation.
- The right to receive medical attention if the law enforcement agency feels it is necessary.
- The right to have property returned promptly to them when no longer needed as evidence.
- The right to minimal inconvenience and to be compensated for their loss whenever possible.
- The right to be provided with a safe waiting area—not necessarily separate from that of the defendants and their families—while at police stations and courthouses.
- The right to be advised of the progress of the case and its result.
- The right to make at least one phone call (in the case of victims being delayed).
- The right to receive information about the conviction, sentencing, and release of the offender.

Victims are also given the opportunity to prepare a written "victim impact statement" in which they can describe to the sentencing judge the harm that they and their families have suffered. The superior court can also allow victims to address the court in person at sentencing, offering a public statement that goes beyond the presentence statement and that actually becomes a part of the public record.

Another law allows judges to order defendants to keep a specified distance from victims or witnesses and not to communicate with them.[3] The law also provides that if a defendant disobeys such an order and tries to influence a witness, he or she may be charged with two new offenses. One is *contempt of court* (disobeying a court order), and the other is *tampering with a witness*. If convicted of both of these charges, the defendant could serve the two sentences consecutively.

A third law allows for *restitution* to the victim. All persons convicted of committing a crime must make payments to the Violent Crimes Compensation Board.[4] If the person convicted fails to make payments, he or she can lose his or her driver's license.

Still another law allows convicts who fail to make restitution to victims or payments to the Violent Crimes Compensation Board to be jailed for contempt of court.

Filing a Criminal Complaint. Most criminal cases are started with the filing of a criminal complaint. The complaint must state who violated the law and set out the facts that show a violation of the law. The *complainant* (the person who signs the complaint) must swear that the facts in the complaint are true to the best of his or her knowledge.

You can file a complaint with the municipal court clerk in the town where the incident occurred. The clerk should help you figure out what statute or ordinance has been violated. If the municipal court clerk's office is not open, you should be able to file a complaint with the county prosecutor's office.

Although your complaint must be accepted, you do not have an absolute right to have your complaint prosecuted. After a complaint is filed, the court clerk will decide whether an arrest warrant or a summons should be issued. If the clerk does not believe that an offense was committed by the person you accuse, your complaint will be referred to a judge who will hold a hearing. The judge may dismiss your complaint if he or she does not have reason to believe that an offense was committed by the person you have named. If your complaint charges someone with an *indictable offense* (a crime punishable by more than six months), it will be sent to the county prosecutor's office. The prosecutor may decide to dismiss your complaint or to *downgrade* it, i.e., to charge the person you say committed a crime with a less-serious offense. The prosecutor's office will probably let you know why it dismissed or downgraded your complaint; however, you will not be able to challenge this decision.

Financial Help for Crime Victims. Victims of violent crimes may be eligible for financial help from the Violent Crimes Compensation Board. The board awards money to victims who qualify for medical expenses not covered by insurance or who have lost wages due to the crime-related injury. A victim counseling service is also provided. Any person responsible for the crime is not eligible to receive compensation.

Your claim will be considered only if

- A crime was committed that resulted in physical injury to you or the death of your spouse, parent, or any relative upon whom you depended for support,
- Police records show that the crime was reported within three months after it happened,
  and
- The claim was made within two years of the date of injury or death. Claims filed after two years will be considered only if there was a good reason for the delay in filing.

In addition, you must have either unreimbursable expenses for medical or other services of at least $100, or you must have lost at least two continuous weeks of earnings. The lost-earnings requirement does not apply if you are disabled or sixty years of age or older at the time of the crime.

In deciding how much to award you, the board will consider monies you received from insurance companies, public funds, or the person who committed the crime.

The maximum amount that can be awarded is $25,000. The board will verify all information reported in the claim application and then send you a written summary, which will include all the facts about the crime and the losses you suffered. The summary will also include either a recommendation as to the amount to be awarded, or a recommendation that the claim be denied. If the claim is denied, the reasons for denial must be explained.

After receiving the board's recommendation you have twenty days to advise the board in writing whether you accept or reject the recommendation. If you do not accept it, you may request a hearing before the board. At the hearing, you will be given the chance to give evidence to support your claim. You have the right to be represented by a lawyer before the board, and the board is required to pay a reasonable fee for your lawyer's services. Emergency financial assistance is also available if you lack funds because of the crime and this causes an undue hardship. You should tell the board if you are unable to buy food, make rent or other payments, or get medical treatment because of a financial hardship.

For more information on filing a claim, contact the Violent Crimes Compensation Board office located nearest you.

People who are robbed, particularly in the inner cities, often do not report the crime to the police. It is important, however, for crime victims to report such incidents. Even if the police report does not help you to recover your property or apprehend the wrongdoer, it can help you in other ways, such as in pursuing insurance claims. It will also help you at tax time, in writing off your loss on your income tax return.

Crime Victims' Participation in Parole Decisions. If the person who victimized you was convicted of a first-degree crime—such as murder, armed robbery, or aggravated sexual assault—or a second-degree crime—such as sexual assault, aggravated assault, or extortion—and was sentenced after July 10, 1984, under New Jersey law you have the right to object to that person's release on parole.[5] A New Jersey law requires the county prosecutor to notify you of your right to appear before the state parole board when the inmate becomes eligible for parole. The parole board must give you a chance to state, in person or in writing, whether the crime or the criminal caused any long-term mental or physical harm to you or your family members and whether the crime has hurt your ability to work or contributed to a loss of earnings.

You can ask for confidentiality if you fear harassment or reprisal by the convict or his or her family. At no time in this process will you and the convict come face to face.

Your Rights and Responsibilities as a Witness. A *witness* is a person who saw a criminal offense as it happened. All witnesses have one important responsibility—to tell the truth to the best of their ability. Witnesses who have been subpoenaed must come to court. If they do not show up, they can be found in contempt of court and punished.

Witnesses have some of the same rights as victims. The New Jersey Crime Victims Bill of Rights, discussed earlier, applies to witnesses as well. Some witnesses to crimes may also be eligible for free counseling under the Violent

Crimes Compensation Law. This will occur if the witness is the family member of a victim and the commission of the crime had a psychological effect on the witness.

Witnesses must answer questions during a trial unless the answers might incriminate them. Generally, the prosecutor does *not* have to tell you that you have the right not to incriminate yourself. However, the prosecutor *must* advise you of your right not to incriminate yourself if you are the target of a grand jury or other investigation. If you do not claim the privilege against self-incrimination and provide testimony, you waive (lose) the privilege.

Once you claim the privilege, one of two things will happen. Either the prosecutor will decide that he or she does not care if you answer the question, or you will be brought before a judge. You will have to give the judge some idea of why answering the question would incriminate you. The judge will then decide whether or not to order you to answer the question. If you find yourself in this situation, it is a good idea to get legal advice.

The prosecutor has one more way of getting you to answer. The prosecutor can request that the attorney general grant you *immunity* and then ask the court to order you to answer the question. With a grant of immunity, whatever you say and whatever evidence comes from what you say cannot be used against you in a criminal proceeding. However, the state can still prosecute you for a crime using evidence it receives from someone else, unless it grants you full immunity.

Public employees must testify about anything that concerns their jobs. If they do not after they are told of this duty, they can be fired. Public employees who testify after they claim the privilege against self-incrimination receive automatic immunity against use of the testimony. While the evidence provided by the testifying employee cannot be used to criminally prosecute that employee, it may be used as a good reason for firing him or her.

ARRESTS, SEARCHES, AND QUESTIONING. Under our criminal justice system, arrests, searches, and questioning are permitted only in certain ways so as to protect the person being restrained or arrested.

Arrests. An arrest takes place when a police officer or a private citizen takes someone into custody or restrains them physically or verbally, so that they may be held to answer for a crime or an offense. The person may be taken into custody immediately or be given an *appearance summons* (similar to a traffic ticket) and released. Arrests may be made with or without a warrant.

An arrest warrant is issued by a court. A police officer may serve an arrest warrant any day of the week, at any hour of the day or night. The police officer must state whether he or she is acting under the power of an arrest warrant. If asked, the officer must also show the warrant and provide the subject a chance to read it, either at the time of the arrest (if it is in the officer's possession) or as the officer obtains the warrant after the arrest.

A police officer may arrest a person without a warrant if he or she

- Has reason to believe that a crime, violation, or offense is being committed or attempted in his or her presence.
- Has reason to believe that the person committed a crime, although not in his presence.
- Has reason to believe that the person was lawfully arrested by another individual.

When making an arrest without a warrant, a police officer must state the reason for the arrest, unless the person is in the act of committing the crime or is being chased. In any arrest without a warrant, in New Jersey a police officer may chase the individual beyond the borders of the town or city covered by his or her police department.

If a person resists an arrest, the police officer may use all necessary means to make the arrest, including force.

A police officer with an arrest warrant may break open a door or window to enter a home to make an arrest if entry is refused after the officer has given notice of the authority and purpose for the entry. A police officer can also break in and make an arrest without notice if he or she reasonably believes that the suspect will escape or destroy evidence, or that the officer will be in danger if notice is given.

The law permits a police officer to approach a person in a public place to request information if there is reasonable suspicion that the person is committing, has committed, or is about to commit a crime. The officer may demand the person's name, address, and an explanation of his or her actions. The person, however, is *not* required to answer and has the right to remain silent under the U.S. and New Jersey constitutions.

If a person is taken into police custody, he or she has the right

- To telephone a lawyer, friend, or family member to notify them of the arrest.
- To speak with a lawyer at the place where he or she is being held.
- To remain silent. (The person can remain completely silent or answer some questions and not others.)

When a person is arrested for a crime, an arrest record is made. The person usually will be fingerprinted and photographed. If the person is found not guilty or the case is dismissed, he or she may apply to have the fingerprints and photographs returned and the record of the case sealed.

If personal property or money is taken by the police, the person must be given a receipt showing the amount of money or the type of property taken.

Searches. When a person is lawfully arrested, he or she may be searched. The immediate area of the arrest may also be searched. If a person is held for questioning by a police officer and the officer reasonably suspects that the officer is in danger, the officer may search the suspect for weapons or objects that could cause serious injury. If a dangerous weapon or object is found, the officer may keep it until the questioning is completed. If there is no arrest, the weapon or object must be returned (provided the person has any necessary permit to carry it). During a proper search, if the police officer finds anything else on the suspect that it is a crime to possess, the officer may seize it and arrest the individual for illegal possession.

In most situations except lawful arrest as just described, the police need a search warrant to search someone. A *search warrant* is a written order, signed by a judge, directing a police officer to search a certain place or person for specified property and to bring that property to court. The warrant must describe the place or person to be searched and the property sought.

A police officer conducting a search must show the search warrant and give notice of his or her authority and purpose before making entry and beginning to search, unless the warrant authorizes the police to break in and search without notice. A police officer, in this case, can break in if refused admission after giving proper notice.

Anything taken by the police during an *unlawful* search may not be used later as evidence against the individual who was searched.

A New Jersey law[6] provides that a person arrested on minor charges may not be strip-searched unless

- The search is authorized by warrant,
- The person consents to the search,
- There is probable cause that the person is hiding a weapon, drugs, or evidence of a crime and a recognized exception to the warrant exists, *or*
- The person is in jail or lockup and the search is based on a reasonable suspicion that the person has a weapon, drugs, or contraband.

Questioning. After a person has received a Miranda warning (see the box on the following page), if he or she wants to speak with a lawyer before questioning, the questioning must stop until the lawyer is present. If a person agrees to allow the police to begin questioning, the person may still change his or her mind and ask that the questioning stop until he or she can see a lawyer.

SUPERIOR COURT PROCEEDINGS. All criminal matters not triable in municipal court are prosecuted in New Jersey Superior Court, Law Division, except those cases involving charges of willful nonsupport or interference with custody, which are heard in the Family Part of Chancery Division.

In a criminal trial, the plaintiff is always the state of New Jersey. The party accused of committing the crime is the defendant. Upon the filing of a sworn complaint, a judge will initially determine whether there is probable cause to

THE MIRANDA WARNING

Before the police begin questioning persons arrested or suspected of a crime, they must give them *Miranda warnings.* The police must inform them

- ✔ That they have the right to remain silent,
- ✔ That anything they say may be used against them,
- ✔ That they have the right to speak with a lawyer before answering any questions and to have a lawyer present when they are being questioned,
  and
- ✔ That, if they cannot afford a lawyer, one will be assigned without cost.

believe the defendant committed the offense with which he or she is charged. If the judge determines that probable cause exists, a summons or arrest warrant will be issued, depending upon the seriousness of the offense and other circumstances. A person arrested under a warrant or without a warrant directly by the police in the case of certain serious crimes (violent crimes and drug-related offenses) has the right to be brought before a judge "without unnecessary delay." A person arrested by the police without a warrant for an offense other than certain specified serious crimes will be given a complaint and summons and released, unless the police determine that the person is dangerous, likely to flee, or has other arrest warrants outstanding, or that the prosecution would in some other way be harmed by immediate release. If the person is not released immediately, he or she is entitled to be brought before a judge.

First Appearance. At the first appearance before a judge, a defendant must be

- Informed of the charge made.
- Given a copy of the complaint, if not already furnished.
- Informed of the right to not make a statement concerning the charge and that anything said may be used against him or her.
- Advised of the existence of any *pretrial intervention* (PTI) program.
- Informed of the right to retain counsel; if the defendant cannot afford a lawyer, the right to have counsel furnished without cost.
- Advised of the right to have a probable-cause hearing and indictment by a grand jury if an indictable offense is charged, and whether either of these may be waived. The judge must then allow the defendant a reasonable time to consult counsel.

Bail. All persons charged with crimes in New Jersey, except in death penalty cases, have a right to be freed on bail before the determination of guilt or innocence. The sole purpose of bail is to make sure the defendant appears in court when required. In fixing the amount of bail, the court must take into account the background, residence, employment, and family status of the defendant. Also, the court has the right to impose terms or conditions appropriate for the release of any defendant. The court may release a defendant on his or her own recognizance, or in the custody of the county probation department.

The law allows a municipal court judge to release a defendant on bail. However, the right of a municipal judge to set bail is severely restricted. A judge of the superior court of the county in which the crime was committed or the arrest made will set bail. In general, bail is made by posting collateral, such as cash, real estate, or other security. Most counties allow for the deposit of cash in the amount of 10 percent of the amount of bail fixed.

The law permits the prosecutor to ask for a *declaration of forfeiture of bail* if any condition of the bail agreement is broken. This usually happens when the defendant fails to appear for a scheduled hearing. This means that if you post bail for someone who leaves the state or does not appear in court for a scheduled hearing, you may lose your bail money. If you posted 10 percent of the bail, you will owe the remaining 90 percent. If you used your home as security, you may lose it.

Probable-Cause Hearing. A probable-cause hearing is a proceeding before a judge at which the state has to show that there is *probable cause* (a good reason) to believe that a crime was committed and that the defendant committed it. The defendant has the right to the assistance of a lawyer and to cross-examine the state's witnesses. But the defendant cannot bring his or her own witnesses to the probable-cause hearing. If a judge decides that there is probable cause, he or she will continue the defendant's bail or, if he or she has been detained, extend the detention. The prosecutor can then move to get an indictment. If the judge decides there is no probable cause, the defendant will be released if detained and any bail previously posted will be continued. However, the prosecutor will still be allowed to seek a grand jury indictment. If the prosecutor does not get a grand jury to indict the defendant within 120 days, bail will be returned to the defendant.

If a defendant is indicted by a grand jury before there is a probable-cause hearing, there will be no such hearing since the indictment itself serves as a finding of probable cause.

Grand Jury Indictment. Anyone who is accused of an indictable crime has the right to have a grand jury decide whether or not he or she should be indicted and have to stand trial, or whether the charges should be dropped. A grand jury consists of a group of twenty-three citizens who are chosen in much the same way as other jurors. Only twelve of the twenty-three—a simple majority—must agree to charge the defendant.

A grand jury can consider evidence that the prosecutor presents to it as well as the testimony of other witnesses. It may also consider evidence that could not be admitted in court. The person who is the target of a grand jury inquiry does not have to testify, and the prosecutor has the power to prevent the defendant or his or her witnesses from testifying. The defendant does not have the right to be present during grand jury proceedings. A person appearing before a grand jury has the right to a lawyer but the lawyer must remain outside the grand jury room. If a defendant is inside the jury room, he or she may leave the room whenever he or she needs to consult with the attorney. Finally, grand jury proceedings are usually secret.

If a grand jury decides to charge a defendant, it will issue an *indictment.* An indictment is a written document that charges a defendant with a crime. It must set forth the basic information about the crime. Only one crime can be charged in each *count* of an indictment. The indictment itself can charge one defendant with a number of crimes in several counts. One indictment can also charge two defendants at the same time, if they were involved in the commission of the same crime. An indictment can be issued before or after a defendant has been arrested. After an indictment is returned, a defendant is entitled to a transcript of everything that is said in the grand jury.

Arraignment. After a grand jury issues an indictment or after a defendant has waived the right to an indictment by a grand jury, the defendant is *arraigned.* At an arraignment, the judge presents the indictment to the defendant and asks for a plea. If the defendant does not have a lawyer and has not waived the right to one, the judge cannot accept a guilty plea. If the defendant has not had a *first appearance,* the judge must tell him or her about the right to a lawyer.

The prosecutor has the power, on his or her own, to dismiss a complaint, downgrade a complaint to a less serious charge, or to move to dismiss an indictment. Many criminal cases are eliminated from the court system in this way.

Discovery. Criminal case *discovery* in New Jersey is designed to give defendants maximum information about the case against them. Upon written request, a defendant must be allowed to look at or copy material that pertains to his or her case.

Plea Bargaining. One of the most important things that can take place before a trial is *plea bargaining.* The law permits the prosecutor and defense attorney to talk about pleas and sentences. At the beginning of these talks, the judge is not allowed to participate. If an agreement is reached, information about the crime(s) to which the defendant will plead guilty, the charge(s) to be dismissed, or the sentence the prosecutor will recommend must be stated to the judge, in open court, at the time the guilty plea is entered.

At this time, the judge may indicate his or her feelings about the proposed agreement. The judge may also condition any approval on receipt of the presentence report, which is prepared by the county probation department.

After the proposed plea-bargain agreement is placed on the record, the judge must question the defendant about his or her proposed plea of guilty. No guilty plea may be accepted unless the court is satisfied (1) that the facts support a plea of guilty *and* (2) that the defendant is voluntarily pleading guilty and understands the nature of the charge(s) and the consequences of the plea.

Assuming there is no guilty plea, whether through a plea bargain or otherwise, the case will then proceed to trial.

Pretrial Intervention. New Jersey courts may remove certain defendants, generally first-time offenders, from ordinary criminal prosecution to allow them to undergo early rehabilitative services. This has been done under the PTI program. The PTI program provides defendants charged with criminal offenses in New Jersey courts with opportunities for alternatives to the traditional criminal justice process of ordinary prosecution.

The purposes of PTI are

- To give defendants rehabilitative services, such as counseling or drug and alcohol abuse treatment, when such services can reasonably be expected to prevent future criminal behavior by the defendant and there is a connection between the crime charged and the need for rehabilitative services.
- To provide an alternative to prosecution for defendants who might be harmed by criminal penalties, when rehabilitative services can be expected to prevent any future criminal conduct.
- To provide a way for the least burdensome form of prosecution for defendants charged with "victimless" crimes.
- To help reduce the number of minor criminal cases, allowing the police and courts to work on cases involving serious crimes.
- To deter future criminal or disorderly behavior by a defendant participating in the PTI program.[7]

A defendant should apply for acceptance in the PTI program as early as possible upon the commencement of proceedings. Applications should be made to the Criminal Division of New Jersey Superior Court in the county where the criminal charge is filed, not later than seven days after the defendant's original plea to the indictment. Any defendant who is charged with an indictable offense may apply. The admissions guidelines set forth in the court rules include

- *Minor violations.* Defendants are ineligible if the likely result of the offense would be a suspended sentence without probation or fine.
- *Prior record of convictions.* Defendants who have been previously convicted are generally excluded from the program.
- *Parolees and probationers.* Defendants who are on parole or probation are generally excluded without the prosecutor's consent and are considered only after consultation with parole and probation departments.

- *Defendants previously diverted.* The program excludes defendants who have been previously granted a diversionary program or conditional discharge.

The application process includes an interview with the defendant by a staff member of the Criminal Division of superior court. A written decision is prepared admitting or rejecting the defendant and is forwarded to the prosecutor and defense counsel. The defendant is accepted into PTI on the recommendation of the Criminal Division of superior court, with the consent of the prosecutor and defendant. The appropriateness of a defendant's admission to PTI is measured by his or her amenability to correction and responsiveness to rehabilitation, as well as by the nature of the offense involved.[8] The judge may then postpone all further action against a defendant on such charges for a period not to exceed thirty-six months. At the end of the period set forth, the judge makes one of the following decisions:

- Dismiss the case against the defendant,
- Further postpone all action against the defendant for an additional period not to exceed thirty-six months,
  or
- Order the prosecution of the defendant to proceed.

If accepted, the conditions for participation are set forth in the PTI order and must be followed for the defendant to successfully complete the program. If for any reason the defendant is *not* accepted, the defendant may appeal the decision to the presiding judge of the Criminal Division of superior court. In cases in which a preindictment application is made, the prosecutor may withhold action on the application until the matter has been presented to the grand jury.

Participant supervision in the PTI program may average from one to three years. Certain standard conditions are imposed on those accepted into PTI, such as random urine monitoring, and assessments for fees, penalties, and fines. Additional conditions may include performance of community service, payment of restitution, and submission to psychological and/or drug and alcohol evaluations with compliance to recommended treatment programs. Upon successful completion of the PTI program, the original charges are dismissed and no record of conviction remains. If, however, the defendant does not successfully comply with all the conditions of the program, the defendant is terminated from PTI and returned to the trial list.

The Trial. The first step before a trial actually begins is the selection of a jury. The right of trial by jury in criminal cases is guaranteed by both the U.S. and New Jersey constitutions. A criminal jury is composed of twelve people, although at any time before a verdict both parties can agree to a jury of fewer people.

Each party to a trial has the right to have jurors who are free from prejudice or bias, with open minds, and without any preconceived opinions as to how the case should be decided. Questions may be asked of prospective jurors concerning any matter which may disclose bias or prejudice or other reasons why a juror should not be selected in the case about to be tried.

In addition, it is the duty of each juror to disclose any fact that might affect his or her ability to render an impartial verdict. If he or she is acquainted with any of the parties, witnesses, or lawyers in the case on trial, he or she should say so without being asked.

When a juror's answers disclose something that might affect the juror's ability to reach an impartial verdict, either party may *challenge the juror for cause*. If the judge believes that the juror's ability to make an impartial verdict might be affected by facts or opinions disclosed in his or her answers, the judge must excuse the juror.

Even if there is no legal reason for a challenge for cause, a trial lawyer may feel that a particular juror should not sit on a particular case. Each side has the right to excuse a limited number of jurors without a reason. This is called a *peremptory challenge*.

In criminal trials, the first juror picked and accepted by both sides is designated by the court as the foreperson of the jury.

After the jury has been selected and sworn and before the trial starts, the judge must give preliminary instructions to the jury.

During a trial, jurors must report promptly for each court session and listen carefully to every question and answer and all evidence presented. Also, jurors should not discuss the case with fellow jurors or anyone else until the case has been formally submitted to the jury by the judge and deliberations have begun. If anyone attempts to discuss the case with a juror or influence his or her decision, the juror has an obligation to report this to the judge.

If, during the trial, a juror wishes to bring to the attention of the judge some matter affecting his or her service, such as a personal emergency, he or she can send a written message to the judge through the court clerk. He or she may ask to discuss his or her problem with the judge in the judge's chambers.

The trial will start with an *opening statement* by the state; this is optional for the defendant. The opening statements serve the same function in a criminal case as in a civil trial. Opening statements are not evidence.

The procedure for calling witnesses in criminal trials is similar to that in civil trials. The state must offer evidence in support of its accusation against the defendant. The state's witnesses are called first. The defendant's attorney may cross-examine these witnesses and the state may then reexamine. At the close of the state's evidence, the defendant may call his or her witnesses and offer evidence in his or her defense. The state can cross-examine and the defendant can then reexamine.

Finally, the state may offer further evidence in rebuttal. The defendant may rebut this additional evidence. In conclusion, both the state and the defendant may *sum up*. These summations serve the same functions as those in civil trials. The defendant sums up first.

After all witnesses have been heard and the attorneys have summed up, the judge will instruct the jury as to the law applicable to the particular facts of the case. Among other things, the judge will inform the jury that the state must prove the truth of all charges against the defendant *beyond a reasonable doubt* to obtain a conviction. It is the duty of the jurors to accept the law as explained to them by the judge, even though they may believe the law is or should be otherwise. The jury must then determine from the evidence presented whether or not the state has proven guilt beyond a reasonable doubt.

When the jury retires for deliberation, it is the duty of the *foreperson* to ensure that the discussion is carried on in a sensible and orderly fashion and that every juror has a chance to say what he or she thinks. Jurors should deliberate with open minds and give respectful consideration to the opinions of their fellow jurors. Most important, they must not be hesitant to change their minds when reason and logic so dictate.

If, during their deliberations, the jurors wish to ask a question of the judge or desire further instructions or testimony to be reread, the foreperson may send written requests or questions to the judge.

To reach a verdict in a criminal case, there must be unanimous agreement by all the jurors. If the jurors are unable to agree, the jury may be considered a *hung jury* and it will be up to the state to decide whether or not to hold a new trial.

CRIMINAL APPEALS. A person who is tried in superior court and convicted of a crime has the right to appeal that conviction, or the terms of the sentence, to the Appellate Division of the superior court. In some cases, the state may appeal the trial court's dismissal of an indictment, accusation, or complaint. But the right of the state to appeal is very limited because both the United States and New Jersey constitutions provide that a criminal defendant shall not be tried twice for the same offense. Courts have held that the state cannot appeal if the trial court dismisses the indictment on the ground that the state's case was inadequate. On the other hand, it has been held that if the trial court dismisses the complaint because it believes that the law under which the defendant was prosecuted is unconstitutional, then the state has a right to appeal. It has also been held that the state can appeal an illegal sentence. The state's time to appeal starts to run when the sentence is imposed, not when the judgment of conviction is entered.

An appeal must be filed within forty-five days of the time a final judgment is entered by the trial court. In cases in which the defendant makes a proper request for a new trial, the time for filing an appeal does not begin to run until the request for a new trial has been denied. The defendant is also excused from the forty-five-day requirement if his or her lawyer drops the case or if the defendant becomes mentally incapacitated.

An appeal is begun by filing a written notice of appeal with the Appellate Division. It must be served upon the county prosecutor and the Appellate Section of the New Jersey Division of Criminal Justice. The defendant must also file a *case information statement* presenting basic information about the appeal on a prescribed form. A copy of the notice of appeal and a request for a transcript must also be sent to the trial court.

The notice of appeal must set forth the defendant-appellant's name and address or the address of the appellant's lawyer. It must also give a short, clear statement of the offense, the trial court's judgment, the date of judgment, and any sentence imposed. If the defendant is in custody, it must state where he or she is being held. It must also provide the name of the trial court and indicate the court to which the appeal is directed.

If the defendant-appellant is indigent and cannot afford to pay the fees for filing the appeal or for a transcript, he or she may apply to the court for an order granting him or her a free transcript. This order, when signed by a judge, constitutes a notice of appeal. Also, if the defendant-appellant is *pro se* (not represented by a lawyer), the clerk of the Appellate Division must notify all the parties that an appeal has been filed. At the time of application for a free transcript, a low-income defendant-appellant can also apply to have an attorney appointed to handle the appeal and will then be referred to the Office of the Public Defender.

A sentence of imprisonment will not be stayed just because an appeal is filed. The defendant, however, may be granted bail pending the outcome of the appeal. Bail will be granted to a convicted defendant pending appeal if it appears that the case involves a substantial question that should be decided by the Appellate Division, and if the safety of any person or the community will not be seriously threatened by releasing the defendant. In cases in which the sentence involves the payment of a fine or probation, the trial judge may stay the sentence pending the outcome of the appeal.

In criminal cases, the appellate court can consider whether a jury verdict was against the weight of the evidence *only* if the appellant made a request for a new trial on that basis to the trial court. The ruling of the trial court on that request will not be overturned unless it clearly appears that there was a miscarriage of justice. If the appeal is based on an error or omission made by the trial court, that error or omission will be disregarded by the appellate court, unless the error was clearly capable of producing an unjust result. If the appellate court does find that the trial court made an error that was clearly capable of causing an unjust result, it can reverse the trial court, even if the error was not brought to its attention by the defendant. If a judgment of conviction is reversed because the appellate court finds that the sentence imposed was illegal, the appellate court can either impose the correct sentence or send the case back to the trial court to impose the proper sentence.

MUNICIPAL COURT PROCEEDINGS. Most cities and towns have municipal courts. The power of these courts is limited to the types of cases listed below, when the incident or violation of law is alleged to have taken place within the boundaries of the municipality. Cases that can be heard by a municipal court judge include

- Violations of motor vehicle and traffic laws.
- Violations of fishing and hunting laws.
- Violations of the municipality's ordinances.
- Disorderly and petty disorderly persons offenses.
- Neighborhood disputes.
- Crimes that have a penalty of less than $1,000 or a year in jail, including theft, receiving stolen property, and forgery, provided that the loss or the value of the item(s) is under $500. Even these cases can be heard in municipal court *only* if the defendant waives the right to an indictment and a trial by jury and the prosecutor agrees.

Your Rights in Municipal Court. As in any other court, basic constitutional protections apply to most municipal court cases, including

- The right to hire an attorney.
- The right to be assigned an attorney if you are charged with an indictable offense and the judge determines that you cannot afford an attorney.
- The right to be assigned an attorney if you are charged with a nonindictable offense, the judge determines that you cannot afford an attorney, and there is a likelihood that if you are convicted you will either go to jail, receive a large fine, or have your driver's license suspended.
- The right to have your case postponed so that you may have a chance to consult with your lawyer and prepare a proper defense.
- The right to be informed of the charges against you.
- The right to remain silent concerning the charges against you.
- The right to plead guilty or not guilty to certain nonindictable charges against you. Examples of nonindictable charges are traffic offenses, disorderly persons offenses, and violations of municipal ordinances.
- If you are charged with an indictable offense, the right to a probable-cause hearing before a judge and to a trial by jury in superior court if a grand jury indicts you.
- For certain indictable offenses, the right to be tried in front of the municipal court judge by waiving, in writing, your right to indictment and to a jury trial in the Law Division of superior court.

- The right to be informed of whether the charges against you are indictable offenses.
- The right to be presumed innocent until proven guilty beyond a reasonable doubt.
- The right to testify or to not testify on your own behalf.
- The right to call or subpoena witnesses to testify on your behalf.

Disorderly Persons Cases. Disorderly persons offenses are minor offenses. They are called "quasi-criminal," meaning that they are not considered quite as serious as full crimes; however, they are still subject to the legal protections and rules covering all criminal prosecutions. Examples of disorderly persons offenses are failing to send a child to public school or provide equivalent education elsewhere, desecrating a public monument, using foul language in public, and smoking on a bus.

Any person can charge you with a disorderly persons offense or a petty disorderly persons offense by filing a complaint against you. The municipal court clerk, the municipal court judge, or the local police can then issue either a summons for you to appear in court or an arrest warrant.

Municipal Court Trials. Most municipal court cases are heard on the return date of the summons. On the date of the trial, cases in which the defendant is represented by an attorney are usually given priority, unless the case will involve a considerable amount of time to hear. Lengthy cases are usually scheduled for a special time.

Prior to the opening of the trial, the judge must make sure that you understand the complaint. The judge must also tell you that you have a right to have a lawyer represent you and that the court can assign a lawyer to represent you if you cannot afford one and are charged with an offense for which you could go to prison or suffer other serious consequences. If you are entitled to a court-appointed lawyer, you will be represented either by the municipal public defender or by an assigned private lawyer. If you are entitled to a court-appointed lawyer or request the opportunity to speak to a lawyer, the judge must postpone your case to give you an opportunity to do so.

When you are before the court, you can either enter a guilty plea or plead not guilty. The judge must talk to you to make sure that if you are pleading guilty it is voluntary, that there is a reason for your plea, and that you understand the consequences of your plea. If you are entering a guilty plea to a traffic offense other than a parking violation, the judge must advise you that the conviction will become part of your driving record.

Some municipalities have prosecutors who appear at each municipal court session and act as prosecutors for all cases presented. In cases in which there is no prosecutor and the complaint was filed by a private citizen, the private citizen can have his or her attorney prosecute the case. If neither the complainant nor the defendant is represented by a lawyer, the judge will question the witnesses to bring out all the facts. It is improper for police officers to question witnesses since they are not parties to the action and cannot prosecute a case without engaging in the unauthorized practice of law.

Regardless of who has the duty to prosecute, the complaining party must prove its case "beyond a reasonable doubt," and you do not have to testify if you do not want to.

Each judge is responsible for the orderly conduct of his or her court. The judge, however, cannot impose an unreasonable dress code on persons who appear in court.

Normally, the judge does not require or permit opening statements, except in complicated cases. Each witness should be sworn individually and his or her name and address noted by the court.

All proceedings in municipal court must be recorded by sound-recording equipment. Witnesses must therefore speak into a microphone when testifying.

If the judge finds you guilty of a traffic or other nonindictable offense, the penalty cannot be imprisonment for more than six months and you will be sentenced immediately. Prior to sentencing, the judge must give you a chance to make a statement. Thereafter, you may be ordered to pay a fine, serve time in jail, or both.

Municipal court traffic cases are discussed in Chapter 10, "You and Your Car."

Appeals of Municipal Court Convictions. You can appeal a municipal court conviction to the Criminal Part of the New Jersey Superior Court, Law Division. When you appeal, you can ask the municipal court judge or the superior court judge to *stay* (stop the enforcement of) any fine or other sentence you received while the appeal is pending.

To start an appeal, you must file a notice of appeal with the municipal court clerk within ten days of the written judgment. Within five days after you file the notice of appeal with the clerk, you must send one copy to the prosecuting attorney—usually the county prosecutor—and one copy to the superior court clerk in that county. You must pay a filing fee (unless you are indigent) and show the superior court clerk that you served the municipal court clerk and the prosecuting attorney with the notice of appeal.

If the municipal court hearing was recorded, you must get a copy of the transcript. If you cannot afford one, you can ask the superior court judge to have the county or the municipality pay for the cost of reproducing it.

If there was a record of the hearing, the superior court judge will hear the case *de novo,* or on the record. This means that the judge will re-examine the case but will usually not hear testimony or consider new evidence. Since the superior court judge will not hear testimony, he or she will accept what the municipal court judge decided about the credibility of the witnesses. If there is no record or if the record is not clear, the superior court judge will hear testimony. The superior court judge can uphold the municipal court judge or set aside the conviction. He or she can also send the case back to the municipal court. The municipal court can then lower the fine or sentence you received but it cannot increase it.

JUVENILE OFFENSES. The law defines a *juvenile* as a person who is under the age of eighteen. New Jersey has set up a special system for handling juvenile problems because the state is required to try to help the juvenile rather than punish him or her.

POLICE MISCONDUCT

The U.S. system of law places a tremendous amount of power and responsibility on police officers.

In decisions interpreting constitutional guaranties, courts have decreed that in cases in which there is evidence of police misconduct involving a search or arrest, it is preferable to allow the accused who might be guilty to go free than to condone improper police conduct. These decisions maintain that to convict someone under such circumstances would encourage police misconduct, and that to allow lawbreaking by police officers under any circumstances places all of society in danger and destroys the very nature of our system of justice.

If you have been charged with a crime in an incident involving police misconduct, you should tell your attorney what happened. If the police officer obtained evidence by violating your rights, your attorney may move to have the evidence *suppressed* so that it cannot be used against you. Your attorney may also advise you to file a formal complaint with the police department involved.

There are also civil remedies. A federal statute creates a right to sue if constitutional or civil rights are violated by a person acting "under color of state law." This includes police officers who are employed by a municipality or the state and may include their supervisors and the municipality that employs them. Suits under this law (often called Section 1983) may be brought in either federal or state court and must be filed within two years of the incident. Police officers or other defendants may defend themselves by claiming that they acted in *good faith.* The U.S. Supreme Court has defined this as a standard for situations in which an official is acting sincerely and with a belief that he or she is doing right.

In New Jersey, police officers enjoy the protection of the Tort Claims Act.[9] This law provides that public employees will not be held liable if they act in good faith in the enforcement of any law. It does not, however, protect officers from liability for acts outside the scope of their employment or for conduct that constitutes a crime, actual fraud, malice, or willful misconduct. Thus, you can sue an officer for committing an act of assault, battery, false arrest, or false imprisonment. However, the officer can defend himself or herself by showing a good-faith reason for doing what he or she did. If a criminal charge against you is dismissed or if you are acquitted, you can also sue for malicious prosecution or *malicious use of process*, although these suits are very hard to win. You will have to show that the officer lacked a good reason for his or her actions and acted with bad intentions.

EXPUNGEMENTS

Expungement is the process of eliminating records of convictions from police and court records. The purpose of New Jersey's expungement law[10] is to give a person who has very few convictions a "fresh start." The law also provides for the removal of all records of arrests for cases in which the arrest did not end in a conviction.

A person who is eligible for expungement must prepare and file a petition for expungement in the superior court in the county where the arrest and/or prosecution took place. A judge then decides whether an order of expungement should be granted. An order of expungement deletes, with some exceptions, the record of the criminal proceedings. It also allows the person to fill out school, job, and military applications truthfully without having to declare that they were once arrested or convicted.

The law *does* allow expunged records to be considered when a person applies for a job with a law enforcement agency, such as departments of corrections, police, and the court system. This does not mean that such law enforcement agencies will never hire persons with records but that those applying must still reveal the existence of an expunged record on a job application.

When an expungement is granted, law enforcement agencies are required by law to keep that person's records private. However, expunged records may be subsequently used for very limited purposes. If a person is arrested following expungement, his or her past records will be considered in deciding eligibility for a PTI program, bail, or probation. If a victim files a claim with the Violent Crimes Compensation Board, the expunged records of the person who was convicted of the crime can be used in connection with that claim. Also, when a person is imprisoned, the Department of Corrections is allowed to use the person's expunged records in deciding how to classify and assign him or her within an institution. Finally, following a conviction and jail sentence, expunged records can be used in deciding eligibility for *parole* (early release).

The expungement procedure is quite simple. A handbook has been prepared by Legal Services of New Jersey to assist you if you cannot afford a lawyer and must do your own work. If, on the other hand, you can afford an attorney, you may want him or her to take you through the process. The following information should help you in deciding whether or not you are eligible to have your records expunged.

ELIGIBILITY FOR EXPUNGEMENT. Eligibility depends on the type and number of criminal records a person has. If the conviction or guilty plea was entered in superior court, then it was for an indictable offense. If, on the other hand, the conviction or guilty plea was entered in a municipal court, it was probably a disorderly persons conviction (punishable by less than six months) or a violation of a municipal ordinance. Motor vehicle convictions, which often occur in municipal court, may not be expunged as they are not considered criminal offenses but rather violations of motor vehicle regulations.

To be eligible to expunge an indictable conviction, you cannot have had any other indictable convictions in any state at any time. You cannot have more than two subsequent disorderly persons convictions after the conviction for the indictable offense. You must wait at least ten years from the conviction, payment of fine, completion of probation or parole, or release from jail, whichever is latest.

The following convictions for indictable crimes occurring *after* September 1, 1979, *cannot* be expunged: murder, kidnapping, aggravated sexual assault, robbery, arson and related offenses, perjury, false swearing, and conspiracies or attempts to commit such crimes. The following indictable crimes committed *prior* to September 1, 1979, also cannot be expunged: murder, manslaughter, treason, anarchy, kidnapping, rape, forcible sodomy, arson, perjury, false swearing, robbery, *embracery* (bribing or influencing a juror), a conspiracy or any attempt to commit any of the foregoing, or aiding, assisting, or concealing persons accused of the foregoing crimes. Also, convictions for certain drug crimes cannot be expunged.

To expunge a disorderly persons conviction, you cannot have had any indictable convictions in any state at any time. You must wait five years from the date of conviction, payment of fine, completion of probation or parole, or release from jail, whichever is latest. You cannot have had more than three subsequent disorderly persons convictions.

To expunge a conviction for a violation of a municipal ordinance (not including traffic offenses), the requirements are the same as for disorderly persons convictions except that the waiting period is two years from the date of conviction, payment of fine, satisfactory completion of probation, or release from jail, whichever is latest.

In some cases, people who are convicted of certain drug offenses when they were under twenty-one years of age can get special consideration.

EXPUNGING AN ARREST RECORD. A record of an arrest can hurt your reputation as much as one indicating a conviction. It is as important, therefore, to expunge an arrest record as it is the record of a conviction.

If a person was arrested for any offense but not convicted (either because he or she found not guilty or the charges were never brought to trial), the person is eligible for an expungement at any time. However, if the person was found not guilty by reason of completing a PTI program, the person must wait six months. If the person was found not guilty by reason of insanity, expungement is not permitted.

In all cases, a person must not have any charges pending or otherwise still open when he or she files a petition for expungement. If a person had one or more charges dismissed or discharged as the result of a plea bargain in which the person agreed to a conviction on other charges, that conviction must be expunged before the arrest record of the dismissed charges can be expunged.

13. Educating Your Children

This chapter discusses various rights and responsibilities of parents, children, and school officials. It includes an overview of the right of access to education and some specific rights and obligations of public school students. It also discusses some particular educational requirements, such as bilingual education, special needs of low-income children, vocational education requirements, and educational rights of the handicapped.

RIGHTS AND RESPONSIBILITIES OF ATTENDING PUBLIC SCHOOLS

New Jersey law requires that free public education be provided to all residents between the ages of five and twenty.[1] The goal of the public school system, as required by the New Jersey Constitution, is to provide students with an education that is both "thorough and efficient."[2] A "thorough and efficient" education has been defined as one that provides the educational opportunity that is needed to equip students to fulfill their roles as citizens and competitors in the market.[3] Children with disabilities are entitled to a free and appropriate education from the time of their third birthday until they are twenty-one years old.

Parents are responsible for sending their children to school between the ages of six and sixteen. They must regularly send them to public school or provide them with an equivalent education elsewhere. Parents can teach their children at home, if the home instruction is equivalent to the school instruction. Parents who do not comply with this law can be charged with a disorderly persons offense and fined.[4]

School officials are also responsible for seeing that all children between the ages of six and sixteen attend school. They must require school attendance and have policies and procedures in place that ensure maximum attendance. Policies that encourage absences are not allowed.

Each school district is required to have attendance officers to look into all attendance problems and warn *truant* children and their parents or guardians of the consequences of continued absence. When they find that a child has not been attending school, the attendance officers must notify the parents or guardians in writing.

School attendance officers have the power to take into custody any child who is found to be illegally absent from school. Juvenile-delinquency charges can be brought against any child between the ages of six and sixteen who is repeatedly absent from school and whose parents are unable to make him or her attend school.[5]

Each school district is also required to have an *issuing officer* who is an employee of the child's school district. The issuing officer is responsible for providing "working papers" or employment certificates required for children to work. (See the section entitled "Children and Employment" in Chapter 5, "You and Your Job," for information regarding children who work.)

RESIDENCY LAW. As a rule, a school district will not allow a child who does not live in the district to attend its schools free of charge. Many districts, however, allow out-of-district students to attend their schools under certain circumstances upon the payment of tuition.[6]

School districts have also tried to keep children who live in the district with someone other than their parents from enrolling in the district schools. The purpose of this policy is to prevent children whose actual home is in one school district from attending school in another district that has a better school system. A child who stays with someone other than his or her parents can enroll in the school district in which he or she is actually residing if the person with whom the child is living is keeping the child free of charge (just as if he or she were the child's parent) and files an affidavit saying that he or she[7]

- Lives in the school district,
- Is taking care of the child for free,
- Will assume school-related responsibilities for the child,
  and
- Intends to keep and support the child for free for a time period longer than the school term.

A school board may ask the commissioner of education to decide if what is said in the affidavit is true. While this is being decided, however, the child must be allowed to attend school. If the commissioner decides that the evidence does not show that the child is fully supported by the resident, the commissioner can authorize the school district to charge the resident tuition for the child.

It is a disorderly persons offense for someone to (1) allow another person's child to live in his or her residence solely for school attendance purposes *or* (2) claim to have given up custody to a person in another district solely for school attendance purposes.

EDUCATIONAL LAWS CONCERNING HOMELESS CHILDREN. Special rules apply when a family temporarily moves from one school district to another as a result of being homeless. In that case, the school district where the parent or guardian last resided prior to being homeless—known as the *district of residence*—is responsible for the education of the homeless child.[8] After consulting with the parent or guardian, the district of residence must determine which of the following educational placements is in the child's best interest:

- To continue the child's education in the school district where he or she last attended school,
- To enroll the child in the district of residence (if not the same as the district where he or she last attended school),

  or
- To enroll the child in the school district where the child is temporarily living.

In making the determination, the district of residence is required to consider the parent or guardian's preference; the continuity of the child's educational program; the eligibility of the child for special instructional programs; and distance, travel time, and safety factors in transporting the child to school.[9]

Transportation services for a homeless child are to be provided by the district where the child attends school, although the district of residence is responsible for the costs of transportation. The district of residence is also responsible for the cost of the child's tuition in another district.

Each school district is required to have a liaison for the education of homeless children to facilitate cooperation among school districts. The liaison of a district where a child is temporarily living is required to notify the liaison of the district of residence of the child's presence within twenty-four hours. The superintendent of the district of residence is then required to make a decision as to the child's educational placement within three school days. If the parent or guardian objects to the placement decision, he or she has the right to appeal: first to the county superintendent of schools, second by requesting mediation through the state's Office of Education for Homeless Children and Youth, and finally, by filing an appeal to the state commissioner of education. The homeless child must be placed in the district designated by the county superintendent pending the outcome of the appeal.

TRANSPORTATION TO SCHOOL. School districts are required to provide free transportation to students who live far from the school building. This means providing transportation beyond two and one-half miles for high school students (grades nine through twelve) and beyond two miles for elementary school students (kindergarten through eighth grade).[10] Distance is determined by measuring the shortest route along roadways or walkways from the entrance of the student's home to the nearest public entrance to the school.

Students who cannot walk even short distances to school because of handicaps must be provided free transportation to school. However, school districts may, if they find it desirable, also provide transportation to students who live shorter distances from school, if the child must walk along dangerous roads to get there. If the school district decides not to provide transportation to your child, you can go to your town council with other parents and ask the council to provide crossing guards or traffic lights. The school system is not responsible for providing a safe route to and from school; however, the town can be.

The school bus driver is responsible for keeping order on the bus; however, the driver may not prevent a student from riding the bus. The driver must report an unmanageable student to the school principal, who has the power to exclude the student from the bus. During the exclusion, the student's parents must provide school transportation.

SCHOOL PUSHOUTS, SUSPENSIONS, AND EXPULSIONS

A child's right to attend school is an important one. Students should neither be encouraged to leave school nor be suspended or expelled except for very bad behavior.

PUSHOUTS. Local school boards are required to have procedures for identifying students who are failing and to provide extra services to them so that they may reach grade level. School officials should not suggest that a student leave school or drop a student from school for failing classes or for poor attendance. Pushing a student out of school takes away the student's right to a free public education.

If your child is in danger of being pushed out, meet with your child's teachers, guidance counselor, and school principal to work out a plan to keep your child in school. The plan that is developed should be aimed at solving or lessening your child's problems in school.

SUSPENSIONS OR EXPULSIONS. School officials may suspend or expel students only if their behavior directly violates one of the school's discipline policies or is harmful to themselves or others. Suspension or expulsions should be used only for serious violations of school rules that call for immediate and strong action, not as punishment for minor violations of school rules

A student may be suspended or expelled for any of the following reasons[11]:

- Breaking school rules more than once.
- Disobeying a teacher, principal, or school aide.
- Hitting or fighting with another student or causing another student to be in danger.
- Hitting or fighting with a teacher, principal, or school aide.
- Taking or trying to steal money or property from another student.
- Destroying or trying to destroy or damage school property.

- Helping other students take over a school building.
- Taking over a school building with other students and not leaving when told to leave by a person in charge.
- Persuading Getting other students to be illegally absent from school.
- Illegal possession or consumption or being under the influence of alcoholic beverages or controlled dangerous substances.

Sending a child home or out into the street may cause the child to get into additional trouble and is therefore not the best punishment for bad behavior. Many schools now have *in-school suspensions.* These programs are usually held in the school but outside the regular classroom. The goal of an in-school suspension is to have the student off the streets and back in class as soon as possible.

RIGHTS OF A STUDENT BEFORE SUSPENSION. A student is entitled to the following rights prior to a suspension of less than ten days:

- Verbal or written notice of the charges against him or her,
- If the student denies the charges, an explanation of the evidence in support of the charges,
  and
- An opportunity to tell his or her side of the story.

If your child is suspended for less than ten days, you and your child may talk to the school principal. A hearing before the board of education is not required. The student also has no right to be represented by a lawyer or to confront or question the witnesses against him or her.

A student who misbehaves may be suspended from school for up to ten days by a principal or district superintendent. However, only your local school board may expel or suspend your child for more than ten days, and then only after it has given the child a hearing.

A student suspended for more than ten days has the right to have a prompt hearing before the board of education. At the hearing, the student can tell his or her side of the story, bring witnesses to testify, and be represented by a lawyer. The student, or his or her lawyer, has a right to confront and question witnesses against the student.

If the parents agree, a suspended student may be sent to a child-study team to decide if the child needs special education. Child-study teams are discussed in more detail later in the chapter. (See the discussion on special education in the section entitled "Disabled Children's Right to Education.")

If your child is suspended, check to see if he or she will be automatically readmitted after the suspension period, or if there are any conditions that must be met.

A student may not be given low grades as punishment for losing time in class during a suspension. A suspended student must be given the chance to make up work missed. The make-up grade must be the same as the grade that would have been received for work done on time.

RIGHTS OF A STUDENT BEFORE EXPULSION. Only the local board of education has the power to expel a student. A student facing expulsion has the right to a prompt and full hearing before the board. Before a hearing, a student has the right to be given a full and detailed statement of the complaint(s) that have been made against him or her. This includes the identity of witnesses and statements or affidavits by them verifying the charge(s) against the student.

At the hearing, the student can tell his or her side of the story. The student can also bring witnesses who support his or her side of the story, as well as a lawyer to defend him or her. At the hearing, the student or his or her lawyer has the right to ask questions of the witnesses against the student. If these witnesses do not appear in person to answer these questions at the hearing, then their statements cannot be considered by the school board.

Before a student is expelled, the student must be sent to the local child-study team for a full evaluation.

STUDENT RECORDS

School records contain grades, reports of misbehavior, evaluations by teachers, evaluations and referrals for special education, I.Q. scores, psychological reports, medical histories, and other information placed in them by school personnel.

School districts may only compile two kinds of student records:

1. *Mandated records.* These are school records that are required by law. They usually include the student's name, home address, age, parents' names, ethnic origin, names of brothers and sisters, place of birth, race, sex, health history, school attendance, student progress, and educational classification.
2. *Permitted records.* These are records that are usually allowed by the rules of the local school board. They can include teacher observations, school-work, standardized tests, and information given to the school by the parent or student. This type of permitted information cannot be given out by the school to other persons or agencies without the parents' permission.[12]

Records not allowed to be placed in a student's file include things said about the student by outsiders and the religion or political party to which the student belongs.

RIGHT TO EXAMINE SCHOOL RECORDS. Parents of minor children and students age eighteen and over have the right to examine or obtain copies of the child's school records.[13] When a student reaches age eighteen, a parent can no longer review the student's records without the student's permission. When a student graduates or permanently leaves the school system, the parent or adult student must be notified in writing that a copy of the entire record will be given to them upon request.

The law requires school officials to review the records of students every year and delete information that no longer accurately describes the student or school situation. School officials must remove this information in a way that leaves no sign that such information was ever there in the first place.

RIGHT TO CHALLENGE INACCURATE OR MISLEADING RECORDS. Parents and adult students also have the right to challenge and, if necessary, correct any inaccurate or misleading information in school records related to the child.[14] Student records can be challenged by parents and adult students on grounds of inaccuracy, irrelevancy, or inclusion of improper information. The parent or adult student may seek to (1) take out inaccurate, irrelevant, or otherwise improper information from the records; *and/or* (2) put in additional and reasonable comments as to the meaning and/or accuracy of the records.

If the school denies the request by a parent or student that a change be made to the school records, the parent or student can appeal the decision. To appeal, a parent or student must notify the chief school administrator in writing of the specific problems relating to the record. Within ten days of notification, the chief school administrator, or his or her delegate, must meet with the parent or student to review the issue set forth in the appeal. If the matter is not resolved satisfactorily, the parent or student may appeal to the local board of education or to the commissioner of education within ten days.

If the appeal is made to the local school board, the board must make its decision within twenty days. If the parent or student is unhappy with the decision made by the local school board, he or she may appeal the decision to the commissioner.

The parent or adult student making an appeal must be given a full and fair opportunity to give evidence that the school record changes he or she requests should be made. The law also requires that a record of the appeal proceedings and outcome be made a part of the student's record.

PRIVACY OF RECORDS. A school may not allow anyone to have access to a student's records without the permission of the parent or adult student, except

- Certified school officials in the same school district who have been assigned educational responsibility for the student.
- Federal and New Jersey educational agencies checking to see that the school is obeying federal laws.
- Any outside individuals or agencies, if the school is ordered to show them specific records by a court (however, unless told by the court *not* to do

so, the school must give the parent or adult student at least three days' notice of the name of the requesting agency and the specific records requested).

- School officials in a school district to which a child intends to transfer.

In addition, some limited "directory information" from a student's school record may be made public by the school, such as the student's name, address, and telephone number. The school must inform the parent or adult student each year what directory information will be made public. A parent or a student over age eighteen may request that the school not include his or her name in a student directory.

Parents and adult students may challenge school officials' decisions to release a student's records without consent, or to deny access to the records to agencies or persons who have been given permission to see them. The rules for appealing a decision by school officials regarding access to student records are the same as those for challenging information contained in the records.

GENDER DISCRIMINATION IN EDUCATION

A federal law known as Title IX[15] makes gender discrimination in public schools illegal. The law says that, with certain limited exceptions, no person shall be discriminated against in any educational program or activity receiving federal financial assistance.

Under the law, no student may be denied the right to take a particular course because of his or her gender. This applies to all courses, including shop, home economics, and vocational and physical education. In fact, a school may not set up separate classes for male and female students for any subjects other than sex education and contact sports.

Title IX also makes it illegal for schools to engage in gender discrimination in school admission policies, admission tests, employment practices, and the granting of financial aid.

The law protects students who are married or pregnant, or who are parents. A female student may not be excluded because of pregnancy from any school activity, including regular classes, extracurricular activities, or special events, such as graduation ceremonies. A school must excuse an absence for pregnancy and readmit a student to the same grade level she held when she left school.

For extracurricular sports, separate teams are permissible provided that the selection of the members of the team is based upon competitive skills, or the activity involved is a *contact sport*. Contact sports include boxing, wrestling, rugby, ice hockey, football, and basketball. However, if a school has a noncontact sports team for only one sex, members of the other sex must be given an opportunity to try out for the team on the basis of ability.[16]

Every school district is required to prepare and publish grievance procedures for the quick and fair handling of gender discrimination complaints. School districts must also have a Title IX coordinator whose job it is to inform students and parents how to file complaints.

A complaint alleging a Title IX violation can be filed at the New York area regional office of the U.S. Department of Education. In addition, a complaint charging gender discrimination can be filed with either the New Jersey Commissioner of Education or the New Jersey Division on Civil Rights.

MINIMUM BASIC SKILLS

The state board of education has set up minimum statewide levels of student proficiency that apply to every public school. Each year, every school district must evaluate student proficiency in these basic skills. The tests used by schools to check the reading and math levels of their students are approved, standardized tests.

If your child is given a basic-skills test, the school must grade the test and tell you how well your child performed. If your child did poorly, the school must tell you what type of help your child will be given. Students who score below their grade level must be given *remedial instruction*—extra help either in the regular classroom or in a special class with other students who also need extra help. As soon as the remedial work is finished, students should be tested again. Students who still need extra help should continue to receive it.

If you feel your child is not getting the help he or she needs, talk to the principal or, if necessary, the superintendent of the school district or the local school board.

Schools that have a large number of students who do poorly on basic-skills tests are given extra money by the state. The schools must use this money to provide extra help to those students who are below the minimum grade level in reading or math.

MINIMUM HIGH SCHOOL GRADUATION REQUIREMENTS

New Jersey has also set up minimum requirements for high school graduation.[17] All high school students must successfully complete the minimum statewide requirements and any local requirements in order to graduate.

Each student entering ninth grade and his or her parents must be given a copy of all state and local high school graduation requirements. In addition, students and their parents at the beginning of each course must be given a list of what is required to pass the course.

HIGH SCHOOL PROFICIENCY TEST (HSPT).[18] All eleventh-grade students must take the High School Proficiency Test in order to qualify for a high school diploma. The HSPT tests students' proficiency in math, reading, and writing. If the student fails the test in eleventh grade, he or she must take it again until passing it. Students who score below the passing rate on any part of the HSPT must be given remedial help before being retested.

Any student who performs below state standards on any part of the HSPT by the end of the eleventh grade must also be evaluated during the twelfth grade. This evaluation must look at the student's overall performance and improvement on tests, in course work, and in other areas.

On the basis of the evaluation given in twelfth grade and an independent evaluation of the facts by a local district review panel, a recommendation regarding each student not meeting statewide basic-skills requirements must be made and sent to the county superintendent of schools by March 1 of the year the student is scheduled to graduate. In its recommendation, the local district review panel must say whether it thinks that the student has completed the statewide proficiency graduation requirement.

If so recommended by the district review panel, the school principal, and the district superintendent, the county superintendent of schools may certify that a student has met the graduation requirement.

Any student who has met all state and local graduation requirements but who does not graduate because he or she failed the HSPT may take the test again the next time it is given in the district.

A child who is handicapped may be excused from the basic-skills proficiency requirement based on the recommendation of the child-study team and the approval of the superintendent of schools.

DIPLOMAS. All students who successfully meet their graduation requirements must receive a state-endorsed diploma. Students who do not receive diplomas because they failed the HSPT will get a diploma as soon as they pass the test.

BILINGUAL EDUCATION

Under federal law, every school district that receives any federal funds must provide classes to teach English to its non-English-speaking students.[19]

New Jersey law requires certain school districts to provide bilingual education as well.[20] The law says that if, at the beginning of a school year, a school district has twenty or more students of limited English-speaking ability in any one language group, the school district must provide a bilingual education program for them. Bilingual education programs must include a full-time program of instruction in

- All courses or subjects required by law,
- Language-development classes in the child's native language,
- English-language classes,

- The history and culture of the native country of the child's parents, *and*
- The history and culture of the United States.

FEDERAL EDUCATIONAL FUNDING
FOR LOW-INCOME CHILDREN

The federal government provides funds to local school districts to help them meet the special educational needs of children in low-income areas, under Chapter I of the Elementary and Secondary Education Act.[21] The law recognizes the negative effect poverty can have on a child's ability to learn, and the problems that a school district in a low-income area can have in raising the money it needs for educational programs.

In response to these problems, the law provides that federal funds must be used to help pay for educational programs designed to help low-income children. New Jersey must send its federal money to school districts having the highest numbers of children from low-income families.

Funds can also be used to meet the special educational needs of handicapped children, neglected or delinquent children, or children of migrant or agricultural workers.

The Quality Education Act of 1990[22] gives New Jersey's educational system the opportunity to meet the needs of students at risk for school failure. The Department of Education has promulgated regulations governing the use of funds for at-risk students.

VOCATIONAL EDUCATION

Under the Vocational and Applied Technology Education Act of 1990,[23] the federal government gives money to the states for vocational education. The purpose of this act is to provide access to vocational training to help people of all ages find employment.

Each year more students apply for high school vocational education classes and schools than can be admitted. As a result, vocational high schools require students to take a placement test. Those who do well on the test and who have done well in elementary and junior high school are admitted. Consequently, many vocational programs have been closed to handicapped students, disadvantaged students, and students with limited English-speaking ability.

The New Jersey commissioner of education has determined that students of limited English-speaking ability should not be required to pass a test in English in order to receive vocational education.

The act also requires that a certain portion of the federal money given to New Jersey be used to provide vocational training programs to economically and culturally disadvantaged students, handicapped students, minorities, and females.

The act further requires that New Jersey ensure that vocational programs are equally available for men and women.

DISABLED CHILDREN'S RIGHT TO EDUCATION

New Jersey guarantees all disabled children from the time of their third birthday an appropriate education at no cost to their parents.[24] Children who are considered disabled include those

- Who have neurological problems that make it hard for them to learn.
- With serious psychological or emotional problems.
- With serious social and behavioral problems.
- With physical handicaps, illnesses, or other health conditions that keep them from being in a regular school program.
- Who are blind or partially sighted.
- Who are deaf or hearing impaired.
- Who are unable to speak or have speech difficulties.
- Whose intelligence is below average.

EVALUATION FOR SPECIAL EDUCATION. Before being placed in a special education program, a child must first be evaluated. The evaluation will determine whether a child is disabled, what the disability or difficulty is, or whether a disabled child's condition has changed.

The evaluation must be done (at no cost to the family) by the school district child-study team. Every school district in New Jersey has at least one child-study team. This team is made up of a school social worker, a school psychologist, and a learning disabilities teacher-consultant. When necessary, the child-study team can also include a school nurse, a psychiatrist, a speech therapist, or other specialists.

A school district may ask its child-study team to evaluate a child when a teacher, a counselor, someone from an agency who knows the child, or the parent tells the district that the child may be disabled. If you know that your child has a disability, you should send a letter to your school principal asking that an evaluation be done. If the school district refuses to test your child, it must notify you in writing of its reasons. You then have the right to ask for a hearing to force the school district to evaluate your child.

Once the school district determines that your child needs to be tested, it must tell you in writing that an evaluation is planned and state the reasons. It must do this even if you asked that your child be tested. This written notice must explain what kinds of tests will be used.

You must also be told that you have a right to refuse the test. If you refuse, the school district may ask for a hearing. At the hearing, school officials will

319

try to show why they think your child needs to be tested. If the administrative law judge (ALJ) agrees with them, he or she will order that your child be tested even though you oppose it.

Once it has been determined that a child must be tested, the school district must ask its child-study team to test your child. The child-study team then has ninety days to complete its evaluation, decide if your child is disabled and in need of special education, and—if your child is found eligible for special education—to develop an individualized education program (IEP).

CHALLENGING THE RESULTS OF THE EVALUATION. If you disagree with your school district about your child's evaluation, try to work out the problem by talking to the teachers, child-study team members, or other people in the school district. If you cannot resolve the disagreement, you have a right to ask the child-study team to order, at public expense, an evaluation by specialists not working for the school district. If your request is denied, the school district must request a hearing and give reasons for the denial of the independent evaluation. If the ALJ determines that the school's evaluation is appropriate, you still have a right to an independent evaluation, at your own expense.

If you prefer to discuss your disagreement with the child-study team and a neutral third party, you can request mediation instead of a hearing. The mediator may be from your school district, the county supervisor of special education, or a representative from the New Jersey Division of Special Education in Trenton. If these mediation meetings lead to an agreement between you and your school district, the mediator will write up the agreement and both sides will sign it.

If the mediation does not resolve the problem, parents have the right to ask for a hearing. To request a hearing, you must write to the Department of Education, Division of Special Education.

INDIVIDUALIZED EDUCATION PROGRAMS. Once the testing is complete and your child has been found to be in need of special education, the school district is required to develop an *IEP* for your child. An IEP is a written plan that school districts must prepare for each disabled child attending school. The IEP then becomes a teaching guide for the child's teachers and school administrators.

In order to design an IEP, the parents meet with the child-study team and the child's teachers to go over all information about the child's educational needs. Going to the IEP meeting is one of the most important things you can do for your child. It is your chance to help your child receive the kind of education he or she needs. You may bring anyone you want with you to the meeting. When you go to the IEP meeting, bring copies of your child's records and anything else you may have that supports what you feel are your child's educational needs. You may tape-record the meeting.

An IEP is like a contract. It states what kind of education your child will receive for one year. The IEP must include

- A statement of the present level of the child's schoolwork,
- Short-term and long-term educational goals for the child,
- A statement of the services to be provided to the child, including a description of all special education services required to meet the child's special needs and how many times a week and for how long such services will be provided,
- A description of how well the child will be able to learn in regular education programs,
- The dates on which services are expected to begin and end, *and*
- The measures used to evaluate the progress of the child's program.

Before the initial IEP can go into effect, you must approve it. Do not approve it at the IEP meeting. Get a copy, take it home with you, and look it over carefully. If you decide that the IEP is what your child needs, sign and return it. If you have problems with it, talk to the child-study team again and try to work out your differences. If the problem cannot be settled, you have a right to refuse to approve the IEP and ask for mediation or a hearing.

An IEP is good for only one school year. It must be reviewed at least once each year. A full retesting of your child must be done at least once every three years by the child-study team.

Note: Parental consent is not required for subsequent IEPs; they can be implemented by the Department of Education with fifteen days' written notice.

PLACEMENT. After the IEP is prepared, the child-study team must decide what school and what type of class your child should attend. New Jersey law requires that disabled children, if possible, be taught in a regular class with other school-age children. The school district must also try to send the disabled child to the school he or she would normally attend if he or she were not disabled. A disabled child who cannot be taught in a regular class should receive an education in a classroom that is as much like a regular classroom as possible.

A child with special educational needs might be

- Placed full time in a regular class with nondisabled children, with extra help to meet the child's special needs,
- Placed in a regular class for most of the day with extra help from a special teacher, or with part of the day spent in another classroom with a small group of students,
- Placed for most or all of the day in a special class where all the children have the same type of disability,

- Placed in either a day or live-in school for disabled children, *or*
- Able to receive individual instruction by a tutor at home but only on a doctor's orders or no other action is appropriate at the time.

PARENT INVOLVEMENT IN PUBLIC SCHOOLS

The federal government requires that state and local school districts receiving federal funds for certain educational programs must allow citizen and parental involvement in the planning and administration of those programs. These federally funded programs include vocational education programs, bilingual education programs, programs providing for the educational needs of low-income children, and programs providing for the education of handicapped students. New Jersey law also provides that local school districts involve the public in important school decisions.

RIGHT TO SEE SCHOOL DOCUMENTS. New Jersey's Right to Know Law (RTKL) gives all citizens the right to examine all documents defined as *public records.*[25] Public records include "all records that by law must be made and kept on file by any public board . . . or by any official acting for any public board." This includes any record received and kept by a public body, no matter how long or complicated. (See Chapter 11, "The Rights and Obligations of Citizenship.")

Personnel records of teachers or school principals and school records of individual students are not public records.

PARTICIPATION AT SCHOOL BOARD MEETINGS. Under the Open Public Meetings Law,[26] parents and the public can attend most school board meetings. Under this law, only those meetings or parts thereof in which the discussion may harm the public interest or invade someone's privacy are to be closed to the public. The law also applies to all meetings of school board committees to which a majority of the board members have been assigned. At school board meetings, parents may take notes and use tape recorders, as long as the tape recorders do not interfere with the meeting.

The time and place of school board meetings and the agenda must be made public at least forty-eight hours before the time of the meeting. However, the advance-notice requirement does not have to be followed if the issues that the school board needs to discuss are so urgent that any delay might cause more harm.

At school board meetings, the public has the right to hear the school board discuss and make decisions. However, the law also gives the school board the power to decide whether the public can actively participate at the meeting. The school board is not required by the Open Public Meetings Law to give parents and community citizens a chance to voice their opinions.

Although the Open Public Meetings Law does not require school boards to give parents attending the board meeting a chance to speak, other laws *do* provide for public participation in some proceedings. Under the New Jersey Public School Education Act of 1975,[27] local school districts are required to involve parents and other community residents in certain important school decisions. For example, school officials must hold public meetings to involve other community residents in setting school education goals. Once district and school educational goals are set, they must be reviewed and updated at least once every five years.

Every school board is also required to hold a public meeting each year to inform parents, teachers, and other community residents of the result of school evaluation reports. At this meeting, parents, teachers, and the public are to be given a chance to talk about the evaluations.

CHALLENGING SCHOOL BOARD DECISIONS

If you want to challenge a decision of the school board, you can appeal by filing a petition with the New Jersey Commissioner of Education.

A copy of the petition should be sent to the school board. You may include in the petition a request that the commissioner stay the decision of the school board pending the commissioner's final decision. The commissioner may either hear your appeal directly or, most likely, transfer your case to the Office of Administrative Law (OAL) for a hearing before an ALJ who will recommend a decision. The commissioner will make a final decision accepting, rejecting, or modifying the ALJ's recommended decision. If you apply for a stay of the school board's decision, the commissioner may grant or deny that application before transferring the case to the OAL. However, after the transfer to the OAL you must seek any such emergent relief from the ALJ. You can appeal the commissioner's final decision to the New Jersey Superior Court, Appellate Division.

14. Your Right to Health Care

This chapter begins by providing an overview of the health care system in general, including federal programs designed to help ensure medical protection for low-income and elderly people. Various health insurance programs provided by large and small employers are discussed, as is the right to receive hospital care regardless of income. This chapter also describes the variety of health benefit plans and programs that operate within New Jersey, your rights to health care, and changes to the health care industry which affect how you receive health care services and what health care services you receive.

THE HEALTH CARE SYSTEM

Perhaps the most characteristic aspect of the health care system in the United States is that most individuals are enrolled in health benefit programs or plans which pay for the majority of the costs of the health care services these individuals receive. This means that most individuals do not pay the full cost for most health care services out of their own budgets. These health benefit programs or plans can be sponsored by public or private employers for the benefit of employees, by federal or state governments for the benefit of certain categories of persons, or by insurance companies or health care companies for purchase by private individuals. If you qualify for one of these health benefit programs or plans, you must learn about any requirements the plan has for obtaining health care and any limitations it has on the types of health care for which it will pay. You must do so in order to protect your health, use health care services responsibly, maximize your benefits, and minimize the cost of the health services for which you will need to pay out of your own pocket if your health benefit plan will not cover the cost of those services.

As payers for health care services, these public and private health benefit plans and programs have had a growing influence on the organization of the health care industry in the United States in the past ten years.

OVERVIEW OF HEALTH PLANS AND PROGRAMS

New Jersey, like all other states, has a patchwork system of health benefit plans and programs in which consumers participate to obtain coverage for the cost of the health care services they have obtained. Health benefit plans sponsored by private employers or health insurance plans purchased by private employers for their employees cover a majority of consumers. Public programs try to fill the gaps for individuals who are not eligible for these plans. Medicaid and Medicare are the two major public programs that the federal government regulates and substantially finances. Large-employer plans, Medicaid, and Medicare cover 74 percent of New Jersey residents. Individual health insurance and small-employer insurance plans cover about 13 percent of New Jersey residents. Another 13 percent, approximately one million residents of New Jersey, have no health insurance of any kind.

Medicaid pays for health services, including prescription drugs, received by welfare recipients and certain other people with low incomes. It also pays for the long-term care, including nursing home care, of many elderly, blind, and disabled people who have exhausted their resources to pay for their own health care and who meet certain income guidelines. Medicare pays for most health services received by elderly, blind, or disabled people, but only if they have made sufficient contributions to the Social Security system. Generally, Medicare does *not* pay for long-term care or prescription drugs.

New Jersey also covers the entire costs of several important health programs, notably the Pharmaceutical Assistance for the Aged and Disabled (PAAD) program, which is paid for through assessments on the casino industry. The PAAD program pays for prescription drugs and other necessary health products for elderly and disabled people who meet the program's financial eligibility requirements.

Individual health insurance and small-employer insurance plans are regulated under the Individual Health Insurance Reform law, *N.J.S.A.* 17B: 27A-2 *et seq.*, and the Small-Employer Health Benefits law, *N.J.S.A.* 17B:27A-17 *et seq.* Two separate boards, the Individual Health Coverage Board and the Small-Employer Health Benefits Board (with a single administrative staff), administer these plans. The boards are funded entirely by assessments on health insurance companies and *health maintenance organizations* (HMOs). Many of the boards' members are government employees. Most of the other members are appointed by health insurance companies and by HMOs. There is minimal consumer representation.

Many New Jersey residents cannot pay for health care or afford health insurance. Whether you are eligible for Medicaid or Medicare may depend on your income, your assets, how old you are, your Social Security contributions, or whether you are disabled according to strict federal disability standards. However, New Jersey law mandates that every resident of the state is entitled to hospital care if he or she needs it, including those residents who have only recently arrived in the state and undocumented aliens. Hospitals must provide hospital services to everyone. In New Jersey, you have the right to hospital care whether or not you can afford to pay for it.

This is a most important right and a bulwark many have fought to preserve. The state has helped to preserve this right by providing subsidies through the charity care program to hospitals furnishing care to those who cannot afford it. However, the statutory obligation of hospitals to provide care without regard to ability to pay is not contingent on these subsidies. This statutory obligation is the most important part of the "safety net" beneath the patchwork system of health care plans and programs in New Jersey.

HEALTH PLANS SPONSORED BY LARGE EMPLOYERS

If you are covered by a health benefits plan sponsored by a large, private employer, you should understand some important things about the plan and your rights under the plan. You should read the *summary plan description* provided to you by your employer. It is more comprehensive than the descriptions in most employee manuals or handbooks and provides much information about what health care services are covered under the plan (and any limitations or conditions), and what rights you have if you dispute decisions about coverage.

Find out whether your employer purchases insurance to cover the costs of the plan or whether your employer's plan is self-insured. A *self-insured plan* is one in which the employer itself pays for all of the costs of the plan. In an *insured plan,* the employer pays a premium to an insurance company or HMO, which in turn is responsible for paying for all of the costs of the plan. This is an important distinction, because self-insured plans are exempt from state health insurance laws. Many provisions in New Jersey law apply only to insured plans. (Unlike New Jersey's Medicaid HMO regulations, many rights under the state HMO law *N.J.S.A.* 26:2J-1 *et seq.*, are illusory from a consumer standpoint. Although there is an elaborate appeal process culminating in a review of HMO member grievances by an external review board, regulations of the Department of Health and Senior Services [DHSS] explicitly permit HMOs to disregard the board's determinations in their unfettered discretion [*N.J.A.C.* 8:38-8.7 (k) and (l)].) If you are in an insured plan, you can appeal to the state insurance commissioner to investigate a complaint you may have about your plan.

CONTINUATION OF COVERAGE IN AN EMPLOYER'S HEALTH PLAN. Since coverage in an employer's health benefit plan is linked to continuing employment with that company, one major concern is what happens if you leave your job, lose your job, or otherwise cease to be eligible for your employer's plan. The federal Consolidated Omnibus Reconciliation Act (COBRA) of 1985 requires that *continuation provisions* be included in health benefit plans offered by employers with twenty or more employees, including both insured and self-insured plans. (State law requires continuation of coverage for small-employer plans.) Persons who would lose their health plan coverage due to certain qualifying events must be offered the opportunity to continue their coverage for limited periods of time at group rates plus a 2 percent administrative fee. In the case of an employee, the qualifying events are (1) termination of employment (for reasons other than gross misconduct on the employee's part) *or* (2) a reduction in hours of employment. In the case of an employee's dependents, qualifying events are (1) the employee's termination of employment or a reduction in his or her hours, (2) death of the employee, (3) divorce or legal separation from the covered employee, (4) entitlement of the covered employee to Medicare benefits, *or* (5) the cessation of a dependent child to meet the plan's definition of a dependent.

The continuation coverage periods are eighteen months in the case of loss of coverage due to termination of employment or reduction in hours (or twenty-nine months if the employee is determined to be disabled under the Social Security Act at the time of termination or reduction in hours) and thirty-six months for all other qualifying events.

The Family and Medical Leave Act (FMLA, 29 *U.S.C.* Section 2601 *et seq.*) requires covered employers to provide up to twelve weeks of unpaid, protected leave to eligible employees for certain family and medical reasons. During an FMLA leave, the employer must also maintain the employee's health coverage for up to twelve weeks of leave (up to the amount normally paid by the employer). Employees must continue to pay any required contributions toward their health benefits coverage.

RECENT CHANGES IN THE HEALTH CARE INDUSTRY. There have been significant changes over the past ten years in how the health care industry is organized. For most of the post–World War II era, hospitals and physicians operated as independent entities and billed consumers for their services (hence the term *fee for service*). Consumers, in turn, submitted those bills to their health benefit plans and, in most cases, the health plans paid for the services. These health benefit plans were known as *indemnity health benefit plans* because they reimbursed (indemnified) participants for their costs. Participants and their physicians chose the health services to be provided; the health plans reviewed the bills to make sure the particular services were covered by the plan and that the costs were within a reasonable and customary range for such services. Health plans did not, generally speaking, exert any independent control over the types or costs of the health services their participants were receiving.

Starting in the 1970s, a small number of persons were also enrolled in HMOs, which would pay for only those health services rendered by the hospitals and physicians under contract to the plans. In addition, whereas indemnity health plans typically paid only for services rendered to treat illnesses and injuries, HMOs paid for preventive care. HMOs were organized to "manage" their members' overall health care by preselecting the doctors and hospitals they were to use, negotiating fees with those providers, and exercising administrative oversight of utilization of health care services. They were relatively successful in controlling overall plan costs, but for the first fifteen years of their existence their appeal seemed relatively limited.

In response to very large increases in the costs of health services during the late 1980s and early 1990s, however, many public and private employers began offering HMOs as alternative choices to employees. Since then enrollment in HMOs nationally has soared. In addition, other forms of managed care, such as point of service plans, have developed. *Managed care* has rapidly become the most widespread method of delivering health care in the United States. It is the most common system offered in employer-sponsored health plans. Several million elderly or disabled Medicare recipients nationwide have chosen or been given the option of managed care. Managed care has also become the usual means through which Medicaid in New Jersey delivers health care services to welfare recipients and other eligible low-income people. Even disabled Medicaid recipients who were previously given a choice must now accept Medicaid managed care. It is expected that managed care will soon become the only choice under Medicaid for patients with mental illness or substance abuse diagnoses. The major features of managed care are described in the following sections; most are incorporated into the various managed care plan designs prevalent today.

PROVIDER NETWORKS. HMOs, insurance companies, other managed care companies, and some employer sponsors of health benefit plans are contracting with doctors, hospitals, pharmacies, laboratories, and other health care providers to form groups (*networks*) within local or regional geographic areas. These providers have usually agreed to reductions from their usual fees in order to participate in the networks. Negotiating lower provider fees is one of the main ways in which managed care organizations have held down their costs. The HMO, insurance company, or other managed care company reviews the credentials of the doctors, hospitals, and other health providers before enlisting them in the network. A public or private health benefit plan or program may contract with one or more HMOs or with an insurance company to make their networks available to the plan's members.

UTILIZATION REVIEW. In most managed care plan designs, network physicians must seek authorization for hospital admissions, certain outpatient procedures, or other health care services. As long as the patient is using a network physician, the patient does not have to take any action. If the reviewer does not approve the services, the costs of these services may not be covered by the health benefit plan at all or may be covered at only a reduced level. Reviewers may include nurses or other health professionals as well as physicians. A plan may require a *preadmission review* (a review performed prior to the patient's admission to a hospital), a *concurrent review* (a review performed while the patient is undergoing treatment in order to authorize additional days in the hospital or additional procedures), and *discharge planning* (authorization for posthospitalization care).

328

CASE MANAGEMENT. *Case managers* typically provide coordination of all of the health care services needed for patients with severe or prolonged illnesses. By coordinating care among many providers, case management attempts to improve the overall quality of care while controlling costs.

HMO AND POINT OF SERVICE PLANS. The health care industry is today organizing around a number of different managed care plan designs. They all contain the elements described in the previous sections, but they vary in the restrictions they place on members in choosing providers. As described earlier, the HMO plan design requires members to obtain health care services only from the plan's network of providers. The HMO will not reimburse nonemergency care received from non-HMO providers. Given the high cost of most health care services, in practice this restriction means that members must obtain their care from the HMO and its providers or not at all. Most HMOs operate in a specific geographic area. If you move permanently out of the HMO's service area, you will no longer be eligible.

The *point of service* (POS) plan design typically includes a provision for both in-network and out-of-network benefits. A member will receive the highest level of benefits when a network provider is used, and much lower benefit coverage if an out-of-network provider is used. Members can decide at the time they are seeking care (hence the term *point of service*) whether to use a network or out-of-network provider.

Both HMO and most POS plans also require members to see their primary care physician first whenever they need health care services. The primary care physician will decide if a specialist is needed and issue a referral to a particular specialist. If a referral is not obtained before seeing the specialist, the cost of the specialist's services will not be reimbursed (HMOs) or may be reimbursed only at the out-of-network level of benefits (POS).

STATE HEALTH INSURANCE REFORM

In 1992 New Jersey addressed some problems affecting the health insurance industry by enacting the Individual Health Insurance Reform law and the Small-Employer Health Benefits law. These laws were amended in 1997 by the Health Care Quality Act, *N.J.S.A.* 26:2S-1, to conform New Jersey Law to the requirements of the federal Health Insurance Portability and Accountability Act of 1996 (29 *U.S.C.* Section 26). The purpose of these laws is to guarantee access to health insurance coverage to individuals and small employers (two to fifty full-time employees), regardless of health status, age, claims history, or any other risk factor. The basic problems the laws sought to remedy were

- Lack of choice and access to health coverage for individuals.
- The inability of many small employers to get and keep good health coverage for their employees.

329

- Over one million uninsured residents of New Jersey.

Many previously uninsured New Jersey residents have become insured since the passage of the laws and are enrolled in plans covered under the laws. Nevertheless, the number of uninsured people in New Jersey remains nearly the same as before the laws were passed. This is probably because some large employers have canceled the coverage of many of their employees (or increased employee premiums) and also because of reduced coverage offered to employees' dependents.

STANDARD PLANS FOR INDIVIDUALS AND SMALL EMPLOYERS. Under the new laws, each insurance carrier in the individual and small-employer markets must offer five standard plans. This makes it easier for individuals and employers to compare prices among competitors. The insurance carriers must offer the standard plans to any qualified individual or small employer. Generally, insurance carriers may not cancel and must renew the plans, except in the case of fraud, nonpayment of premiums, or failure to continue to meet eligibility requirements. Certain other exceptions have been added by the Health Care Quality Act, including special provisions for HMOs. A carrier cannot cancel and must renew policies, without regard to a person's illness or claims history.

The standard plans are all offered as indemnity plans. In addition, an HMO plan is available. All but one of the standard plans—Plan A—include comprehensive coverage. Plan A is a basic plan that provides limited benefits for hospital expenses, as well as only some of the services offered by the other standard plans. Very few people are covered under this plan, although it is the cheapest. The other standard plans all include comprehensive coverage for

- Office visits.
- Hospital care.
- Prenatal and maternity care.
- Immunization and well-child care.
- Screenings, such as mammograms, pap smears, and prostate exams.
- X-ray and laboratory services.
- Certain mental health and substance abuse services.
- Prescription drugs.
- Preventive care.

The standard plans offer a range of deductibles or copayment options.

THE INDIVIDUAL HEALTH INSURANCE PROGRAM. New Jersey residents, regardless of their age or health status, are guaranteed that if they can pay for it, they will get health insurance under the standard health benefits plan designed by the Individual Health Coverage Board, and that their insurance will be renewed (*N.J.A.C.* 11:20-1 *et seq.*). In general, New Jersey residents are eligible to buy individual health insurance if they are not eligible under a group plan provided by an employer and are also not eligible for Medicare. They may purchase a single plan, a husband-and-wife plan, a plan for a parent and child(ren), or a family plan.

You can never be denied coverage because of your health. However, if you have been uninsured for more than thirty-one days prior to the effective date of your new policy, you will have to wait up to one year before expenses for preexisting conditions are covered. Under certain circumstances you may not be subject to a limitation on preexisting conditions if you apply for coverage within sixty-three days of termination of your group coverage. During the waiting period, you are covered for all other (non-preexisting) conditions. After the waiting period, you are covered for *all* illnesses and injuries.

Individual health benefit plans are *community rated.* This means that a carrier must offer the same plan to everyone at the same rate, regardless of an applicant's age, gender, profession, health status, or geographical location in the state. Rates vary from company to company and from plan to plan.

THE SMALL-EMPLOYER HEALTH BENEFITS PROGRAM. This program guarantees that eligible small employers who wish to purchase health insurance for their employees may do so under the standard plans (*N.J.A.C.* 11:21-1 *et seq.*). They are also guaranteed that they may renew this coverage. Small employers are not required by the law to provide health benefits for employees. To be eligible, the small employer must employ between two and fifty full-time employees. The Small-Employer Health Benefits Act requires insurance carriers to notify employers if and when they are no longer eligible to be covered by a small-employer plan. An employer may lose eligibility if, for example, he or she begins to employ more than fifty full-time employees. The notice must be given to the small employer at least sixty days before the insurance carrier terminates the health benefits plan. Notification is not required in cases of nonpayment of premiums, fraud, or misrepresentation by the employer or eligible employees.

To be eligible to participate in a small-employer plan as a full-time employee, you must work a minimum of twenty-five hours per week. If you are covered by a small-employer plan, you will generally not have to wait before having your expenses for preexisting conditions covered, unless you are a *late enrollee,* i.e., you did not enroll within the initial 30-day enrollment period provided under the terms of the plan. However, an insurance carrier may impose, only on groups of from two to five employees, a waiting period of up to 180 days for preexisting-condition coverage.

Standard plans for small employers are rated under a modified form of community rating. This means that carriers can offer a plan at different rates based on age, gender, family status, and the location of a business in the state.

They may not, however, offer different rates to different people on any other basis. Modified community rating allows the highest rates charged to small employers to be no greater than 200 percent of the rate charged to the lowest-rated employer.

Small employers with between two and nineteen employees must offer employees the option to continue their group health coverage at their own expense when the are terminated for reasons other than for cause or when they go to part-time status. Employees who cease to work twenty-five hours per week—as required to be eligible to participate in a small-employer plan—must be offered continuation of coverage. *Continuation of coverage rights* is similar to federal COBRA rules for employees with twenty or more employees. Insurance carriers must provide notice of continuation of coverage rights in the certificate of coverage issued to each employee. Small employers must also notify employees of their continuation of coverage rights at the time of any event that qualifies them for these rights, such as a change to part-time status or termination other than for cause.

Small employers may purchase nonstandard plans. An amendment to the act permanently grandfathered prereform, nonstandard plans. Small employers are, therefore, not required to switch to one of the standard plans. However, the nonstandard plans offered by insurance carriers in the small-employer market must comply with the most important health insurance reform rules.

A little more than half of all enrollees in small-employer plans are enrolled in one of the standard plans. These plans provide for guaranteed issuance and renewal, modified community rating, limited preexisting-conditions exclusions, and continuation of coverage rights for employees who have been terminated and employees who cease to work full-time.

THE RIGHT TO HOSPITAL SERVICES

Under state law, low-income people are entitled to free or low-cost hospital care. The New Jersey Health Care Reform Act of 1992 states that "no hospital shall deny any admission or appropriate service to a patient on the basis of that patient's ability to pay or source of payment" (*N.J.S.A.* 26:2H-18.64). According to the New Jersey Health Care Cost Reduction Act of 1991, "access to quality health care shall not be denied to residents of this state because of their inability to pay for the care" (*N.J.S.A.* 26:2H-18.51c).

CHARITY CARE. As yet there is no stable funding mechanism for charity care, or *hospital assistance* as it is often called. Nevertheless charity care has been subsidized for many years under one funding mechanism or another. This is expected to continue. It should be noted, however, that hospitals have a statutory obligation to provide appropriate care to all New Jersey residents who need it without regard to the patient's ability to pay and without regard to whether the hospital receives a subsidy or not. The hospital cannot make you prove you are eligible for charity care *before* providing medical treatment.

New Jersey acute care hospitals must, therefore, provide medically necessary care to everyone and must provide free care or reduced-cost care to low-income New Jersey residents who are not eligible for Medicaid or Medicare and whose hospital bills are not fully covered by private health insurance. Charity care rules do not cover hospitals run by the federal government, such as Veterans Administration (VA) hospitals, or the state, such as psychiatric institutions.

The hospital bills that charity care covers include bills for doctors provided by the hospital. It does *not* cover bills for doctors who treat you while outside the hospital or doctors you call in yourself to treat you while in the hospital. Charity care also does not cover anesthesiology fees, radiological interpretations, or outpatient prescriptions. It *does,* however, cover outpatient and inpatient care at acute care hospitals throughout New Jersey.

If you have health insurance, the charity care program will not pay for amounts covered by that insurance. If you receive Medicare, charity care can be used to cover your copayment, which Medicare does *not* pay. You are not barred from receiving charity care just because you have partial insurance or Medicare coverage. If you are, or might be, financially eligible for Medicaid, you will be required to apply for it before seeking charity care. Medicaid covers most health services, including hospital care. Medicaid coverage is retroactive for up to three months. If you are eligible, Medicaid is better than charity care since it covers more than just hospital bills. If a hospital requires you to apply for Medicaid before applying for charity care, you should do so even if you think you are not eligible for Medicaid. The hospital will give you the name, address, and phone number of the Medicaid office nearest you. If you are rejected for Medicaid, get a written rejection and then go back to the hospital to apply for charity care again.

The Application Process. Each hospital is required to give you a written notice about charity care when you are admitted. The hospital must give a person who is billed for someone else's hospital care—such as a parent or a spouse of the patient—the same notice as the patient gets. The hospital also must prominently post a sign about charity care. The notice and sign will tell you whom to see in the hospital to apply for charity care.

You must apply for charity care within one year from the date you leave the hospital. If you apply but are turned down because you did not have enough information about your income or assets to satisfy the hospital, you will have to supply that information within the one-year period. If you don't apply in time, you could lose your right to charity care. The hospital must inform you about charity care, but the burden is on you to make the application.

Ask the hospital financial or billing office for the application forms for charity care. Sometimes the admissions desk has the forms, too. After the form is filled out, ask for a copy of it and keep it. Hospitals may accept applications more than a year after the service was provided but are not required to do so. If they do, they will still be eligible for charity care reimbursement. If the hospital fails to give proper written notice and more than a year passes before you find out about charity care, the hospital's failure to give you proper written notice may give a court grounds to order the hospital to take your application even after a year has passed.

When you apply for charity care, the hospital will ask you for identification. You can use any of the following:

- Driver's license.
- Voter registration card.
- Alien registry card.
- Birth certificate.
- Employee identification card.
- Union membership card.
- Insurance or welfare plan identification card.
- Social Security card.
- Passport.
- Visa.
- Death certificate (if someone else applies retroactively for charity care on your behalf after you die).

A person *not associated* with you can also identify you. This means somebody outside your family, such as a police officer or a local business-person. There are other acceptable forms of identification. You must also be able to prove through documentation that your income and your assets really are low enough to make you eligible for charity care. You may do this in many ways, for example by presenting your pay stubs or a letter from your employer on company letterhead stating your exact income for the applicable time period. If you had no income during the applicable time period, you can attest to that by signing a notarized document stating that you had no income.

Eligibility. In order to qualify for charity care, your family income (before federal and state taxes are taken out) must be less than or equal to 200 percent of the federal poverty level. If your family income is more than 200 percent of the poverty level but less than 300 percent, you will qualify for reduced-cost care. In computing their income, patients may deduct qualified medical expenses, which are any out-of-pocket medical expenses that the patient has to pay for, such as physician services and prescription drugs.

If you are single, you are allowed to have up to $7,500 in assets and still be eligible for charity care. Families are allowed up to $15,000. Your car, your furniture, and a house that you live in are *not* counted. Examples of items that are counted as assets include bank accounts, stocks, bonds, Treasury bills, and equity in real estate other than one's primary residence. Furthermore, there is a *spend-down* provision: *Only* those assets in excess of the allowable limit after being applied toward medical expenses (including the hospital bill, doctor bills, and prescription drugs) are counted. This means out-of-pocket expenses *you* paid—not money paid by an insurance company. If you still own other property worth more than the asset limit, you are not eligible for charity care.

If you qualify for reduced-cost care, how much you pay depends on how much your family income is. You will be charged 20 percent, 40 percent, 60 percent, or 80 percent of the bill, depending on your income. Families with incomes higher than the maximum for charity care (200 percent of the poverty level) but less than the maximum for reduced-cost care (300 percent of the poverty level) may qualify for extra help if they have a very high bill or many bills in one year. You do not have to pay more than 30 percent of your income in any twelve-month period for hospital bills. Hospital costs in excess of 30 percent of your income are to be considered charity care that you do not have to pay for.

Notices and Hearings. The hospital must notify you in writing whether your application for charity care was approved within five working days from when you applied. If denied, the notice must explain why, that you can reapply if your financial situation changes, and how you can appeal. If you think you should have been found eligible for charity care, you can appeal by writing a letter to the DHSS, Health Care for the Uninsured Program, within thirty days of when you received the written denial from the hospital.

Resolving Disputes, Collections, and Appeals. The DHSS has taken the position that it may only mediate eligibility disputes and has no authority to contradict a hospital's eligibility determinations. According to the DHSS, "patient rights are protected by more direct access to the court system should they need to further pursue eligibility determinations." It is possible that you could take an appeal directly to the New Jersey Superior Court, Appellate Division.

If you do not pay a hospital bill, the hospital or a collection agency will probably sue you in a collection action in a trial division of superior court. You can defend that action by proving in court that you were eligible for charity care. Many collection agencies are unaware of patients' rights to charity care and will withdraw their claim once it is explained to them or their lawyer. If the DHSS's mediation fails to resolve the dispute, you will need a lawyer to uphold your rights. You should first seek DHSS intervention, however, because the DHSS has considerable leverage over hospitals and in some very clear situations may be able to exercise its influence quickly in your favor.

A hospital may attach your state income tax refund if you have not paid the bill and the hospital decides that you were not eligible for charity care when you received hospital services. However, under a procedure provided by the Division of Taxation, you have a right to a hearing before an administra-

335

tive law judge (ALJ), and ultimately a right of appeal to the New Jersey Superior Court, Appellate Division. The Division of Taxation will notify you of your appeal rights if the hospital attempts to recover an alleged debt by attaching your state income tax refund. You have the right to show that you were eligible for charity care despite the hospital's unilateral determination that you were not eligible.

MENTAL HEALTH SERVICES

The state is obligated to provide treatment for mentally ill people who cannot care for themselves or who are considered dangerous to themselves or others. A person is considered dangerous to himself or herself or others if he or she has threatened or attempted suicide or serious physical harm, may suffer serious harm as a result of his or her inability to care for himself or herself, or may seriously injure another person or property.

For those who cannot afford private treatment, New Jersey has public hospital facilities. People can be admitted to these hospitals either by voluntary admission or through an involuntary commitment proceeding. If a person seeks *voluntary admission* into a psychiatric facility and a public institution determines that the person requires treatment and has no other treatment options, he or she can be admitted to a state or county facility.

If a patient who has voluntarily entered a psychiatric facility requests to be discharged, he or she must be released within forty-eight hours. If the treating doctors believe that *involuntary commitment* is necessary, they must initiate a court proceeding. The hospital cannot detain the patient beyond forty-eight hours without a court order.

INVOLUNTARY COMMITMENT. Mentally ill persons who are dangerous to themselves or others but who refuse treatment may be admitted to a psychiatric institution through an involuntary commitment proceeding. A person who is believed to need mental health services may be referred to a county screening service. Each county must have at least one such office to evaluate people and determine what their needs are for mental health treatment. If a screening service determines that a person needs to be committed, he or she can be referred to a psychiatric facility that then completes the commitment process. If a person is unable or unwilling to go to a local hospital for screening, under certain circumstances a screener can go to the person's home to evaluate his or her condition. A person cannot be held for more than seventy-two hours without a court order permitting commitment.

If a psychiatric facility initiates a proceeding, it must submit to the court a certificate from a treating psychiatrist describing the patient's condition, as well as one from the screening service that authorized admission to the hospital. An individual with responsibility for a person may also start commitment proceedings. If a commitment proceeding is started without a screening service, two certificates about the patient's medical condition must be submitted. At least one must be from a psychiatrist.

If the court finds that there is probable cause to justify commitment, it can issue a temporary order for confinement. A hearing must then be held within twenty days of admission. The patient must have an attorney at this hearing. If the court finds no need for involuntary commitment, the patient must be discharged within forty-eight hours. If commitment is ordered, there must be periodic court review to determine whether continued commitment is necessary.

RIGHTS OF PSYCHIATRIC PATIENTS. New Jersey has a bill of rights for psychiatric patients that provides them with the right to receive medical and other professional treatment, education, and training (for individuals between the ages of five and twenty), and the right to participate in treatment decisions. Within five days of admission to a hospital, patients must be given written notice of their rights, which include the right to be free of unnecessary medication, experimental or intrusive treatment, physical restraints, isolation, and corporal punishment. Voluntary patients must also be given written notice of their right to refuse medication. Patients are also entitled to privacy and religious freedom and to have visitors, phone calls, exercise, and their own clothes. If clinically appropriate, a doctor may restrict these rights. However, a hospital can never restrict a patient's right to call his or her lawyer or doctor.

PROGRAMS FOR THE AGED AND DISABLED

There are two important government programs that exclusively fund health care services for the aged and disabled. They are Medicare, a federal program, and PAAD, a state program.

MEDICARE. Medicare is a federal health insurance program for

- People sixty-five years of age or older,
- People of any age with permanent kidney failure, *and*
- Certain disabled people.

The Medicare program is administered by the Health Care Financing Administration. Local Social Security offices accept applications for Medicare. (You can locate your Social Security office by looking in your telephone directory under "Social Security Administration.") Someone at the Social Security office can provide you with information about the program. If you are physically unable to go to the office, a representative will visit you to take an application.

Medicare has two parts: hospital insurance, which is known as Part A, and medical insurance, which is known as Part B. The hospital insurance, Part A, helps pay for inpatient hospital care, certain follow-up care after you leave the hospital, and certain nursing home care. The medical insurance, Part B, helps pay for your doctors' services and many other medical services and items. The medical insurance program is voluntary; to be covered you must pay monthly premiums.

Part A—Hospital Insurance. You are eligible for Medicare Part A beginning the month in which you become age sixty-five if you are eligible for Social Security or railroad retirement benefits, or if you have worked for a certain minimum period of time. If you are receiving Social Security or railroad retirement benefits, your Part A coverage will start automatically at age sixty-five. You do not have to retire at sixty-five to have Part A coverage. But if you plan to keep working, you will have to file an application for Part A in order for your coverage to start. To find out if you are eligible and to make sure your coverage starts on time, contact a Social Security office about three months before you turn sixty-five.

Many disabled people under age sixty-five are also entitled to Medicare benefits after they have been entitled to Social Security or railroad retirement disability benefits for twenty-four months.

You are eligible, regardless of your age, if you need maintenance dialysis or a kidney transplant because of permanent kidney failure and you are insured or are getting monthly benefits under Social Security or the railroad retirement system. Your wife, husband, or child may also be eligible if she or he has permanent kidney failure and needs maintenance dialysis or a transplant. If you, your spouse, or your child needs kidney dialysis or a kidney transplant, contact a Social Security office to apply for Medicare. You can apply by phone, or a representative can visit you to take an application if you are unable to go to the office. If you are eligible for Medicare, your coverage generally will start with the third full month after the month you actually begin maintenance dialysis treatments. Under certain conditions, your coverage could start earlier.

If you are sixty-five years of age or older but not otherwise eligible for Medicare Part A, you can buy it and pay a monthly premium. To buy Medicare Part A, you also must enroll and pay the monthly premium for Medicare medical insurance, Part B. You can apply at any Social Security office.

Medicare Part A can help you pay for medically necessary inpatient hospital care, inpatient care in a skilled nursing facility, home health care, and *hospice care* for the terminally ill. Some Part A coverage is based on *spell of illness.*

A spell of illness starts when you enter a hospital. It ends when you have been out of a hospital or other facility that provides skilled nursing or rehabilitation services for sixty days in a row. After that, you begin a new spell of illness the next time you enter the hospital; you will have to pay another deductible as well as other cost-sharing amounts. There is no limit to the number of spells of illness you can have.

If you need inpatient care, Medicare Part A helps pay for up to ninety days in any participating hospital during each spell of illness. For the first sixty days, Medicare Part A pays for all covered services except for a deductible amount, which you must pay during each spell of illness. In 1998, the deductible is $764. For the sixty-first through ninetieth days, you will have to pay $191 per day in 1998. These and most other deductible amounts will increase each year. After the ninetieth day during any spell of illness, you can pay the full charges yourself *or* pay up to $382 dollars per day (in 1998) for up to sixty *lifetime reserve* days. Reserve days entitle you to benefits for all covered services above $382.

Covered services include a semiprivate room, all meals, regular nursing services, operating and recovery room costs, intensive care and coronary care, drugs, lab tests, X-rays, medical supplies and appliances, and rehabilitation services.

Under special conditions, Medicare Part A can help pay for care in a psychiatric hospital, a U.S. nonparticipating hospital, or a Canadian or Mexican hospital.

If you need inpatient, skilled nursing, or rehabilitation services after a hospital stay, Medicare Part A helps pay for up to 100 days in a participating skilled nursing facility during each spell of illness. You must have been in the hospital for at least three consecutive days during the thirty days before entering the nursing home and meet certain other conditions. Medicare Part A pays for all covered services for the first twenty days. Covered services include a semiprivate room, all meals, regular nursing services, rehabilitation services, drugs, medical supplies, and appliances. You pay up to $95.50 a day (in 1998) for up to eighty more days.

Medicare Part A can pay the approved cost of home health visits for recipients who are homebound and who meet certain other conditions. You don't have to have a hospital stay before home health services are provided. Covered services include nursing, physical therapy, occupational therapy, speech therapy, home health aides, medical social services, supplies, and equipment other than drugs. These services must be provided by local home health agencies that participate in Medicare.

Part B—Medical Insurance. You do not need any Social Security work credits to be eligible for Medicare Part B. Almost anyone who is sixty-five years of age or older or who is eligible for Part A can enroll for Medicare Part B. You must pay a monthly premium for this insurance. The monthly premium in 1998 is $43.80. This amount is adjusted every January.

If you are receiving Social Security or railroad retirement benefits, you will automatically be enrolled for Part B at the same time you become entitled to Part A, unless you say you do not want it. However, not everyone is automatically enrolled in Medicare Part B. You will have to apply for Part B if you

- Plan to continue working past age sixty-five,
- Are sixty-five but are not eligible for Part A,
- Are a disabled widow or widower between fifty and sixty-five who is not getting disability checks,
  or
- Live in Puerto Rico or outside the United States.

Medicare Part B helps pay for your doctors' services and other medical services and supplies that are not covered by Part A. Most of the services needed by people with permanent kidney failure are covered only by Part B.

Medicare Part B covers doctors' services no matter where you receive them—in a doctor's office, the hospital, your home, or elsewhere. Covered doctors' services include surgical services, diagnostic tests and X-rays that are part of your treatment, medical supplies furnished in a doctor's office, services of the office nurse, and drugs that are administered as part of your treatment and cannot be self-administered.

Part B covers outpatient hospital services you receive for diagnosis and treatment, including care in an emergency room or outpatient clinic of a hospital. It can also cover an unlimited number of home health visits (the same as provided by Part A) if all required conditions are met.

Under certain conditions, Medicare Part B covers

- Physician services and supplies furnished as part of those services.
- Ambulance transportation.
- Artificial limbs and eyes.
- Chiropractors' treatments for subluxation of the spine.
- Diagnostic testing prior to a hospital stay.
- Durable medical equipment, such as a wheelchair or oxygen equipment.
- Independent laboratory tests.
- Optometrists' services for fitting corrective lenses after cataract surgery.
- Oral surgery (but not routine dental care).
- Outpatient maintenance dialysis.
- Outpatient physical, speech, and occupational therapy services.
- Outpatient psychiatric services (under special payment rules).
- Mammography.
- Podiatrists' services.
- Surgical dressings, splints, casts, colostomy supplies, and braces.
- Training for home dialysis.
- X-rays and radiation treatments.

Each year, you or your health insurance pay the annual Medicare Part B deductible of $100 (for 1998). Thereafter you or your health insurance will pay 20 percent of covered charges. These charges may not exceed the charges allowed by Medicare. You or your health insurance will also have to pay any additional amounts that your physician is allowed to charge. Part B generally will pay 80 percent of the approved charges for other covered services you receive during the rest of the year. In a few cases, Part B will pay for *all* costs.

Part B payments, however, are not based on your doctors' or your suppliers' current charges. Doctors and medical suppliers can *take assignment*. If so, they submit their charges directly to the Part B carrier (which processes the claim) and may not charge more than the amount allowed by Medicare. (Part A hospital charges are billed to an *intermediary*.) A doctor who does not take assignment must still send your claim to the carrier and cannot charge more than 15 percent over the amount allowed by Medicare.

Applying for Benefits. If you must apply for Medicare benefits, there is a seven-month *initial enrollment period* for Part B. This period begins three months before the month you first become eligible for Medicare and ends three months after that month. For example, if you are eligible for Medicare in July, your initial enrollment period starts April 1 and ends October 31.

If you do not apply for Medicare during your initial enrollment period and later decide you want it, you can sign up during a *general enrollment period*. A general enrollment period is held January 1 through March 31 of each year. However, if you enroll during a general enrollment period, your protection will not start until July of that year and your monthly premium will be 10 percent higher for a certain period of time than it would have been if you had enrolled when you first became eligible for Medicare.

What Medicare Does Not Cover. Medicare provides basic protection against the high cost of illness after you are age sixty-five or while you are severely disabled. However, it will not pay all of your health care expenses.

Some of the services and supplies for which Medicare does *not* pay are

- Services or supplies that are determined unnecessary for the diagnosis or treatment of an illness or injury.
- Most prescription drugs.
- Routine physical checkups or tests directly related to such examinations.
- Most nursing home care.
- Routine foot care (except for diabetics).
- Custodial care, such as help with bathing, eating, and taking medicine.
- Dentures and routine dental care.
- Eyeglasses and examinations to prescribe or fit eyeglasses.
- Hearing aids and examinations to prescribe or fit hearing aids.
- Private-duty nurses.
- Private hospital rooms (unless medically necessary).

Appeals. The most common reason for a carrier or intermediary to deny Medicare claims is that the provided service was not "medically necessary."

Medicare recipients have the right to challenge these determinations. If you are found ineligible for Medicare, you must challenge that decision through the Social Security Administration. This appeal procedure is the same as for a Social Security appeal. (See the section entitled "Appealing Disability Determinations" in Chapter 15, "The Rights of the Disabled.")

You must appeal a decision you think is wrong within sixty days. Contact your local Social Security office to begin the appeal process. You can appeal to the federal courts if you are not satisfied with Social Security's decision. You will definitely need a lawyer to do so.

Private Health Care Plans. Many private health insurance companies say that their policies for people who have Medicare are designed to cover only costs that Medicare will not pick up. They recommend that their policyholders also sign up for Medicare Part B to have full protection. If you have private health insurance, it may not pay for some of the services that are covered by Part B. For example, some private plans will not cover visits to a doctor's office.

If you are not sure about the protection you may have, get in touch with your insurance agent to discuss your health insurance and how it relates to your Medicare protection. He or she may be able to help you decide what other coverage you should have. Be sure not to cancel any private health insurance you now have until the month your Medicare coverage begins.

Medicare Supplements. The Medicare program is not a comprehensive health insurance program and therefore does not cover all of your medical expenses. Many people look to supplemental health insurance to fill in the gaps of their Medicare coverage. Federal law has standardized Medicare-supplement policies to ten basic plans. They pay part or all of Medicare's deductibles and coinsurance amounts. (As a general rule, Medicaid recipients and HMO enrollees do not need supplemental health insurance.)

Federal law and the New Jersey Department of Insurance require all Medicare-supplement policies to provide at least the following benefits in the "core" plan:

- Part A copayments: pays the copayment Medicare charges ($191 per day in 1998) after the sixtieth day in a hospital.
- Pays 100 percent of hospital expenses after 150 days (when Medicare runs out), up to a total of 365 lifetime reserve days.
- Part B copayments: pays 20 percent of Medicare's approved amount.

A Medicare-supplement policy is not required to pay for the kinds of services and supplies that Medicare does not cover at all, such as eyeglasses, prescriptions, and private-duty nurses. It also is not required to pay doctors' fees in excess of the amount considered reasonable by Medicare. A carrier may not refuse to sell you a Medicare-supplement policy for health reasons during the six-month period following your sixty-fifth birthday. However, a waiting period of up to six months may be imposed before covering a condition. All Medicare-supplement policies must be guaranteed to be renewable, and a carrier may not cancel solely for health reasons.

PHARMACEUTICAL ASSISTANCE FOR THE AGED AND DISABLED. PAAD is a state-funded program that helps senior citizens and disabled persons pay for prescription drugs, insulin, insulin syringes, needles, and certain diabetic testing materials (*N.J.A.C.* 10:51-1 *et seq.*).

If you qualify for PAAD, you will be issued a PAAD card. With that card, you will have to copay (in 1998) $5 toward the cost of a prescription.

The Bureau of Pharmaceutical Assistance for the Aged and Disabled within the DHSS administers the program. The Casino Revenue Fund is the primary funding source for the program.

Eligibility. To be eligible for PAAD you must meet the following residency, income, and age requirements:

- You must have been a New Jersey resident for at least thirty days prior to the date of application. (Your residence must have been a legally established residence and not a seasonal one.) You do not have to be a U.S. citizen.
- Your countable income cannot exceed $17,550 (in 1998) for a single person or $21,970 (in 1998) for a married couple.
- You must be sixty-five years of age or older, or at least eighteen years of age and receiving Social Security disability benefits.

If you have private health insurance that provides pharmaceutical benefits equal or superior to the PAAD program or if you receive Medicaid benefits, you will not be eligible for PAAD. You are eligible if your health insurance plan offers limited or partial coverage.

Applying for PAAD. To apply for this program you must fill out an application, which you can get at any county nutrition site, pharmacy, Office on Aging, or PAAD office, among other locations. If approved, you should receive a temporary prescription card within thirty days of your application. A permanent card that will be good for one year will be sent to you in the mail.

Before your PAAD card expires, you will have to fill out a renewal application. A form is automatically mailed to you about four months before your PAAD card expires. If you are still eligible, you will receive a new PAAD card, which will be good for another year.

You must notify PAAD of any changes that affect your eligibility. If you become ineligible because of an increase in income or other change in circumstances, you may have to repay PAAD for benefits you received.

If you are found ineligible for PAAD or if your application is denied, you are entitled to appeal the decision by submitting a written request for a fair hearing to the PAAD office at the DHSS. You must submit the request within twenty calendar days from the date the notice of ineligibility was mailed.

343

MEDICAL ASSISTANCE FOR THE POOR

One of the most important safety nets for the medical needs of low-income people is Medicaid.

MEDICAID. Authorized under federal law, Medicaid is a means-tested entitlement program financed by both the federal and state governments but administered by the state (*N.J.A.C.* 10:49-1 *et seq.*). Only persons who fall into particular categories, such as people receiving federal cash assistance, children of low-income families, or pregnant women are eligible. Fifty percent of Medicaid expenditures in New Jersey are paid for by the federal government and fifty percent by the state. Medicaid finances health and long-term care services.

Each state has considerable flexibility in running its Medicaid program and, as a result, it has been said that there are fifty different Medicaid programs. New Jersey is notable for offering a wide range of services in its Medicaid program; however, until the advent of Medicaid managed care, the state offered low reimbursement rates to providers (with the exception of hospitals).

Eligibility. Under the federal Personal Responsibility and Work Opportunity Reconciliation Act of 1996 (PRA, 2 *U.S.C.* Section 901 *et seq.*), people who would have been eligible for cash assistance under the former Aid to Families with Dependent Children (AFDC) program, which PRA repealed, are eligible for Medicaid. If you lose eligibility because of income from employment, you will continue to be eligible for Medicaid for two more years. Supplemental Security Income (SSI) recipients are automatically eligible for Medicaid. The following groups are also eligible for Medicaid:

- Infants up to age one and pregnant women whose family income is below 185 percent of the federal poverty level (there are no resource limits).
- Other children up to age eighteen whose family income is below 133 percent of the federal poverty level (there are no resource limits).
- People who are age sixty-five or over, blind, or disabled who have incomes below the federal poverty level (and resources below specified limits).

Several groups are also eligible for Medicaid under special federal provisions. Two of them are (1) persons receiving care under home and community-based service programs, for example, the AIDS Community Care Alternative Program (ACCAP) *and* (2) certain Medicare beneficiaries. These are discussed in more detail later in the chapter.

Applying for Medicaid. You may apply for Medicaid at the county welfare agency (CWA). People receiving assistance from SSI programs are automatically given Medicaid when they qualify for SSI benefits. Thus, they do not apply separately for Medicaid.

Medicaid applications can also be processed at certain hospitals and federally qualified community health centers. If necessary, additional documentation can be mailed to the CWA. Pregnant women may be found *presumptively eligible* by a Medicaid provider and receive prenatal care for a temporary period without providing any documentation to the provider or the CWA before the end of the temporary period.

Services Paid for by Medicaid. Medicaid directly reimburses participating providers for care to Medicaid recipients. Medicaid also pays for transportation to and from doctors' offices, hospitals, and clinics. Providers who choose to participate in the Medicaid program—including doctors, dentists, hospitals, nursing homes, and pharmacies—may not charge recipients for services covered by Medicaid. In the past, Medicaid reimbursement for physician services was so low that Medicaid recipients often could not find a doctor easily. Until recently most providers were reimbursed on a fee-for-service basis.

Hospital care, including emergency room care, was always reasonably reimbursed and available. Many Medicaid recipients who could not find a Medicaid doctor near where they lived would seek nonemergency care in hospital emergency rooms. Medicaid managed care is rapidly replacing the fee-for-service system. One of the purposes of Medicaid managed care is to ensure an adequate supply of all providers through changing the reimbursement methodology, increasing the supply of accessible doctors, and decreasing the inappropriate use of hospital emergency rooms.

Medicaid in New Jersey pays for many services, including

- Inpatient hospital services.*
- Outpatient hospital services.*
- Prenatal care.*
- Physician services.*
- *Early and periodic screening, diagnosis, and treatment* (EPSDT) services for children under age twenty-one, including private-duty nursing if medically necessary, and services for conditions identified in the screening examination.*
- Nursing home services.*
- Clinic services.
- Intermediate care facility (ICF) services for the aged and disabled.
- ICF services for the mentally challenged.
- Optometrist services and eyeglasses.

- Prescription drugs.
- Prosthetic devices.
- Dental services.
- Family-planning services and supplies.
- Laboratory and X-ray services.
- Nurse-midwife services.

The services marked by an asterisk (°) (*mandatory services*) must be provided under federal law. New Jersey has chosen to provide the other services (*optional services*) as well; the federal government funds them to the same extent as mandatory services. However, since the state is not required to provide the optional services, it may discontinue them for budgetary or other reasons.

Certain medical services require approval by the Medicaid office before they can be given, except in an emergency. It is the duty of the doctor, dentist, or other provider to get prior approval, if required, before giving treatment. It is a good idea to ask your doctor if Medicaid has approved your treatment before you accept services.

Medicaid provides three months' retroactive coverage. When you apply for Medicaid, if you submit your medical bills for treatment received in the three months prior to the date you applied for Medicaid, they will be paid.

The Medically Needy Program. The Medically Needy program extends Medicaid benefits to cover some specific medical services, especially nursing home services (*N.J.A.C.* 10:70-1 *et seq.*), for certain groups of people whose income and resources are too high to qualify for AFDC or SSI but who do not have enough money to meet their medical expenses. The following groups of people are potentially eligible for the Medically Needy program: pregnant women, dependent children under twenty-one years of age, persons sixty-five years of age or older, and persons who are blind or disabled.

The major significance of the Medically Needy Medicaid program in New Jersey is that it provides a means for elderly people whose incomes are too high to qualify for SSI—and who therefore cannot qualify for the regular Medicaid program—to become eligible for Medicaid nursing home services and other long-term care (*N.J.A.C.* 10:49-5.3(a)4). They will be eligible provided their income is less than the cost of their care. They must still meet the resource eligibility requirements of the Medicaid program. After they are determined to be eligible, recipients must pay most of their income to the nursing home, and the Medicaid program will pay the difference between that amount and what the nursing home charges. Medicaid pays for about half of all nursing home care in New Jersey. This is a very important program for elderly people because Medicare does not cover nursing home services.

Appealing a Medicaid Decision. If you are determined to be ineligible for Medicaid or if Medicaid decides that a particular medical service or device is not medically necessary and will not be paid by Medicaid, you can request a *fair hearing* (*N.J.A.C.* 10:49-10.3). Your hearing request should be made to your CWA within twenty days of the date you receive notice from Medicaid of its adverse decision. If you were previously on Medicaid and you appeal within ten days, your Medicaid benefits will continue until there is a final decision.

After you tell Medicaid that you wish to appeal their decision, your case will be referred to an administrative law judge (ALJ) who will make a recommendation (*initial decision*) within ninety days. If you disagree with it, you or your attorney can write a *letter of exceptions* to the Division of Medical Assistance and Health Services. The division will make a final decision within forty-five days of receiving the initial decision. If you have applied within the time allowed for continuing benefits, you will continue to receive them until the final decision is issued. If you disagree with the final decision, you can appeal to the New Jersey Superior Court, Appellate Division.

If you are a member of a Medicaid HMO, you can also appeal a decision of the HMO—for example, to reduce or deny services, or to deny access to a specialist—through the internal grievance procedure that each HMO must have and which must be described in your HMO's handbook. You do not have to complete any of the stages in the grievance process before appealing the decision to Medicaid itself and using the appeals procedure previously outlined (*N.J.A.C.* 10:74-11.1 and 11.2).

Medicaid for the Elderly or Disabled. If you are over sixty-five, blind, or disabled, but your income or resources are too high for you to receive SSI *and* get Medicaid services, you can still get Medicaid under the New Jersey Care program (*N.J.A.C.* 10:72-1 *et seq.*). Your monthly income must not be more than the federal poverty level for that year. The amount of countable resources that you can have (in 1998) is $4,000 for one person or $6,000 for a couple.

Certain resources are exempt, that is, not counted toward the limit. These include

- The home in which you live.
- Household goods and personal effects.
- Life insurance policies with a face value of less than $1,500 per person.
- A car that is necessary for transportation to work or a health facility for regular medical treatment for a health problem, altered for use by a disabled person, or that is needed to perform essential daily activities.

347

Otherwise, a household can exclude $4,500 for the value of a household car or cars.

Some low-income Part A Medicare recipients are entitled to have Medicaid pay their Medicare premiums, deductibles, and copayments. These individuals are called *Qualified Medicare Beneficiaries* (QMBs). If you are receiving Medicare and also qualify for Medicaid under the New Jersey Care program, you are a QMB. As such, you are entitled to have the Medicaid program, through the CWA, pay for the following Medicare premiums, deductibles, and copayments on your behalf:

- Medicare Part B premiums (and Part A if not received premium free).
- Medicare Part A and Part B deductibles.
- Substantial copayments for (1) doctor bills, (2) outpatient care, (3) hospital stays over sixty days, *and* (4) skilled nursing home care over twenty-one days.

You qualify as a *Specified Low-Income Medicare Beneficiary* (SLMB) if you have income between 100 and 120 percent of the federal poverty level. SLMBs are entitled to have the state pay their Part B premiums. But you must apply for QMB coverage at your CWA, not at the Social Security office.

Medicaid and AIDS. The ACCAP is a home and community-based services program for needy persons with AIDS, needy persons with AIDS-related complex (ARC), and children under age thirteen diagnosed as HIV positive (*N.J.A.C.* 10:49-22.7). ACCAP provides all Medicaid services except nursing home coverage, and also provides case management, private-duty nursing, medical day care, personal care assistant services, certain narcotic and drug abuse treatments at home, intensive supervision for children who live in foster homes, and hospice care. Hospice care services are provided by Medicare-certified hospice agencies and are available to ACCAP recipients on a daily, twenty-four-hour basis. Hospice provides optimum comfort measures (including pain control) and support to an individual certified by an attending physician as terminally ill with a life expectancy of less than six months.

Medicaid Services for Children. The EPSDT program is designed to help discover, as early as possible, the ills that handicap Medicaid-eligible children. EPSDT is supposed to provide continuing follow-up and treatment so that handicaps are not neglected. It is the most comprehensive federal prevention and treatment program available for children. EPSDT should provide—for all Medicaid-eligible children from birth to age twenty-one—a comprehensive and periodic evaluation of a child's health, developmental, and nutritional status, as well as vision, dental, and hearing care (*N.J.A.C.* 10:49-18.1). Any problem discovered during an EPSDT checkup (called a *screen*) must be referred for treatment.

A medical screen includes

- A comprehensive health and developmental history.
- A comprehensive, unclothed physical exam.
- Appropriate immunizations.
- Lab tests.
- Health education, including counseling to both parents and children.

In addition to the medical screen, a child is entitled to

- A vision screen, which includes diagnosis and treatment for defects in vision, including eyeglasses.
- A dental screen, which provides relief of pain and infections, restoration of teeth, and maintenance of dental health.
- A hearing screen, which provides diagnosis and treatment for defects in hearing, including hearing aids.

Children are entitled to *periodic* screens at intervals that meet reasonable medical and dental standards. There are separate checkup schedules for general physical and developmental conditions and for dental, hearing, and vision care. In addition, a new federal law requires Medicaid to pay for so-called *inter-periodic* screens. This means that when physical or mental illnesses or conditions are suspected, the child has a right to a screen when medically necessary to diagnose the problem even if it's not yet time for another periodic screen. Medicaid must pay for the interperiodic screen. Medicaid must also pay for any necessary Medicaid-covered diagnosis or treatment to correct or improve any defect or mental or physical illness discovered during a screen, including private-duty nursing services for very sick children.

MEDICAID MANAGED CARE. Most Medicaid recipients in New Jersey now receive Medicaid services through an HMO; nearly all will very soon (*N.J.A.C.* 10:74-1 *et seq.*). SSI recipients still have a choice about joining a managed care program or not but that is expected to change by 1998. Welfare recipients and women and children who are eligible because of low income but who are not eligible for welfare must join an HMO in most counties. By 1998, this will be true of all counties.

HMOs are responsible for providing the full range of Medicaid services in New Jersey in return for a flat fee per enrollee paid by Medicaid. This is an advantage over the former fee-for-service system in many ways. Each Medicaid recipient is guaranteed to have a doctor, someone who can be held accountable for making sure that children receive all EPSDT services. The Department of Human Services has set up quality-control mechanisms to make sure that minimal standards are met. Medicaid patients, however, no longer have access to hospital emergency rooms without a referral from their doctors, except in the case of emergencies. For many recipients, this means that high-quality care may not be as conveniently located or even available.

Medicaid recipients are entitled to a choice between at least two HMOs (and in practice have had a much wider choice), although this is not expected to last. They also have a choice of doctors within an HMO. The doctor is either directly employed by the HMO or, more usually, is paid a flat fee by the HMO for each Medicaid recipient enrolled with him or her.

HMOs must all sign a standard contract with Medicaid. State regulations and the contract set out the standards HMOs must meet, their obligations to their enrollees, and the rights of Medicaid recipients participating in managed care. They include geographic-access standards stating how close enrollees must live to their physicians, hospitals, pharmacies, and other providers. They also include appointment-scheduling standards, such as how quickly you must be given a routine appointment for a condition that is not chronic, and how quickly the HMO must give you appointments with specialists and for dental care, laboratory services, and so on. HMOs must actively reach out to schedule a first visit within six months of enrollment.

In addition to contracting with HMOs, the state has contracted with an organization called the Health Benefits Coordinator (HBC). HMOs are not supposed to enroll Medicaid recipients directly in mandatory managed care, though some of them sometimes do. Medicaid recipients are supposed to do that through the HBC.

If you have problems with an HMO, you should first ask the HBC representative to intervene, then use the grievance procedure that is outlined in every HMO handbook. If you do not receive satisfaction on your complaint, remember that you have a right to a fair hearing. You don't have to go to the HBC or through the grievance procedure before asking for a fair hearing. If the matter is serious and you are eligible for Legal Services, you should ask a lawyer or paralegal in a Legal Services office near you for assistance.

CATASTROPHIC ILLNESS IN CHILDREN RELIEF FUND. The Catastrophic Illness in Children Relief Fund is another important health program for children (*N.J.A.C.* 10:155-1 *et seq.*). It is not a Medicaid program and is financed by state funds only. It provides financial help to families whose children have suffered a catastrophic illness. A child must be under age nineteen and a resident of New Jersey. An illness is considered to be "catastrophic" under the following circumstances:

- The child must have incurred medical expenses for an illness or condition.
- The medical expenses must not be fully covered by any other federal or state program, insurance contract, or any trust funds or settlements relative to the medical condition of the child.

- The remaining medical expenses must exceed a threshold of 15 percent of the first $100,000 of a family's annual income and 20 percent of income over $100,000.

If a child has out-of-pocket medical expenses above the applicable threshold, the child passes the initial screen of eligibility for the Fund's assistance. The Fund rarely pays for all out-of-pocket medical expenses. There is an upper limit, or cap, of $100,000 per year on the amount of medical expenses the Fund may pay for a child. Nevertheless, in hardship cases the upper-limit requirement can be waived. The Fund determines how its available money will be distributed among providers and vendors.

Eligible expenses are those uncovered medical expenses a child incurred during any prior consecutive twelve months back to 1988. Income is measured for the same twelve-month period.

If there is insufficient money in the Fund, a *sliding payment schedule* will be used to distribute the available money. At that point, the Fund will consider assets and other factors that affect the ability to pay for care.

You may apply to the Fund through any of its local agencies. The local agency is responsible for assisting you to apply, sending your application to the Fund, and referring you to other programs and benefits, including Medicaid and charity care.

If the Fund denies your child's application, you may appeal to the Catastrophic Illness in Children Relief Fund Commission. You may do so no later than thirty days from the date of the notice of denial. The commission may waive the deadline for cause. The commission may refer the case to the Office of Administrative Law (OAL) for an initial decision, or may make a final decision without first referring the case to the OAL. You may appeal the commission's final decision to the Appellate Division of superior court.

NEW JERSEY KID CARE PROGRAM. This program provides subsidized health insurance coverage for children up to age 18 who are financially ineligible for Medicaid but whose family income is below 200 percent of the federal poverty level. Medical services are provided through HMOs.

Unfortunately, a child with family income greater than 133 percent of the federal poverty level and who is therefore ineligible for Medicaid will also be ineligible for this program, until he or she has remained uninsured for a minimum of twelve months. Exceptions are granted for children who are losing Medicaid eligibility and have no other coverage at the time of termination.

15. The Rights of the Disabled

This chapter discusses various programs available to disabled persons under both federal and state law. It also discusses specific laws prohibiting discrimination against disabled people, as well as the specific rights of disabled people to education, court interpreters, and accessible transportation. In addition, the rights for handicapped accessible transportation, court interpreters, and education are discussed, as are specific laws covering discrimination and disability benefits available to disabled persons.

Disabled people have certain special rights under federal and state laws, including the right to Social Security Disability Insurance (SSDI) and Supplemental Security Income (SSI) disability benefits, if eligible. The state of New Jersey has designated New Jersey Protection and Advocacy, Inc. to protect the legal rights of people with disabilities. It receives federal and state funding to provide a range of services to people with disabilities, including individual and class representation and information and referral services.

THE AMERICANS WITH DISABILITIES ACT

The Americans with Disabilities Act[1] (ADA) is a sweeping federal civil rights law that provides protections surpassing previous civil rights legislation for disabled people. In enacting the ADA, thereby guaranteeing the civil rights of people with disabilities, Congress found that

- Forty-three million Americans have mental or physical disabilities.
- Society has tended to separate people with disabilities.
- Disabled people face widespread discrimination.

As a result disabled people face educational and job disadvantages and suffer from stereotypes that overlook the individual ability of the disabled individual to participate in and contribute to society.

The general purposes of the ADA are to ensure equality of opportunity, full participation, independent living, and economic self-sufficiency for disabled people, and to eliminate discrimination against them while providing a major role for the federal government in enforcing the law.

The ADA primarily applies to people who meet the ADA definition of *disabled.* To be considered disabled, an individual must meet one of the following three tests. He or she must (1) have a substantial impairment with respect to a major life activity, (2) have a record of such impairment, *or* (3) be regarded as having such an impairment.

The ADA has five titles, dealing with employment, public services, public accommodations, telecommunications, and miscellaneous issues.

The employment title stipulates that businesses must provide reasonable accommodations to protect the rights of employees with disabilities in all aspects of their employment, such as hiring, wages, and benefits. For example, the ADA might require a business, as a reasonable accommodation to the needs of a disabled employee, to alter the layout of a workstation or modify equipment. This provision, however, applies only to employers of fifteen or more persons.

The public services title of the ADA prohibits public services, such as state and local government, from denying services that are available to people without disabilities to people with disabilities. Under the public services title, all new construction and modifications must be accessible to people with disabilities. Furthermore, if the goal is readily achievable, barriers to services in existing facilities must be removed. This provision applies to businesses of all sizes, no matter how many or how few employees they have.

Under the telecommunications title, telephone companies must make telephone relay services available to people who use telecommunication devices for the deaf.

The miscellaneous title includes a prohibition against coercing, threatening, or retaliating against the disabled for asserting their rights under the ADA.

EMPLOYMENT. The ADA states that no employer shall discriminate against a "qualified individual with a disability" in regard to job application procedures, hiring, advancement, compensation, job training, discharge, and other terms and conditions of employment.

All employers that employ at least fifteen people are covered by the ADA. In order for a disabled person to be protected under the act, the person must be *qualified*—that is, the person must be able to perform the essential functions of the job the person holds or desires. This includes being able to perform the job if the employer makes reasonable changes in the workplace to accommodate such persons, including (1) making the facilities readily accessible and usable by disabled people *and* (2) making changes in job or work schedules; acquiring or modifying equipment or devices; changing examinations; providing training materials; or providing qualified readers or interpreters.

Under the law, an employer may not

- Separate or classify job applicants or employees in a way that adversely affects the opportunities of such employees because of their disabilities.
- Exclude or deny equal jobs or benefits because of a persons' disabilities.
- Give medical examinations or ask questions about disabilities, unless the examinations and questions are job related and necessary for the business.

An employer must (1) make reasonable changes in the workplace to accommodate the worker's physical or mental limitation, unless this change would cause undue hardship on the operation of the business, *and* (2) give applicants fair tests that measure the applicant's qualifications and do not discriminate against the applicant's test performance because of disability.

The law does not protect an employee when the employer acts based upon an individual's use of illegal drugs. It *does* protect disabled people who are no longer using illegal drugs or who have been or are being rehabilitated.

PUBLIC SERVICES. Discrimination in public services because of disability is prohibited under the ADA. This covers

- Any state or local government.
- Any department or agency of a state or local government.
- The National Railroad Passenger Corporation and any commuter authority.

A public service agency must provide services to all disabled people, as defined in the ADA, who qualify for the services provided by that agency. The agency must make reasonable changes to rules, policies, and practices; remove architectural or transportation barriers; or provide aids or services to help disabled people who are qualified for services.

Discrimination because of disability is also prohibited in public transportation, including buses, commuter trains, and intercity trains.

Any new vehicle that is purchased or leased by a transportation system (e.g., a bus) must be "readily accessible to and usable by individuals with disabilities, including individuals who use wheelchairs." Train systems must have at least one car per train that is accessible to disabled people.

On intercity, single-level passenger trains, the cars must

- Be able to be entered by a person who uses a wheelchair.
- Have space to park and secure a wheelchair.
- Have a seat to which a passenger in a wheelchair can transfer, and a space to fold and store the wheelchair.
- Have a rest room usable by a person who uses a wheelchair.
- Provide food service to a passenger who uses a wheelchair if the train has a dining car.

Newly constructed transportation facilities (stations) must be accessible to and usable by persons with disabilities, including those who use wheelchairs. Changes must be made to existing facilities to make them accessible to and usable by disabled people. In general, the changes must make bathrooms, telephones, and drinking fountains accessible. This should be done as soon as practicable, but a facility or its operator has twenty years to comply.

A transportation system operating on a regular schedule must provide extra transportation services for disabled persons who cannot ride on the system. For example, some people may need another person's help to board a vehicle and some people may not be able to get to the station. A transportation system must meet the needs of those persons.

PUBLIC ACCOMMODATIONS AND SERVICES OPERATED BY PRIVATE ENTITIES. Discrimination because of disability is also prohibited in public accommodations and services operated by private companies. These include

- An inn, hotel, motel, or other place of lodging, except for a building that has not more than five rooms for rent and is occupied by the owner.
- A restaurant, bar, or other establishment serving food or drink.
- A motion picture house, theater, concert hall, stadium, or other place of exhibition or entertainment.
- An auditorium, convention center, lecture hall, or other place of public gathering.
- A bakery, grocery store, clothing store, hardware store, shopping center, or other sales or retail establishment.
- A laundromat, dry cleaner, bank, barber shop, beauty shop, travel service, shoe repair service, funeral parlor, gas station, office of an accountant or lawyer, pharmacy, insurance office, professional office of a health care provider, hospital, or other service establishment.
- A terminal, depot, or other station used for specified public transportation.
- A museum, library, gallery, or other place of public display or collection.
- A park, zoo, amusement park, or other place of recreation.
- A nursery, elementary, secondary, undergraduate or postgraduate private school, or other place of education.
- A day care center, senior citizen center, homeless shelter, food bank, adoption agency, or other social service center or establishment.
- A gymnasium, health spa, bowling alley, golf course, or other place of exercise or recreation.

Disabled persons are entitled to the full and equal enjoyment of the goods, services, facilities, privileges, and advantages of any place of public accommodation. The definition of discrimination includes

- Denying disabled people the opportunity to take part in or benefit from the services of a business.
- Failure to provide equal benefits to disabled and nondisabled persons.
- Having eligibility rules that screen out disabled people.
- Failure to make reasonable changes that are necessary to provide such services and facilities to disabled people.

- Failure to take steps to ensure that disabled people are not denied benefits and are treated the same as nondisabled people.
- Failure to remove barriers and make changes in passenger cars used to transport people where such changes are "readily achievable."

Services must be provided in as integrated a setting as possible, and a disabled person must be allowed to participate in an integrated setting even if the facility provides separate services.

Newly constructed facilities must be "readily accessible to and usable by" disabled people "except where . . . it is structurally impractical." Facilities must be altered to make them readily accessible to and usable by persons with disabilities. Bathrooms, telephones, and drinking fountains must also be "readily accessible."

Private clubs and religious organizations are generally not covered by the law.

ENFORCEMENT OF THE ADA. Anyone who feels that any provisions of the law are being violated should contact a lawyer. The U.S. government also has an important role in enforcing the law. Complaints about discrimination in employment may be made to the Equal Employment Opportunity Commission (EEOC), either in Washington, D.C., or in New Jersey. Complaints about public accommodations, privately owned facilities, or commercial establishments should be made to the U.S. Department of Justice, Civil Rights Division. After assessing your particular needs, they will make a determination as to where to refer you.

If you have a problem regarding telephone and other telecommunications common carrier services within New Jersey, complaints should be addressed to the New Jersey Board of Public Utilities (BPU). Problems concerning services between New Jersey and another state (*interstate services*) or foreign communications should be addressed to the Federal Communications Commission (FCC), Common Carrier Bureau, Enforcement Division, Informal Complaints and Public Inquiries.

There is no special form to fill out to file an informal complaint with the FCC. You can simply send a typed or legibly printed letter. The letter should include your name, address, telephone number(s) involved with your complaint, a telephone number where you can be reached during the business day, and the name of your local telephone company.

Formal complaints must be accompanied by a filing fee and must be in the format prescribed in the FCC commissioners' rules.[2] A complaint must show facts that, if substantiated, establish that a violation of the Federal Communications Act[3] or an FCC rule or policy has occurred. Formal complaints filed with the FCC usually require the assistance of an attorney.

THE DEVELOPMENTALLY DISABLED ASSISTANCE AND BILL OF RIGHTS ACT

A developmental disability is a severe, chronic disability, manifested during the developmental period, that results in impaired intellectual functioning or deficiencies in essential skills. The term *developmental disabilities* is an umbrella one, describing a group of conditions, including mental retardation, cerebral palsy, autism, and spina bifida. Severe learning disabilities, some severe head injuries, and some severe sensory impairments are also sometimes considered to be developmental disabilities.

The Developmentally Disabled Assistance and Bill of Rights Act[4] states that persons with developmental disabilities have a right to appropriate treatment. The treatment should be designed to maximize the developmental potential of the person. The law places a duty on both the federal and state governments to make sure that public funds are not given to any residential program that does not meet certain minimum standards. It further requires that nonresidential programs receiving public funds provide treatment and services that are appropriate to the persons served.

THE DEVELOPMENTALLY DISABLED RIGHTS ACT

The Developmentally Disabled Rights Act[5] specifically safeguards the rights of persons in institutions. It provides that persons in institutions shall receive humane treatment. It also requires a written *individualized habilitation plan* (IHP) to be prepared for each person with a developmental disability. The plan must list the habilitation goals and the services needed to meet those goals. The law also requires that every developmentally disabled person between the ages of five and twenty-one be provided a thorough and efficient education suited to that person's age and abilities. (See the section entitled "Disabled Children's Right to Education" in Chapter 13, "Educating Your Children.") The law also governs the rights of developmentally disabled persons who are transferred from a state institution to a community residential facility.

SERVICES AND VOCATIONAL REHABILITATION FOR THE DISABLED

The Division of Developmental Disabilities (DDD) in the New Jersey Department of Human Services is responsible for meeting all of the habilitation and related needs of people with developmental disabilities. This includes a whole range of day programs, housing, and some guardianship for developmentally disabled children and adults. The DDD has a public guardianship program for people with developmental disabilities who are over age eighteen,

357

who have been found incompetent by a court, and who have no family or friends who are able or willing to act as legal guardian of the person. The court will appoint this program as legal guardian only for disabled persons who are receiving residential, training, or other services as a qualified client of the DDD. The program is carried out by the DDD's Bureau of Guardianship Services (BGS). The BGS does not receive a fee for its services. It will only act as guardian of the *person*, not of the property of a disabled individual. More information may be obtained from one of the regional offices of the BGS located around the state. The central office of the DDD is located in Trenton.

The Division of Vocational Rehabilitation Services in the New Jersey Department of Labor provides vocational training, evaluation, and placement for eligible disabled persons, including mentally ill persons. Its central office is also located in Trenton.

To apply for any of the services provided, you will have to contact the office in your county. If you are blind or visually impaired, vocational rehabilitation services are available to you through the New Jersey Commission for the Blind and Visually Impaired.

TITLE V, THE REHABILITATION ACT OF 1973

Title V, the Rehabilitation Act of 1973,[6] prohibits a program or activity receiving federal funds from denying benefits or services to any person because of a disability, including mental illness, if the person is otherwise qualified for the benefit or service. If your rights are violated under this law, you often have to file a complaint with the civil rights office of the federal agency that funds the activity or program against which you have a complaint before you have the right to file a complaint in federal district court. In some cases, you may be able to go directly to court.

This law also requires the creation of an Architectural and Transportation Barriers Compliance Board (ATBCB) to ensure that disabled persons have access to federal government buildings and public transportation. Complaints about failure to provide services may be sent directly to the ATBCB.

Several other laws require all federal agencies and employers with government contracts to develop affirmative action plans to hire disabled persons. (See the section entitled "Employment Discrimination" in Chapter 5, "You and Your Job.")

TRANSPORTATION FOR THE DISABLED

Under the New Jersey Senior Citizen and Disabled Resident Transportation Assistance Act,[7] $7\frac{1}{2}$ percent of New Jersey's casino tax fund is appropriated for transportation services for senior citizens and individuals with disabilities. Of those funds, 75 percent are made available to the counties through New Jersey Transit to provide locally coordinated services for senior citizens and people with disabilities; the remaining 25 percent of the funds are available to New Jersey Transit to provide "additional and expanded services" to these people. With this funding, New Jersey Transit has modified rail stations for accessibility and has administered a statewide bus accessibility program.

New Jersey Transit offers a reduced fare for disabled and elderly passengers traveling on most New Jersey bus routes and trains during off-peak hours. All new public buses must have wheelchair lifts, and certain train stations must be made accessible to wheelchair users.

The Office of Special Services of New Jersey Transit makes available to qualified nonprofit groups specialized vehicles, bought with federal funds, for the transportation of senior citizens and persons with disabilities. This office is also in charge of overseeing the use of specialized vehicles by public and private nonprofit social service agencies in each county. Further information about accessible transportation, routes, and wheelchair reservations can be obtained from New Jersey Transit, Office of Special Services.

THE AIR CARRIER ACCESS ACT OF 1986.[8] This federal law specifically prohibits discrimination by airlines on the basis of handicap. It also requires the U.S. Department of Transportation to issue regulations protecting the disabled against discriminatory practices by airlines.

TELECOMMUNICATIONS FOR HEARING- AND SPEECH-IMPAIRED PERSONS

The ADA requires telephone companies to provide services that allow a hearing- or speech-impaired person to engage in communication that is equal to that of those who do not have impairments.

The Telecommunications for the Disabled Act of 1982[9] requires that certain *essential telephones* be compatible with hearing aids that are specially designed for telephone use. Under this federal law, essential telephones include coin-operated phones, phones that alert others to emergencies, and phones that are frequently used by hearing-impaired persons.

NEW JERSEY'S LAW AGAINST DISCRIMINATION

New Jersey's Law against Discrimination[10] explicitly prohibits discrimination against any person because of an actual or perceived disability, including mental illness. The law covers discrimination in employment, public accommodations, publicly assisted housing, and other property issues, including real estate transactions. The law also prohibits any unlawful employment practice against a disabled person, unless the individual cannot adequately perform his or her job duties despite reasonable accommodations to his or her needs. (See the section entitled "Employment Discrimination" in Chapter 5, "You and Your Job.")

If you are discriminated against under this law, you may file either a lawsuit in superior court or a complaint with the New Jersey Division on Civil Rights (DCR), which enforces the New Jersey Law against Discrimination. The DCR can help you if you believe that you have been discriminated against in employment, housing, or public accommodations.

LAWS AGAINST HOUSING DISCRIMINATION

In the area of housing, there are several relevant laws.

THE FAIR HOUSING ACT AMENDMENTS OF 1988. The purpose of this federal law is to prevent housing discrimination against people with disabilities including mental illness.[11] It seeks to (1) end segregation of the housing available to people with disabilities, (2) give people with disabilities the right to choose where they wish to live, *and* (3) require reasonable accommodation to the needs of people with disabilities in securing and enjoying appropriate housing.

THE SENIOR CITIZEN AND DISABLED PROTECTED TENANCY ACT. The New Jersey Senior Citizen and Disabled Protected Tenancy Act[12] provides that senior citizens and qualified disabled persons (regardless of age) cannot be evicted from their homes for forty years when a building is being converted to a condominium or cooperative. This law also protects eligible tenants from unfair rent increases.

In many federally subsidized and public housing projects, disabled tenants are in a protected class, similar to the elderly, and have priority in obtaining housing. Chapter 2, "Your Rights as a Tenant," discusses federal laws and regulations that protect the disabled from unfair discrimination in regard to housing and that provide them with specific rights.

INDIVIDUALS WITH DISABILITIES EDUCATION ACT

The Individuals with Disabilities Education Act (IDEA)[13] guarantees that all disabled children, ages three through twenty-one, are entitled to a free and appropriate education. In 1986, Congress amended the law to include a section relevant to disabled infants and toddlers from birth through two years of age and their families. The amendments created a $300 million federal grant program for early-intervention services to these children and their families. In 1986, Congress also enacted the Handicapped Children Protection Act[14] to provide for the payment of attorneys' fees when the parent of a disabled child between the ages of three and twenty-one wins a court case against a school district that is not providing an appropriate education for the child. Congress also passed the Education of the Deaf Act of 1986,[15] which reaffirms the importance of quality education and training for deaf persons.

THE COURT INTERPRETERS ACT

The Court Interpreters Act[16] requires that interpreters be provided for defendants and witnesses in any civil or criminal federal court case that is brought by the U.S. government. It requires that sign- and foreign-language interpreting services be provided at no cost to persons who need them.

Under New Jersey law,[17] New Jersey state courts are required to appoint a "qualified interpreter" to assist any hearing-impaired person who is a witness, a party to, or the parent of a juvenile involved in a case. You have a right to an interpreter throughout all court proceedings before any court, and during preparation with an attorney for those proceedings.

An interpreter is deemed a *qualified interpreter* only if he or she has been certified by the National Registry of Interpreters for the Deaf, Inc. and is listed by the Division of the Deaf in the New Jersey Department of Labor, or by the New Jersey Registry of Interpreters for the Deaf. The Interpreter Referral Service of the Division of the Deaf has the expertise to match the particular needs of the deaf person with the particular skills of the several qualified interpreters available. To get a qualified interpreter, contact the Interpreter Referral Service of the Division of the Deaf. The interpreter is to be provided free of charge to the hearing-impaired person.

VOTING RIGHTS FOR DISABLED PERSONS

Two laws deal with the voting rights of disabled persons. The Voting Accessibility for the Elderly and Handicapped Act[18] requires that polling places and registration facilities for federal elections be accessible to people with mobility impairments. This law also provides for certain voting and registration aids to persons with disabilities. Telecommunication devices for the deaf must be available to provide information about registration and voting to persons with hearing disabilities. Instructions about voting must also be printed in large type and be clearly displayed at registration and polling places. The law also makes voting easier for disabled people who physically cannot go to the polls to vote. They do not need to obtain a medical certificate in order to cast an absentee ballot. New Jersey law has similar requirements governing state elections.

Under the Voting Rights Act of 1965,[19] a voter who needs help to vote because of his or her blindness, disability, or inability to read or write, may be assisted to vote by a person of his or her choice.

If you have a complaint about denial or interference with voting rights, contact the New Jersey Department of State, Election Division.

DISABILITY BENEFITS

Public employers, some private employers, and the Veterans Administration (VA) provide disability benefits; however, by far the most important source of financial support for disabled people is the Social Security Administration. It administers the following types of disability benefits for people who meet the very strict Social Security definition of *disabled:*

- Disability insurance benefits to people who have earned enough Social Security credits to qualify for SSDI benefits on their own work record. (See the discussion on Social Security credits in Chapter 9, "Securing the Future for Senior Citizens and Their Families.")
- SSDI benefits to widows and widowers with disabilities on the work record of a spouse.
- SSI benefits to people with disabilities who qualify because of income.
- SSI disability benefits to disabled children who might be eligible for SSI disability benefits on their own.
- SSDI benefits to disabled children over age eighteen (so-called *adult children*) whose disability must have started before age twenty-two and who might be eligible for SSDI benefits on the work record of a parent.

There is a five-month waiting period after you become disabled before you become entitled to SSDI benefits. There is no waiting period for SSI disability benefits. On the other hand, you cannot receive SSI disability benefits for any period before your claim was filed, whereas SSDI benefits can be paid retroactively for up to twelve months, not including the waiting period.

QUALIFYING AS DISABLED. Social Security's disability rules are different from those of private pension plans and other government disability programs. The fact that you qualify for disability benefits from another program or plan or have a statement from your doctor saying that you are disabled does not necessarily mean you will be eligible under Social Security's rules.

To qualify as disabled, you must have a physical or mental impairment that is expected to last for a continuous period of at least twelve months, or result in death. You will not qualify for disability benefits if your mental or physical impairments were caused by alcoholism or drug addiction. You must also demonstrate that because of the impairment, you are unable to engage in any *substantial gainful activity.* This means not only that are you unable to return to your former work, but also that you are unable to do *any* work. In deciding your ability to work, factors such as your age and education will be considered. To prove that you are disabled, you will need medical evidence from your doctor and other sources to show how severe your condition is and how it prevents you from working. The Social Security office will send your claim to the Division of Disability Determinations in the Department of

Labor. Social Security must also consider nonmedical evidence related to your ability to function from day to day and combine the medical and nonmedical evidence in reaching a decision. Disability can still be established by medical evidence alone if a condition such as heart disease, arthritis, or mental illness is sufficiently severe. However, if the medical evidence alone is insufficient, functional ability must also be considered.

To qualify for disability benefits, children must have a physical or mental condition that can be medically proven and that results in "marked and severe functional limitations" of substantial duration. The Personal Responsibility and Work Opportunities Reconciliation Act of 1996 mandated a narrower definition of disability for children than for adults. The major difference is that children must have "a medically determinable physical or mental impairment, which results in marked and severe functional limitations." Congress intended to eliminate benefits for less severely disabled children. The law disproportionately denies SSI disability benefits to children who have serious mental, emotional, and behavioral disorders. Most of the children who have been denied SSI benefits or who have had their SSI benefits terminated under this law have mental, emotional, or behavioral, not physical, problems.

Disability Determination in HIV Cases. Persons who have been diagnosed with AIDS qualify for disability benefits. AIDS is caused by the HIV retrovirus. HIV suppresses the immune system, weakening the body's ability to fight infections. HIV itself cannot be detected in the body; however, antibodies to it can be. Persons infected with HIV may have no symptoms, have symptoms but none of the diseases that qualify them for a diagnosis of AIDS, or have symptoms that lead to a diagnosis of AIDS. Asymptomatic persons will not qualify for disability benefits on the basis of HIV infection alone. Those who have been infected with HIV but have not been diagnosed as having AIDS will find it very difficult to receive disability benefits even though they may be very sick.

The Social Security Administration has detailed guidelines for evaluating disability cases involving HIV infection. These guidelines apply to disability determinations for SSI disability and SSDI benefits. The guidelines include separate lists for adults and children of many severe HIV-associated conditions. If any of these HIV-associated conditions are documented as present, you will be found to be disabled.

Terminal Illness. Certain SSDI and SSI disability benefit cases must be marked as *potential TERI* (terminal illness) cases by the Social Security Administration and must be more speedily processed than other cases at all levels of claims processing and administrative appeals. The Social Security Administration lists certain conditions that require TERI processing. These are: chronic dependence on a cardiopulmonary life-sustaining device; awaiting a heart, liver, or bone marrow transplant; chronic pulmonary or heart failure requiring continuous home oxygen; having a malignant disease such as cancer and being confined at home or institutionalized; and being comatose thirty days or more.

In addition, there must be TERI processing in the following situations:

- Where there is an allegation by the claimant, his or her representative, family friend, doctor, or nurse that the claimant has a terminal illness,
- Where there is an allegation or diagnosis of AIDS (an allegation or diagnosis of HIV infection is not enough),
  or
- Where the claimant is registered in a Medicare-designated hospice or is receiving hospice care (for example, in-home counseling or nursing care).

TERMINATION OF DISABILITY. You will continue to receive disability benefits unless your condition improves or you return to "substantial" work. Your case will be reviewed periodically to determine if your condition has improved. This means new medical evidence may be needed from time to time, or you may be asked to take a special medical exam or test. Children must have their cases reviewed every three years, unless their condition is not expected to improve. Children who qualify because of their low birth weight must be reviewed a year after their birth.

MEDICAID OR MEDICARE. If you are eligible for SSI, you are automatically eligible for Medicaid. A separate application is not necessary. A letter of acceptance and a Medicaid identification card will be sent to anyone who is eligible for SSI. Medicaid benefits are paid retroactive to three months before your claim for SSI was filed. People who are losing SSI may still be eligible for Medicaid on other grounds. Therefore they should not be automatically terminated from Medicaid when they lose SSI.

After receiving SSDI benefits for twenty-four months, you will qualify for Part A Medicare (hospital insurance protection). At that point you may sign up for Part B Medicare (medical insurance protection). You must pay a monthly premium for Part B. However, people who qualify for SSDI benefits on the basis of chronic kidney disease qualify for Medicare immediately. (See the discussion on Medicare in Chapter 14, "Your Right to Health Care.")

RETURNING TO WORK. There are special rules for people who would like to return to work but are concerned about the effect this might have on their SSDI or SSI disability benefits. These rules offer special plans that permit people to work on a trial basis without suddenly losing their monthly benefits and their Medicare or Medicaid coverage. During a trial work period of up to nine months, you can work, receive paychecks, and still receive full SSDI benefits as long as you are still disabled. If you are receiving SSI disability benefits, your payments might be reduced or discontinued while you are working but may resume if you stop working within a year of starting.

If you do lose SSI and Medicaid because of your earnings but you still meet the SSI assets requirements ($2,000 for an individual in 1998), you will still be able to receive Medicaid if your earnings cannot make up for the loss of Medicaid and SSI, and you might not be able to keep working if you do not receive Medicaid. You would then be eligible for Medicaid as a *qualified severely impaired individual.*

If you *do* lose SSDI benefits because you continue working after the trial work period, you will continue to receive Medicare for three more years. After you have worked a total of four years and exhausted your Medicare eligibility, you may purchase Medicare coverage. However, the Medicaid program will pay for your Medicare hospital insurance (Part A) if you are a *qualified disabled and working individual.* This means that your income must be less than 200 percent of the current federal poverty level, your assets must be less than twice the current SSI asset level, and you must not be otherwise eligible for Medicaid. You must apply to the New Jersey Department of Health and Senior Services (DHSS), which can also provide you with the current financial requirements and any additional information about the program.

APPEALING DISABILITY DETERMINATIONS. The procedure for appealing disability determinations is the same as the procedure for appealing any other decision of the Social Security Administration. You can challenge a decision that you are no longer disabled enough to continue getting SSDI or SSI disability benefits as well as a decision that you were not disabled in the first place.

When Social Security makes a decision regarding whether or not you are disabled, it must send you a written notice. If you do not agree with the decision, you have a right to appeal.

Most people handle their own disability appeals, at least at the beginning stages. However, you have a right to be represented by a qualified person of your choice (such as a laywer) when you appeal a decision.

Reconsideration. Asking for a *reconsideration* is usually the first step to take in appealing a decision Social Security has made.

You must ask for reconsideration in writing. You must do so within sixty days of the date you receive the notice regarding your case. The date of receipt is assumed to be five days after the date on the notice, unless you can show that you received the notice later or did not receive it at all.

If Social Security has decided that your benefits should be reduced or eliminated, you have a right to have the payments continue unchanged while Social Security reconsiders your case. If you want this done, you must apply for reconsideration within ten days (rather than sixty days) of the date you received the notice.

Hearings. If you disagree with the reconsideration decision, you may request a hearing. You must request a hearing in writing no later than sixty days from the date you received the decision.

A Social Security administrative law judge (ALJ) will schedule a hearing. A notice telling you the date, time, and place of the hearing will be mailed to you at least ten days in advance. A hearing is usually held in the city where the Social Security office that handles your case is located.

You or your lawyer may attend the hearing and present your case in person. The ALJ will then take testimony from you and from any of your witnesses. The ALJ may also ask you or any witnesses questions about your case. You or your lawyer may question the witnesses, present new evidence, and examine the evidence that the judge will use to make a decision, including your case file. If you do not attend the hearing, the ALJ will base the decision on all the evidence submitted in your case, plus any additional evidence or statements you later submit within the time allowed for doing so.

The ALJ must make a written decision on the case within ninety days of the date on which your request for a hearing was made, unless the hearing was delayed at your request. A copy of the decision will be sent to you.

Review by the Appeals Council. If you are not satisfied with the ALJ's decision, you can appeal to the Social Security Appeals Council. You must request a review of your case by the Appeals Council within sixty days of the date on which you received the hearing decision.

Within thirty days, the Appeals Council will decide whether to review the hearing decision. If the council agrees to review your case, it will review the entire case record and a transcript of the hearing. You may request the right to appear and present oral arguments before the council. The Appeals Council's decision or refusal to review your case represents Social Security's final decision on your case.

Taking Your Case to Court. After Social Security has made its final decision in your case, if you are still not satisfied, you may file an appeal in federal court. The appeal must be filed no later than sixty days from the date on which Social Security made its final decision. This is the final step in the review process, and you will probably need a lawyer to pursue it.

16. Your Rights as a Veteran

To reward people who served in the armed forces, the U.S. government and the state of New Jersey offer special benefits to veterans, their spouses, and their dependents. This chapter primarily discusses federal veterans benefits, including service-connected disability compensation, need-based disability pensions, medical care, and education assistance. There are, however, many other federal benefits available to veterans, most of which are administered by the Veterans Administration (VA).

One way to get current information on VA benefits and claims procedures is to call the VA regional office in Newark. Counselors can answer questions about benefits eligibility and application procedures and refer you to other VA facilities, such as medical centers. The VA regional office processes claims for and administers VA benefits, which include disability compensation, disability pensions, home-loan guaranties, life insurance, educational assistance, vocational training for disabled veterans, burial allowance, and survivors' compensation, pension, and educational assistance.

VA medical center admissions offices are the immediate source for information about medical care eligibility, admissions procedures, and scheduling. They can provide information on all types of medical care, including nursing home and dental care, drug and alcohol dependency, prosthetics, readjustment counseling, and Agent Orange, radiation, or Desert Storm exposure examinations. In New Jersey, there are several VA medical centers, which can be found in the blue pages of your phone book. New Jersey's programs for veterans are run by the New Jersey Department of Military and Veterans Affairs.

ELIGIBILITY FOR BENEFITS

To receive veterans benefits, the person seeking them must be eligible and entitled to them. You are eligible for most veterans benefits if you received an honorable or a general discharge. (Educational benefits under the Montgomery GI Bill, however, require an honorable discharge.) You may be eligible for veterans benefits if you received an undesirable or bad-conduct discharge from a special court-martial. You are not eligible for veterans benefits if you received a dishonorable discharge or a bad-conduct discharge from a general court-martial. If you have a discharge that bars you from receiving VA benefits, you can apply to have the discharge upgraded.

There are two other types of general eligibility requirements for receiving VA benefits. First, a veteran must have served in the armed forces for a certain length of time and during a particular time period in order to receive certain benefits. Second, spouses and dependents of veterans must also meet certain requirements concerning their relationship to the veteran; children must meet certain age requirements.

TYPES OF BENEFITS

There are a number of different types of veterans benefits, which have their own specific eligibility requirements. The VA runs two major disability benefits programs for veterans: (1) service-connected disability compensation *and* (2) a disability pension for total disability that is not due solely to service-connected conditions. The service-connected disability compensation program is not needs based; however, the pension program is.

DISABILITY COMPENSATION. Disabled veterans can receive disability payments, without regard to income or age, if they are disabled because of an injury or disease that is *service connected.* Service connected means that the injury or disease happened during the time the person was serving in the armed forces, or a condition was made worse because of military service or treatment at a VA medical center. The disability cannot be a secondary effect of willful misconduct or abuse of alcohol or drugs.

The law assumes that the person was healthy when he or she entered the military and that certain diseases that show up (even if not diagnosed) during a certain period of time after leaving the service are service connected. There are also many other laws and rules that apply to decisions on what is considered to be service connected. For example, for veterans who served in Vietnam, the Agent Orange Act of 1991 states that chloracne (a skin condition) and non-Hodgkin's lymphoma and soft-tissue sarcomas (two rare types of cancer) are service connected.

In 1993, Vietnam veterans suffering from Hodgkin's disease, porphyria cutanea tarda (a liver disorder), respiratory cancers (including lung, larynx, and trachea), and multiple myeloma were added to the list of those entitled to service-connected disability payments, based on their service in Vietnam and their presumed exposure to Agent Orange and other herbicides. A veteran can also prove that a post-traumatic stress disorder (PTSD) is service connected. The veteran must show that he or she experienced an in-service stressor, that he or she currently has a PTSD, and that the PTSD is related to the in-service stressor. It doesn't matter how much time has passed between the veteran's discharge and the filing of a PTSD claim.

The amount of the disability payment varies according to how severely the disability impairs the veteran's ability to work. Disability ratings for VA benefits are made in increments of 10 percent; benefit payments are made every month. The rates are adjusted annually by a cost of living increase. Larger amounts are paid when the VA determines that an eligible veteran has suffered certain specific, severe disabilities. These are all decided on an individual basis.

A veteran who is a patient in a nursing home, who is determined by the VA to be in need of the regular aid and attendance of another person, or who is permanently housebound may be entitled to additional benefits.

If a veteran is rated at 30 percent or more disabled, he or she will receive extra benefits for his or her dependents. The additional amount depends on the number of dependents and the degree of disability. A disabled veteran evaluated at 30 percent or more disabled is also entitled to receive a special allowance for a spouse who is in need of the aid and attendance of another person.

Also, if the veteran experiences 100 percent disability due to specific causes, the state of New Jersey will pay $750 per year.

Surviving spouses, children, and parents of a veteran are eligible for certain VA benefits, called *dependency and indemnity compensation* (DIC), if the veteran's death was service connected. DIC benefits are also payable to these survivors even if the veteran's death was not service connected if the veteran was continuously rated totally disabled for a period of ten or more years, or if so rated for less than ten years, was so rated for a period of not less than five years from the date of discharge from military service.

The amounts of these survivorship payments are calculated based on the former service member's highest pay grade or, in the case of dependent parents, on their financial need as reflected in their annual income. Surviving spouses and parents receiving DIC may be granted a special allowance for *aid and attendance* if they are patients in a nursing home or require the regular aid and attendance of another person. The person providing the assistance need not be paid to receive the allowance.

Surviving spouses who are qualified for DIC who are not so disabled as to require the regular aid and attendance of another person but who, due to disability, are permanently housebound, may be granted a special allowance in addition to the DIC rate.

When a member of the armed forces who served in a combat zone dies as a result of wounds, disease, or injury received there, no state income tax is due for the taxable year the death occurred, nor for any earlier years served in the combat zone.

DISABILITY PENSION. The only VA disability pension program available for new applicants is the Improved Pension program. It is paid to veterans for total disability that is not due solely to service-connected conditions and to veterans (and their survivors) who served during wartime whether or not in a war zone. To qualify, the veteran must

- Have served ninety consecutive days on active duty with at least one day during an official period of war,
- Be totally and permanently disabled (not due to the willful misconduct of the veteran, or traceable to military service),

- Have a low income,
  and
- Have only limited assets.

The amount of money you receive depends on how much other income you have and how many dependents you have. The Improved Pension program is intended to bring your income to an established support level. The support level is reduced by the annual income you receive from other sources —such as Social Security—or the countable income of any spouse or dependent children. Not all income is counted toward the reduction. For example, Supplemental Security Income (SSI) and other welfare benefits are not counted. (Additionally, your income itself is reduced by any out-of-pocket medical expenses above an annual amount you pay.) The annual payment to you from the Improved Pension program is reduced only by the amount of any countable income you, your spouse, or your dependent children have. The disability pension is not, however, payable to those who have assets that could be used to provide adequate maintenance.

A veteran who is a patient in a nursing home or otherwise determined by the VA to be in need of the regular aid and attendance of another person, or who is permanently housebound, may be entitled to benefits in addition to those outlined above.

Surviving spouses and dependent children may also be eligible under the Improved Pension program; however, the established support level, and consequently the annual payment, is lower.

RELATIONSHIP OF SOCIAL SECURITY, SSI, AND VA BENEFITS

Your Social Security Disability Insurance (SSDI) benefits or your Social Security retirement benefits cannot be reduced because you receive VA disability compensation benefits. Conversely, your VA disability compensation benefits cannot be reduced because you receive any benefits from the Social Security Administration, including SSI.

Your SSI benefits, however, whether based on your disability or your age, *will* be reduced by the amount of any VA disability compensation benefits or any VA disability pension benefits you receive. On the other hand, SSI payments of *any* kind are not considered income in calculating your entitlement to a VA disability pension. SSDI benefits and Social Security retirement benefits *are* counted as income in calculating your eligibility for VA disability pension benefits.

APPORTIONMENT OF COMPENSATION AND PENSION

A veteran's children, spouse, or dependent parents may file an application with the VA to have a portion of the veteran's benefits paid directly to them. This is called *apportionment.* The VA will authorize an apportionment if the veteran is not living with his or her spouse or children and is not reasonably discharging his or her support obligations. Compensation and pension benefits may also be apportioned when a veteran is *incompetent* (not of sound mind) and hospitalized.

APPLYING FOR BENEFITS

To apply for compensation or pension benefits, you should complete the correct VA form at the VA's regional office in Newark. In most cases, the process will be routine. Once your claim is filed, the VA will send you a "C" number that you should use on all letters to the VA. An employee of the VA should start to process your claim by asking for additional, substantiating information.

If you submit a *plausible* claim—one that is meritorious on its own or capable of substantiation—the VA regional office must, in appropriate cases:

- Search for and retrieve all relevant records that the federal government has concerning you.
- Obtain all of your private medical records.
- Conduct a thorough medical examination, including (if necessary) a medical examination by a specialist.

You should apply for benefits immediately without waiting to collect documentation because compensation benefits and pension benefits are not payable prior to the date of application, even if you would otherwise be eligible for these benefits.

Nevertheless, it is extremely important that you provide a carefully documented claim. Do not rely on often overworked VA employees to obtain all the records that are necessary for a fair consideration of your claim. Work with a well-trained representative to understand what evidence is necessary to establish your claim.

After the VA regional office in Newark has gotten all the facts together, it must give you the benefit of the doubt if the evidence for and against your claim is evenly balanced.

If the VA regional office in Newark denies your claim, it will send you a notice of decision. You can appeal by filing a notice of disagreement within one year of the decision. The VA regional office in Newark must then send you a *statement of the case,* which explains why your claim was denied. You must then file a substantive appeal within sixty days of the date you received the statement of the case, or by the end of the one-year period after receipt of the notice of denial, whichever is longer.

Your appeal will be heard by the Board of Veterans Appeals (BVA), the highest administrative level within the U.S. Department of Veterans Affairs.

The BVA will decide the appeal based on the information in your file unless you request a *personal hearing.*

There are three kinds of personal hearings:

1. You can have a BVA *field hearing* at the VA regional office in Newark before a hearing officer acting as an agent of the BVA. This will take two to four months to schedule after your request. The hearing officer can change the decision if there is new and material evidence. Otherwise the transcript of the hearing is sent for review by a panel of the BVA in Washington, D.C., together with the rest of your file and any written comments or references to the transcript that your attorney may submit.
2. You can have a *personal hearing* in Washington, D.C., before the BVA panel that will actually hear the appeal. This is obviously expensive and takes from six to twelve months to schedule.
3. You can have a hearing before a *traveling panel* of the BVA at the VA regional office in Newark. However, this will take from one to two years to schedule.

Any decision of the BVA must include a written statement of the BVA's findings and conclusions, and the reasons for those findings and conclusions, on all material issues of fact and law presented on the record. The purpose of this requirement is to enable a claimant to understand the decision and the reasons for it, as well as to enable a court to subsequently understand and evaluate the VA's action.

If the BVA denies your claim, you basically have three options. One is to immediately appeal to the court of veterans' appeals, a federal court, which sits in Washington, D.C.[1] (If your claim is granted by the BVA, the VA cannot appeal.) Second, instead of immediately appealing to the court of veterans' appeals, you can first ask the BVA to reconsider your claim and, if your claim is again denied, then appeal to the court of veterans' appeals. (For information about the court's rules and procedures, contact the clerk's office in Washington, D.C.) Third, you can start the entire adjudication process over again by asking the VA regional office in Newark to reopen your claim and make a new decision on the basis of new and material evidence.

You have the right to be represented by an attorney. The major service organizations, such as the American Legion and the Veterans of Foreign Wars, provide trained representatives to help veterans obtain VA benefits.

Both the claimant and the VA can appeal a decision of the court of veterans' appeals to the U.S. Court of Appeals for the Federal Circuit, and to the U.S. Supreme Court.

MEDICAL CARE

The VA provides hospital care, nursing home care, outpatient care, home-based hospital care, respite care, and readjustment counseling. You should apply at the medical facility where you wish to receive treatment by submitting the correct VA form. You must have been discharged under conditions other than dishonorable to be eligible for VA medical treatment.

The VA must provide hospital care and may provide nursing home care, if you

- Have a service-connected disability.
- Were formerly a prisoner of war.
- Have income below a specified amount.
- Were exposed to radiation from A-bomb testing, or to Agent Orange in Vietnam.
- Are eligible to receive Medicaid.
- Receive a VA non-service-connected disability pension.

The VA must provide appropriate and timely medical care to any eligible woman veteran for gender-specific conditions. Women veteran coordinators have been designated at each VA medical center and regional office to counsel women veterans.

Hospital care is discretionary for veterans with non-service-connected medical problems and incomes higher than required for mandatory hospital care. Such veterans must pay an amount equal to what would have been paid under Medicare for the first ninety days of care—that is, the amount of the Medicare deductible. Half of this amount is payable for each additional ninety days. These veterans also must pay $10 for each day of hospital care and $5 for each day of nursing home care.

Outpatient care may be provided to you if you have or were discharged for a service-connected disability. Treatment for service-connected disabilities sometimes can be provided by private doctors at VA expense.

Medical care may be provided to the spouse or child of a veteran who has a service-connected total disability or who died of a service-connected disability.

Unless it is an emergency, it is a good idea to call ahead to the veterans facility to determine if an appointment can be made in advance. If you are denied medical care, you can appeal that decision by following the procedure described under "Applying for Benefits" (discussed earlier in this chapter).

EDUCATIONAL BENEFITS

There are several educational assistance programs available to veterans and their spouses and children. However, only two major educational benefits programs for veterans are in effect today.

Veterans who served between December 31, 1976, and July 1, 1985, may qualify for the Veterans' Educational Assistance program (Vietnam-Era GI Bill). They must have been discharged under conditions other than dishonorable.

These veterans must have contributed to an educational fund while still on active duty. Their contributions will be doubled by the program once they begin attending an approved school. A ten-year deadline from date of discharge must be met to receive the payments. Most Vietnam-era veterans are therefore no longer eligible for educational benefits. However, unused portions of the money contributed by the veteran can be refunded upon request.

Veterans who entered active duty after June 30, 1985, qualify under the Montgomery GI Bill. They must have a high school diploma or the equivalent and a fully honorable discharge. Contributions under this program were automatically deducted from active-duty pay unless the member requested no withholding. The contribution will be doubled and paid in monthly amounts once the veteran begins attending an approved school.

Also eligible for Montgomery GI Bill benefits are those people who had any remaining entitlement under the Vietnam-Era GI Bill on December 31, 1989, and served on active duty without a break between October 19, 1984, and July 1, 1985. To convert from the Vietnam-Era GI Bill to the Montgomery GI Bill, you must have met the requirements for a high school diploma or an equivalency certificate *before* December 31, 1989. Completion of twelve credit hours toward a college degree meets the requirement.

Dependents of disabled veterans and certain surviving family members of veterans may also qualify for educational assistance. There is a deadline to apply of ten years from either the date the veteran is found permanently and totally disabled with a service-connected disability, or the date of the veteran's death. There are exceptions to this ten-year deadline: Spouses of veterans missing in action may also qualify.

JOB PREFERENCES

If you apply for a job with the federal government, you will be classified as a *preference eligible.* Preference eligibles are divided into two categories: (1) veterans and (2) disabled veterans. The spouse of a veteran can also be considered a preference eligible if the veteran—because of a service-connecteddisability—cannot qualify for any federal civil service jobs. Preference eligibles who pass Civil Service examinations have ten points added to their score if they are disabled, or five if they are nondisabled veterans. Preference eligibles must also be given a job retention preference if their employer has to lay off workers.

The state of New Jersey also gives veterans a job preference, but its way of rewarding veterans is different. Wartime veterans who pass state civil service examinations are given *absolute preference* over nonveterans when applying for state, county, and municipal employment. Absolute preference is not extended to promotions. An agency that is hiring must offer a job to a veteran if the veteran is one of the top three people on the list for that job;

when only nonveterans are involved, the agency has a choice of selecting *any* of the top three candidates.

Veterans with service-connected disabilities who pass civil service examinations are given preference over other veterans and nonveterans for state, county, and municipal employment. To be eligible, a veteran must have served at least ninety days' active duty during wartime.

Spouses, widows, widowers, and the parents of disabled or deceased veterans are eligible for veterans' preference under specific circumstances. (In the case of spouses, entitlement occurs only after a disabled veteran waives his or her rights and terminates if the spouse should ever remarry.)

For further information regarding New Jersey's procedure for veterans' preference under civil service, contact the New Jersey Department of Personnel, Veterans' Preference Unit.

REEMPLOYMENT RIGHTS FOR RETURNING VETERANS

Under the Veterans' Reemployment Rights[2] (VRR) law, a person who leaves a civilian job in order to voluntarily or involuntarily enter active duty in the armed forces is entitled to return to his or her civilian job after release from active duty if he or she meets the five basic eligibility criteria of the VRR law:

1. He or she must hold an "other than temporary" civilian job.
2. He or she must leave the civilian job for the purpose of entering military service.
3. He or she must not remain on active duty longer than four years, unless the period beyond four years is "at the request and for the convenience of the federal government."
4. He or she must be released from active duty "under honorable conditions."
5. He or she must apply for reemployment with the preservice employer or successor in interest (for example, a new owner of the company) within ninety days after separation from active duty.

A person meeting these criteria is entitled to reinstatement (within a reasonable time) to a position of like seniority, status, and pay. The veteran is also protected from discharge without cause for one year from the time of reemployment. (Companywide layoffs are considered just cause, so long as your seniority rights have been protected.) If you became disabled while serving in the military and cannot perform your job, you are entitled to another job that you can perform with the same seniority, status, and pay as your former job, or to the nearest extent possible.

You should reapply for your job verbally or in writing to your supervisor or someone who is authorized to represent the company for hiring purposes. Reemployment should be as soon as possible, normally within two weeks.

A key part of the VRR law is that you should be treated as if you had never left your job. This means that when you report back to work, it must be with the same seniority, status, pay increases, and any other benefits—such as pensions, missed promotions, and/or missed transfers—you would have had if you had not been absent for military service. If part of your pension plan requires an employee contribution, you may have to contribute the amount for the period of time that you were on active duty.

If you have questions or problems about your reemployment rights, contact the U.S. Department of Labor, Veterans Employment and Training Service.

17. Public Benefits Programs

This chapter gives a very broad outline of federal and state laws affecting low-income recipients of public benefits in New Jersey. The most important programs are the federal Food Stamp program; the federal Special Supplemental Food Program for Women, Infants, and Children (WIC); the federal Supplemental Security Income (SSI) program; the state-funded General Assistance (GA) program; and the joint federal and state Temporary Assistance for Needy Families (TANF) program, which replaced the former AFDC (Aid to Families with Dependent Children) program. This chapter first discusses unemployment benefits.

UNEMPLOYMENT COMPENSATION

Unemployment is often the precursor of poverty. Unemployment benefits provide income for a limited time to certain unemployed people to enable them to find other employment before needing help from other public programs.

Federal law establishes basic standards for unemployment compensation programs enacted under state law. State unemployment compensation programs must meet federal standards to receive federal funding incentives. Under this program many workers in New Jersey can collect unemployment benefits if they lose their job.[1]

ELIGIBILITY FOR UNEMPLOYMENT BENEFITS.
Workers who are out of work through no fault of their own are eligible for unemployment benefits. However, workers who quit "without good cause attributable to the work" are not eligible. This is the most common reason for denying people unemployment benefits. Whether a worker is eligible for unemployment benefits often depends on his or her reason for leaving a job. "Good cause" has to be connected with your job. If you had to quit because of circumstances directly related to your work, for example, because of illness caused by fumes from chemicals on the job, then you would have good cause for leaving that is attributable to the work. If you meet other eligibility requirements, you would receive unemployment benefits.

However, if a worker left to take a higher-paying job or because he or she got tired of the commute to work, although these might be good reasons, they are considered to be personal, that is, not related to the job. In New Jersey such a worker would be denied benefits.

If denied benefits because he or she has voluntarily quit a job, a worker will not be eligible for unemployment benefits unless he or she has become employed again. The reemployed worker must also have worked for four weeks, earned at least six times his or her weekly benefit rate, and lost his or her job for a reason that qualifies the worker to receive benefits. If a worker is fired for misconduct connected with the work and the misconduct is *gross* because it was an act punishable as a crime, the worker's disqualification for unemployment benefits will be the same as that of a worker who voluntarily quits a job.

If a worker is fired because of his or her misconduct, he or she will have to wait six weeks before collecting benefits if the misconduct was connected to the worker's job.

An act is considered to be *misconduct* if it is (1) improper, (2) connected with one's work, (3) "willfully malicious," (4) within the individual's control, *and* (5) an intentional breach of the worker's obligations toward the employer.

To receive unemployment benefits, you have to show you are able to and available for work. A physical or mental defect that prevents an applicant from being able to work will disqualify him or her for unemployment benefits. An applicant must also be ready, willing, and able to accept suitable work. You must (1) report to the local office of the New Jersey Department of Labor (DOL Division of Unemployment and Disability Insurance at the requested date and time; (2) make it clear that you are ready, willing, and able to work and that you are actively seeking work; (3) accept suitable work if it is offered to you; *and* (4) fill out and return your work-search forms to your local office, as directed.

Workers need only accept "suitable" employment. But if a recipient of unemployment benefits refuses suitable work, he or she cannot receive unemployment benefits for four weeks. The DOL will consider the following factors when it decides if a job is suitable:

- The degree of risk involved to the worker's health, safety, and morals.
- The individual's physical fitness, prior training, experience, and prior earnings.
- The individual's length of unemployment and prospects for securing local work in the individual's customary occupation.
- The distance of the available work from the individual's residence.

Work is not suitable if it is an opening due to a strike or labor dispute; if the hours, pay, or other conditions are "substantially less favorable" than other similar, local jobs; or if, as a condition of being employed, the individual would be required to join a company union or to resign from or refrain from joining any bona fide labor organization. (Special considerations apply for farm workers.)

If you become sick or disabled while you are collecting unemployment benefits, tell your local office you want to apply for *disability during unemployment benefits.* However, do not stop looking for work until you have told the local office about your condition, or you may not be eligible for benefits during that time.

If you become sick or temporarily disabled while you are working, apply for *temporary disability* benefits, not disability during unemployment benefits.

AMOUNT OF BENEFITS. The amount of benefits you will receive depends on how much money you earned before filing your claim. Your *weekly benefit rate* is about 60 percent of your average wage; however, there is a *cap* (upper limit) to what you can receive. The cap for 1997 was $374 per week. This is the maximum amount per week you may receive even if your weekly benefit rate is more than this amount. You can receive benefits for only twenty-six weeks, except in some periods of high unemployment when special rules are adopted.

If you are not receiving the maximum weekly benefit and have an unemployed spouse or unmarried children under the age of nineteen (or under age twenty-two if the child is still in school), you can also receive *dependency benefits.* However, you can never get more unemployment benefits than the maximum weekly amount.

Any unemployment benefits you are awarded will be reduced in part by other income you receive, such as amounts from Social Security, a pension, or a part-time job.

Unemployment checks are sent every two weeks. After your application for unemployment is approved, there is a "waiting week" before your first check will arrive.

INTERSTATE CLAIMS. All states and the commonwealth of Puerto Rico agree to cooperate in interstate claims. For general information about interstate claims, workers can contact the DOL, Interstate Office.

FILING A CLAIM. You can apply for unemployment benefits at any of the local offices of the Division of Unemployment and Disability Insurance of the DOL. The local office asks you for the names and addresses of all employers during the past year, how long you worked for each, how much you were paid, and the reason for leaving each job. The local office will then ask each listed employer for information regarding your wages and reason for leaving.

After the local office receives information from the worker and employers regarding a claim, a deputy at the local unemployment office decides whether the worker is eligible for unemployment benefits.

If the deputy decides the worker is eligible, he or she will send a notice saying so. The former employer will also get a copy of this notice and has the right to appeal.

If the deputy thinks the worker may not be eligible for unemployment benefits, a fact-finding meeting with the worker is scheduled. The employer does not attend the fact-finding meeting, although the deputy will have contacted the employer for information. After the fact-finding meeting, the deputy decides whether the worker is eligible and writes a decision. The worker or the employer can appeal the decision. DOL must receive appeals *in writing*, within seven days of delivering the notice of denial, or within ten days of mailing the notice of denial.

APPEALS EXAMINER HEARING. If you appeal, a hearing will be scheduled. You and your employer will be notified by mail of the date, time, and place of the hearing. A person called an *appeals examiner* (sometimes also called the *appeals tribunal*) will hold the hearing, consider the case, and make a decision. Employers may be represented at the hearing.

Workers have the right to

- A fair and impartial hearing.
- Examine the file and obtain copies of items in it.
- Require (subpoena) witnesses to come to the hearing.
- Examine and cross-examine witnesses at the hearing.
- Represent themselves or bring an attorney, other advocate, friend, or relative to represent them.
- Prior to the hearing date, request that the hearing be rescheduled if the worker is unable to come.
- Bring copies of documents to the hearing and offer them as evidence.

After the hearing, the appeals examiner will make a written *appeals tribunal decision* that will be mailed to the worker.

Board of Review Decision. If the worker or employer appeals in writing within ten days from when the appeals examiner mails the appeals tribunal decision, then the Board of Review will consider the case. You can mail your appeal directly to the Board of Review in Trenton, but it must be postmarked or received *within ten days* of the mailing date of the appeals tribunal decision. The simplest way to file *on time* is to go to your local Division of Unemployment and Disability Insurance office within ten days of the mailing date of the appeals tribunal decision and ask to file a written appeal. (Bring the appeals tribunal decision with you.) Usually the Board of Review will make its decision based on the papers filed and not hold a hearing. Either party can ask the board to consider written arguments.

Court Review. Board of Review decisions may be appealed within forty-five days to the Appellate Division of the New Jersey Superior Court. Appeals from the Appellate Division are to the New Jersey Supreme Court.

OVERPAYMENTS. Sometimes DOL decides that a worker was not eligible for the benefits he or she received. If so, DOL will ask for the benefits to be repaid. The worker will receive written notice of *overpayment.* If the worker is unable to pay the money back in full, the DOL may take steps to collect the money, including taking future tax refunds, homestead rebates, or unemployment benefits, or getting a money judgment against the worker in court.

If a worker has not repaid the money and applies for unemployment again, the DOL will offset the money owed from the new claim. No new benefits will be paid until the money the worker owed has been subtracted. (If the worker was overpaid because the DOL made a mistake, then only *half*—not all—the amount overpaid will be subtracted from the new benefits.)

If you believe you have not been overpaid or that you were overpaid due to a mistake made by the DOL, you should file a written appeal *immediately* when you first receive the written notice of overpayment. (See the following section.) You may receive this notice of overpayment at a time that you are working and not even applying for unemployment benefits. You should still *immediately* appeal or you will lose unemployment benefits when you do need them at a later date.

If you are permanently disabled, you may not have to pay the money back if you did not hold back information from the DOL or provide information you knew was false. You can file for a *waiver* at your local unemployment office and should do so as soon as possible if appropriate. The New Jersey Superior Court, Appellate Division, has held that DOL can *forgive* or not require repayment in cases in which the worker is not permanently disabled.[2]

TIME TO APPEAL. The time allowed to appeal benefits denials and over-payment decisions is very short.

To appeal a denial of a new claim, the DOL must receive appeals *in writing* within ten days after it mails its denial of benefits, or within seven days after delivery.

To appeal a request for repayment of an overpayment, the DOL must receive appeals *in writing* within ten days after it mails its notice, or within seven days after delivery.

The simplest way to file an appeal on time is to go to your local unemployment insurance office and ask to file a written appeal. (If you are unable to file an appeal in writing, ask a worker at the unemployment insurance office for help.)

A few workers have been successful in filing late appeals when they had good reasons for being unable to appeal on time and they were clearly eligible for benefits. According to a decision of the New Jersey Supreme Court, which ordered DOL to write regulations that allow workers to show that they had good reason for filing appeals beyond the ten-day limit, inflexible time limits for filing appeals are unlawful.[3]

ALIEN ELIGIBILITY. Under federal and state law, in order to be eligible for unemployment benefits, people who are not U.S. citizens must meet certain requirements. At the time the services were performed, aliens must be

- Lawfully admitted for permanent residence ("green card" holders) at the time the services were performed,
- Lawfully present for purposes of providing services (including current work authorization, regardless of immigration status),
  or
- Permanently residing in the United States under color of law.

Anyone who has a claim to some immigration status in the United States can argue that they are permanently residing in the United States under *color of law.*[4] Possibilities include persons applying for asylum, persons applying for adjustment of status through a relative or employment, or persons who the Immigration and Naturalization Service (INS) knows are here but for whatever reason will not deport. However, undocumented aliens are not eligible for government benefits. (See Chapter 11, "The Rights and Obligations of Citizenship.")

WELFARE REFORM

The federal Personal Responsibility and Work Opportunity Reconciliation Act of 1996 (Personal Responsibility Act or PRA)[5] dramatically transformed public benefits programs for low-income people in New Jersey and the United States as a whole. This federal law made the most sweeping change in federal welfare law in sixty years. In its wake, New Jersey has enacted a new welfare program known as Work First New Jersey (WFNJ). WFNJ enacted both GA (the welfare program for single adults and childless couples) and TANF (the welfare program for families with children). WFNJ enacted TANF to replace AFDC, and a new GA program following many of the principles of TANF. WFNJ implements some of the choices the federal legislation allowed the states to make. It also enacts some important changes not required by federal law.

By far the most dramatic changes in welfare law are those affecting low-income families with children now receiving TANF benefits through WFNJ. Under TANF, states have a much greater role than before in developing welfare programs for families with children. But TANF also introduced some major changes that every state must follow to receive federal funds.

Significant changes have also been made to the GA program. These were not required by federal law since GA is an entirely state-funded program. However, WFNJ attempts to make the rules in TANF (for families) and GA (for childless individuals) as similar as possible. One result is that, although the name of the program remains the same, the GA program in New Jersey is quite different from before.

By contrast with the comprehensive changes made by the TANF provisions of the PRA, the PRA did not change the basic structure of the Food

Stamp program or the SSI program, and there were almost no changes in the WIC program. One significant change in the Food Stamp program is that under PRA, there are new restrictions on the eligibility of able-bodied, single adults. These are discussed later in this chapter.

A very significant change in the SSI program is that children (especially children with mental, emotional, or behavioral problems) will now have to qualify on the basis of a more restricted definition of childhood disability than before.

The most dramatic change in the Food Stamp program is that most noncitizens will no longer be eligible for food stamps. The new rules on alien eligibility for food stamps and their exceptions are discussed later in this chapter, as well as the alienage provisions in the SSI, GA, and TANF programs. Alienage restrictions in TANF are significantly different from alienage restrictions in GA. The alienage restrictions in TANF and GA are both less restrictive than those in the Food Stamp program.

Unlike the unemployment compensation program, eligibility for all the aforementioned public benefits programs is *means-tested;* that is, eligibility is dependent on income and assets (also called resources). Each program has some special rules for the types of income and resources that are disregarded or excluded in determining eligibility. They also have special rules concerning whose income and resources may, must, or must not be included. The basic meaning of income and resources is the same. *Income* is often divided into two categories: *earned income* and *unearned income.* Earned income includes cash, wages, tips, and (sometimes) in-kind income, such as free shelter. Unearned income is all income that is not earned, such as public benefits, gifts, child support, interest, and dividends. *Resources* (also called assets) include all personal property, such as bank accounts, stocks, bonds, and insurance policies, and all real property, such as land or a house.

SUPPLEMENTAL SECURITY INCOME

SSI is a federally funded program run by the Social Security Administration for certain low-income people who have not contributed enough to qualify for Social Security benefits. SSI provides monthly cash benefits to low-income U.S. citizens and most noncitizens.

Recipients must be sixty-five years of age or older, blind, or disabled (including disabled children). They must also satisfy the income and resource requirements of the program.

The Balanced Budget Act of 1997 (BBA) amended provisions of the Personal Responsibility and Work Opportunity Reconciliation Act of 1996 that imposed harsh restrictions on the eligibility of noncitizens for SSI. Under BBA most legal immigrants who were receiving SSI benefits based on age or disability on August 22, 1996, will continue to receive them as long as they remain qualified for SSI, without regard to their alien status. Most legal immigrants who were lawfully residing in the United States on August 22, 1996, but who were not receiving SSI disability benefits on that date, will be eligible for SSI disability benefits if they later become disabled. They will not, however, become eligible for benefits based on attaining age sixty-five if they were living in the United States before August 22, 1996, but were not receiving disability benefits because they were at that time not old enough to receive SSI based on age.

Most legal immigrants who arrived in the United States after August 22, 1996, will not be eligible for SSI benefits until after they have worked in the United States for ten years. However, refugees and certain others in similar alien categories are eligible for disability benefits for up to seven years, even though they entered the United States after August 22, 1996.

The federal government runs the SSI program and pays most of the benefits. New Jersey adds a small supplemental amount that is included in the monthly SSI check paid to each New Jersey recipient. SSI recipients are eligible for health coverage through Medicaid by virtue of being eligible for SSI.

Chapter 15 ("The Rights of the Disabled") discussed the SSI program for the blind and disabled, including disabled children, who do not qualify for Social Security benefits. Chapter 9 ("Securing the Future for Senior Citizens and Their Families") discussed SSI for low-income people over age sixty-five who do not qualify for Social Security benefits. Chapter 14 ("Your Right to Health Care") discussed the eligibility of SSI recipients for Medicaid. Later in this chapter, restrictions on alien eligibility for public benefits, including SSI, are discussed.

FOOD STAMPS

The Food Stamp program provides *coupons* (food stamps) to eligible households to cover all or part of their household's food budget. It is a nutrition program to help low-income people buy food and improve their diets. Food stamps are coupons that low-income people can spend at supermarkets and other grocery stores, if the store accepts food stamps. Soon, most food stamp recipients in New Jersey will be given an electronic benefits card instead of coupons. Using this card, recipients will be able to purchase food almost as if they were using a credit card.

Recipients can buy most food items with their food stamps. There are certain things recipients cannot buy, however, including alcohol, cigarettes, soap, toilet paper, and pet food. In addition, recipients cannot buy hot food that has been prepared to be eaten.

In New Jersey, the county welfare agencies (CWAs) determine eligibility for food stamps and ensure compliance with program rules under the direction of the New Jersey Department of Human Services (DHS). Although the DHS issues regulations governing the Food Stamp program, these regulations are based on federal regulations.

APPLYING FOR FOOD STAMPS. Recipients must apply for food stamps at the CWA in the county where they live. Recipients must fill out an application form and be interviewed by a caseworker employed by the CWA. It is very important to send in the application form as soon as possible because recipients get food stamps from the date of application even if the form is not completely filled out. The application form must, however, have the applicant's name, address, and signature, and the date.

Recipients must apply as a *household,* not as individuals or families. Households can be of different sizes and/or composition. A household can consist of only a single person. There can even be more than one household sharing the same house. The general rule is that people living in the same house who buy and prepare food together cannot form separate households but must apply for food stamps as one household. Some people must apply together as a single household even if they do not buy and prepare food together. Husbands and wives cannot apply as separate households. Parents and children must also apply for food stamps as a household.

ELIGIBILITY. Eligibility is based on both financial (income and resources) and nonfinancial factors (such as citizenship and work requirements). Most households (those without elderly and disabled members) must have *gross* incomes below 130 percent of the federal poverty level. All households, including those with elderly and disabled members, must have *net* incomes below 100 percent of the federal poverty level. Net income is the household's countable income after allowable deductions. (For example, households can deduct some portion of high housing costs.)

Benefits vary depending on the size of the household and net income. If a household has no net income, it receives the maximum allotment of coupons.

When households apply for food stamps, the CWA decides if the household is eligible for food stamps and, if so, how many. The CWA makes this determination based on the household's income and resources. Income is money an applicant receives on a regular basis. Not all of it is counted under Food Stamp rules. The income limits are tied to the federal poverty guidelines and are adjusted every year in October. Resources are money or property that you have or own, such as cash in hand, stocks, bonds, cars, land, and buildings. The CWA is not allowed to count an applicant's house and the land on it, personal belongings, or tools, among other exceptions. The CWA will not count the first $4,650 of the fair-market value of one vehicle per household.

At the interview with the caseworker, he or she will ask applicant(s) to verify certain things about the people in the household, such as their income and resources. There are different ways of providing this verification. The important thing is that applicants must cooperate with their caseworkers in providing this verification.

Certain people are not eligible for food stamps even if they are U.S. citizens and their verifiable income and resources are low enough to meet the guidelines. Under Food Stamp rules, the following people (with some exceptions) cannot receive food stamps:

- People who are on strike, unless they were eligible for food stamps before the strike,
- People in hospital or jail,
- People enrolled at least half-time in a college,
- People disqualified because they deliberately broke Food Stamp program rules,
  and
- People who quit a job without good cause.

NOTIFICATION. The CWA must notify applicants and recipients in writing of any action that affects their receipt of food stamps. All notices must state in clear, simple language what the decision is. Any decision that denies benefits to an applicant or recipient must state the particular regulation under which the CWA is acting. Applicants and recipients (or their attorney) can check to see if the decision is correct under the law.

RIGHT TO A HEARING. The notice must also explain your right to a fair hearing before an administrative law judge (ALJ). It must also explain how and when you can receive continued assistance pending the outcome of the hearing. If you want to challenge the CWA's action, you have to request a fair hearing either through the CWA or through the Division of Family Development (DFD) within the DHS.

You can request a hearing on any action or failure to act on the part of the CWA that took place in the past ninety days. If your benefits are reduced, suspended, or terminated, you can have your benefits continued until the hearing, but only if you ask for the hearing within ninety days of the date of the notice. However, you should request a hearing within fifteen days after you receive the notice. Your food stamps will be reduced (if that is the reason you are requesting the hearing) while you wait for the outcome. However, if you win your case, you will receive retroactive food stamp benefits.

RESTRICTION ON ELIGIBILITY OF ABLE-BODIED ADULTS. Under the PRA, food stamps are cut off to able-bodied adults aged eighteen to fifty who do not have dependents after three months—unless exempt—if, during a fixed thirty-six-month period they did not

- Work at least twenty hours per week (averaged monthly),
- For twenty hours or more per week, participate in a Job Training Partnership Act, Trade Adjustment Act, or Food Stamp Employment and Training program activity, other than a job-search training program, *or*
- Participate in a Food Stamp workfare program.

An individual may be reinstated for an additional three months if he or she works or participates in one of the above approved programs for eighty hours in one month. Individuals will be exempt if they are medically certified as mentally or physically unfit for employment.

The PRA allows states to apply for waivers (on restrictions) for areas with high unemployment (i.e., with an unemployment rate of 10 percent or higher) or for areas with "insufficient jobs." New Jersey has applied for and received both kinds of waivers. The restrictions on food stamps for able-bodied adults will not affect people who live in those areas. About 80 percent of current food stamp recipients in New Jersey who might be affected by the new law live in areas that have received waivers.

RESTRICTIONS ON ALIEN ELIGIBILITY
IN THE FOOD STAMP PROGRAM

Under the PRA, noncitizens, including lawful, permanent residents ("green card" holders), are ineligible for food stamps and SSI, with the following exceptions:

- Refugees, aliens seeking asylum, and those whose deportation is withheld (only for their first five years in the United States; if they have already been in the United States for more than five years, they will lose Food Stamp benefits).
- Veterans, those on active duty, and their spouses and unmarried dependent children.
- Immigrants who have worked in the United States for ten years. The immigrant's spouse and minor children can be credited with qualifying work *quarters*. (To count as a qualifying quarter after December 31, 1966, the individual must not have received any public benefits during the quarter. Methods of proving quarters of coverage are different for the Food Stamp and SSI programs.)

New Jersey is one of a few states that have created state-funded food stamp programs to provide food stamps for some legal immigrants who are ineligible for federal food stamps because of the alien restrictions in the PRA. The state purchases food stamps from the federal government and provides them to certain applicants who would qualify for federal food stamps but for the alien restrictions. However, not all of those who would have been eligible for federal food stamps but for the restrictions in the PRA will be eligible for state-funded food stamps in New Jersey. To qualify for state-funded food stamps under state regulations, recipients must also be disabled, under age eighteen, or over age sixty-five. The disability standard in the state food stamp regulations is very flexible. For example, many disabled people will qualify for state food stamps although they are not sufficiently disabled to meet the much narrower definition of disability in the SSI program.

Under state regulations, individuals who are found to be eligible for the New Jersey food stamp program must apply for U.S. citizenship. They must do so within sixty days of being found eligible for the program or within sixty days of the date on which they are eligible to apply for U.S. citizenship, whichever is later. This provision is probably unconstitutional.

THE SUPPLEMENTARY FOOD PROGRAM
FOR WOMEN, INFANTS, AND CHILDREN

WIC is a health and nutrition program designed to prevent health-related problems caused by inadequate nutrition. Like the Food Stamp program, it is federally administered by the U.S. Department of Agriculture (USDA). In New Jersey the Department of Health and Senior Services (DHSS) is responsible for administering the program. The WIC program is administered by DHSS through about 20 local agencies and 135 satellite sites. These satellite sites are located in community health centers, hospitals, and prenatal, family planning, and child health clinics.

WIC provides benefits and services to low-income pregnant women, new mothers, and children under age five. WIC also provides various other support services, such as checking immunization records (in some cases giving immunization shots) and screening for lead poisoning.

Nationally the WIC program has achieved great success in reducing the incidence of nutrition-related health problems among the low-income women and children it reaches. One reason is that pregnant women cannot receive the diet supplements provided by WIC without accepting medical checkups.

ELIGIBILITY. To be eligible for WIC, your family's gross income must be at or below 185 percent of the federal poverty income guidelines for your family size. All income is counted, including wages, public assistance benefits, pensions, child support, alimony, and any other source.

You are automatically income eligible for WIC if you receive food stamps, TANF, or Medicaid; if you are a member of a family that has a TANF recipient;

or if you are a pregnant woman or infant receiving Medicaid. State Medicaid agencies must *notify* you of the availability of WIC if you are eligible for Medicaid and are pregnant or nursing, or have a child under age five. The Medicaid agencies must also specifically *refer* you to the local WIC agency.

WIC participants must also demonstrate that they are at nutritional risk for reasons such as inadequate diet, anemia, or abnormal weight. A health professional where she applies will examine a woman and her children to see if they have a medical condition that needs better nutrition. The health professional will also check the diets of applicants to see if there is any dietary deficiency that might harm their health. Many women have some nutritional deficiency while they are pregnant. Children often have some nutritional need that is not being met.

The WIC program does not guarantee benefits to all eligible people, because the program may not have enough funding to serve all eligible women, infants, and children who apply. However, if you meet the eligibility requirements, you should apply. Applications are accepted according to established priorities. The highest priority is given to pregnant women, breast-feeding women with infants (i.e., under one year old), and infants who have one of a specified list of medical problems. In New Jersey, applicants in all priority groups have been receiving benefits, and the New Jersey WIC program has not had a waiting list in recent years.

APPLYING FOR BENEFITS. You can apply at the WIC agency serving the area where you live. (In New Jersey there are no restrictions based on alien status, even though the PRA gave states the option to impose such restrictions.) If you cannot find the agency, call the toll-free, family-health-line phone number for information. The local WIC agency must provide you with information and referral to the Medicaid program as well as to the Food Stamp, child support enforcement, and AFDC programs.

Participants receive vouchers that they may redeem at local supermarkets. In exchange for these vouchers, WIC participants "purchase" specific, highly nutritional food products, including infant formula, milk, cheese, eggs, cereal, juice, and peanut butter. The WIC program also counsels parents about nutrition.

DENIALS. If your application is denied, you will be informed in writing. You will be told the reasons why you are ineligible and advised that you have a right to request a fair hearing. The notice will tell you how to request a hearing and what your rights are at the hearing. You are also entitled to a fair hearing if you are disqualified or terminated from the program and you disagree with the action. You must request a hearing within sixty days of the date the local agency gives you written notice of its action.

WORK FIRST NEW JERSEY

The TANF program is the major source of income support for poor families in New Jersey. It replaced the AFDC program. The GA program is the major source of income support for poor, single adults without dependent children in New Jersey. Both GA and TANF are part of WFNJ, the state welfare program that was enacted and went into effect on April 1, 1997. Revised WFNJ regulations went into effect on January 20, 1998.[6]

BENEFIT LEVELS. The new law did not change benefit levels, which have remained the same since 1987. A family of three with no income is eligible to receive a maximum cash assistance of $424 per month. The GA program has two standard levels of cash assistance. A single adult with no income is eligible to receive a maximum of $210 per month, if he or she is considered "unemployable." If considered "employable," a single adult is eligible to receive a maximum of $140 per month. Families and single adults receive less cash assistance if they have "countable" income as defined in special rules.

Both TANF and GA recipients are also eligible for other public benefits, in particular food stamps. Both food stamps and cash assistance decrease as earnings increase, unless earnings are disregarded under special rules.

MEDICAL CARE. TANF recipients are usually financially eligible for Medicaid. They do not, however, qualify for Medicaid by virtue of being qualified for TANF. Before welfare reform, many poor families with children had qualified automatically for Medicaid because they were receiving AFDC, the welfare program that TANF replaced. Welfare reform ended that automatic link when it eliminated the AFDC program. However, under federal Medicaid law families with children remain eligible for Medicaid if they would have qualified for AFDC under the prior law. In the vast majority of cases, recipients of TANF are eligible for Medicaid.

GA recipients are not eligible for Medicaid whatever their income; however, the GA program will pay for a physician's care, drugs, and almost everything else covered by Medicaid, except inpatient and outpatient hospital care and methadone maintenance treatment for substance abusers. GA recipients are financially eligible for charity care if they need inpatient or outpatient hospital care. Applications for charity care must be made at the hospital. (See Chapter 14, "Your Right to Health Care.") Some hospitals provide methadone treatment for detoxification purposes; however, none provide methadone maintenance treatment.

EMERGENCY ASSISTANCE. TANF and GA recipients who are homeless can also receive Emergency Assistance (EA), which primarily provides emergency shelter assistance but also provides emergency food and clothing allowances if there are special circumstances. SSI recipients may also be eligible for EA.

The same EA rules apply in the TANF, GA, and SSI programs. You cannot get EA unless you are eligible for TANF, GA, or SSI.

There are certain circumstances under which individuals or families eligible for TANF, SSI, or GA can obtain additional assistance, including emergency shelter, from the EA program. The applicant for EA must meet one of the following criteria:

- The applicant has become homeless because of fire, flood, or other natural disaster.
- The applicant has become homeless because of domestic violence.
- The Division of Youth and Family Services (DYFS) has certified that placement of children in foster care is imminent, only because a family is being subjected to a serious health- or life-threatening situation because of the lack of adequate housing.
- The applicant can document that there is a pending eviction or an actual eviction, or previous housing is no longer available and the applicant can show that he or she did not have a *realistic capacity to plan for substitute housing*. (An example of lack of realistic capacity to plan for substitute housing is when an applicant for EA has not had enough time to find somewhere else to stay. Another example is when the applicant has spent all of his or her available funds on necessary household and living expenses.)

If found eligible for EA, the TANF, SSI, or GA recipient will be provided one or more of the following services in addition to those normally available in the TANF, SSI, and GA programs:

- The EA program may pay up to three months of rent that is due, or pay up to three months of owed mortgage payments. The program may also pay up to six months of owed utility payments.
- The EA program may pay for accommodations in an emergency shelter facility, or in a motel or hotel.
- The EA program may pay for a security deposit for rent and utilities. It may also provide money to cover moving expenses.
- The EA program may provide a rent subsidy to pay for housing of a permanent nature (such as an apartment) rather than a hotel or motel. This is called Temporary Rental Assistance (TRA).
- The EA program may provide or pay for emergency food, clothing, or household furnishings.

Under the WFNJ state legislation, EA is limited to twelve cumulative months, unless the applicant becomes homeless again because of fire, flood, or other natural disaster. This means that normally you cannot receive more than twelve months of EA in a lifetime. However, TANF families can get up to two six-month extensions in cases of extreme hardship. No more than 10 percent of TANF recipients who are receiving TRA may get a second extension. Up to 10 percent of SSI and GA recipients who are receiving TRA may receive one six-month extension beyond the twelve-month time limit, but again only in cases of extreme hardship. Remember that you will be eligible for EA, no matter how many months of EA you have already received, if you become homeless again because of fire, flood, or other natural disaster.

TIME LIMITS IN WFNJ. Besides the time limits for receiving EA, there are two other very important time limits in the WFNJ state legislation. First, there are limits on how long you can receive WFNJ benefits. Second, there is a time limit on how long you can be on WFNJ before taking part in one of several specified work activities.

How Long You Can Receive WFNJ. You cannot receive more than a total of sixty months of WFNJ in your lifetime as an adult, unless you are one of a small number of people who are exempt from this requirement. This means that no matter how great your need or the reason for it, you will no longer receive WFNJ if you have *already* received sixty months of it in your lifetime as an adult.

You cannot receive more than a total of sixty months of combined GA and TANF in your lifetime. Even if you didn't use up the sixty months all at once, once you have reached a total of sixty months of benefits, you are no longer eligible to receive them.

However, any WFNJ benefits that a child receives do not count toward the sixty-month maximum to which the child will be entitled when he or she becomes an adult. In addition, a child can receive more than sixty months of benefits while a child, under certain circumstances. A child cannot receive more than sixty months as a child in a family in which the adults have already received sixty months of WFNJ benefits. A child could, however, continue to receive benefits if he or she became part of another family if that family never received WFNJ benefits or if their sixty-month time limit had not expired.

Exempt People. Certain people are completely exempt from the sixty-month limit. For these people, WFNJ benefits will not be time limited at all. Additionally, some people may be able to get a short extension of WFNJ benefits beyond the sixty-month time limit.

The following WFNJ recipients are completely exempt from the sixty-month time limit:

- People over sixty years of age.
- The parent or another relative of a disabled child or other dependent, who must provide full-time care for the disabled child or other dependent.
- Permanently disabled people.
- People who are "chronically unemployable."

Extensions of the Benefit Period under WFNJ. Under certain circumstances victims of domestic violence may receive more than sixty months of benefits. In addition, certain WFNJ recipients may receive a lifetime extension of no more than twelve months beyond the sixty-month limit, and for no more than six months at a time. They may receive this extension if

- The recipient or the recipient's dependent child would be subject to extreme hardship or incapacity.
- The recipient is working full-time but is still financially eligible for benefits because part of the recipient's earned income is not counted under WFNJ rules.
- The recipient has not received an opportunity to engage in work activities under WFNJ.
- The recipient was working full-time and still financially eligible for benefits but was terminated from employment through no fault of the recipient.

HOW LONG YOU CAN RECEIVE WFNJ BEFORE WORKING. Recipients must comply with all work activity participation requirements as a condition of receiving benefits. Recipients with dependent children can be required to commence participation in a work activity at some time prior to receiving twenty-four months of benefits. However, recipients shall not be required to take part in a work activity if child care is unavailable for the recipient's dependent child, including a child over six years of age for whom after-school care is unavailable.

Deferrals of the Work Requirement. Recipients may get a temporary deferral of the requirement to take part in a work activity if

- The recipient is a woman in the last three months of her pregnancy.
- The recipient is a person certified by an examining physician to be unable, because of a physical or mental disease, defect, or impairment, to engage in any gainful employment for any period of more than twelve months.
- The recipient is the parent or relative of a child under the age of twelve weeks, who is providing care for that child.
- The recipient is a victim of domestic violence.

Approved Work Activities under WFNJ. There are many types of approved work activity under WFNJ, including the following:

- Community work experience (CWEP), i.e., unpaid work.
- Training on the job.
- Searching for a job and getting assistance in becoming ready for a job.
- Vocational educational training and job-skills training directly related to employment.
- Secondary education (under certain circumstances) and postsecondary education when combined with CWE or another work activity. (A postsecondary student in a course of study related to employment shall

not be required to take part in another work activity for more than fifteen hours a week.)

Protections for Current Workers. WFNJ legislation provides that an adult recipient taking part in a work activity under WFNJ shall not displace a regular employee by being placed or utilized in a position at a particular workplace

- That had previously been filled by a regular employee but the position became vacant through a demotion, reduction of hours, or a layoff in the previous twelve months, or the position was eliminated in the previous twelve-month period.
- In a manner that infringes on a wage rate or employment benefit, or violates contractual overtime provisions.
- In a manner that violates a collective bargaining agreement or statutory provision that applies to the workplace.
- If there is a contractual or statutory recall right to that position at the workplace.
- If there is an ongoing strike or lockout at the workplace.

Work Activities That May Be Considered Employment. WFNJ provides that two forms of work activity most akin to regular employment, CWEP and alternative work experience (AWEP), are not to be considered employment except for the purposes of specifically listed statutes. CWEP and AWEP are forms of unpaid work that WFNJ recipients may be required to undertake. Participation in CWEP and AWEP may be considered as employment for the purposes of the following New Jersey statutes:

- The Law against Discrimination.
- The Public Employees Occupational Safety and Health Act.
- The Conscientious Employee Protection Act.
- The Worker and Community Right to Know Act.
- The Workers' Compensation Act.
- The Family Leave Law.

For a discussion of these statutes, see Chapter 5, "You and Your Job."

Punishment for Not Working. If a recipient fails to actively cooperate with WFNJ requirements, including work requirements, he or she will receive a punishment called a *sanction.*

The sanctions become more severe for second and third offenses. Only a person who is the head of a household may be sanctioned for a first offense. He or she may be ineligible for benefits for thirty days. For some subsequent offenses, the entire family, including children, can be cut off from benefits for ninety days.

However, recipients can earn *record credits.* If a recipient has not received a sanction for twelve months or more, any existing sanction will be removed from the recipient's record. In that instance, a third offense is considered to be and would result in the same sanction as a second offense.

WFNJ Services That Support People Who Are Working. WFNJ recipients receive the following services to support them when they take part in required work activities:

- Child-care services. This continues for up to twenty-four consecutive months after a recipient is no longer eligible for WFNJ because of earned income.
- Transportation services in the form of an allowance or a subsidy to purchase transportation.
- Medical assistance in the form of Medicaid for recipients with families with dependent children. This continues, under present law, for up to twenty-four months after other income might disqualify the family for Medicaid. Under present law, single individuals and childless couples receive more limited medical assistance, not including hospitalization. For hospitalization expenses, these people must still rely on the charity care program. (See Chapter 14, "Your Right to Health Care.")

New Rules under WFNJ. New rules that have gone into effect making receipt of WFNJ benefits more difficult include the following:

- A person will not be eligible to receive benefits if it is determined that he or she voluntarily quit a job less than ninety days before applying for welfare.
- A person who commits a felony drug offense after August 22, 1996, will not be eligible for WFNJ benefits for a period of ten years after the conviction.
- A person who fraudulently gives a wrong address in order to receive any federal means-tested benefit, such as TANF, will be ineligible for all such benefits, including WFNJ.
- A person who makes a false statement in order to receive benefits will be ineligible for six months for a first offense, twelve months for a second offense, and permanently for the third offense. If such a person actually receives benefits because of the false statement, the person can be convicted of a fourth-degree crime.
- A person who is a fugitive from confinement, custody, or prosecution, or who is violating probation or parole will not be eligible for WFNJ.
- A person who has resided in New Jersey for less than twelve consecutive months will only receive the amount of cash assistance he or she would have received in his or her prior state of residence if that amount is less than the recipient would be entitled to under WFNJ. The recipient will receive the regular WFNJ amount if he or she would have received more cash assistance in the prior state of residence. (This provision is almost certainly unconstitutional and has been challenged in court by Legal Services of New Jersey.)

- There are special restrictions on unwed teenagers who are pregnant or caring for a child. If unmarried and under the age of eighteen, a teenager may be required to live with her parents, legal guardian, or other adult relative. She may also be required to regularly attend high school or an equivalency program and to engage in a work activity if she has completed high school. There are several exceptions to this precondition to receive WFNJ benefits.
- A person who, without good cause, fails to actively cooperate with the program or participate in work activities may lose cash assistance.
- A person will not receive an increase in cash assistance as a result of parenting an additional child during the period that the recipient is eligible for benefits, unless the child was born as a result of rape or incest or an act of domestic violence.

DUE PROCESS PROTECTIONS AND OTHER RIGHTS PRESERVED FROM THE OLD LAW. The WFNJ legislation provides that applicants or recipients have the right to a fair hearing before an impartial ALJ from the Office of Administrative Law. Applicants and recipients have this right whenever their claim for benefits is denied, reduced, terminated, or not acted upon within a reasonable time. Recipients shall continue to receive their current benefits pending the outcome of the hearing. After the ALJ makes an initial decision, the DHS, through the DFD, will make a final decision. If the applicant disagrees with the final decision, he or she has a right to appeal to the New Jersey Superior Court, Appellate Division. The appeal must be filed within forty-five days of the final decision. It will probably be necessary to have a lawyer to do so.

Applicants and recipients of food stamps whose claims for benefits have been denied, reduced, or not acted upon within a reasonable time have similar rights of appeal—beginning with an ALJ, to DFD, to the appellate court. Federal law guarantees the right to appeal decisions under the Food Stamp program. TANF recipients probably have few right of appeal under the PRA; however, these rights *are* guaranteed under the WFNJ legislation for both TANF and GA recipients.

The WFNJ legislation also retained an important provision protecting people who need help immediately. In order to protect such people from administrative delays in processing their applications, the law says that they must be given cash and other assistance on the day of application. The only stipulations are that they must apparently meet all program requirements and need help right away.

RESTRICTIONS ON THE ELIGIBILITY OF ALIENS FOR TANF AND GA. Welfare reform under the PRA as well as WFNJ made no changes as to the eligibility of undocumented immigrants for welfare benefits. They *remain* ineligible. However, many legal aliens who would have been eligible for AFDC now will not be eligible for TANF. Notably, persons "permanently residing in the United States under color of law" (or *prucol*) were previously eligible under AFDC but are no longer eligible under TANF. Although the new GA program is more restrictive than the old, *prucols* arriving in the United States before August 22, 1996, are eligible for GA.

With some exceptions, new immigrants (that is, those arriving in the United States after August 22, 1996) will be *ineligible* for TANF for five years; after that they are eligible only if they are *qualified aliens* under the PRA. Thereafter they will be eligible but are unlikely to qualify in most cases because the incomes of their sponsors will be attributed to them. This is expected to make most new immigrants financially ineligible for TANF. Certain victims of domestic violence who are qualified aliens, however, will be immediately eligible for TANF, even if they arrived in the United States after August 22, 1996.

Qualified aliens are defined as (1) lawful, permanent residents ("green card" holders); (2) refugees, aliens seeking asylum, or people whose deportation has been suspended; *or* (3) parolees and those granted conditional entry. Qualified aliens who arrived in the United States before August 22, 1996, are eligible for TANF under WFNJ. If they arrived in the United States after that date they will be barred from receiving TANF under WFNJ for five years, unless they fall into a category that has been exempt from the five-year ban.

These include certain aliens admitted for humanitarian reasons: refugees, aliens seeking asylum, and people whose deportation has been suspended. However, immigrants in these categories will only be eligible for TANF during their first five years in the United States.

Other exceptions are veterans and those on active military duty, as well as their spouses and unmarried dependent children. Also excepted are lawful, permanent residents ("green card" holders), but only if they can be credited with forty qualifying quarters of work (ten years) for Social Security purposes. They will not be credited with any quarter after the end of 1996, unless they did not receive federal means-tested benefits in that quarter.

The WFNJ alien eligibility requirements for GA generally mirror those for TANF. However, there are two significant differences. As mentioned above, immigrants who arrived in the United States before August 22, 1996, and who can show that they are permanently residing in the United States under color of law (*prucol*) are eligible for GA even if they are not qualified aliens, and therefore would not be eligible for TANF.

GA regulations allow eligibility for aliens who are *prucol,* provided that they arrived in the United States before August 22, 1996. "Permanently residing in the United States under color of law" is interpreted differently in each program. It is not an immigration category, but a phrase used to allow eligibility in some public programs. It has been given a broad meaning in the GA program, allowing eligibility for people who are living in the United States with the knowledge and often tacit permission of the INS.

Under PRA, people who are *prucol* are no longer eligible for food stamps, SSI, or TANF. PRA did not affect the eligibility of *prucols* for unemployment benefits.

The GA program requires aliens to "naturalize" as a condition of receiving benefits. This is the second significant difference between alien-eligibility requirements for TANF and GA. Lawful, permanent resident applicants for GA—but not for TANF—who have resided in the United States for the period required to qualify for citizenship must initiate the naturalization process in order to be eligible for benefits. Having applied for citizenship, the GA applicant will not receive GA benefits for more than six additional months, unless he or she attains citizenship or unless he or she satisfies the following requirements:

- Passes the civics and English-language components of the naturalization examination,
  or
- Is exempt from those components,
  and
- Is awaiting a final, delayed determination by the INS through no fault of the applicant. (It is most probable, however, that courts will find these naturalization requirements imposed by the state to be unconstitutional.)

Notes

1. You and the Law

1. *N.J.S.A.* 59:1-1 *et seq.*

5. You and Your Job

1. *N.J.S.A.* 34:8-43.
2. 29 *U.S.C.* Section 1501 *et seq.*
3. 29 *U.S.C.* Section 201 *et seq.*
4. *N.J.S.A.* 34:11-56a24.
5. *N.J.S.A.* 34:11-4.4.
6. *N.J.S.A.* 34:11B-1 *et seq.*
7. 29 *U.S.C.* Section 2601 *et seq.*
8. 29 *U.S.C.* Section 141 *et seq.*
9. New Jersey Constitution, Article 1, Paragraph 19.
10. 29 *U.S.C.* Section 401 *et seq.*
11. 29 *U.S.C.* Section 651 *et seq.*
12. *N.J.S.A.* 34:6A-25 *et seq.*
13. 29 *U.S.C.* Section 657 *et seq.*
14. 29 *U.S.C.* Section 660(c).
15. *N.J.S.A.* 34:5A-1 *et seq.*
16. 42 *U.S.C.* Section 2000e *et seq.*
17. 8 *U.S.C.* Section 1324(b).
18. *N.J.A.C.* 4A:7-1.3(a).
19. 29 *C.F.R.* Section 1604.11(f) (1990).
20. DCR, *Your Employment Rights* (Nov. 1986), p. 11; DCR, *Sexual Harassment* (1989), pp. 5-6.
21. 29 *U.S.C.* Section 621 *et seq.*
22. 29 *U.S.C.* Section 791(b).
23. 29 *U.S.C.* Section 794.
24. 29 *U.S.C.* Section 793.
25. 29 *U.S.C.* Section 626.
26. 29 *U.S.C.* Section 206(d)(1).
27. *N.J.S.A.* 34:11-56.1 *et seq.*
28. *N.J.S.A.* 34:19-1 *et seq.*
29. *N.J.S.A.* 34:19-5.
30. *N.J.S.A.* 34:15-1 *et seq.*
31. *Mendoza v. Monmouth Recycling Corp.,* 288 NJ Super 240 (App Div 1996).
32. *N.J.S.A.* 43:21-25 *et seq.*
33. *N.J.S.A.* 34:2-21.1 *et seq.*
34. *N.J.S.A.* 34:9A-1 *et seq.*
35. 5 *U.S.C.* Section 2101 *et seq.*
36. 5 *U.S.C.* Section 7101 *et seq.*
37. 5 *U.S.C.* Section 7324(a).
38. *N.J.S.A.* 11A:1-1 *et seq.*
39. *N.J.S.A.* 34:13A-1 *et seq.*
40. *N.J.S.A.* 11A:2-23.

8. Law and the Family

1. *N.J.S.A.* 2A:53-15.
2. *N.J.S.A.* 18A:37-3.
3. *N.J.S.A.* 9:17B-3.
4. *N.J.S.A.* 9:17B-1.
5. *N.J.S.A.* 9:8-21-1; *N.J.S.A.* 30:4C-12.
6. *N.J.S.A.* 9:6-1 *et seq.; N.J.S.A.* 30:4C-12.
7. *N.J.S.A.* 30:4C-12.1.
8. *N.J.S.A.* 9:6B-1 *et seq.*
9. *N.J.S.A.* 30:4C-15 *et seq.*
10. *N.J.S.A.* 9:3-41 *et seq.*
11. *N.J.S.A.* 9:3-37 *et seq.*
12. *N.J.S.A.* 9:3-45.
13. See, for example, *In the matter of the adoption of two children by H.N.R.,* 285 NJ Super 1, 666 A2d 535 (1995); *In the matter of the adoption of a child by J.M.G.,* 267 NJ Super 622 (Ch Div 1993).
14. *Katterman v. DiPiazza,* 37C A2d 955 (App Div 1977); *In ref.* 406 A2d 986 (Ch Div 1979). See also *In re J.C.,* 129 NJ 1 (1992).
15. *N.J.S.A.* 3B:12-1 *et seq.*
16. N.J. Court Rules 5:8A and 5:8B.
17. N.J. Court Rules Appendix IX-A.
18. *Lepis v. Lepis,* 83 NJ 139, 416 A2d 45 (1980).
19. *N.J.S.A.* 9:2-4.
20. *N.J.S.A.* 2A:34-28.
21. 28 *U.S.C.* Section 1738A.
22. *N.J.S.A.* 9:2-7.1.
23. *N.J.S.A.* 2C:25-1 *et seq.*
24. *N.J.S.A.* 2A:52-1 *et seq.; R* 4:72-1 *et seq.*

9. Securing the Future for Senior Citizens and Their Families

1. 29 *U.S.C.* Section 1001 *et seq.*
2. 5 *U.S.C.* Section 8402.
3. 5 *U.S.C.* Section 8401 *et seq.*

4. *N.J.S.A.* 43:15A-1 *et seq.*
5. *N.J.S.A.* 18A:66-1 *et seq.*
6. *N.J.S.A.* 43:16-A1 *et seq.*
7. *N.J.S.A.* 3B:12-25.
8. *N.J.S.A.* 52:27G-20 *et seq.*
9. *N.J.S.A.* 3B:13A-1 *et seq.*
10. *N.J.S.A.* 26:2H-53 *et seq.*

10. You and Your Car

1. 49 *U.S.C.* Section 32701 *et seq.;* 15 *U.S.C. Section 1981 et seq.* given in 1988 edition.
2. *N.J.S.A.* 39:10-26 *et seq.*
3. *N.J.S.A.* 56:12-29 *et seq.*
4. *N.J.A.C.* 13:45A-26C.2.
5. *N.J.S.A.* 56:8-1 *et seq.*
6. *N.J.S.A.* 2A:44-21; *Associates Commercial Corp. v. Wallia,* 211 NJ Super 231 (App Div 1986).
7. *N.J.S.A.* 39:6B-1 *et seq.; N.J.S.A.* 39:6A-1 *et seq.*
8. *N.J.S.A.* 39:6A-8.

11. The Rights and Obligations of Citizenship

1. 28 *U.S.C.* Section 1871.
2. 28 *U.S.C.* Section 1875; *N.J.S.A.* 2B:20-17.
3. *N.J.S.A.* 22A:1-1.1.
4. *N.J.S.A.* 19:31-6.3.
5. *N.J.S.A.* 19:31-6.11.
6. 5 *U.S.C.* Section 552(b).
7. 5 *U.S.C.* Section 552(a).
8. *N.J.S.A.* 10:4-6.
9. *N.J.S.A.* 47:1A-1 *et seq.*
10. 5 *U.S.C.* Section 552(a).
11. *N.J.S.A.* 10:5-43
12. 8 *U.S.C.* Sections 1324a and 1324b.

12. The Criminal Justice System

1. *N.J.S.A.* 2C:1-4.
2. *N.J.S.A.* 52:4B-34 *et seq.*
3. *N.J.S.A.* 2C:2-85.1.
4. *N.J.S.A.* 2C:43-3.1a(6)(a).
5. *N.J.S.A.* 30:4-123.55.
6. *N.J.S.A.* 2A:161A-1.
7. *N.J.S.A.* 2C:43-11 *et seq.*
8. *State v. Leonardis,* 71 NJ 85 (1976).
9. *N.J.S.A.* 59:1-1 *et seq.*
10. *N.J.S.A.* 2C:52-1 *et seq.*

13. Educating Your Children

1. *N.J.S.A.* 18A:38-1.
2. N.J. Const., Art. VIII, Section 4, Para. 1.
3. *Abbott v. Burke,* 119 N.J. 287, 313 (1990).
4. *N.J.S.A.* 18A:38-31.
5. *N.J.S.A.* 18A:38-27.
6. *N.J.S.A.* 18A:38-19.
7. *N.J.S.A.* 18A:38-1(b)(1).
8. *N.J.S.A.* 18A:7B-12(c).
9. *N.J.A.C.* 6:3-8.6(c).
10. *N.J.S.A.* 18A:39-1.
11. *N.J.S.A.*18A:37-2.
12. *N.J.S.A.* 18A:36-19.
13. *N.J.S.A.* 18A:36-19; N.J.A.C. 6:3-6.5.
14. *N.J.A.C.* 6:3-6.7.
15. 20 *U.S.C.* Section 1681.
16. 34 *C.F.R.* Section 106.41.
17. *N.J.A.C.* 6:8-7.1(c).
18. *N.J.A.C.* 6:8-7.1(b).
19. *Lau v. Nichols,* 414 US 563 (1974).
20. *N.J.S.A.* 18A:35-15–26.
21. 20 *U.S.C.* Section 3801.
22. *N.J.S.A.* 18A:7D-1 *et seq.*
23. 20 *U.S.C.* Section 2301 *et seq.*
24. *N.J.A.C.* 6:28-2.
25. *N.J.S.A.* 47:1A-1 *et seq.*
26. *N.J.S.A.* 10:4-6.
27. *N.J.S.A.* 18A:7A-2.

14. Your Right to Health Care

1. 26 *U.S.C.* Sections 162, 4980(B); 29 *U.S.C.* Sections 1002, 116-1168; 42 *U.S.C.* Section 30bb-1.
2. *N.J.S.A.* 26:2H-1 *et seq.*
3. *N.J.A.C.* 10:69A-1.1 *et seq.*

15. The Rights of the Disabled

1. 42 *U.S.C.* Section 12101 *et seq.*
2. 47 *C.F.R.* Section 1.70-1.735.
3. 47 *U.S.C.* Section 151 *et seq.*
4. 42 *U.S.C.* Section 6000 *et seq.*
5. *N.J.S.A.* 30:6D-4.
6. 29 *U.S.C.* Section 794 *et seq.*
7. *N.J.S.A.* 27:25-25.
8. 49 *U.S.C.A.* Section 41705.
9. 47 *U.S.C.* Section 610 *et seq.*
10. *N.J.S.A.* 10:5-1.
11. 42 *U.S.C.* Section 3601, *et seq.*
12. *N.J.S.A.* 2A:18-61.22.
13. 20 *U.S.C.* Section 1400 *et seq.*

14. 20 *U.S.C.* Section 1415(e)(4)(B).
15. 20 *U.S.C.A.* Section 4301.
16. 28 *U.S.C.* Section 1827.
17. *N.J.S.A.* 34:1-69.7 *et seq.*
18. 42 *U.S.C.* Section 1973ee.
19. 42 *U.S.C.* Section 1973aa-6.

16. Your Rights as a Veteran

1. Veterans Judicial Review Act (38 *U.S.C.* Section 7251).
2. 38 *U.S.C.* Section 2021 *et seq.*

17. Public Benefits Programs

1. *N.J.S.A.* 43:21-1 *et seq.*
2. *Hopkins v. Bd of Review,* 249 NJ Super 84 (App Div 1991).
3. *Rivera v. Bd of Review,* 127 NJ 578 (1992).
4. *Brambila v. Bd of Review,* 124 NJ 425, 432 (1991).
5. 2 *U.S.C.* Section 901 *et seq.*
6. *N.J.A.C.* 10:90-1 *et seq.*

Glossary

accelerating (a debt) requiring immediate payment of the entire amount owed on a debt.

adoption the process by which natural parents' rights are terminated and a new parent-child relationship is created.

affidavit a written statement that is sworn before a notary public.

agency shop a workplace in which employees are not required to join the union, but only to pay agency fees instead of union dues.

alimony a sum of money that one divorced spouse pays the other.

annual percentage rate the yearly cost of borrowing money in percentage terms.

answer a document filed with the court by a defendant, responding to all of the claims asserted by a plaintiff in a complaint.

appeal a proceeding challenging the decision of a lower court or an agency.

arbitration a hearing in which an impartial party, or arbitrator, decides a dispute between two parties.

> **binding arbitration** an arbitration in which the parties agree in advance to accept the arbitrator's decision as final.

> **fee arbitration** a hearing to determine the reasonableness of an attorney's fee.

arraignment a court proceeding at which a judge reads an indictment to the charged defendant and asks the defendant to enter a plea of guilty or not guilty.

arrest the process by which a person is taken into custody or restrained so that he or she may be held to answer for a crime or other offense.

> **arrest warrant** a document issued by a judge that allows the police to place a person under arrest.

assault the action by which one person causes or attempts to cause bodily harm to another.

attorney's fees fees paid to an attorney; at the end of a lawsuit one party can be ordered to pay the other's attorney's fees where this is allowed by a statute or court rule.

at will (employment) the condition under which an employee works without a contract and may be fired without justification.

bail the posting of money in order to be released from custody.

> **bail order** rules set by a judge to govern the terms under which an arrested person may be released on bail.

bait and switch the practice of advertising an item that is not in fact in stock or for sale.

beneficiaries people who will receive money or property under a will, contract, policy, pension plan, or other arrangement.

breach of the peace a violation or disturbance of public order.

brief a written statement submitted to the court in a case, setting forth the facts of the case and the party's legal argument.

burden of proof the responsibility of a party to prove disputed facts in a case.

case information statement a written statement filed with the court at the beginning of an appeal, setting forth basic information about the case.

certification of completion a written statement given by a homeowner to a contractor upon the completion of home repair work, expressing satisfaction with the work.

challenge for cause an objection to the seating of a juror based on the juror's partiality or other inability to render a fair decision.

charge a judge's instructions to a jury at the end of a trial, before jury deliberation begins.

child custody arrangements governing which parent will take care of a couple's children when the couple separates.

joint custody a custody arrangement under which both parents share the child. Generally, the child will live part of the time with one parent and the rest of the time with the other.

child support money paid by the noncustodial parent to the custodial parent to provide for the care of their children after separation.

citation (cite) the notation of where a law or legal case is published.

closing a proceeding to finalize the transfer of property or the loaning of money, at which deeds, mortgage papers, or other documents are completed and exchanged.

　　closing statement a written statement provided at a closing setting forth the relevant information, such as the amount of money or property exchanged.

codicil an amendment or addition to an existing will.

collateral security on a loan.

common law law that is created by court decisions rather than statute or regulation.

complaint a document that begins a lawsuit and sets forth all of the plaintiff's claims against the defendant.

confession of judgment a defendant's written confession of a debt or liability that allows a judgment to be entered against him or her.

conservatee a competent person who voluntarily allows another person (a conservator) to be appointed by a court to help manage his or her affairs.

conservator a person appointed by a court to manage the affairs of another person (a conservatee) who is competent but requires assistance.

constitution the law of a country or state that establishes its system of government and the extent and limits of the government's powers.

consumer report a report giving basic information to creditors concerning a potential borrower's credit history.

　　investigative consumer report a part of a consumer report or credit report containing personal information.

contempt of court a charge brought against a person for disobeying a court order.

contingent fee a method of compensating a lawyer by which the lawyer is paid a fixed percentage of the client's recovery, if there is one.

contract an agreement between two or more people or groups involving mutual promises to perform acts.

copayment a cost-sharing arrangement under which a person covered under a health insurance plan pays a specified charge for a specified service, such as $10 for an office visit.

cosign the act of making oneself jointly responsible with another person for an obligation, such as a loan.

count a statement or charge of a crime in an indictment; each count in an indictment charges a separate crime.

credit borrowed money; the ability to buy goods and pay later.

　　closed-end credit credit given on a single transaction.

　　open-end credit continuing credit, under which payments for purchases are made over a period of time, as is the case with most credit cards.

creditor a person who is owed money.

crime an offense that can result in a jail sentence of more than six months.

criminal mischief an act by which one person intentionally damages the property of another.

cross-examine to question opposing witnesses.

damages awards of money that injured parties can receive through litigation. There are many different types of damages, including compensatory, punitive, and liquidated damages.

decertification election   an election in which employees may vote to leave their union.

default judgment   a decision entered against a party that fails to answer a complaint or appear in a case.

defendant   a person or entity being sued.

deficiency   the amount still owed on a product purchased on credit after the product has been repossessed and sold.

defined benefit plan   a pension plan in which benefits are based on a formula set out in the plan.

defined contribution plan   a pension plan in which the benefits depend upon the amount of contributions made by the employer and employee and how well the plan's investments perform.

deposition   a form of discovery in which the parties meet at a designated time and place and one party asks the other oral questions.

descendant   a relative in the direct line of descent, such as a child or grandchild.

developmental disability   a severe, chronic disability manifested during the developmental period that results in impaired functioning or deficiencies in essential skills.

direct examination   a lawyer's or party's questioning of his or her own witnesses.

discharge   a legal release from obligations and debts.

disclosure statement   information regarding credit charges provided by a creditor to a borrower.

discovery   the formal exchange of information in which parties engage during the course of litigation and in advance of trial.

disorderly persons offense   an offense that is harmful to the public peace and welfare, such as defacing a public monument.

> **petty disorderly persons offense**   a minor offense, such as fighting in public or creating public annoyance or alarm.

dissenting opinion   an opinion by one or some of the judges hearing an appeal disagreeing with the opinion of the majority.

docket number   the identifying number assigned to a case by the court clerk, which should be used on all court papers.

door-to-door sale   a sale that is made away from the seller's place of business.

duty of fair representation   the obligation of a labor union to represent all employees, even if they are not union members, in a fair, nonarbitrary, and nondiscriminatory manner.

earned income   income received from work.

easement   the right of one person to use another's property.

emancipation   the point in time at which a child reaches adulthood and his or her parents are no longer obligated to provide support.

endorsement   the signing of a check or other negotiable instrument.

equitable distribution   the division of real and personal property, acquired by a couple during marriage, that takes place at the time of divorce.

executive or closed session   a portion of a meeting held by a public body that takes place in private, excluding the public.

executor   a person designated under a last will and testament to oversee the distribution of property and other estate matters.

expunge   to remove records of a person's criminal convictions or arrests from police and court records.

fair hearing   a hearing at which an administrative law judge decides a dispute between an individual and a government agency.

federal poverty level   income guidelines established annually by the federal government to measure whether family income is low enough to qualify for various programs.

fee arbitration a hearing to decide on the reasonableness of fees charged by an attorney.

fee for service the traditional health care payment system, under which a provider receives payment for each service.

felony a serious crime, such as murder.

finance charge the total cost of borrowing money or buying on credit, including interest.

foreclosure the process by which a lender or mortgagor repossesses the home or other real estate of a person who borrows money to purchase property and fails to make loan payments.

garnish to direct that a person or entity with control over the money or property of a debtor, such as an employer, apply the debtor's money or property to pay a debt to a third party.

giving full faith and credit giving full effect to the orders or judgments of another state's courts.

grand jury a jury that hears preliminary information about a criminal case and decides whether a trial should be held.

grievance an employee's claim against an employer for violating the union contract or interfering with established rights.

guardian a person appointed by a court to care for or manage the affairs of a child or an incompetent person.

> **guardian ad litem** a temporary guardian appointed by a court to represent a child or an incompetent person in a court proceeding.

harassment the treatment of one person by another in an offensive or abusive manner.

hardship increase a rent increase above what is permitted by a rent control ordinance based on a landlord's demonstration of need.

hardship stay a delay of a decision because of the hardship that would result to the affected person. Hardship stays are granted both to tenants who face eviction and to aliens who face deportation.

health maintenance organization (HMO) an organization that delivers and manages health services under a risk-based arrangement.

holder in due course a third party who purchases a negotiable instrument for the payment of money without knowledge of the original transaction, making that third party immune from claims by the original purchaser.

holographic will an informal, handwritten will.

hung jury a jury that cannot reach a verdict.

immigrant visa petition a request made by a potential immigrant to come to the United States with legal status.

immunity protection against being charged with criminal conduct.

indemnity insurance a health insurance product allowing insureds total freedom to choose providers.

indictable offense an offense for which an accused person must be charged by a grand jury; not a minor crime or disorderly persons offense.

indicted charged with a crime by a grand jury.

indictment a document charging a defendant with a crime or crimes, issued by a grand jury.

injunction a court order directing a person or group to take or refrain from a particular action.

interrogatories written questions submitted by one party to another during discovery. Interrogatories must be answered and sworn to under oath.

intestacy laws laws that govern the division of property when a person dies without a valid will.

joint and survivor benefits pension benefits that pay a reduced amount to the participant during his or her lifetime with continuing benefits for the life of the spouse when the participant dies.

judgment an order entered by a judge deciding the rights of parties at the close of a case.

jurisdiction the authority or power of a court to hear and decide cases.

just cause in employment law: A valid reason that must be given by an employer for firing or taking other disciplinary action against an employee, if required by law or a union contract.

in tenancy matters: A valid reason, set by statute, that must be given by a landlord for evicting a tenant.

juvenile-family crisis a situation in which the conduct of a minor or his or her family creates a serious threat to the minor's health and safety.

law statutes, regulations, ordinances, case decisions, and other guidelines that govern people's legal rights and obligations.

legal residence the place where a person is considered to live according to the law—based on factors such as voter registration or driver's license and registration—despite the fact that that person may spend a great deal of time elsewhere.

letter of instructions directions that supplement a last will and testament, governing such things as distribution of minor items of personal property.

letters testamentary a document that authorizes the executor of a deceased's estate to administer the estate.

lien a claim on property securing the payment of a debt.

lifetime benefits pension benefits paid to a participant at retirement for his or her lifetime.

liquidated damages a fixed or clear amount of money damages.

living will a will in which a person's wishes regarding types and limits of medical treatment to be provided to him or her in the event of incapacitation are set forth.

managed care a health care system under which the overall care of a patient is overseen by a single provider or organization.

misdemeanor an offense that is of a less serious nature than a felony.

mortgage an agreement securing a loan of money on the borrower's home.

    first or purchase mortgage a mortgage taken on the purchase of a home.

    home repair mortgage a mortgage to finance work on a home.

    revolving home equity loan a credit arrangement allowing a person to take out credit, secured by his or her home, from time to time.

    secondary mortgage a second mortgage on a home.

negligence the failure to act with reasonable care.

negotiable instrument a written, unconditional promise to pay a specific amount of money on demand to the person holding it. Checks are negotiable instruments.

notarization the process by which a signature is witnessed by a notary public.

notary public a public officer who administers oaths and witnesses signatures.

notice of appeal a written statement that must be filed by a party appealing a case decision.

notice to cease a written notice from a landlord to a tenant requesting that the tenant stop certain conduct.

notice to quit a written notice from a landlord to a tenant requesting that the tenant vacate the premises on a particular date.

nuisance an unreasonable interference with the use and enjoyment of property.

    private nuisance interference with one's private property.

    public nuisance interference with the public rights to health, safety, peace and quiet, comfort, or convenience.

opening statements statements made by both parties at the beginning of a trial, explaining what the case is about and summarizing the facts and evidence to be presented.

ordinance a law passed by a city or town.

own recognizance An individual's word that he or she will not flee, according to which that person is released from custody without posting bail.

palimony an award of money, similar to alimony, between unmarried partners who end their relationship.

parole an early release from prison on certain conditions.

partial permanent disability a disabling illness or injury that affects a part but not all of one's body and that will not improve.

peremptory challenge an objection to the seating of a juror without a legal basis. Each side to a case is entitled to exercise a certain number of these challenges.

petition a form of complaint or document that begins a court proceeding.

petition for certification a formal request that the New Jersey or U.S. Supreme Court hear an appeal from a lower appellate court in a case in which appellate review is not required.

plaintiff a person or entity that initiates a lawsuit.

plea bargaining discussions between the prosecution and defense about what charges the defendant may plead guilty to rather than stand trial, and possible sentences to be imposed.

political asylum the legal status granted to an alien who cannot return to his or her country of origin because of persecution or fear of persecution.

power of attorney the grant by one person (the principal) of certain powers to another so that the other person can act in his or her place.

    durable power of attorney a power that continues when the principal becomes disabled.

    springing power of attorney a power that takes effect only if the principal becomes disabled.

precedent past court opinions that are relied on in subsequent decisions.

preference eligible a special status given to veterans seeking civil service jobs.

prenuptial agreement a contract between future spouses to govern certain terms of their marriage and provide for the distribution of property and other arrangements in the event of death or divorce.

privileged of or pertaining to information that parties have the right to guard from disclosure.

probable cause good reason to believe that a certain act has been committed.

probate the process under which a will is filed with the surrogate's court and proved to be genuine.

product liability the responsibility of a business or manufacturer for the safety of the products it sells or makes.

pro se acting on one's own behalf in legal proceedings.

receivership the process by which a court appoints an outside person to take control of a building or organization.

regulations laws passed by administrative agencies.

relocation assistance financial and other help given to a tenant who must move under certain conditions.

remand to send a case back to a lower court or administrative agency to render a new decision.

rent abatement a reduction in a tenant's rent granted by a court because of unsatisfactory conditions in the tenant's house or apartment.

rent control laws   laws that govern by how much and when a landlord can increase a tenant's rent.

rent strike   an action in which tenants join together and withhold rent to protest their living conditions.

repossess   to take back goods on which money is due.

representation fee   a fee paid by nonunion employees to the union representing their workplace for services that they receive.

representative payee   a person who receives payments for the benefit of another.

rescind   to cancel.

residuary legatee   a person who receives all remaining unaccounted for property after distribution has been made under a will.

resources   a person's real and personal property.

restitution   money paid to replace something that is taken or damaged.

retainer   money paid in advance for services.

revocation of acceptance   the situation in which a person changes his or her mind and decides to return a product that he or she has accepted.

search warrant   a document issued by a judge allowing the police to search a certain place or person for specific property.

security deposit   money given by a tenant to a landlord to protect the landlord against any damage the tenant may cause to the house or apartment.

security interest   an interest in property that backs a loan of money. Even if there is a security interest, a creditor must still go to court before taking the debtor's property.

sovereign immunity   governmental freedom from liability.

statutes   laws enacted by the U.S. Congress or state legislatures.

statutes of limitations   laws that create time periods limiting the time in which different types of lawsuits can be filed.

stay   to stop the enforcement of a court order or judgment.

subpoena   an order directing a person to appear in court to testify or to produce documents at a certain place and time.

summations   closing statements made by both parties at the conclusion of a trial.

summons   a document served with a complaint on a defendant to a lawsuit to notify him or her to answer the complaint or appear in court.

surcharge   an additional charge beyond what is actually owed.

temporary disability   an illness or injury that leaves one temporarily unable to work.

temporary restraining order (TRO)   an emergency, temporary court order directing a person or group to take or refrain from taking an action.

tenants by the entirety   a form of property ownership generally applied to property held by spouses, under which the entire property is owned by both spouses and belongs to one automatically upon the death of the other.

tenants in common   a form of property ownership under which co-owners own separate shares of the property, which can be divided.

testator   a person who makes a last will and testament.

total permanent disability   an illness or injury that leaves one completely unable to work on a regular basis and that will not improve.

transcript   a written version of the record of a hearing or trial.

trespass   a physical invasion of property.

trustee   a person appointed or required by law to oversee property for the benefit of another.

unconscionable   extremely harsh or unfair.

unearned income   income that a person receives without working for it.

unfair labor practice any action taken by an employer or a union that violates a provision of the Labor Management Relations Act, including interfering with employees' rights to organize and refusing to bargain.

union shop a workplace in which employees are required to join the union under the union contract.

unsecured debt a debt that is not backed by an interest in property.

variable rate loan a loan on which the interest rate may vary.

verdict a decision reached by a jury at the close of a trial.

vested the characteristic of having worked a sufficient amount of time to be entitled to collect accrued pension benefits at retirement age even if one stops working.

visitation arrangements for a noncustodial parent or relative to visit with his or her children.

wage execution an order allowing a debt to be satisfied by directing the debtor's employer to take money out of the debtor's wages for the creditor's benefit.

waiver a giving up of rights or a relaxation of restrictions.

warrant for removal an order from a judge allowing a court constable to evict a tenant on three days' notice.

warranty a promise to repair or replace defective goods or to refund money.

> **express warranty** a written or oral promise or representation about a product.

> **full warranty** a complete warranty promising to repair or replace the goods.

> **implied warranty** a warranty that is not written or spoken but exists under the law.

> **limited warranty** a warranty covering only certain things that may go wrong.

> **warranty of fitness for a particular purpose** a warranty that is implied if a person relies on a seller to give him or her a product to meet a particular need.

> **warranty of habitability** a landlord's implied promise that rented premises will be in safe and decent condition.

> **warranty of merchantability** an implied warranty that exists when a person buys a product from a seller who regularly sells that product.

writ of execution a court order allowing a sheriff to seize a person's property to satisfy a debt.

writ of possession a court order directing a sheriff to evict homeowners or tenants from their home.

Index

Page numbers for entries occurring in boxes are followed by a b, and those for entries occurring in tables, by a t.

abandoning residence, 281
abandonment: of a child, 203; of property, 82, 85
absolute preference, 374–75
ACCAP. *See* AIDS Community Care Alternative Program
accelerating (debt), 79–80, 82, 178–79
accrued benefits, 233–34, 235
ACLU. *See* American Civil Liberties Union
actual damages, 165, 169, 186
ADA. *See* Americans with Disabilities Act
ADEA. *See* Age Discrimination in Employment Act
administration expenses, 248
administrative law judges (ALJs): car problems and, 254; disability determinations and, 366; employment discrimination and, 116; Food Stamp program decisions and, 386; hospital bill disputes and, 335–36; job safety violations and, 109, 112; Medicaid decisions and, 347; motor vehicle infraction cases and, 259; New Jersey pension decisions and, 240; school board decisions and, 323; special education evaluation and, 320; state employee hearings and, 129; unfair labor practices and, 107; Work First New Jersey decisions and, 396
adoption, 203–5, 223
ADR. *See* Alternative Dispute Resolution
adult children, 362
adultery, 210, 214
advance directives, 243–44
advance-fee loans, 134, 147–48
advertising: of cars, 251; Consumer Fraud Act on, 140–43; by lawyers, 10
AFDC. *See* Aid to Families with Dependent Children
affidavits, 13–14; of proof, 59; of support, 281
affirmative action, 358

Age Discrimination in Employment Act (ADEA), 114–17, 128, 130
agency fees, 105
agency shops, 105
Agent Orange, 367, 368
Agent Orange Act of 1991, 368
agricultural (farm) workers, 125–26, 378
aid and attendance allowances, 369
AIDS, 70, 348, 363, 364
AIDS Community Care Alternative Program (ACCAP), 345
AIDS-related complex (ARC), 348
Aid to Families with Dependent Children (AFDC), 344, 346, 377, 382, 390, 396–97
Air Carrier Access Act of 1986, 359
alcohol abuse: disabilities caused by, 362, 368; as grounds for divorce, 210
aliens, 279–84; amnesty for, 282; Food Stamp program and, 383, 387–88; General Assistance and, 396–98; inadmissibility and, 279, 283; obtaining legal status, 282–83; Special Supplemental Food Program and, 389; Supplemental Security Income and, 224, 383–84, 387; Temporary Assistance for Needy Families and, 396–98; undocumented, 120, 283; unemployment compensation and, 381–82. *See* also immigrants
alimony, 209, 212, 213–14; bankruptcy and, 189, 191, 194; credit applications and, 163; taxes and, 216, 278
ALJs. *See* administrative law judges
Alternative Dispute Resolution (ADR), 156
alternative work experience (AWEP), 394
American Civil Liberties Union (ACLU), 13
American Jurisprudence, 9
American Legion, 372
Americans with Disabilities Act (ADA), 352–56, 359

411

revolving home equity loans, 75, 174, 177
right of rescission, 74, 75–77, 85
right to cure, 83–84, 85
Right to Know Law (RTKL), 268, 269, 272–73, 322
right-to-sue letters, 115
rip-offs. *See* scams
RISA. *See* New Jersey Retail Installment Sales Act
rollback taxes, 73
Rooming and Boardinghouse Act, 67–68
roominghouses, 48, 66–69
RTKL. *See* Right to Know Law
Rules of Professional Conduct, 11
Rutgers Law School, 5

safe and decent housing right, 37–40, 58
sanctions, 394–95
sanitation problems, in rental dwellings, 41
scams: car repair, 132; consumer, 132–35; credit "repair," 134, 169; and immigrants, 135; mail-order purchase, 133; 900 number, and senior citizens, 142; Social Security, 135
school attendance officers, 308
school board decisions, challenging, 323
school board meetings, 322–23
school documents, 322
screens, 348–49
searches, 291–92
search warrants, 292
seat belt law, 260
Secondary Mortgage Loan Act, 78, 79
second mortgages, 75, 177
Section 1983, 304
secured debts, 162, 179–81, 189
securities, financial, 157
security agreements, 137
security deposits, 24–28, 29; constructive eviction and, 34, 35; displacement and, 27–28; interest on, 25–26; notice of, 25; return of, 26–28; sale of building and, 27
security interest, 74, 76, 137, 145, 174–75, 179; bankruptcy and, 192–93; contractors and, 90–91
self-employment, Social Security and, 228
self-help evictions, 47–48
self-incrimination, privilege against, 290
self-insured plans, 326
self-proving wills, 246

seller-lenders, 162
sellers, complaining to, 155
selling practices, 140–43
Senior Citizen and Disabled Protected Tenancy Act, 64, 360
senior citizen housing, 30–31, 69, 70
senior citizens, 224–50, 325; abuse of, 219; advance directives and, 243–44; condominium and cooperative conversions and, 63, 65–66; conservatorship and, 242–43; as crime victims, 288; estates of, 247–50; guardianship for, 240–42; health care programs for, 337–43; housing discrimination and, 360; Medicaid and, 347–48; Medically Needy program and, 346–47; 900 number scams and, 142; pet ownership rights and, 30–31; Supplemental Security Income and, 224–27; transportation for, 358–59; utilities and, 93b. *See also* Medicare; pensions; retirement plans; Social Security; wills
separate maintenance payments: bankruptcy and, 189, 191, 194; credit applications and, 163; taxes and, 216, 278. *See also* alimony
separation, of married couple, 209–10
service contracts, 138–39, 153, 256
Seton Hall University, 5
settlements: in eviction cases, 50–51; in small-claims cases, 19–20, 159
700 numbers, 132
sewers, 73
sex discrimination. *See* gender discrimination
sexual harassment, 113
Shepard's Citations, 9
shutoffs, utility, 94–96
siblings, visitation rights of, 218
sign-language interpreters, 20, 361
skilled nursing facilities, 338, 339
SLMB. *See* Specified Low-Income Medicare Beneficiary
small-claims court, 6t, 9, 18–19, 157–61; collecting the judgment, 19, 160–61; for consumer problems, 157–61; criteria for suing in, 159; filing a suit in, 18, 158–59; getting sued in, 161; settlement out of court, 19–20, 159; tenant-landlord disputes and, 27, 44, 159
Small-Employer Health Benefits Act, 325, 329, 331

About the Authors

Melville D. Miller, Jr., is president of Legal Services of New Jersey. Leighton A. Holness is a senior attorney with Legal Services of New Jersey.

Legal Services of New Jersey is a nonprofit corporation that coordinates the provision of legal services in civil matters to New Jersey residents who cannot afford counsel.